Global cases in logistics and supply chain management

To My Father Ronald
For a life time of encouragement

Global cases in logistics and supply chain management

Edited by
David H Taylor

THOMSON

LEARNING Australia • Canada • Mexico • Singapore • Spain • United Kingdom • United States

Global Cases in Logistics and Supply Chain Management

Copyright © David H Taylor 1997

The Thomson Learning logo is a registered trademark used herein under licence

British Library Cataloguing-in-Publication Data
A catalogue record for this book is available from the British Library

First edition 1997
Reprinted 1998, 1999 and 2001

Produced by Gray Publishing, Tunbridge Wells, Kent
Printed in China by L.Rex

ISBN   1 86152 395 5

Thomson Learning
Berkshire House
168 – 173 High Holborn
London WC1V 7AA
UK

http://www.thomsonlearning.co.uk

Contents

Part 2 Purchasing and supplies management

Part 3 Manufacturing logistics

Part 4 Distribution planning and strategy

Part 5 Warehouse planning and operations management

Part 6   Inventory management

Part 7   Transport management

Part 8   International logistics and international market-entry strategies

Reference maps

Note: All cases presented in this book have been prepared as a basis for class discussion rather than to illustrate effective or ineffective handling of administrative situations.

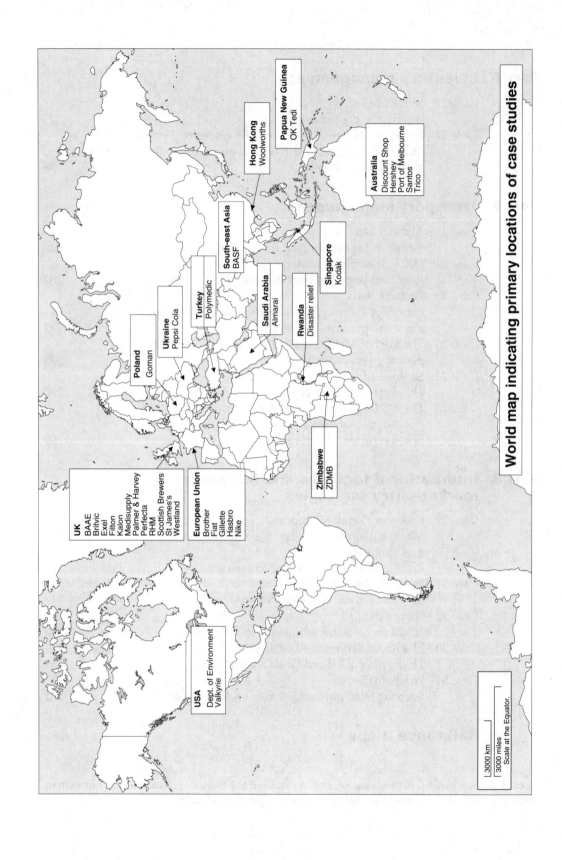

World map indicating primary locations of case studies

USA
Dept. of Environment
Valkyrie

UK
BAAE
Britvic
Exel
Filton
Kalon
Medisupply
Palmer & Harvey
Perfecta
RHM
Scottish Brewers
St James's
Westland

European Union
Brother
Fiat
Gillette
Hasbro
Nike

Poland
Goman

Ukraine
Pepsi Cola

Turkey
Polymedic

South-east Asia
BASF

Saudi Arabia
Almarai

Rwanda
Disaster relief

Zimbabwe
ZDMB

Singapore
Kodak

Hong Kong
Woolworths

Papua New Guinea
OK Tedi

Australia
Discount Shop
Hershey
Port of Melbourne
Santos
Trico

3000 km
3000 miles
Scale at the Equator.

Foreword

Case studies have proved a valuable tool in the training and development of modern managers. The growing recognition of the importance of logistics as a management process, and the development of logistics degree programmes have made this collection of case studies long overdue.

Eleven industry sectors are covered in this book – reflecting the potential 'reach' of logistics, and the universality of its contribution.

As President of the Institute of Logistics I commend the efforts of David Taylor in preparing the logistics casebook and instructor's manual.

David Quarmby
President
Institute of Logistics

Classification of cases by industrial sector

Aircraft/aerospace
  British Airways Avionic Engineering
  Filton Aerostructures
  Westland Helicopters Ltd
Electronics
  Brother International
  Valkyrie
Food and drink
  Almarai Ltd
  Britvic Soft Drinks
  Goman Marketing Co.
  Hershey Foods Corporation
  Palmer & Harvey Ltd
  Pepsi Cola International
  Rank Hovis McDougall plc
  Scottish Brewers
  Zimbabwe Dairy Marketing Board
Chemicals
  BASF
  Kalon Paints
General consumer products
  Gillette
  Hasbro Europe
  Eastman Kodak Singapore
  Nike Europe
  Perfecta Beds

Medical industries
  Medisupply
  Polymedic
  St James's Hospital and Lucas
  Engineering Systems
Mining/extractive/oil
  OK Tedi Mining Limited
  Santos Ltd
Motor car manufacture/component supplies
  Fiat Auto Spa
  Trico
Retailing
  The Discount Shop
  Woolworths plc
Transport
  Exel Logistics
  The Port of Melbourne
Other sectors
  The US Department of Environment
  The Rwandan Refugee Crises 1994

Contributors

Editor

David Taylor is a Senior Lecturer in of the Department of Transport and Logistics and at the University of Huddersfield, UK. He is also Director of the University's Centre for Transport and Logistics Management. In 1994–5 he held the position of Visiting Research Fellow in the Department of Marketing, Logistics and Property at The Royal Melbourne Institute of Technology in Australia. His main areas of interest are international logistics and logistics strategy. He holds a first degree from London University, an MSc in Transport Studies from Cranfield University and an MBA from the University of Sheffield. Before entering the academic field he worked as marketing and distribution manager for Wm Skidmore Ltd, a manufacturer of medical equipment, and as a distribution planner for NFC, a major UK distribution company. In recent years he has carried out numerous training and consultancy projects for companies in Britain, eastern and western Europe, Russia, the Middle East, south-east Asia and Australia.

Authors

Martin Ashford in 1995 became Head of Logistics for the *Financial Times* newspaper London. He started his career with P&O Containers and then worked for six years for the Distribution and Logistics Division of Touche Ross Management Consultants where he specialized in European logistics assignments covering a wide range of clients and all aspects of logistics.

Colin Bamford is Professor and Head of the Department of Transport and Logistics at the University of Huddersfield, UK. He has published various books and articles on transport economics and distribution management.

John Beaty is an independent logistics consultant and also a Lecturer in the Department of Marketing, Logistics and Property at The Royal Melbourne Institute of Technology in Australia. He specializes in warehouse planning and management and has had extensive experience as a military logistician, as a logistics manager in the retail sector and latterly as a logistics consultant and teacher.

Valerie Bence is a Research Officer in the Centre for Logistics and Transportation at Cranfield University in the UK. She provides research support for faculty and writes teaching material, working papers and articles as well as case studies for use within the graduate programmes.

Paolo Bianchi is Principal Consultant with A.T. Kearney SpA in Milan, Italy. He has been with the firm since 1984 and is responsible for projects in automotive practices and business process re-engineering.

Ian Black is a Lecturer in the Centre for Logistics and Transportation at Cranfield University, UK. One of his main interests is in the development if models that simulate the performance of different designs of logistics and physical distribution systems.

Daniel F. Carr is a logistics executive at Hewlett-Packard Corporation in Seattle, Washington, USA. He has many years of practical experience in logistics management in the electronics sector and holds an MBA from Michigan State University.

Martin Christopher is Professor of Marketing and Logistics at the Cranfield University School of Management in the UK. He has written numerous books and articles on logistics and is on the editorial advisory panels of a number of professional journals in the fields of logistics and marketing. He has lectured all over the world and carried out consultancy for many major companies.

Marion Court is a Senior Lecturer in the Department of Transport and Logistics at the University of Huddersfield, UK. Prior to entering the academic world in 1993 she had had extensive industrial experience in distribution and transport management with NFC and BOC and as a logistics consultant.

Paul D. Cousins is a Lecturer in Strategic Purchasing and Supply Management at Bath University's, School of Management. His main interests are purchasing strategy, relationship management and measurement, and strategic performance measurement systems. He is the author of a forthcoming book *Collaborative Strategies for Competitive Advantage.*

Peter Dapiran is Senior lecturer in Logistics in the Faculty of Business and Economics, Monash University, Melbourne, Australia. He has had wide experience in industry as a logistics practitioner and in recent years has written a number of logistics case studies.

Eddie Dennis is Distribution Planning Manager for P&H McLane Ltd. He is responsible for the development of the company's national distribution strategy and holds an MSc in Transport and Distribution Management.

Martin Dresner is an Associate Professor of Logistics and Transportation in the College of Business and Management at the University of Maryland, USA. He received his MBA from York University, and his PhD from the Faculty of Commerce and Business Administration at the University of British Columbia, Canada.

Stephen Errey is Senior Consultant with Distribution Projects Ltd of Chester, UK. He has carried out many logistics and distribution assignments in the UK and overseas including a number in Africa.

Paul Corns is a Lecturer in the Department of Transport and Logistics at the University of Huddersfield, UK, and specializes in logistics, warehouse management and marketing.

Martin Green is Head of the Logistics Planning Unit for ASDA Stores, UK. Before joining ASDA in 1994 he had spent ten years as a logistics consultant with Touche Ross Management Consultants where he was responsible for a wide range of logistics assignments across many industries.

Adrian Grey is Operations Division Personnel Manager for Almarai Ltd, Saudi Arabia. He is an Irish national and has worked in the Middle East for a number of years. He is responsible for the personnel recruitment and training for Almaria.

Peter Gilmour is Professor of Management in the Graduate School of Management, Macquarie University, Sydney, Australia. He specializes in logistics and supply chain management and has published numerous articles and books on the subject.

Mark Harrison is Logistics Director at Perfecta Beds, part of the Silentnight Group which is a market leader in the UK. He holds a master's degree in Logistics and Distribution from Cranfield University.

Peter Hines is a Senior Research Fellow at Cardiff Business School, Cardiff, UK where he is the Deputy Director of the Lean Enterprise Research Centre. Much of his work has focused on intercompany relationships and in particular on supplier co-ordination and development. His first book *Creating World Class Suppliers: Unlocking Mutual Competitive Advantage* was published in 1994.

David Jessop is Professor Emeritus of Purchasing and Supply at the University of Glamorgan, UK. He also works as Senior Research Fellow at Cardiff Business School and as a consultant.

Alan McKinnon is Professor of Logistics in the School of Management at Heriot-Watt University, Edinburgh, UK. He has been teaching and researching in the fields of logistics and freight transport for 17 years and has published extensively on the subject. He has been an adviser to numerous public and private sector organizations on freight transport issues and, between 1990 and 1995, was European Editor of the *International Journal of Physical Distribution and Logistics Management*.

Andrew McClintock has been working in logistics for 15 years. His early career was spent as a manager with British Steel and then after an MSc in Distribution at Cranfield, he set up his own consultancy – specializing in quality and logistics management. In 1994, he held the position of Senior Logistics Officer for the UN in Zaire. He also lectures widely in the UK and overseas.

David A. Menachof took up the position of Senior Lecturer in Maritime Business at University of Plymouth, UK in 1996. Prior to that he was Associate Professor at the University of Charleston, South Carolina, USA. In 1994–5 Dr Menachof was awarded a Fulbright Scholarship to teach marketing, logistics and quality management at Odessa State University in Ukraine.

Adrian Murray is Head of Logistics in the Department of Marketing, Logistics and Property at the Royal Melbourne Institute of Technology, Australia. Before taking up a career in academia he had many years experience as a ship's master in the merchant navy followed by management positions in the road transport industry.

Will Murray is a Senior Lecturer in the Department of Transport and Logistics at the University of Huddersfield, UK. His main research interests are in the areas of management development for logistics and reducing commercial vehicle accidents. He has published numerous articles and has undertaken consultancy projects both in the UK and overseas.

Denis Nettle is a Senior Lecturer in the Department of Management at Victoria University of Technology, Melbourne, Australia. His research focuses on operations management and quality management, and he has recently published work on the development of the quality management movement in Australia.

Jane Parkin is a Senior Lecturer in the Department of Computer Studies and Mathematics at the University of Huddersfield, UK. She specializes in computer applications in transport and distribution.

John Oska is Regional Logistics Manager for BASF South-east Asia. He has had many years practical experience in logistics in both the business and military spheres and holds a master's degree in logistics.

Krzysztof Rutkowski is a professor at the Warsaw School of Economics Poland. He has particular interests in distribution and logistics management and in recent years has been involved in a number of co-operative programmes with universities in western Europe and the USA. His co-author *Professor Fred Beier* is based at the Carlson School of Management in the University of Minnesota, USA.

Ian Sadler is a Lecturer in Manufacturing and Logistics at Victoria University of Technology in Melbourne, Australia. His research interests include formulation of manufacturing and logistics strategies, logistics analysis and flow process simulation. He has been involved in teaching, consulting and publishing papers in all these areas.

Philip Schary is Professor of Logistics at Oregon State University, USA. He has worked in logistics for over 30 years and has been an influential figure in the development of the discipline. He has published many articles and books in the field and has lectured and consulted in many parts of the world.

Brian Shortland is Logistics Manager for Kingfisher Asia. He is based in Hong Kong and is responsible for organizing the international movement of products from all parts of south-east Asia to the UK for Woolworths and other companies within the Kingfisher retail group.

Tony Whiteing is Senior Lecturer in Transport and Logistics at the University of Huddersfield, UK, and co-ordinates the university's programme of logistics research. He has been involved in transport and logistics research since the late 1970s and holds a PhD from the University of Leeds.

David Wilson is a Lecturer in the Department of Information Systems, Faculty of Computing and Information Technology, Monash University, Australia. He specializes in logistics operations management and has previously taught at Melbourne University and RMIT University. He has had extensive industrial experience both as a logistics and operations manager and as a consultant.

George Wilson is Transport Manager with OK Tedi Mining Ltd in Papua New Guinea. He has had experience in transport management throughout the world with a variety of companies and the military. He holds a post-graduate qualification in transport and logistics management.

Acknowledgements

I would first like to thank all the authors that have contributed to the book. Most cases have been written specifically for this book by people who recognized the need for cases in the field of logistics and were prepared to respond my request for help in spite of their busy schedules.

Thanks are also due to in the companies and organizations which have allowed their operations to be described and to the great many people in these organizations that have assisted by providing the necessary data.

During part of the period in which this book was written I held the position of Visiting Research Fellow in the Department of Marketing Logistics and Property at the Royal Melbourne Institute of Technology in Australia. Thanks are due to members of that department for their support in the project and particularly to the Faculty of Business at RMIT for the award of a research grant to assist with the costs of collating and editing the work.

Special thanks are due to Gill Smith in the Department of Transport and Logistics at the University of Huddersfield who, during the two years it took to compile this book, gave unstinting and cheerful administrative and secretarial support which went far beyond the call of duty. Sincere thanks also go to Ron Pegg of the University's Computer Services Group, who repeatedly resuscitated my computer and rescued this book from electronic oblivion.

Finally I must thank my wife Chris and children Richard, Rosalind and Katie for their support and also for their patience and tolerance of a husband and father, who at times during the course of this project got rather grumpy!

David Taylor

Preface

This was book was conceived to fill a gap in the resources available for the teaching of logistics and supply chain management. In the last 10 years increasing numbers of specialist logistics courses have been developed by universities, professional institutes and management training organizations in countries throughout the world. In addition more and more general business and management courses such as the MBA are including modules on logistics and supply chain management. As a result there has been a growing demand for cases to help bridge the gap between theory and practice.

Over the same period logistics has become an increasingly international activity, not only in its study, but more importantly in the operation of logistics systems and the development of global supply chains. The book attempts to reflect this internationalization by bringing together 34 cases drawn from around the world, all of which deal with real situations faced by companies in the 1990s.

It is hoped the collection will help to educate both current and future managers who are directly involved in logistics, and those in other management fields who need an understanding of the role which logistics and supply chain management can play in enhancing corporate performance.

Scope of the book

Logistics management is concerned with the movement, storage and processing of materials and information across the whole of the supply chain, from acquisition of raw materials and components, through manufacturing, to delivery of finished products to end users.

Modern supply chain management demands a multidisciplinary and cross-functional approach to business which transcends the traditional functional boundaries and management disciplines that chararacterize many organizations. In consequence, many of the cases in the book will be of relevance to students and managers not just in the field of logistics but in various other business areas such as marketing, organizational behaviour, operations management and business policy.

Objectives of the book

In compiling this set of cases I had four general objectives.

1. To create a collection of cases which cover all major aspects of supply chain management
Cases cover the whole spectrum of supply chain activity including:

- purchasing and supplier management
- manufacturing logistics
- inventory management
- transport management
- distribution management
- warehousing management
- customer service management
- information management
- logistics and supply chain strategy.

While many cases deal with a specific aspect of the logistics activity such as purchasing or inventory management, the holistic nature of the logistics approach, demands that almost all cases require consideration of the individual functions and issues within the context of the wider supply chain.

2. To gather a collection of international cases

Prior to the publication of this book it is probably true to say that most logistics cases (certainly those published) had emanated from North America. This collection has attempted to be more geographically dispersed. Inevitably there is some bias towards the editor's home region of Europe, but as many cases as possible have been derived from other parts of the world. Authors have been asked, where ever possible, to present cases in such a way as to give students an understanding of the particular business environments and logistics characteristics of the different countries and regions involved.

A further international aspect of the book relates to the supply chain activities of case companies. Although the companies are classified by their country of origin, many of the supply chains described are international. Such a perspective is important, if not essential, in these days of global business activity.

3. To develop 'action-oriented' cases

Each of the cases in the book has two underlying objectives: first to provide a source of information on a specific issue, situation or organization, knowledge of which is in itself educationally valuable. However, the cases are not intended to just give an informative description. The second, and more important objective, is to demand action from the case user in terms of problem analysis, decision making and formulation of recommendations.

4. To produce cases which marry theory and practice

A critical aspect in achieving this objective has been the involvement of practicing logistics managers and/or consultants with academics in the production of the cases. Many cases have an academic and a practitioner as joint authors; some have been written just by practitioners; whilst for those where an academic is the sole author, appropriate acknowledgement is given to the company managers who provided the vital supply of real data and practical insight.

David Taylor

Courses and subject areas to which the book is relevant

The cross-functional and multidisciplinary nature of supply chain activity means that it is anticipated that this book will be of value to students on a variety of courses including those listed below.

Logistics and supply chain management

All the cases will be of relevance to students or managers involved in logistics or a supply chain activity. Some cases deal with the broad issues of logistics strategy, while others deal with specific functional aspects of logistics such as transport, warehousing or inventory management.

Marketing management

The primary objective of logistics management is to provide appropriate customer service. Customer service is the link between logistics and marketing. If logistics management is successful, it will result in good customer service, which can then be promoted as a key element in the company's competitive marketing strategy.

Many, if not all, of the cases in this book give consideration to customer service. In some instances it is the main issue (e.g. Palmer & Harvey); in many others it is considered as one of the objectives of logistics reform. The cases thus provide a valuable resource for marketing students in understanding the contribution that logistics can bring to the firm's marketing strategy and of the necessity for a close working relationship between marketing and logistics functions.

Operations management

A number of cases are concerned directly with specific aspects of operations management such as manufacturing operations (e.g. Trico, Kalon, Valkyrie, Fiat); transport operations (e.g. Polymedic, Santos), capacity planning (e.g Port of Melbourne); materials handling (e.g. BAAE, The Discount Shop) and materials sourcing (e.g. Filton, Westland Helicopters).

These and other cases will be valuable for courses in operations management not only by giving examples of specific operations management problems, but also by setting these problems in the wider context of operations across the whole supply chain.

International business and international marketing

Many of the cases deal with issues of international business.

Cases are based on organizations or situations in various parts of the world (see the map locating the case companies). One major objective of these cases is to give an understanding of the particular business, physical and cultural environments in different regions (e.g. Almarai in Saudi Arabia, Pepsi Cola in the Ukraine). Logistics initiatives require considerable change on the part of organizations and individuals and it is often crucial for the logistics planner to understand and take full account of national or regional cultural and environmental characteristics when planning and proposing change.

A further and particularly important aspect of international business is that nowadays many businesses have become international or global in their activities. Management of international supply chains is of paramount importance to global business; indeed it is increasingly recognized as critical to the success or failure of the global corporation. Some cases specifically deal with global supply chain management (e.g. Woolworths, Valkyrie). Others cover issues within the various emerging economic regions such as the Single European Market (SEM) (e.g. Brother, Nike, Hasbro) or Asia Pacific (e.g. BASF, Kodak, Hershey) or Third World scenarios (e.g. OK Tedi in Papua New Guinea, Rwandan disaster relief, Zimbabwe Dairy Marketing Board).

The cases contain much relevant information to aid the understanding of international business environments and the need for cultural knowledge and sensitivity when planning international business activities

Business strategy

A significant proportion of the cases are strategic in that they are concerned with the contribution that improved supply chain management can make to corporate performance and corporate strategy. A number present situations that were considered by the most senior management of the companies concerned, e.g. Fiat (European manufacturing and marketing strategy); Kalon (reforming corporate strategy); BASF (Asian regional logistics strategy); Pepsi (Ukraine marketing and distribution policy); Gillette, Nike and Hasbro (marketing and logistics strategies for the SEM).

These cases provide good examples of the contribution which enhanced supply chain management can make to corporate performance and may go some way towards filling the 'logistics gap' in corporate strategic planning theory and practice.

Organizational behaviour/change management

The essence of logistics management is the adoption of a process-based rather than a functional-based approach to business. Attempts to improve the supply chain of any organization inevitably require considerable organizational change. Supply chain management cuts across traditional boundaries within the firm, requiring greater co-operation between functional groups, e.g. purchasing, manufacturing, distribution and marketing. It requires individuals to accept new perspectives, objectives and ways of working, e.g. sub-optimization in parts of the supply chain to achieve greater overall improvements in corporate performance. It requires organizations within a supply chain, e.g. component suppliers, manufacturers and distributors, that have previously worked independently and often antagonistically, to form new types of relationships. Consequently, in practice probably the single most critical aspect of achieving supply chain change and improvement is the need to achieve changes in organizational and individual behaviour. Logistics managers need to be extremely sensitive to organizational issues. Conversely, logistics is an area which is increasingly recognized as crucial by those responsible for organizational structures, personnel management and training.

Many of the cases in the book provide examples of the need for organizational change and challenge students to consider the realities of achieving such change and as such will be a valuable resource for courses in organizational behaviour. Some cases which have a particularly strong focus on organizational issues include:

- Brother (achieving co-operation between diverse European subsidiaries)
- BASF (achieving change across subsidiaries in 16 Asian countries by a German multinational)
- Filton and Westland (changing traditional business relationships with suppliers)
- Rwanda (managing in the chaotic environment of a multiorganization disaster relief operation)
- US Department of Environment (managing change in a government organization).

Audiences for which the book is intended

University courses

Undergraduate and post-graduate.
1. Logistics/supply chain management and the various sub-disciplines:
    purchasing and supply
    distribution
    transport
    inventory management
2. Marketing and international marketing
3. International business
4. Operations management
5. Organizational behaviour
6. Retailing
7. General management/business, e.g. MBA

Courses of professional institutes

Logistics
Purchasing and supply
Production and inventory control
Transport
Marketing
Operations research
Management

Management training courses

Many of the cases will provide valuable real examples for management training at levels
from executive through to middle and junior management.

Additional materials to assist in using the cases

The instructor's manual

A comprehensive instructor's manual is available from the publisher. This contains teaching notes for every case, designed to permit teachers to make the most effective use of cases

The notes for each case are in the following standard format for ease of reference:

1. Case synopsis.
2. Teaching/learning objectives.
3. Main issues raised.
4. Specific questions/student assignments.
5. Description of actual developments in the companies subsequent to the case.
6. Suggestions for using the case, teaching approaches, suitable audiences.

Internet data availability

A number of the cases contain presentations of significant amounts of data in tabular form. Full analysis of the case may require students to manipulate this data by computer.

To reduce time wasting in transferring data from the printed text to the computer, data from the cases listed below has been posted at the following Internet address and can be downloaded by teachers or students.

Internet address:

> http://www.opsmanagement.itbp.com

The cases with data available on the Internet are:

Britvic	Eastman Kodak	Perfecta Beds
Brother International	Medisupply	Rank Hovis McDougall
Hasbro Europe	Nike Europe	US Department of the Environment
Hershey	Palmer & Harvey	Zimbabwe Dairy Marketing Board

The analysis of logistics and supply chain management cases

David Taylor
Department of Transport and Logistics, University of Huddersfield, UK

Since the mid-1970s there has been significant development in the theory and practice of logistics management and as a consequence there is now a much greater degree of understanding of how supply chains operate and how they might be improved.

Although each supply chain situation and indeed each case in this book is unique, an understanding of the theories and techniques of logistics management provide a framework with which to systematically approach the analysis of supply chain problems.

The purpose of this introductory chapter is to outline a framework for analysing supply chain situations. However, it must be emphasized that this is not a prescriptive approach that can be applied without thought to all situations, rather it provides a series of checklists of factors to consider. The case analyst must determine which checklist, or part thereof, is relevant to the case in question.

Some cases deal with the full scope of an organization's supply chain from raw material supplies through to delivery of a finished product to the end user; while others deal with just one part of the supply chain such as retailing or manufacturing; or just one logistics activity such as transport or inventory management. Analysis of cases dealing with particular functions will usually require knowledge of specific techniques and may require detailed operational analysis; nevertheless it is always advisable to set the specific logistics problem in the context of the overall supply chain system and consider the effects of changes in one function on other functions both up and down the supply chain.

Defining logistics and supply chain management

There are many definitions of logistics coined by authors, consultants and practitioners. However, for the purposes of this book the definition of logistics developed by the US Council of Logistics Management in 1986 will suffice:

> The process of planning, implementing and controlling the efficient, cost-effective flow and storage of raw materials, in-process inventory, finished goods and related information from point-of-origin to point of final consumption for the purpose of conforming to customer requirements.

This definition highlights the key features of logistics:

- it is concerned with movement and storage of materials
- it is concerned with managing the information flows that underpin the flow of materials
- its scope ranges across the whole supply chain from point of origin of raw materials to final consumption of finished products
- it requires a single logic to plan and organize this flow of materials throughout the supply chain
- it has two key objectives: (i) achieving appropriate customer-service standards and (ii) doing so in a cost-effective manner.

Logistics management and supply chain management are essentially synonymous terms, in that logistics management is a systematic and holistic approach to managing the flow of materials and information across the whole supply chain from raw materials sources to end-user consumption.

Many logistics problems initially manifest themselves within the confines of an individual firm and indeed within an individual functional area of the firm. For example, a company may realize that it has insufficient warehouse capacity or that there is insufficient flexibility in production, or that inventory levels are too high. Yet the real cause of the problem and indeed the solution may lie outside the immediate functional area or even outside the firm.

Approaching such problems from a logistics perspective therefore requires the student to consider the issue at three levels:

- Level 1   the specific function in which the problem occurs, e.g. the warehouse
- Level 2   the other functions within the firm which relate to the flow of materials or information, e.g. purchasing, manufacturing, marketing
- Level 3   the wider supply chain beyond the bounds of the firm, e.g. suppliers, distribution channel members, end users.

To analyse a problem only at level 1 would be a functional approach and not a logistics approach. Some authors argue that level 2 is a logistics management approach, while level 3 is a supply chain management approach. It is suggested here that a logistics approach requires consideration of all three levels, even though in practice it may not be easy to implement changes beyond the bounds of the functional area in which the problem occurs and even more difficult to effect change beyond the bounds of the firm.

Logistics objectives

Improved customer service and reduced supply chain costs are the outputs of logistics management and it is through the achievement of these two objectives that logistics contributes to corporate performance. When analysing any logistics problem it is important to always keep these two fundamental objectives in view.

Customer service

In many industries in the 1990s customer service has become a key competitive issue and there has been an increasing realization that efficient management of the flow of materials through the supply chain is critical to achieving high levels of service.

In the 1960s and 1970s authors such as Peter Drucker talked of distribution being the neglected area of marketing or the 'economy's dark continent'. The 1980s and 1990s have seen companies attacking not just distribution, but the wider concept of logistics and realizing that improvements in logistics can improve service and reduce costs and thereby give the firm a significant competitive advantage which can then be exploited as a key element of marketing strategy. Indeed it is through customer service that the marketing and logistics functions interface.

Logistics costs

The second objective of logistics is to minimize cost. Logistics costs frequently represent a significant element of a firm's total cost. In companies where logistics has not been well managed there is usually considerable scope for cost saving and there may well be a temptation for management to concentrate on the cost reduction objective to the detriment of customer service performance. However, it is critical that the required customer service standards are clearly defined and safeguarded before cost reduction measures are implemented.

It is usually the case that measures aimed at cost reduction result in more easily quantifiable benefits particularly in the short run, whilst measures aimed at service improvement tend to have less easily quantified and longer run outcomes such as enhanced customer satisfaction and greater customer loyalty which eventually work through to increased profits.

The starting point for any logistics project should therefore be a clear definition of the customer service standards required to give a competitive advantage. Once those standards have been defined the logistics manager should devise the most cost-effective systems to achieve the service targets.

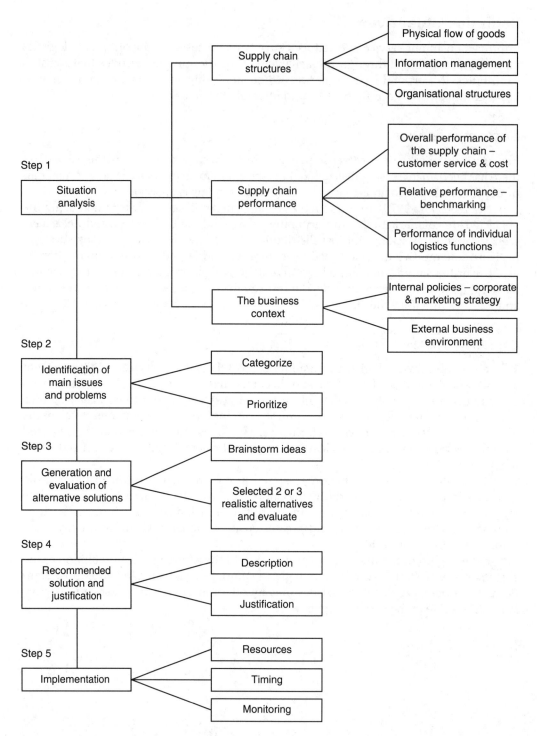

Figure 1   The case analysis framework.

A framework for analysing logistics and supply chain cases

The five-step process outlined overleaf in Figure 1 can be used to approach most case studies. In the following notes most emphasis is given to step 1 because in practice a thorough and accurate situational analysis will often in itself highlight the main problems and issues (step 2) and in many instances point directly towards appropriate solutions (steps 3 and 4)

Step 1. Analysis of the existing situation

Supply chain structures

At first sight supply chain systems often appear to be quite complex involving many functions within a firm and many organizations along the supply chain. The complexity may be increased by confusion within organizations over responsibilities for logistical activities and an uncoordinated approach to the management of material and information flows.

The schematic diagram in Figure 2 provides a framework with which to approach the analysis of supply chains.

The figure shows there are three major issues which need to be considered when analysing supply chain problems:

- the physical flow of goods
- the information flows and systems which underpin the flow of goods
- the organizational and management structures which control the supply chain.

Whether a case situation relates to the whole supply chain or to only part of it, it is advisable to consider each of these three aspects.

The physical flow of goods
The flow of goods through the logistics pipeline is the most obvious aspect of supply chain activity. A good starting point in analysing most cases is to produce a schematic diagram (as in Figure 2) showing the flow of goods from point of origin of raw materials or components, through manufacturing and out through the distribution channels to the end-user.

Such diagrams should be schematic and as simple as possible. For example, if there are 50 suppliers of components it would be unnecessary to show 50 boxes in the suppliers column, better to state '50' as a figure; on the other hand if the primary manufacturer has three plants these could all be drawn into the column under 'manufacturing'

Supply chain diagrams should not attempt to illustrate geographical locations. Although relative locations of organizations in the supply chain may be important, particularly when considering global supply chains, the schematic diagram is only intended to show the structure of the fixed points in the chain (e.g. factories or warehouses) and movement patterns between those fixed facilities (the flows).

(a) **Fixed points in the chain.** The first step is to categorize the various functional stages in the supply chain, e.g. manufacturing, storage wholesaling, retailing, etc. and then group organizations into the following categories.
- The primary manufacturer – this is defined as the organization producing the final

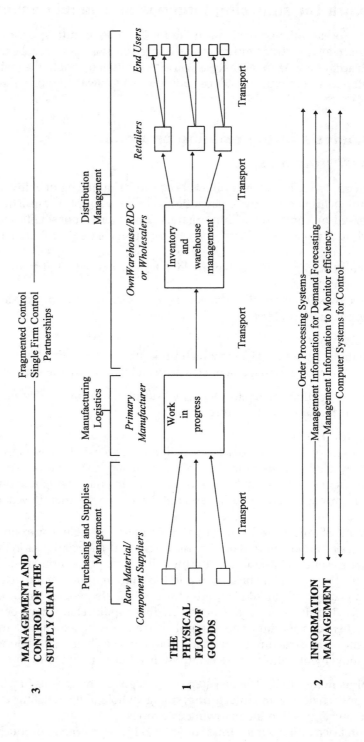

Figure 2 The supply chain management model.

product as used by the end-user (sometimes referred to as the original equipment manufacturer or OEM). In many supply chains the primary manufacturer is the pivotal point of the chain.

- Upstream of the primary manufacturer there are likely to be component suppliers and beyond them raw material suppliers. It may be beneficial to identify first-, second- and even third-tier suppliers to the OEM. There may also be consolidation centres between the component suppliers and the manufacturer to accumulate or sort supplies inbound to the manufacturing process.
- Downstream of the manufacturer are likely to be a variety of fixed facilities in the distribution channel. It is useful to think of distribution as all activities that take place after the OEM finished product leaves the end of the factory production line. Initially there may well be the manufacturer's finished product storage facilities, perhaps a warehouse at the factory site or distribution centres in 'field' locations closer to the market place. Thereafter the product is likely to move through distribution channels, be these wholesalers and retailers (common for consumer goods) or distributors (common for industrial goods).

It is advisable always to chart the supply chain as far as the end-user, because it is possible that difficulties for the final customer may arise between the last organization in the chain and the actual consumption or use of the product. For example, a medical equipment manufacturer selling products through distributors into hospitals may consider that the supply chain ends when the product is received by the hospital's purchasing or stores function. In fact considerable problems in terms of inventory levels and product movement may arise between the hospital stores and the use of the equipment by the end-user, be that a surgeon or nurse. Increasingly companies are looking at influencing the total supply chain even within the customers' organization in order to ensure best customer service to the actual end-user.

(b) **Movement patterns along the chain.** After identification and categorization of the organizations which comprise the fixed elements of the supply chain, the second step is to chart the flows and movements which provide the links between the fixed elements.

Conceptually transport should be the last issue to consider when analysing existing supply chains and indeed when planning new supply chains, because transport requirements are determined by the number and geographical proximity of the fixed elements in the chain and the volumes to be moved. When considering the links it is important to view the chain as a whole. Transport flows should be clearly indicated on the schematic diagram and in reality they may be more complex than simple direct flows between the fixed facilities.

It is often beneficial when analysing transport movements to additionally produce a simple geographical map to show the main fixed locations in the supply chain and the major movement patterns between them. A knowledge of the basic geography of an area is essential in analysing transport systems. For example, some potential transport options may be precluded because of physical barriers such as unbridged river estuaries or mountain ranges. Furthermore, mapping the locations of *all* fixed elements in the supply chain from raw material suppliers, through factories, wholesalers and retailers may reveal geographical juxtapositions that suggest opportunities for co-ordination of transport across the chain. For example, backloading outbound delivery vehicles with inbound component supplies. (A series of maps are contained at the end of this book as a starting point for geographical analysis.)

It is also important when considering transport to identify transport requirements right up to the end-user's point of consumption, as again problems and potential customer difficulty may occur beyond the point of final purchase. For example, in the UK, retailers selling 'flatpack' or 'knockdown' furniture recognized that some customers faced difficulty in transporting such furniture home from the store and consequently developed a service for the loan of car roof-racks or trailers to enable customers to conveniently complete the last leg of the supply chain.

Most supply chains have not been planned as a single system; rather they have evolved on the basis of many decisions taken independently at different times and different points in the chain. As a result chains are often complex and inefficient. The schematic mapping of the system is an essential first step in untangling this complexity and the production of a flow diagram is often a very good indicator of some of the major supply chain problems.

Information management

The second major group of issues to consider when analysing logistics cases are those related to information management.

Information management is critical to effective supply chain operations. In Figure 2 four key issues related to information management are identified.

(a) **Order processing information.** The first thing to consider is the operational systems required to process orders through the supply chain. Customer demand triggers orders and the systems which are in place to capture the order and progress it down the supply chain must be identified. The order moves in the opposite direction to and initiates the physical flow of goods.

A second flow of information accompanies the movement of the physical product through the system, for example, despatch notes, delivery notes and invoices. Again this must be identified and its efficiency analysed.

Just as the physical flow of goods can be mapped, it is also useful to produce a schematic diagram to show the flows of information. This should indicate the fixed points through which the information passes, e.g. sales department, warehouse, transport department, and the mechanisms by which information is transmitted, e.g. telephone, fax, electronic data interchange (EDI).

Again the production of flow diagrams is an essential first step in understanding the mechanisms of the supply chain information flows and in highlighting potential problems.

(b) **Demand forecasting information.** The second key aspect of information management in logistics is the information required for demand forecasting. A fundamental starting point for modern logistics management is the requirement for forecasts of future demand in order to plan the capacities of the supply chain functions such as production or transport and to determine the levels and locations of inventory required to meet customer demand.

In many organizations demand forecasting is the responsibility of the marketing or sales department, in others it is the responsibility of production, while in some it effectively does not take place at all. Accurate demand forecasts are essential to successful logistics planning and it is therefore important to identify the functions and system involved in demand forecasts and assess the accuracy of these forecasts.

(c) **Management information.** The third aspect of information management relates to the availability of the management information which is necessary to monitor the efficiency of logistics operations.

A great variety of such information is required ranging from data to monitor the performance of specific operations, e.g. vehicle utilization levels or warehouse productivity, to information which indicates the performance of the overall logistics system such as inventory levels throughout the supply chain.

In many companies there is a paucity of management information for logistics, partly because logistics is often a new function and no-one has previously collected relevant information and partly because most information is generated by and for the financial functions of the firm and may not be in an appropriate form for logistics managers. An important early step in logistics improvement is to clearly define the management information required to monitor the performance of supply chain activities and to establish if or how that information can be made available.

(d) **Computer systems.** The fourth aspect of information management which requires analysis is the physical systems to facilitate the flows of operational information and provide the requisite management information. In most modern organizations this will centre around the computer systems and requires assessment of the capabilities of both hardware and software and increasingly of the network linkages between computers.

It should not be forgotten however that in some organizations and some situations, e.g. less-developed countries, computers may not be in evidence and indeed may not be appropriate; in which case analysis should be made of the alternative systems which are in place to handle information.

The organization and management structures which control the supply chain

The third major consideration when analysing logistics systems relates to the organizational structures which control the supply chain.

The essence of logistics is to develop an integrated approach to the management of the whole supply chain. It is therefore necessary to understand the pre-existing structures, functions and attitudes which control the existing supply chain system.

Analysis of management structures should be carried out at two levels:

• the individual firm, and
• the supply chain as a whole.

Even within the individual companies that comprise the supply chain, e.g. a manufacturer or a retailer, it is common to find responsibility for different logistics activities split between functions. For example, in-bound transportation, warehousing of components and inter-plant transportation might be the responsibility of the production function; warehousing of finished products and outbound transportation the responsibility of the distribution function; while customer service and inventory levels could be controlled by sales or marketing.

The traditional organizational structure of most companies is into vertical functional groups, while materials and information flow horizontally across these functions. It is important to identify the groups involved in the flows and to determine their perspectives and objectives in relation to logistics activity.

It is also important to assess the perspective of a company's senior management to supply chain activities and improvement. Various studies have shown that senior management understanding of, and backing for, logistics change is an essential ingredient for success. It is therefore necessary to assess the senior management's view of logistics as this will be critical to the likely success of future plans.

The relationships of the various individual organizations which make up the supply chain must also be examined. Most supply chains are comprised of a large number of companies, e.g. numerous component suppliers, numerous retailers or wholesalers. All these companies are independent commercial entities, each with their own business objectives and profit goals. As a result, the control of many supply chains has traditionally been fragmented between these companies and relationships were often adversarial.

In some instances one firm (often a major manufacturer) may have gained control of other organizations either upstream (e.g. component suppliers) or downstream (e.g. retailers) in a process of vertical integration in order to gain control of a greater part of the supply chain and thereby permit more systematic management of the system. This has been the case with some Japanese car manufacturers who often own component suppliers, and even have interests in the steel works supplying the raw material, as well as having control of the dealerships which distribute finished products.

In recent times there have been initiatives in many industries towards the formation of 'partnerships' between supply chain members. A prime purpose of this is to move towards a situation where logistics improvements can be implemented along the supply chain as well as within individual organizations.

A further important issue which should be examined when analysing the control of the supply chain is that of power relationships between the organizations and groups making up the chain. It is important to assess which organizations are most powerful, as in reality it is likely that only the most powerful members of the chain will be able to force through logistical initiatives which require significant changes of operational practice across the chain and may result in a disproportionate sharing of benefits. For example, it is unlikely that a small scale supplier of components will be able to initiate logistics changes which require significant changes in practice from a large manufacturer customer. Alternatively very significant logistics improvements have been made in UK food supply chains, forced through by a small number of very powerful supermarket groups which have been able to impose their wishes on food manufacturers and agricultural producers.

A final, but very important, point to bear in mind in relation to organizational issues is where supply chains are international or companies are multinational. There is a need for considerable cultural sensitivity and diplomacy when dealing with supply chain partners that are based in different parts of the world and that may have very different perspectives on business practices and on logisitics management initiatives.

Supply chain performance

In order to study the benefits of any logisitics improvements which may later be suggested and to help in determining where to target effort, it is necessary to assess the current performance of the supply chain.

This should be done at three levels:

- the overall performance of the supply chain
- the relative performance of the supply chain
- the performance of individual logisitics functions.

Overall performance

It is necessary to evaluate and quantify the existing performance of the current logistics system in terms of both customer service and total logistics costs. This will then provide a benchmark against which to evaluate the success of any proposed changes.

(a) **Customer service.** It is first necessary to identify or develop a set of key customer service performance criteria and obtain measures of the standards actually achieved by the company or the function.

In analysing customer service performance it is necessary to clearly differentiate the various levels of customer. Many firms consider their customer to be the organization which pays their invoice, for example a manufacturer's customer might be a wholesaler; a wholesaler's customer a retailer. Although these are customers and their service requirements must be met, from a supply chain perspective it is always advisable to identify the end-user, i.e. final consumer of the product, and consider their service needs; it is after all the payment from the end-user that actually provides the funds to make the payments all the way along the chain.

Another level of customer which might also be considered is the internal customer; that is the next group or function within any one organization to receive the material or information flow. For example the production department may pass the finished product to the factory warehouse, the factory warehouse passes it to the transport department and transport passes it to the regional distribution centre. The service requirements of each one of these internal customers should be identified and the performance between the functions quantified.

(b) **Logistics costs.** It is also desirable, although frequently not at all easy, to collate figures to indicate total logistics costs. Effort should be made to obtain at least a best estimate of total logistics costs because it is likely that initiatives introduced later into any one area of the system may give cost benefits in that area but have trade-offs with cost dis-benefits in other parts of the supply chain. Unless the overall cost picture is known at the outset, it is impossible to accurately identify such trade-offs and determine whether individual initiatives are of overall benefit.

Where detailed figures on particular elements of logistics costs are not available within the company, it may be appropriate to use standard published figures, such as those produced by the UK Institute of Logistics, as a best estimate.

Relative performance

A further aspect of analysing the current situation of a company's supply chain is to benchmark its performance against outside organizations. Benchmarking has become increasingly popular in recent years and can include many aspects of supply chain activity such as

- customer service performance
- logistics costs
- systems and technology for operational functions, e.g. warehouse control, transport routing and scheduling, production management
- inventory levels.

The aim of benchmarking is to assess the company's performance in relation to best practice. Benchmarking can be accomplished in many ways including direct studies of other firms, possibly on a reciprocal basis with non-competing companies, use of studies published in trade or academic literature, attendance at conferences and trade shows.

Although it is often difficult to directly obtain information about a competitor's supply chain performance, the logistics manager must ultimately make some judgement as to the firm's performance relative to the competition. The aim of supply chain management is to gain an advantage in terms of customer service and cost over competitors. It is therefore important to form as clear a view as possible of the firm's position in these issues relative to the main competitors.

Performance of individual logistics functions

So far the suggested approach to logistics analysis has concentrated on the supply chain at a macro-level in terms of the flows of materials and information, control structures and performance. Such an overview is an essential prerequisite of the logistics approach, which by definition deals with the supply chain as an integrated whole rather than with individual functions in isolation. However, alongside this macro-level analysis in most cases it will be necessary to undertake detailed analysis of one or more individual functions within the supply chain. For example, it may be necessary to analyse inventory control systems, transport operations, supplier relationships or production control systems.

For any individual functions it is necessary to develop a clear picture of what is happening. Here again the three major features highlighted in Figure 1, the physical flow of goods, the underlying management information systems and the organizational control structures provide a suitable framework with which to approach the situation analysis. Clearly, however, within each function there will be many specific issues that need to be considered, which will require the use of the particular tools and techniques relevant to the specific function. For example, in analysing an inventory issue it may be appropriate to use the technique of Pareto analysis or the concept of stockturn ratio; whilst in analysing a transport problem it may be necessary to evaluate the use of vehicle carrying capacities or fleet operating costs.

Logistics in the business context

Internal corporate policies

So far the situational analysis has been concerned with the nature and performance of the supply chain itself. It is also necessary to evaluate the corporate context in which the logistics functions operate. A brief assessment should be made of both the corporate business strategy and the marketing strategy with particular reference to those issues which directly affect or could be affected by logistical activities. For example, if the corporate plan states the need to reduce costs in order to become more price competitive, this may focus logistics planning on cost reduction initiatives. Alternatively the marketing plan may highlight the need to improve customer service as a key competitive element. If logistics is to contribute to corporate performance and competitive strategy, logistics managers must have a clear picture of corporate goals.

The external business environment
The final aspect of the situational analysis is to consider factors in the company's external business environment which may impinge directly on supply chain issues. Potentially there are many such influences, a few examples are given below.

- Increasing power of a major customer may force the company to introduce supply chain initiatives to meet that customer's inventory and delivery requirements.
- Increasing price competition from lower cost overseas producers may require initiatives in the supply chain to both reduce cost and improve service in order to remain competitive.
- Changes in the cost and/or efficiency of external service providers such as contract distribution companies or transport modes may impact on logistics policy.
- Development of new politico-economic regions such as the single European market may create opportunities for different logistics approaches.

The business environment is external to the company and as such is largely uncontrollable by the firm. The requirement is for the firm to continually scan the environment and identify changes, be they opportunities or threats, that might influence supply chain policy. The aim is to develop policies in response to, or preferably in anticipation of, changes in the environment.

To SWOT or not? A note on SWOT analysis
SWOT analysis (Strengths–Weaknesses–Opportunities–Threats) is a common technique used as the basis for situational analysis in marketing and business strategy studies. It can also be useful for categorizing issues in the situational analysis of logistics cases. However, experience shows that there is a danger if SWOT analysis is used that some students, particularly those who have studied marketing, may stray into a marketing analysis of the situation rather than a logistics analysis. In so doing too much emphasis may be given to aspects of the wider marketing policy such as price/promotion/product issues to the detriment of logistics analysis.

In the context of a logistics analysis, strengths and weaknesses will be concerned with controllable elements of the supply chain operations such as inventory, transport or order processing systems. Opportunities and threats will require identification of externalities which either directly affect or can be affected by supply chain policies.

A word of warning therefore: if SWOT analysis is used in logistics cases, ensure it is relevant to a logistics analysis rather than a marketing analysis.

Step 2. Identification of major issues and problems

Identify

Identification of the main issues and problems is usually not only the most difficult but also the most crucial part of case analysis. Consequently, considerable thought should be given to the process. If the main issues and problems are not correctly identified, it is highly unlikely that appropriate recommendations can be made. The more comprehensive and rigorous the situational analysis, the more likely it is that the key problems and issues will emerge.

This section should not just concentrate on problems even though in many cases these will be paramount, but should also identify relevant issues, some of which may be opportunities rather than problems. For example, if a major customer introduces a new EDI ordering system, this may create an opportunity to improve the speed and accuracy of order intake and also reduce the costs of order processing.

Categorize

The first step is to list all problems and issues that have been identified. The second step is to categorize the issues raised. There are various ways that this can be approached including:

(a) problems that must be solved   vs   opportunities that could be seized
(b) strategic issues   vs   operational issues
(c) Figure 1 gives an alternative framework for classifying issues and problems in relation to the various functional and organizational aspects of the supply chain.

Whatever basis is used, categorization of problems into meaningful related groups is an important step in moving towards sensible solutions.

Symptoms vs causes. It is very important to differentiate between symptoms and causes. In cases, as indeed in reality, it is often the symptoms that are most overtly stated. For example, a manager may identify lack of warehouse capacity as a problem. In fact this might only be a symptom either of poor inventory management or of production policies which generate stock in excess of demand. The analysis must try to identify the real underlying problem and it is often the case that the problem lies in another part of the supply chain from the symptom, which is why a logistics approach, rather than a traditional functional approach, can be so beneficial.

Prioritize

The final step is to prioritize the problems and issues, perhaps identifying one or more major problems and then a number of minor issues. Alternatively problems can be split into those requiring immediate action and those which require longer term solutions. Whichever way problems are categorized and prioritized it is important to define the issues in a way that calls for action-oriented solutions.

Step 3. Generation and evaluation of alternative solutions

Once the problems have been identified there follows the creative process of generating ideas and possible solutions.

Generating options

As many different ideas as possible should be developed, each with quite different approaches to the problem. It is particularly beneficial to undertake the ideas generation process in 'brainstorming' groups, as it is usually the case that such discussions have a synergistic effect and result in more and different solutions than any one person might develop.

In generating solutions it is often helpful to think at three levels:

- the specific functional issue, e.g. purchasing, inventory, transport, etc.
- the corporate context , e.g. the requirement to achieve cross-functional changes within one company, such as between the marketing, production and distribution departments
- the supply chain context, e.g. possible changes within and between other organizations in the supply chain such as relationships with suppliers, or requirements for distributors to adopt different procedures.

A further helpful tool is the supply chain diagram shown in Figure 1, which not only provides a framework for situational analysis but also provides a checklist of issues to consider when generating solutions.

The generation of solutions is in practice closely linked to the situational analysis, in that a good situational analysis should lead to a clear identification of the main issues and problems, which itself often points to appropriate solutions or courses of action.

Evaluating options

Cursory consideration of possible solutions will usually sift out the impractical or illogical suggestions. The aim should be to produce two or three realistic alternative solutions, each of which should be briefly described and evaluated in terms of the operational requirements, costs, benefits, etc.

One of the most important, possibly the most important, aspects of evaluating alternatives is the need to make a realistic assessment of the practicalities of implementing the proposal and the likelihood of the option being adopted by the organizations concerned.

Traditional business planning adopts the following sequential approach:

- generate options
- select the preferred option
- consider how implementation can be achieved.

In practice, however, many theoretically ideal or optimum solutions, which may have great benefits for companies, never progress beyond the drawing board because the planners did not consider the realities of implementation at the planning stage. There is a strong argument that identification of the obstacles to and mechanisms for implementation should be identified and overtly stated at the point at which ideas are generated. Implementational realities then become a key element in the process of screening and selecting alternatives. A sub-optimal proposal that has a realistic chance of implementation is better than the optimum solution, which for cost, organizational or other reasons has very little chance of being implemented.

A further aspect of implementation is the need to 'sell' ideas to stake holders in the company or wider supply chain. This is an issue which is especially relevant with logistics proposals, as almost by definition, a logistics solution will require an approach that crosses traditional functional boundaries and demand that people adopt different practices, targets or perspectives than they have been used to. Such changes are inevitably difficult to achieve. It is therefore advisable to think clearly at an early stage about how proposals can be packaged and presented to stake holders in order to gain co-operation. The mechanism for 'selling' the proposal should be a major consideration in the option screening process.

Step 4. Recommended solution and justification

The evaluation of alternatives in Step 3 should lead to a decision on the preferred course of action. A full description of the chosen solution should be given together with a justification of its choice in terms of expected costs and benefits.

With all the cases in this book a decision should be reached or a firm recommendation given. It is unacceptable to claim that there is insufficient information in the case to reach a decision or propose a solution. The cases generally contain most of the information that was available to the decision-makers in the situations described. Where it is felt that data or detail are lacking it must be remembered that, in reality, most decisions in business are made on the basis of imperfect or incomplete information.

Step 5. Implementation

The final aspect of case analysis is to carefully consider the implementation of the recommended solution. A list of practical implementation questions should be addressed such as:

Resources
- Who will be responsible for implementation?
- How can the benefits of the proposals be 'sold' to concerned individuals, groups, departments, both within the organization and within the wider supply chain?
- What will be the cost of the implementation process?

Timing
- What time scale is required?
- In what sequence will implementation occur?

Monitoring
- How will the costs and benefits be measured and monitored?

In practice evaluation of the realities, difficulties and costs of implementation should have formed an important part of the screening of alternatives in Step 3. It was argued earlier that a rigorous and realistic evaluation of implementation requirements should be the first criterion in screening ideas, because unless solutions have a realistic chance of implementation they are of no value and it is therefore pointless to develop the proposals in detail.

An explanation of implementational realities should form a significant part of any case report.

The business report

The final important element in the case study process is the preparation of a business report. Business reports must be clear, concise and readable otherwise it is unlikely that the analysis will either be understood (or even fully read) or acted on. It is critical for students to realize that analysing supply chain situations and developing proposals is only the first step in achieving change and in many respects it is the easiest and often the most enjoyable part of the exercise. The real difficulty usually lies in persuading others that your ideas are valid and worth adopting. Preparation of a top-quality business report is an essential step in the process of achieving change. Figure 3 outlines a structure that can be used in presenting business reports.

---

1 *Header page*

2 *Executive summary*
This should normally be no more than one page (approximately 300 words) in length. It should indicate the
  • main problems/issues
  • main recommendations
  • expected benefits if recommendations are implemented
Note: the executive summary is a critical section of a business report, as it might be the only section read by the key decision makers. Great care should be taken in writing the executive summary in order to ensure only the most relevant points are included and that they are presented as clearly and concisely as possible.

3 *Contents page*

4 *The main body of the report*
This should contain:

A Resumé of the current situation
This must be brief.
Imagine you are writing the report for the management of the company who already know the situation. You should not reiterate the facts as presented in the case. Instead the key aspects of the situation should be presented from a logistics perspective.
   A schematic supply chain diagram may be a useful and concise way to illustrate the current situation and may allow presentation of the information from a different perspective and in a more organized manner.
   In practice the situational analysis will have taken considerable time and effort but that will not normally be reflected in the space devoted to explaining the situation in the report.

Statement of main issues and problems
Again it is important not to just reiterate and list the problems as they appear in the case. Instead problems rather than symptoms should be identified and presented in a categorized and prioritized format.

Outline of alternative policies or options
Two or three alternative solutions or improvements may be briefly presented together with a brief statement of their pros and cons.

Recommendations
A clear and concise statement should be given of the preferred solution or recommended policy together with a justification of its choice.

Implementation
A listing should be given of the main aspects of the preferred solution and against each should be indicated by whom, when, how and at what cost implementation will take place.

Analysis of benefits and costs of recommendation
By way of conclusion an analysis should be given of the overall costs and benefits of the recommended course of action

---

Figure 3 Guidelines for the format and structure of a business report.

A note on the classification of cases in this book

Cases have been classified into broad topic groups (e.g. purchasing and supplies management and manufacturing logisitics) as a way of structuring the contents of the book in order to ease usage of the text. However students should be wary of assuming that topic headings are necessarily a reliable guide to the main issues and problems of the cases. Many of the cases deal with a variety of logistics issues. Furthermore the fundamental philosophy of the logistics approach is that problems should be analysed from the perspective of the whole supply chain rather than in the narrow confines of particular functional areas.

PART ONE

Logistics and supply chain strategy

Logistics operations in south and east Asia

John Oska
Regional Logistics Manager, BASF SE Asia

Introduction

In the early 1990s the expansion of BASF, a German-based chemical manufacturer, was accelerating in the Asian region. A regional headquarters had been established in Singapore in 1989 to take advantage of the development in the region and to cope with the predicted growth in turnover and local production (Figure 1.1). Prior to this, the region had been served by an office located in the head office and main production facility in Ludwigshafen, Germany. Within Asia, the company had grown on a steady basis, partially through acquisition, and was represented in most countries by wholly and partly owned subsidiaries or joint ventures. A number of local production sites had been established. At the time the new headquarters had been created, there was a growing

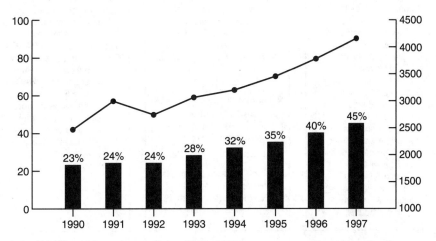

Figure 1.1 BASF south and east Asia: 1990–1997 turnover and local production.

awareness of the importance of logistics to the company, particularly because of the distance from Europe. There was also the vision that the creation of streamlined logistics processes would lead to significant benefits to operating performance in the regional companies. However, owing to a lack of expertise in this field within the headquarters, little was done in the early years other than targeting the inventory levels of selected subsidiaries. In late 1993, the post of Regional Logistics Manager was created with a view to improving logistics in the region. In this new role, the incumbent was faced with the inviting prospect of developing a logistics strategy for the region.

Company background

BASF is one of the world's largest chemical companies. From its beginnings as a producer of coal-tar-based dyestuffs in 1865, BASF has grown into an enterprise covering the spectrum of modern chemistry from crude oil to highly sophisticated products.

BASF is a homogeneous enterprise, concentrating on chemicals and related business-es. Since the mid-1960s it has broadened the scope of its international operations, increasingly establishing production facilities in many parts of the globe, and thus maintaining its traditional closeness to customers.

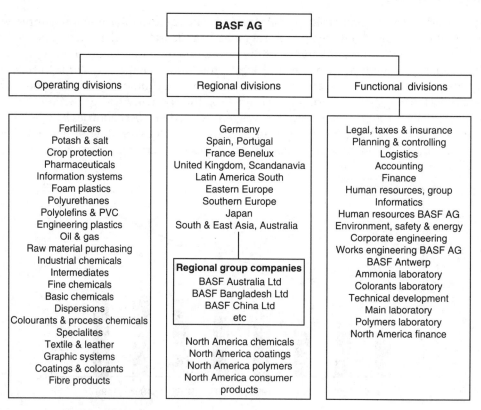

Figure 1.2 BASF company operations.

Some 112,000 people work for BASF in over 300 group companies world-wide. The company headquarters is in Ludwigshafen, Germany, its first production site. Major production sites also exist in Belgium, Spain, the UK, Italy, United States and Brazil. In total, production facilities exist in 39 countries serving a customer base in 170 countries. Turnover during the past ten years has ranged between DM40 and 50 billions.

Company operations are divided into six main sectors (oil and gas, chemicals, agricultural products, plastics and fibres, dyestuffs and finishing products, and consumer products) of 22 major product groupings, each represented by an operating division (Figure 1.2). The total number of products manufactured is over 8000. Support is provided by a further 18 functional divisions, such as logistics, information systems and finance. A further subdivision is provided by regional divisions, of which there are 14 world-wide, and under whose authority individual group companies are located. The total organization is thus represented by a three-dimensional matrix comprising operating, regional and functional divisions.

Regional operations

Limited operations within Asia have existed since the start of the twentieth century. However, only following BASF's global expansion in the 1960s did major operations commence in the region. The company is represented by over 30 companies in 16 countries throughout the region, of which 12 have production facilities. Representation extends from Pakistan in the west to South Korea in the north and New Zealand in the

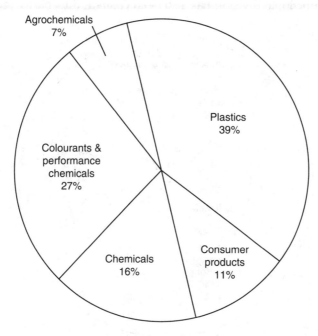

Figure 1.3 BASF in south and east Asia/Australia: sales by business fields. Total 1994: DM3.3 billion.

east; Japan forms a separate regional division. Headquarters for the region is based in Singapore. Of the group companies, several are joint venture operations accommodating local interests and regulations.

Historically, as with other parts of the world, many of the companies have been formed through the acquisition of local companies and others have been taken over from local agency operations. As such these have brought with them local operating procedures, structures, corporate culture and principles. Until 1989, these activities were managed directly from Germany, but owing to the expansion in the region and the future business potential, operations were moved to Singapore. At that time, a specific logistics responsibility was not created.

Turnover throughout the region in 1994 was approximately DM3.3 billion, of which approximately one-third was manufactured in the region (Figure 1.3). The largest supplier of the remaining product to the region was the company's main production site in Ludwigshafen, Germany. Sales by sub-region are shown in Figure 1.4.

Company operations

Each individual group company operates as a separate legal entity with responsibility for part or all of the BASF product line. Separate legal companies have not been structured to perform service functions, such as information systems or transport. However, some companies have been created to manufacture and distribute a single product line or range. Where multiple product ranges are distributed from a company, operating divisions, usually grouped on product lines, are created within the company. In most cases, a central functional division has also been created, thus partly replicating two of

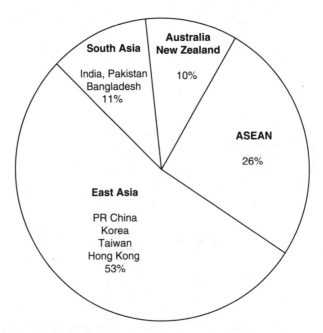

Figure 1.4   BASF in south and east Asia/Australia: sales by area (total 1994: DM3.3 billion).

the three types of division present in the wider company environment. Generally, the functional divisions include responsibility for finance and accounts, logistics, information systems, and personnel and administration (Figure 1.5).

Within the group company, lines of responsibility exist to all three types of division: for profitability of a particular product line, the operating division takes precedence; for total company performance the regional division is foremost; and in regard to functional matters, the functional division is responsible. Generally, where requirements conflict, collaboration is sought from all the higher divisions involved.

Although total company performance is the responsibility of the regional division, each product group is also responsible to the parent company's operating division. Thus, for example, total inventory levels are monitored by the regional division, whereas inventory levels within a product group may be set by the operating division.

Company logistics operations

Because each company was formed differently, logistics activities have developed throughout the region on a piecemeal basis. Although some attempt was made to provide a standard structure, the diversity of company types, i.e. production or merchandising, local cultures, etc., dictated that there was little similarity in operations. Thus in each company the level of logistical sophistication varied considerably. There was general agreement that purchasing, warehousing and transportation were logistics activities, but

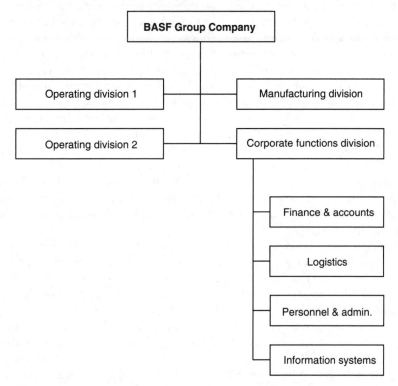

Figure 1.5 BASF typical functional structure in group companies.

others such as customer service, inventory management, product identification and production scheduling were usually outside the gambit of logistics. Most of these activities fell under the control of either marketing, production or finance. Even the three activities considered to be within the logistics domain were generally subject to strict control or oversight by other departments.

Because of the independent nature of company development, there was little in the way of commonality between each group company. Most had developed information systems to suit themselves: they were primarily accounting based and transactional, of different standards and structures, developed in-house or by contractors, and had varying degrees of logistics sophistication. In the main, almost no decision support tools were available for such activities as inventory planning or modelling, distribution planning, production planning and forecasting.

Most personnel within logistics were not specialists in logistics; their training and activities were focused on serving the marketing departments. Many staff had come to logistics from other fields, such as production or marketing. Often their backgrounds were in chemical-related activities which the organization, being a chemical company, valued highly. However, while their professional knowledge of chemicals was good, it proved inadequate in logistics expertise.

Generally, training and education standards for logistics staff needed improvement, as most staff had gained on-the-job training and there was little in the way of formal training. As with most countries in Asia, almost no formal education was available to logistics professionals. Although many key positions in the companies were covered by delegation of personnel from the parent company in Germany, this was rare in logistics as this field rated a lower priority than others.

Local planning from a logistics perspective, other than warehousing, was virtually non-existent. Thus any improvements to processes, systems or procedures were based mostly on experience rather than any professional understanding of the latest trends and developments in industry. Being a service function, staff generally had been trained and encouraged to react to the needs of other departments rather than offering advice or opinions on how better to manage the logistic function.

Even in the fields for which some responsibility was held, such as transport, the operating divisions normally managed the transport function – the logistics personnel simply arranged the transport booking, paid the accounts and searched for lost consignments, but carrier selection and negotiation was an operating division responsibility. Although advice was offered by the logistics department, each operating division generally had its own objectives to satisfy.

Therefore, the emphasis was usually in obtaining the lowest price for any particular service. The organization was usually structured to suit such an operation, and customer service was usually not maximized. Further, as decision making had never been vested in the logistics departments, improving logistic processes was not the highest priority; these decisions were made by the operating divisions and logistics simply provided the infrastructure to fulfil their needs. As there was little understanding of the strategic implications of decisions on logistics processes, conflicting logistics strategies were sometimes adopted.

During the late 1980s and early 1990s this situation gradually started to change, but was resisted in many companies. Some companies did embrace the changes, but to a greater or lesser extent. Thus most logistics departments assumed a full physical distribution management function, but not total logistics management. In a few cases, total logistics management was centred within the logistics department. Where centralization occurred, understanding of its need or of the benefits that might follow was lacking. Many personnel in other departments were concerned that the primary focus of the company would change from the customer to internal bureaucracy.

Regional logistics operations

Until the early 1990s, few activities had been undertaken to develop a co-ordinated approach to logistics activities in the region. A minor effort had been made to determine whether a regional warehouse would be economically viable, but other than this little had occurred. The region was a low priority because of its relatively small size and distance from the centre of operations in Europe.

As with individual group companies, similar problems with suboptimization existed at the regional level. Thus, for example, a product would be available in one country while another would wait three months to obtain supply from Germany. Similarly, many companies independently purchased the same raw materials. Because computer support was fragmented, there was little possibility of obtaining any data centrally for comparative or other purposes. While one country might be able to solve a particular problem, such expertise was usually not transferred to other countries.

At the regional level, the strategic approach to logistics was one of cost minimization. Within the region, little effort had been expended in determining the capacity of logistics services to add value to the various businesses. Logistics was therefore viewed simply as a cost to be avoided. This problem was further exacerbated as there was little ability to measure logistics performance, either as a cost or as a service. Each company had its own performance standards and its own methods for measuring logistics costs. Thus, for example, each company measured its inventory level in a different way. Further, cost data were not collected in any usable form other than for accounting reporting purposes.

While each company grappled with its own inadequacies in logistics, there was no scope to standardize on a single structure, process or philosophy. However, with the transfer of the regional headquarters to Singapore, it became increasingly apparent that much activity was required to bring companies up to a suitable standard. Nevertheless, given the timing of the move to Singapore during a period of recession which had particularly grave consequences on the chemical industry, there was no scope to employ additional personnel nor lavish funds to rectify many of the known deficiencies.

In order to improve logistics, at both the company and regional level, a single regional logistics management position was created in the regional headquarters. The person appointed was a 40-year-old Australian national who had several years experience of working within the logistics function of BASF Australia and held a post-graduate qualification in logistics. The scope of the position was to prepare a long- term strategy to improve logistics within the region. However, on commencing the task, the incumbent was informed that 'there are particular limitations including the restriction on employing additional personnel in the near future'. Although not direct limitations, further constraints were the resistance to change within each of the companies, as each on its own was not necessarily convinced of the need to upgrade its logistics capabilities, and a lack of direct responsibility for logistics functions in each company.

After an initial tour of the majority of companies, the shortcomings in logistics capabilities had been confirmed. In addition to the failings evident at the time of appointment, further concerns became apparent: the cultural differences between western and eastern ideas could prove a significant obstacle to tackling problems, and even the differences between countries within the region were at times obvious. For example, acceptance of outside ideas and the extent of the structured hierarchy would have a significant impact on change management. In many of the countries there was a resistance to change, significantly greater than that evident in some more 'progressive' countries. Therefore, convincing personnel from other departments, and even those within the logistics environment, would prove to be a difficult undertaking. Finally, the massive infrastructure problems evident in many countries would be a significant barrier to modernizing logistics practices. Even with the best intentions, without good telecommunications, etc., it would be a slow process to improve logistics functions within many countries.

European distribution strategy*

David Taylor
Department of Transport and Logistics, University of Huddersfield, UK

Introduction

On 10 January 1993, Martin Crossley, recently appointed European Parts Manager for Brother International, arrived at his office early, told his secretary that he did not want to receive any telephone calls or visitors that day, took off his jacket and settled down to work. On his desk were two documents, one a report summarizing his recently completed review of the company's European parts operation, and the other a spreadsheet he had completed the previous day showing an analysis of the parts inventory situation at the company's largest European sales office, which happened to be in Britain. In four weeks' time he had a meeting with the company's European Chairman to outline his preferred strategy to improve and develop the company's parts supply system, and although he did not know what proposals he was going to make, he did know that he had an awful lot of work to do.

Company background

Brother International is a major Japanese manufacturer supplying a wide range of electrical and electronic goods. It is a leading producer of word processors, laser printers, personal computers and colour copiers, which are supplied from factories in Japan. In Europe the company has one manufacturing plant located at Ruabon in Wales which produces typewriters and microwave ovens.

The European market is served through 20 sales offices located in 13 European countries (Exhibit 2.1). Brother International Europe (BIE), based in Manchester, UK carries out a co-ordinating role for the sales offices but has no direct line responsibility. The sales offices are each independent profit centres and report directly to headquarters

*Data available on the Internet (see page xxii).

Exhibit 2.1 European countries in which Brother International has sales offices

United Kingdom	Denmark	Norway
Sweden	Finland	The Netherlands
Germany	Austria	Italy
France	Switzerland	Belgium
Ireland		

---

in Japan. One area for which BIE does, however, have responsibility is the co-ordination of the procurement of spares and parts required by the European sales offices.

As with many electronics companies, the 1980s saw a period of very rapid growth and expansion for Brother. The company had aggressive marketing policies which targeted a doubling in sales volume every two years and by 1990 the company's total turnover in Europe had reached £400 million. During this growth period relatively little management resource had been devoted to distribution issues, as the company was essentially sales led. As a result the development of systems for distributing finished products and spares had tended to lag behind the growth in sales and there was increasing concern within the company about the level of after sales service being offered to customers. Virtually all of the company's product range required after sales service in terms of maintenance and repair and there was thus a continual demand for parts, the majority of which were supplied exclusively by Brother. The parts operation had grown in line with the growth in the business and by 1992 was supplying parts to the value of some £5 million at cost. Demand for parts lagged behind the sales of new products, with maximum demand occurring a few years after the initial product sale and then trailing off as products reached the end of their life-cycle.

By the early 1990s there was a growing feeling of dissatisfaction in the company with the parts supply systems operating in Europe. There seemed to be an increasing number of complaints from customers and service engineers about waiting times for parts. Managers and staff in the European sales offices were unhappy about the availability of parts from stock and with the accuracy and speed with which parts orders were fulfilled. Meanwhile senior finance managers in BIE were expressing concerns that the level and cost of holding inventory in Europe was too high. However, no-one in the company had clearly identified the real nature or cause of the problem.

In response to these growing concerns the company decided in 1992 to appoint a European Parts Operation Manager. The brief was to review the parts system and make the necessary alterations to achieve an acceptable parts management situation. The person selected was 37-year-old Martin Crossley, who had previously held positions as parts manager with other major companies and had recently completed a master's degree in Logistics Management. Interestingly, Crossley was the first professional logistician to be appointed anywhere within Brother's world-wide operation. On taking up his appointment Crossley's first task was to gain a clear picture of the current systems for parts supply within Brother's European markets. The following sections outline his findings.

Brother International Europe

At BIE headquarters in Manchester there was one administrator responsible for the processing of parts orders between local sales offices (LSOs) and the factories in Japan and Europe. Each of the 20 European LSOs passed their orders for parts to BIE in Manchester either by fax or by letter. BIE accumulated the orders and faxed them daily to Brother's Japanese headquarters.

Once available, parts would be transported direct from factories to the individual LSOs, while confirmation of order despatch from the factory was communicated to BIE and then on from BIE to the LSOs. Factories did not communicate details of order status, back-orders or expected delivery dates on non-available products unless specifically requested. There were frequent delays in the processing of paperwork both at factories and at BIE, such that it was not uncommon for goods to arrive at LSOs weeks in advance of the relevant paperwork. Because of the slowness in order processing, the BIE parts administrator was frequently inundated with 'fire-fighting' calls to chase orders or give order status reports, which further exacerbated the delays in routine order processing. Furthermore, BIE had no systems to give accurate information on promised and actual delivery dates, order status, order cancellation, etc.

Systems at local offices

Soon after taking up his post Crossley devoted a month to visiting the major LSOs around Europe in order to try to understand their operating systems and problems. Each local office operated autonomously and was entirely responsible for its own profitability and post-sales support. As the offices were primarily sales functions, they were usually managed by a sales manager. Each LSO also had a team of installation and service engineers and a stores function for spares and parts.

Staff at all levels in the sales offices seemed to be dissatisfied with the parts operation. Almost universally, the warehouse staff were working overtime and felt they were not on top of the job. Crossley's initial assessment, however, was that most offices were over-staffed in relation to the volume of work being handled, particularly in terms of warehouse and stock control personnel. Customer service was low and stock investment was high, particularly in slow-moving lines. Most local offices had little or no management information to facilitate systematic control of stock and, in relation to parts supply and he felt that most local managers had no real grasp of what was required to run a modern parts operation. Each local office had independently developed their own management and control systems and had stand-alone computer systems using a wide variety of hardware and software. None of the local computer systems had direct links to BIE.

Each LSO manager had his own view on the causes and potential solution to the parts problem which reflected individual personal perspectives and cultural differences between the various European countries. When Crossley explained his new role within the company to the local managers, he was normally met with either scepticism or hostility and frequently was perceived as another interfering busy-body from European HQ. He realized at a very early stage that persuading the local managers to adopt any change was going to be a difficult task.

Parts profile

Brother's parts and spares range included approximately 65,000 items. The majority were small and lightweight (e.g. electronic components, mechanical components, nuts and bolts), while a small number were bulky and very heavy (e.g. replacement motors for industrial sewing machines). All products required some form of special handling, the main criterion being to keep them free from dust and damp, which usually meant packaging in sealed plastic bags. As components would sometimes be issued to end-users, presentation was also important. Most components had an indefinite physical shelf-life with no danger of deterioration providing basic precautionary steps were taken.

Supply channels

The majority of spare parts were supplied from Japan – Crossley's initial estimate was 97% – with the remainder supplied from the Welsh factory and a small number coming from external third-party suppliers. All parts orders from LSOs were passed via BIE to Japan HQ, which identified the relevant factory in Japan or Europe to supply the parts and these would then be shipped direct from the factory to the local office. It was not uncommon for different product lines on the same order to be shipped from different factories. Paperwork confirming order dispatches would be sent to BIE, but because of work overload there was frequent delay in co-ordinating and passing on this information to local offices. The few items within the spares range that were homogeneous, and could be obtained either more cheaply or more quickly from third-party suppliers, were procured locally by LSOs.

Distribution channels

The local sales offices traded with dealers (mainly retailers) who in turn dealt with end-users. The normal route was for a dealer to place orders with the local sales office and to receive product from the LSO. In emergency situations dealers might communicate orders direct to BIE and would receive parts direct from factories. Confirmation of such transactions and payments would, however, pass through the normal BIE–LSO channel, albeit with time delay and some confusion.

End-users normally dealt with the dealers, but again in some circumstances they would contact LSOs directly. As most of the Brother products required proprietary parts for maintenance, customers were effectively tied into the Brother parts service. In practice therefore, there was a completely inelastic demand for Brother parts while customers retained the Brother product. Clearly, however, poor service on parts might prejudice future orders for new products.

Order lead times

The total order cycle time was typically four months from an LSO placing an order to receipt of goods at a European LSO. Generally this comprised three months lead time to despatch from factories and approximately one month transportation lead time from

Japan. However, seven months was not uncommon and in extreme cases 18 months. Fifty per cent of orders had an order cycle time of over three months.

Transport

The transport lead time from factories in Japan to European LSOs was on average 50 days by sea freight and 20 days by airfreight. The figures for both sea and air included approximately ten days for customs and terminal clearance. Variability of transit times, particularly by sea, was high and it was not uncommon for sea freight to take three months from factory gate to arrival at LSO. Transport from the Welsh factory to LSOs could normally be guaranteed within three or four days.

Company policy was that sea freight should be used for Japanese supplies but emergency requests could be shipped by air. The number of orders being transported by air had undoubtedly increased during the latter half of the 1980s. Although there were no figures available to indicate usage of transport modes, as each local office independently made emergency requests, when Crossley entered the company in 1992, he estimated that perhaps 70% of parts were being shipped from Japan by air, while for some LSOs airfreight was used for 90% of shipments. In addition to the extra cost of airfreight, the emergency orders were prioritized at the factories, which further delayed routine orders. He also suspected that many emergency orders were duplicates of earlier routine orders that had not yet arrived but were now urgently required by irate customers. In such circumstances, when the original order did arrive, it would be added to the LSOs safety stock. There were no figures available to indicate the transport costs of servicing the European operation as transport costs were absorbed by the individual factories in Japan.

Inventory situation

Each local office was responsible for managing its own inventory. Typically, LSOs were holding a range of about 22,000–23,000 parts items and in consequence had considerable space and staff devoted to stores management; however most LSO staff lacked any specialist understanding of inventory or warehouse management. The majority of sites were either overcrowded or preparing to expand the space allocated to holding spares, yet in Crossley's view there was not a single site where space requirements could not have been reduced. Local office managers were responsible for ordering and all had their own rules of thumb and personal strategies to obtain and control stock. As most managers had risen through the ranks of the sales force and had little or no formal training in stock control or demand forecasting, few local offices had developed procedures for systematic ordering of stock and there was a lack of relevant and reliable information to measure stock performance. Their difficulties in trying to manage the very large product range were compounded by long and unreliable delivery lead times. A further factor, which few managers had recognized, was that many of Brother's products, such as computers and laser printers, had increasingly short product life-cycles, with the effect that over-ordered parts inventory could rapidly become obsolete. Furthermore, as most parts were entirely specific to Brother products, they were as such non-marketable, so that obsolete stock could not even be disposed of by discounting or promotional efforts.

Exhibit 2.2   Extract from the parts sales and stock report for the UK local sales office (07/09/92)

Part number	Description	Average monthly demand units	Stock cover months	Stock available units	Stock value £'s	Number on order order	Last receipt
407113001	Plain needles	15,980	4.6	23,073	1384.38	50,000	07/06/92
X00009092	KM nolan leaflets 501s	8237	3.5	28,990	9831.50	0	24/08/92
485436011	Blank cards	3331	7.8	25,971	39,735.63	0	23/08/92
K00000003	Accessory leaflets in 100s	3104	3.8	11,884	1663.76	0	22/07/92
404648001	Purl needles (ribber)	2587	19.8	1197	71.82	50,000	07/06/92
404800001	Plain needle	1934	41.4	80,101	4806.06	0	27/05/92
40488305	Weight	1118	3.1	3447	1482.21	0	07/06/92
100117001	Bobbin	1028	6.0	1129	71.95	5000	26/07/92
485451001	Punches	923	9.1	6405	29,078.70	2000	04/08/92
146425001	Screw	892	2.2	0	0.00	2000	14/07/92
410766001	Cast on wire long standard	855	2.4	15	1.80	2000	06/05/92
4033890061	Cast on thread	809	10.8	8742	471.94	0	27/06/92

Although no local office actually quantified the customer service level on parts, Crossley's estimate was that it was on average about 75%. Customers and staff were aware that the system was increasingly failing to meet their needs. In order to try and maintain service to customers, managers were adopting a variety of survival policies, including:

- over-ordering in relation to actual demand in order to build up safety stocks
- increasing use of emergency airfreight
- cannibalization of parts from new finished products held in stock at local offices in the hope that replacement parts would be available to rebuild the new product before it was required for sale.

Crossley quickly realized that he needed to develop an objective view of the inventory situation throughout Europe. He therefore requested all local offices to provide details of the sales and stock situation for all parts lines. The data presented in Exhibit 2.2 are an extract from the first page of a 450-page computer printout which listed all parts stocked at the British LSO. As this was the largest European sales office, representing 25% of total European parts business, and was also located adjacent to BIE in Manchester, Crossley decided to base his analysis on the figures from this office. His initial approach was to convert these raw data into a more manageable form. The 23,500 stock-keeping units at the UK office were classified into 13 bands related to levels of monthly demand as shown in column 1 of Exhibit 2.3; against each of these bands a variety of information was then recorded or calculated.

As Crossley pondered the spreadsheet and reviewed his various ideas to improve the situation he knew that whatever he proposed, the required investment would have to be justifiable within the context of a £5 million European parts operation, which the company did not regard as a mainstream activity. He also knew that in order to get approval from the company's European Chairman (a Japanese national), he would have to put forward some very convincing arguments to justify any changes.

Exhibit 2.3   Aggregated stock and sales data from the UK LSO (figures as at period 9 1992)

A Category of sales Units/mth	B Actual SKU lines	C Cum SKU Lines	D Stock Value £	E Cum stock Value £	F Stock units Acutal	G Cum	H Unit COS Actual	I Cum	J Unit demand vol/mth Actual	K Cum	L %
>10,000	1	1	1384	1384	23,073	23,073	0.06	0.06	15,980	15,980	17.55%
>5000	1	2	9831	11,215	28,090	51,163	0.35	0.22	8237	24,217	26.60%
>1000	6	8	47,828	59,043	124,039	175,202	0.39	0.34	13,102	37,319	40.98%
>100	83	91	348,030	407,073	180,684	355,886	1.93	1.14	22,957	60,276	66.20%
>50	96	187	56,562	463,635	51,995	407,881	1.09	1.14	6850	67,126	73.72%
>35	81	268	75,637	539,272	29,025	436,906	2.61	1.23	3350	70,476	77.40%
>20	172	440	51,732	591,004	29,913	466,819	1.73	1.27	4608	75,084	82.46%
>15	113	553	25,307	616,311	20,537	487,356	1.23	1.26	2007	77,091	84.66%
>10	197	750	20,696	637,007	21,048	508,404	0.98	1.25	2561	79,652	87.47%
>5	481	1231	53,591	690,598	30,780	539,184	1.74	1.28	3645	83,297	91.48%
>2	914	2145	64,238	754,836	44,155	583,339	1.45	1.29	3389	86,686	95.20%
>1	10,050	12,645	268,891	1,023,727	135,121	718,460	1.99	1.42	2094	88,780	97.50%
<1	10,850	23,495	510,128	1,533,855	256,346	974,805	1.99	1.57	2277	91,057	100%

M COS COS/mth	N Cum	O % SKUs Actual	P Cum	Q % COS Actual	R Cum	S Out of stock SKUs	T %	U COS Stockturn	V Cum Stockturn	W Stk units/ SKU	X Vol units/ SKU
958	958	0	0	0.94	0.94	0		8.31	8.31	23,073	15,980
2882	3841	0	0.01	2.82	3.76	0		3.52	4.11	28,090	8237
5051	8893	0.03	0.03	4.94	8.7	8		1.27	1.81	20,673	2183.67
44,219	53,112	0.35	0.39	43.25	51.95	8	9.64	1.52	1.57	2176	276.59
7451	60,564	0.41	0.8	7.29	59.24	23	23.96	1.58	1.57	541	71.35
8729	69,294	0.34	1.14	8.54	67.78	14	17.28	1.39	1.54	358	41.36
7967	77,261	0.73	1.87	7.79	75.58	31	18.02	1.85	1.57	173	26.79
2473	79,735	0.48	2.35	2.42	77.99	20	17.7	1.17	1.55	181	17.76
2518	88,253	0.84	3.19	2.46	80.46	34	17.26	1.46	1.55	106	13
6346	88,599	2.05	5.24	6.21	86.67	90	18.71	1.42	1.54	63	7.58
4930	93,529	3.89	9.13	4.82	91.49	128	14	0.92	1.49	48	3.71
4167	97,697	42.78	51.91	4.07	95.56	735	7.31	0.19	1.15	13	0.2
4531	102,282	46.18	100	4.43	100	490	4.52	0.12	0.8	23	0.2

SKUs = stock-keeping units; COS = cost of sales; cum = cumulative.

Key to spreadsheet columns in Exhibit 2.3

Column A	Arbitrarily determined sales bands measured in units per month
Column B	Actual number of stock-keeping units (SKUs) per band, i.e. the number of line items
Column C	Cumulative total of SKUs
Column D	The total value of stock held within each individual band
Column E	Cumulative total of column D
Column F	This is the actual stock on hand on the day that the print was produced
Column G	Cumulative total of column F
Column H	The value of stock (column D) divided by the quantity of stock on hand (column F), giving the average unit cost of sale for each band
Column I	Cumulative value of stock (column E) divided by cumulative stock quantity column G
Column J	Volume of demand in units per month, i.e. sales
Column K	Cumulative unit demand volume per month
Column L	The cumulative percentage of volume sales per category against total monthly sales
Column M	The average value of cost of sales for each band (column H multiplied by column J)
Column N	Cumulative cost of sales per month
Column O	The percentage of SKUs against total SKUs (column B divided by total of column C)
Column P	Cumulative percentage SKUs
Column Q	Percentage of COS against total COS (column M divided by total of column N)
Column R	Cumulative percentage COS
Column S	The number of SKUs actually out of stock on the day that the print was produced
Column T	The percentage of out of stock against the total out of stock (column S/column B × 100)
Column U	Cost of sales stockturn, column M × 12 (annual cost of sales)/column D (value of stock on hand)
Column V	Cumulative stockturn, column N ×12/column E
Column W	Quantity of stock on hand divided by the number of SKUs per band (column J/column F), i.e. stock per SKU
Column X	Volume of units sold divided by the number of SKUs per band (column J/column B), i.e. demand per SKU

Acknowledgement

The author wishes to acknowledge the time and detailed assistance given in the preparation of this case by Martin Crossley, European Logistics Manager, Brother International.

Creating a European logistics strategy

Professor Martin Christopher
The School of Management, Cranfield University, UK

Introduction

David Harland, Director of Materials Management Europe at Gillette, was putting the finishing touches to the keynote speech that he was shortly to deliver to the 1993 Annual Conference of the United Kingdom Institute of Logistics. This major event would provide an opportunity to describe the changes that had been made over the seven years since he had joined the company in 1986. In considering the substantial progress that had been made towards achieving a European logistics strategy, David Harland also reflected on the major issues that had been learned and what things he might have done differently if he were starting the project over again.

Company background

The Gillette company is a long-established company with a corporate brand name that is recognized world-wide. Its declared mission is to achieve leadership in the following categories: male grooming, male and female shaving and deodorants and anti-perspirants, writing instruments, dental care and small electrical appliances. The corporate strategy is to run the business on a global basis maximizing the power of Gillette's well-established brands. To quote Alfred Zeien, the Chairman of the company: 'We sell the same products world-wide ... we treat all markets the same ... when people shop they do not think very differently from Americans.' Even though there was still a recognition of local requirements and differences in demand, the intention was to build a global business around a common approach with respect to the development and marketing of Gillette products around the world.

When David Harland joined the company in 1986 he found that despite the company's commitment to a global marketing strategy there was a lack of integration of its logistics

Function	Responsibility			
	National	Regional	Europe HQ	North Atlantic HQ
Factory operations	◖		◗	
Master scheduling	●			
Finished goods inventories	●			
Purchasing	●			
Sales forecasting	●			
Warehousing	●			
Distribution	●			
Order processing	●			
Packaging design	◖		◗	
Computer design	●			
I.T. Support	◖		◗	

Figure 3.1 Decision-making responsibility in Gillette – early 1980s.

management, particularly across Europe. Responsibility for logistics was very fragmented with localized manufacture and distribution management. A European HQ had been established in London, but decisions on everything from inventory levels to purchasing decisions were made locally (Figure 3.1). There were 13 warehouses across Europe all carrying virtually identical stock, except that packaging varied locally.

Even allowing for all this inventory, service levels to retail customers were low. Order fill averaged only 78%, and the order cycle time varied from five days to more than 20 days. Service performance was increasingly important as European retailers continued to grow their purchasing power and to place ever greater demands for service on their suppliers.

Many of the markets in which Gillette competed were highly volatile with high levels of promotional activity requiring special promotional packs or over-wraps. In situations such as this, forecasting was difficult and consequently there was always great pressure placed on manufacturing to make frequent changes to its production schedules. Manufacturing worked on a monthly planning cycle and hence needed to have reliable forecasts to cover the planning period as well as any extended lead times required by suppliers.

A different approach

To David Harland, it seemed inevitable that if the company wanted to develop further its global approach to marketing, it would need to underpin this with a greater degree of central co-ordination and planning. A European logistics strategy required a number of fundamental decisions to be made at a European level rather than locally. In particular he felt that areas of particular strategic importance were:

- finished goods inventories
- warehousing and distribution operations

- systems development
- work-in-process inventory
- purchasing.

The centralization of responsibility for finished goods inventory necessitated the establishment of a European planning function. The task of the function was to obtain sales forecasts from each local market, monitor finished goods stock levels at each warehouse and develop production plans and stock movement schedules to drive the flow of finished goods to warehouse to ensure a high service level. Although, in retrospect, this seems a logical move, there was a great deal of resistance by local business managers to the centralization of responsibility for what they saw as their stock of finished goods. The belief was widespread that service levels would suffer as inventory levels were pushed down.

There was also resistance to the next organizational move which was the setting-up of a European warehousing and distribution function. Again, a close working relationship between local business managers and the local warehouse managers, or contractors, made for a difficult transition.

This was paralleled by the creation of a European systems development group which was crucial to the evolution of common systems and the co-ordination of local information technology projects to support integrated materials management.

By 1990 the company was ready to move to the next stage of sophistication in planning. Up to this point all planning had been done in monthly buckets, with the consequence that stocks were still at a high level, although service had improved dramatically. Since a European-wide forecasting system had been installed it had become clear that they could forecast overall European demand centrally much more accurately than they could by adding up all of the local sales forecasts. This led to the implementation of weekly planning, backed-up by capacity-constrained master scheduling. The essence of this is that basic factory operations, namely the production of blades and razors, were driven by accurate, stable European forecasts while the more volatile packaging requirements are driven by national, item-level forecasts. Differences between the two were buffered by the work-in-process inventory which, in turn, required the centralization of its responsibility. Although, in reality, there was close partnership between European and factory planning teams, the centralization of control over work-in-process has been a major step forward, not only at the European level, but also across the North Atlantic business.

A major contribution to integrated materials management was made in 1991 when responsibility for all purchasing was centralized. This did not mean that purchasing teams within the factories were disbanded, merely that they now reported to a central executive with a brief to act locally but think North Atlantic. The benefits of this to the company have been significant reductions in purchase prices achieved. Gillette are currently standardizing purchasing systems and working on a number of projects to reduce inventories of raw material and work-in-process which would not have been possible without a fully integrated materials management organization.

Figure 3.2 shows how the location of various responsibilities had changed by the early 1990s. The materials management part of the manufacturing and technical operations organization in Europe is shown in Figure 3.3; Each factory now reports to the Vice-

Function	Responsibility			
	National	Regional	Europe HQ	North Atlantic HQ
Factory operations				●
Master scheduling			●	
Finished goods inventories			●	
Purchasing			●	
Sales forecasting	◖		◗	
Warehousing			●	
Distribution			●	
Order processing	●			
Packaging design			◖	◗
Computer design		●		
I.T. Support		◖	◑	

Figure 3.2 Decision-making responsibilities in Gillette – early 1990s.

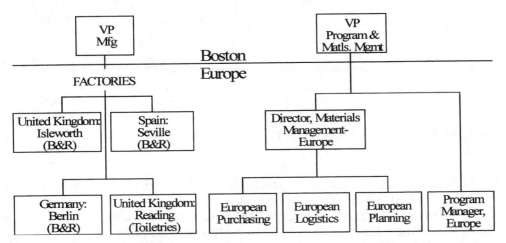

Figure 3.3 Gillette North Atlantic and European manufacturing and technical operations.

President of Manufacturing in Gillette's North Atlantic headquarters. The materials management functions in both Europe and North America report to the Vice-President, Program and Materials Management, Gillette North Atlantic.

Warehousing strategy

It was apparent that once a European logistics management structure was in place there would no longer be a need for 13 warehouses. In order to achieve the desired order-to-delivery time across Western Europe of two days it was determined that eight warehouses would be required. These were located in Isleworth, UK; Copenhagen,

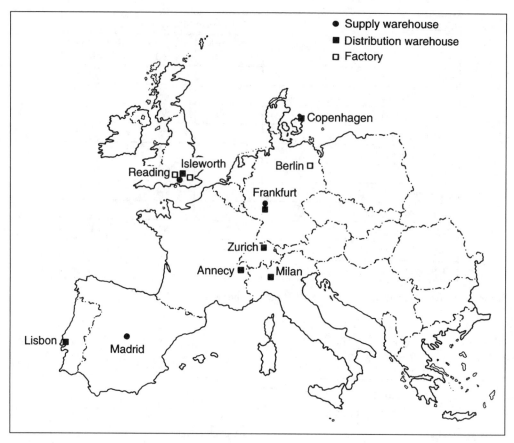

Figure 3.4 European warehouse network.

Denmark; Frankfurt, Germany; Zurich, Switzerland; Milan, Italy; Annecy, France; Madrid, Spain; and Lisbon, Portugal (Figure 3.4).

In Germany, Gillette needed a regional distribution centre located within a 100 km radius of Frankfurt. Its function was to be both a supplier warehouse receiving all production from their largest European factory in Berlin and a regional distribution warehouse holding stock and supplying customers in Austria, Belgium and The Netherlands as well as Germany. Ultimately, it might even cover national markets further afield.

With this facility in operation, it was now possible to eliminate distribution warehouses in Austria, Belgium and The Netherlands. However, because of the promotional demands of Belgium and The Netherlands it was necessary to retain third-party operated stockless depots in these countries where customer orders and promotional packs and merchandisers are made up from stock delivered daily from the German distribution centre. A similar regional distribution plan was implemented in Scandinavia. Four separate stocked warehouses were closed and a contract was agreed with the Danish company, DFDS, who set up a new regional distribution centre. All customer orders and promotional packaging for the whole of Scandinavia are carried out at this facility. At the same time, the rationalization of divisional warehouses in Spain enabled Gillette to set up a third-party operated facility south of Madrid.

Gillette originally owned and operated its own warehouses. The company has since moved progressively towards more contract operation. The policy is one of concentrating investment in core activities and outsourcing logistics operations when and where conditions are appropriate. The growth of the third-party provider industry has ensured that there is no shortage of bidders willing and able to provide a very competitive service in warehousing operations. Transportation had been totally in the hands of outside companies for many years.

Gillette Europe had used contract carriers for the last 20 years or so, but the role played by third parties in warehouse operations had been mixed. Warehouses operated by Gillette and those run by third-party operators had worked very well, although warehousing contractors were changed from time to time for reasons of service or cost. However, Gillette's return on capital performance improvement on the one hand, and the expansion of the third-party warehousing and distribution industry on the other, had made it increasingly difficult to justify their own warehouses. The question is not so much whether they should run their own versus a third-party operator, but the extent to which various logistics management functions and the systems to support them should remain with Gillette or be handed over to third parties. The policy established by the company differentiates between planning activities, which will remain with Gillette, and operations functions and systems, which will be considered for placing in the hands of appropriate third parties.

Planning systems

It would not have been possible to sustain a high level of customer service and obtain the inventory reductions available through the warehouse rationalization programme without centralized planning. A DRP system was installed in 1988, probably the first to be installed by a consumer goods company for total European finished goods planning. As with most application systems, the largest element of cost and implementation time was devoted to interfacing DRP to every sales office, warehouse and factory around Europe. It took more than three years to reach an acceptable level of data integrity and transmission reliability. The operating concept is very simple. On a monthly cycle, sales forecasts from each country are updated and transmitted to the central planning office, and closing stocks at the end of the previous period are transmitted along with updates to the last production schedules from each factory. Each DRP regeneration creates an updated set of production schedules and a set of movement instructions for replenishment of each distribution warehouse.

The performance of the whole planning system was recently enhanced by switching to a weekly planning cycle facilitated by the replacement of in-house developed MRP systems which were restricted to monthly cycles. At the same time, the opportunity was taken to centralize rough-cut capacity planning and master scheduling.

Results

At the completion of the five-year programme to achieve an integrated logistics strategy and management structure for Europe the results were impressive.

The results of the five-year materials management programme can be summarized as follows.

- Customer service performance greatly improved: order fill rate, which averaged 78% in key markets in Europe in 1987, reached 98% in 1993.
- Logistics operations costs rose by less than inflation over the period and represented a smaller percentage of sales in all markets.
- Despite an increase in SKUs of more than 50%, an increased rate of new product launches and more sourcing of products from outside Europe, inventory levels had not risen.
- Total materials management head-count was reduced in both warehouse operations and planning functions.

Pitfalls

In preparing his presentation for the Institute of Logistics conference, David Harland reflected on the lessons that had been learned from the experiences of creating a European logistics strategy and management framework. After some thought he concluded:

In total the programme has been successful; but there have been a few problems. These can be categorized under people, systems and customer service.

(i) People

The most common reaction to the centralization of any activity is the fear of loss of control by local management. In every situation entailing the transfer of responsibility for an operation from that of national or regional managers, there has been resistance. Although this resistance appeared to be irrational and even illogical in the context of a European vision, the reaction is understandable since it is only human to believe that the formula for success in the past will continue to apply in the future, especially when it is proposed that as a consequence of change one's own job and power is diminished. It has, however, been gratifying to see that, after the fact, each step has been embraced enthusiastically and that local management has admitted that their fears are not justified. In retrospect, I would say that no matter how many presentations and seminars are held for groups of people, the most effective means of reassuring managers is a face-to-face discussion to build up trust and understanding.

Overlaid on the top management issues, such as those discussed, have been those arising from national differences. Despite a strong European business culture and the general acceptance of the advantages of a European union by senior management, the difficulties in this respect are much greater than had been anticipated. It also has to be said that for an American or British company working across Europe with English as the working language it should not be a surprise that meetings need to be longer. There are bound to be occasional errors of communication and peculiarities of vocabulary as each local manager does his best to work in a foreign language.

Also on the subject of people, it has been the case that European centralization has created excellent career opportunities for some managers. The gradual movement towards third-party operation has shifted the emphasis from warehouse management skills to those of negotiation and management control and this has been achieved through training and some re-assignment. At the more senior levels the creation of a North Atlantic-wide entity has led to more trans-Atlantic assignments. This has been particularly valuable in the planning function.

(ii) Systems

Although I believe that the redesign of systems should follow after strategic and operational plans have been developed, in practice changes in technology and the life cycles of large IT installations tend to result in hardware and software investments which do not always follow user requirements. This effect has not been as great in the area of planning and warehousing as it has been in manufacturing and commercial systems. Gillette has undergone during the last eight years a total change from mainframes through mid-range machines and is now moving to a client–server environment. This created a momentum for application software replacement that was not always user driven. I anticipate this will be less of a problem in the future.

Another factor that has affected our application systems plans within Europe has been the shortage of European product. American-developed applications software has often not sufficiently recognized the needs of Europe, necessitating costly revisions. Associated with this has been the lack of investment by certain software houses in support of European customers. The fact that companies which have not invested are suffering a decline in business as a consequence is of little consolation to those companies who have bought their particular software packages.

Software purchasing decisions are probably the most difficult to make since it is often extremely difficult for those with authority to understand what they are buying. Conversely, those with the knowledge of the application systems capabilities have generally too little influence on the buying decisions and may perhaps not be involved until a very late stage. This can be very serious given that software generally outlives the life of the vendor who provided the software and the hardware on which it runs.

Probably the most significant aspect of systems implementation within the context of European materials management at Gillette has been the performance of international data transmission networks. In the early to mid-1980s, when we began implementation, we had to rely on dial-up telephone links between computers. This was slow and limited by the availability of operating staff at each end. By the late 1980s public X-25 data links were available, but transmissions still had to be scheduled and they were expensive and unreliable for international communication. It was not until the early 1990s when large, value-added network providers came on the scene that low-cost, high-quality, international data communication became a reality.

We now really could claim to have a European data network supporting centralized planning and forecasting on a virtually real-time basis.

(iii) Customer service targets

Although defined customer service performance targets are a necessary pre-requisite to the development of a logistics strategy, I draw attention to them here as a pitfall both because of their importance and the degree of misunderstanding which frequently arises between sales management and logistics management. The single most important dimension affecting the warehousing strategy is that of order cycle time. That is the cycle that begins with transmission from the customer through order processing, warehouse consolidation, picking and despatch and finally onward distribution. Whenever we came under pressure to cut order cycle times we looked for ways to streamline order processing procedures in order to cut processing times and were generally successful, thus freeing up more time for the physical distribution side of the order cycle.

Another very important measure of customer service performance is that of order fill rate. While not affected directly by the warehouse network, it is a prime measure of the effectiveness of the forecasting and planning side of the business. One of our management reporting deficiencies in the early stages of implementing the European materials management programme was the lack of any customer service reporting system. We were also limited by the inability of our DRP system to utilize forecast error and order fill rate parameters in the setting of safety stock levels by warehouse and product family. This deficiency will be rectified in the new generation of planning systems to be installed shortly.

Acknowledgement

This case study was prepared by Martin Christopher based on material presented by David Harland (Director of Materials Management Europe, Gillette) to the 1993 Institute of Logistics Annual Conference, and subsequently published in the Institute's journal *Logistics Focus*, **2**(7), September 1994.

Developing European logistics strategy*

Martin Ashford

Head of Logistics, The Financial Times, *London (formerly with Touche Ross Management Consultants)*

Introduction

On 1 January 1993, the Single European Market came into existence and with it a whole new world of cross-border trade was inaugurated. All customs barriers between the then 12 countries (Belgium, Denmark, France, Germany, Greece, Ireland, Italy, Luxembourg, Netherlands, Portugal, Spain and the UK) of the European Union (EU) were removed and it became possible to move most goods in free circulation anywhere within the EU without restriction. (Imports from other parts of the world have to clear customs at the time of importation into an EU country. Thereafter, they are defined as being in free circulation and can cross the EU's internal borders without restriction.) There was much talk of the 'single market' of Europe, in which businesses would compete on a 'level playing field' to be achieved through 'harmonization' of national regulations.

As usual, the reality of the situation was rather more complex than the hype. To logistics professionals, the Big Bang of 1993 was arguably a non-event. There were two main reasons for this as follows.

- Harmonization was (to use a very British understatement) incomplete. Major differences remained where government policies impacted on logistics. Examples included excise duties on road vehicles and fuel, maximum weight limits for goods vehicles and employment on-costs such as social security contributions. Equally significant were the national and regional differences in input costs such as wage levels and land prices, brought about by market conditions rather than direct government intervention.
- Many businesses had already been taking a more-or-less pan-European view of their operations, in some cases years in advance of the formal removal of border controls.

*Data available on the Internet (see page xxii).

Xerox is often cited as an example, having long ago centralized its European spares operation in The Netherlands. Many heavy and process industries had been forced into rationalizing their European production capacity in order to achieve economic scale in manufacturing, and this production-driven change had taken logistics along with it.

None the less, the creation of the Single European Market was linked, directly or indirectly, to some fairly fundamental changes. For example, the need for bilateral international haulage permits disappeared in 1993, and restrictions on 'cabotage' (cabotage may be defined, conveniently if not strictly, as the carriage of goods between two European countries by a vehicle from a third European country) were to be removed gradually, while regulation of the French road transport industry (including compulsory tariffs) was dismantled progressively from 1986 onwards.

Nineteen-ninety-three was a symbolic date in a gradual process of Europeanization. It spurred many businesses to think again about how they ran their logistics and other operations across the continent. Two such businesses, Hasbro and NIKE, are the subjects of these case studies. Both are US multinationals. Both are leaders in their consumer markets. And both of them called in consultants from Touche Ross to help them to devise a European logistics strategy. In many other ways, however, they are very different from each other.

We pick up both stories in 1992 ... .

Case 4 • Hasbro Europe

Company background

Hasbro is one of those companies whose corporate identity is less well known than some of its brands and products. These include many of the most famous names in the toy shop: Sindy, GI Joe, Transformers, Playdoh, My Little Pony, Trivial Pursuit, Pictionary, Cluedo and Tonka to name but a small selection.

The company competes head to head with Mattel for the number one world-wide position in the non-electronic toys and games industry. Far from child's play, the toys sector is a tough business characterized by the following.

- There is a massive peak in sales in the build-up to Christmas. If your product arrives late from the factory, you may have missed the market for another 12 months.
- There are high costs and long lead times in tooling up production. If your product starts to sell like hot cakes in October, you probably will not be able to get more made in time for Christmas, and you will miss the market.
- 'Fashion' or 'cult' status products are produced with ever shorter product life cycles. Who buys Cabbage Patch dolls any more?
- There are high marketing and promotional costs, with TV advertising often broadcast around children's TV series. If the programme goes out and the product is not in the shops, you miss the market. If you make the product and then find that the television companies in Europe do not buy the programme, there may be no market to miss.

In this environment, many well-known toy companies have come badly unstuck when they misjudged the market or backed the wrong product. Famous names have been bought up by competitors until the market has become dominated by a few major multinationals. Hasbro Inc. is a case in point. Having previously absorbed Milton Bradley and Playskool, in 1991 it took over Tonka Toys which had merged with Kenner Parker. This gave the total corporation world wide sales in the order of $2 billion, of which $0.7 billion was in the main countries of Western Europe.

Hasbro Europe is headquartered at Stockley Park, near London's Heathrow airport. The offices are modern and very attractive, in a showcase development. The consultants soon found that, to understand the business, they had to visit each of the national subsidiaries, whose General Managers all held strong views on the best way to operate within their territory.

In some countries there had been a measure of rationalization of warehouses and contracts, following the Tonka acquisition. Other countries, however, still had multiple stockholding sites and some were struggling to cope with the growth in volumes that they were experiencing. A question in the consultants' minds was whether there was really scope here for a pan-European approach to logistics, given the diversity of national issues and interests. Conversely, it could be argued that a Europe-wide approach was *essential*, as the only alternative to piecemeal and uncoordinated local initiatives. The challenge was to come up with a recommendation for the shape of the logistics network, and to do that meant first understanding the business.

Products

One of the reasons for Hasbro's success was the relatively balanced portfolio of products that it sold. Its presence in the volatile market for girls and boys toys was balanced by strengths in both the pre-school sector and in family games and jigsaws. Details of the range are shown in Exhibits 4.1 and 4.2 and can be summarized as follows.

- **Pre-school toys:** the Playskool range and Playdoh. Many of these were voluminous and depended for their appeal partly on the image projected by their packaging, which was designed to sell to grandparents and others buying gifts for very young children. This was summed up by a French manager as 'nous vendons le rêve' ('we are selling dreams'). Most of the packs had a limited number of language variants; for example, there might be a French version, an English version and a third version with several other languages on it.
- **Girls' and boys' toys:** a very wide range, including the TV-series spin-offs, mostly imported from China. Many were relatively small and low priced (pocket-money toys) and were sold to the trade in mixed cases of ten to 20 pieces, referred to as assortments. For most of these, the small size of the pack, coupled with the need to appeal directly to the child, had led to each country having its own language-specific branding and packaging; for example, the product sold in the UK as Care Bears was known in France as Bisou-Ours. A limited number of larger products, notably cuddly toys (Plush) and Tonka trucks, were sold in a single multilingual pack type for all countries.
- **Jigsaw puzzles:** Hasbro was the leader in this niche market. Manufactured in The Netherlands, the product was bulky and sold on the basis of the picture, not the name. For this reason almost all puzzles were made in a single multilingual pack type.

Exhibit 4.1   Hasbro Europe: product group characteristics

Product group	Total 1992 items '000	Total 1992 sales $000	Average items/carton	Average cube/item	Total 1992 vol. 000 m3	Average m3/$000
Hasbro products						
Playskool Baby	4147	42,771	9.3	0.00908	37.7	0.880
Preschool	5369	59,173	9.2	0.00810	43.5	0.735
Puzzles	3591	13,335	14.9	0.00329	11.8	0.886
Games	14,920	181,544	10.0	0.00613	91.5	0.504
Crafts	1108	15,998	6.5	0.00838	9.3	0.580
Nintendo	536	17,993	48.0	0.00060	0.3	0.018
Pony	3094	18,089	11.1	0.00291	9.0	0.498
Sindy	2123	22,267	11.2	0.00461	9.8	0.440
Other girls'	1122	34,930	4.6	0.02056	23.1	0.660
Transformers	2675	19,797	13.4	0.00269	7.2	0.363
GI Joe	4046	23,884	26.0	0.00297	12.0	0.503
WWF	3514	16,968	22.0	0.00160	5.6	0.331
Other Boys	1854	10,020	21.1	0.00262	4.9	0.485
Plush	1196	9999	9.1	0.00691	8.3	0.826
Kenner Parker (KP) products						
Playdoh	3571	24,930	14.2	0.00459	16.4	0.657
Pictionary	676	16,283	6.0	0.00633	4.3	0.263
Trivial Pursuit	1315	33,939	4.0	0.00638	8.4	0.247
Other games	6339	83,681	7.8	0.00585	37.1	0.443
Tiny Tears	596	8175	11.2	0.01068	6.4	0.779
Other girls'	2663	28,790	10.4	0.00512	13.6	0.474
Boys toys	2708	22,858	12.3	0.01480	40.1	1.754
Tonka Trucks	328	4901	8.0	0.02642	8.7	1.770
Polystil	1604	9242	13.4	0.00417	6.7	0.724
Polystil Racing	320	6554	13.2	0.01087	3.5	0.531
Hasbro total	49,294	486,770	11.2	0.0055552	273.8	0.563
KP total	20,119	239,352	9.1	0.0072101	145.1	0.606
Total	69,413	726,122	10.5	0.0060349	418.9	0.577

Average sell price   US$10.46

- **Games** include very successful children's games such as Mousetrap, Bed Bugs and Kerplunk as well as adult games including Trivial Pursuit and Pictionary. In some cases, Hasbro owned rights to these games in a number of countries but not in all. In any case, a separate language variant was made for each main country. The differences between the variants might be in the packaging only (Mousetrap) or might include fundamental differences in the contents (Italian-language Trivial Pursuit would not be likely to sell well in Germany or France!).

In total, as seen in Exhibit 4.2, there were some 1400 SKUs (an individual product or reference for the purposes of warehousing and ordering) or, including assortments, 2600. These exclude the language variants which would lift the total figure to over 8000.

Overall, some 50% of items were sold in packs having only one language on them, meaning that they were specific to a single country (or close neighbours: French product was equally saleable in the French-speaking areas of Belgium or Switzerland). For each of these, there had to be pack variants for each main country. A further 30% of SKUs

Exhibit 4.2 Hasbro Europe: assortments and language variations by product group

Product groups	1992 SKUs	1992 Assort-ments	% SKUs with mono-lingual pack	multi-lingual pack	variants of languages	Total SKUs including language	including language and assortment	1992 Forecast items sold (thousands) total	mono-lingual	multi-lingual	variants
Hasbro products											
Playskool Baby	80	122	5	10	85	236	360	4147	207	415	3525
Preschool	167	296	10	15	75	501	888	5369	537	805	4027
Puzzles	143	620	0	95	5	157	682	3591	0	3411	180
Games	129	132	90	5	5	722	739	14920	13428	746	746
Crafts	9	9	100	0	0	54	54	1108	1108	0	0
Nintendo	8	8	100	0	0	48	48	536	536	0	0
Pony	27	103	100	0	0	162	618	3094	3094	0	0
Sindy	69	141	40	0	60	290	592	2123	849	0	1274
Other girls'	30	39	100	0	0	180	234	1122	1122	0	0
Transformers	31	122	0	0	100	93	366	2675	0	0	2675
GI Joe	32	110	10	0	90	106	363	4046	405	0	3641
WWF	27	69	90	10	0	149	380	3514	3163	351	0
Other boys'	7	16	90	10	0	39	88	1854	1668	185	0
Plush	33	96	0	100	0	33	96	1196	0	1196	0
Kenner Parker (KP) products											
Playdoh	22	48	0	0	100	66	144	3571	0	0	3571
Pictionary	5	5	100	0	0	30	30	676	676	0	0
Trivial Pursuit	26	26	100	0	0	156	156	1315	1315	0	0
Other games	113	113	50	50	0	396	396	6339	3169	3169	0
Tiny Tears	18	34	80	20	0	90	170	596	477	119	0
Other girls;	69	129	80	20	0	345	645	2663	2130	533	0
Boys toys	78	115	40	0	60	328	483	2708	1083	0	1625
Tonka Trucks	44	44	0	100	0	44	44	328	0	328	0
Polystil	132	132	0	100	0	132	132	1604	0	1604	0
Polystil Racing	81	81	100	0	0	486	486	4	320	0	0
Hasbro total	792	1883				2769	5508	49294	26116	7110	16067
KP total	588	727				2072	2686	20119	9171	5753	5196
Grand Total	1380	2610				4841	8193	69413	35287	12863	21263
Percentages									50.8%	18.5%	30.6%

existed in a limited number of language variants. Only 20% or so had truly multilingual packs that could be sold anywhere in Europe.

Sales and markets

As mentioned previously, a fundamental feature of the business is the impact of Christmas. The seasonality curve is shown in Exhibit 4.3. Coupled with factory order lead times in the order of several months (sometimes six months), this obliged the company to build up stocks in its warehouses in advance of the autumn peak. In consequence, average stocks in Europe exceeded three months of sales.

Hasbro's largest single market was in France, with Germany, the UK and Spain not far behind. The consultants prepared Table 4.1 to summarize actual sales in 1991 and predictions made at the time for growth up to 1996. It is stressed that here, as throughout

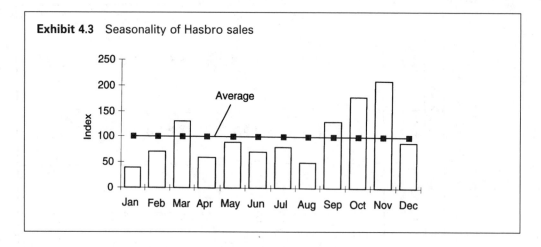

Exhibit 4.3   Seasonality of Hasbro sales

Table 4.1   Hasbro: actual and predicted sales value

	1991: US$ millions	Growth prediction for 1996*
Germany – Hasbro Milton Bradley	74	Medium
Germany – Kenner Parker	48	Medium
France – Hasbro Milton Bradley	116	Medium
France – Kenner Parker	75	Limited
UK – Total	132	Medium
Spain – Total	73	High
Benelux – Hasbro Milton Bradley	32	Limited
Benelux – Kenner Parker	18	Medium
Italy – Total	40	High

*Growth of at least 30% was expected in all cases. Limited growth means less than 45% in total between 1991 and 1996, medium growth implies between 45% and 80% over the forecast period, whilst high denotes a growth expectation of at least 100%.

this case study, that figures are presented in accordance with best predictions made at the time. Inevitably, the actual growth to 1996 might be different to the rate expected when the forecast was made.

Table 4.1 shows two key points. Firstly, although major growth was expected everywhere, this was expected to be particularly strong in the southern countries. Secondly, in several of the countries, figures were still being produced separately for the previously autonomous Hasbro Milton Bradley and Kenner Parker sides of the business. At the time of the study, in all countries *except* France, the two subsidiaries had at least been merged organizationally. Operationally, as will be shown, this was not necessarily the case.

A more detailed geographical breakdown of predicted sales for 1996, as estimated in 1991, is shown in Exhibit 4.4.

The customers of the business were retailers of all sizes. The biggest phenomenon in the market was the rise of Toys 'R' Us, whose store-opening programme was rapidly taking share from other outlets. In France, however, the market was still dominated by hypermarkets. In Italy, by contrast, retailing is far more fragmented and Hasbro was delivering to small stores.

These differences impacted on the size of deliveries and on the way in which orders were taken. In the UK, where most large retailers (such as Argos) had their own distribution centres, nearly 70% of volumes were shipped to just 30 drop points, often as full

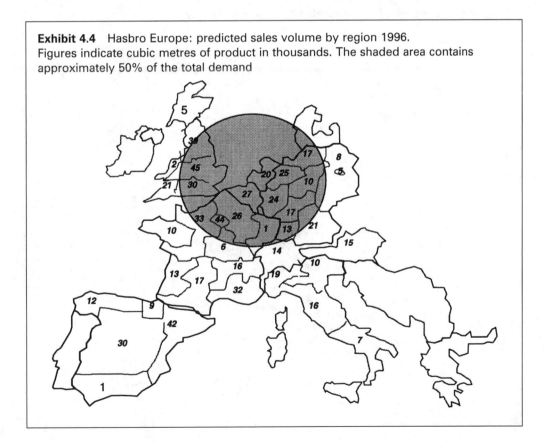

Exhibit 4.4 Hasbro Europe: predicted sales volume by region 1996.
Figures indicate cubic metres of product in thousands. The shaded area contains approximately 50% of the total demand

loads. In Germany, the top 30 addresses took just 20% of volumes. Depending on the country, then, Hasbro made more or less use of a range of haulage contractors, from full load truckers through groupage operators to parcel carriers.

Large retailers with their own warehouses were encouraged to place a single large order at the start of the autumn season, with some flexibility on the date of delivery. After that, they would place replenishment orders to top up their stocks on a weekly basis. Hypermarkets, however, did not operate their own distribution centres and required deliveries direct to each store, with an initial delivery of multiple pallet quantities followed by replenishments which might be just a few cases. Whatever the order size, they applied very strict time windows for delivery. Small retailers were less demanding and would order a few cases every month or less frequently.

There was a trend in the industry towards placing Christmas orders later and later. This was a major concern to Hasbro: it already had to build up substantial stocks in its own warehouses, and later ordering by major retailers meant ever higher peak stocks and corresponding finance costs. It also pushed the despatch activity into shorter time windows. In certain countries, additionally, Hasbro had sometimes to allow customers

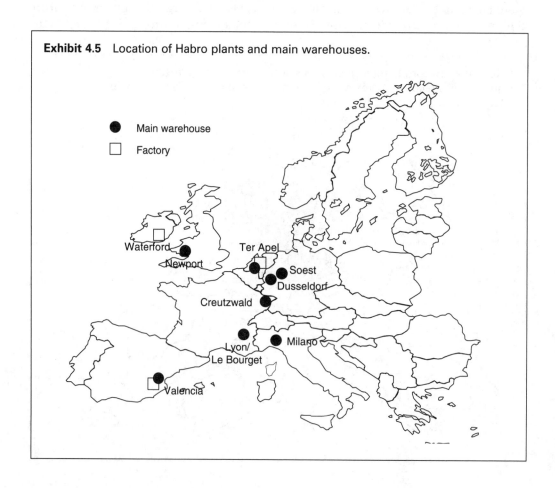

Exhibit 4.5 Location of Habro plants and main warehouses.

to return a percentage of unsold goods in January. Negotiations on discounts, order dates and the allowable percentage of returns were an annual ritual of critical importance to the business.

Sourcing and production

Hasbro, and its predecessors, had progressively moved production of many lines into the Far East. None the less, it still had important production facilities in three locations in Europe: Waterford (Ireland), Ter Apel (The Netherlands) and Valencia (Spain). These, and the main warehousing locations, are shown in Exhibit 4.5.

The rough split of production volumes was as follows.

- **Waterford:** 25% of European sales volume, being primarily the games and crafts ranges. Waterford had plastic moulding capacity in which substantial investments had been made. In addition it had recently taken over Playdoh production.
- **Ter Apel:** 15% of volume, being the whole of the jigsaw puzzle production plus games. This factory specialized in cardboard products.
- **Valencia:** 10% of volume, including some games, a proportion of toys (some of the GI Joe range, for example) and around a third of the preschool range.
- **China and other Far East:** 50% of volume, including the great majority of the girls' and boys' toys. The price of making plastic toys with a high labour content in the Far East was generally substantially below what could be achieved in Europe, even allowing for shipping costs.

Hasbro had already rationalized its European production sites, and further concentration was not envisaged. It had recently closed factories at Coalville (Leicestershire, UK) and Creutzwald (near Metz, France). The latter remained open as a storage facility only.

The time between placing an order on the factory and the availability of the product ex-works was typically in the order of four months. A variety of factors caused this delay, including the need for economic production batches to be built up out of a number of smaller orders and the seasonal nature of demand (volume had to be spread more evenly for manufacturing purposes). In addition, for some toys, the tooling would be rotated around several factories in Europe, the Far East and the USA. Thus, the plant in Waterford might only have the use of the tools for a few months in the year.

Distribution

Each country managed its own operations, including purchasing, stockholding, order processing and final delivery. There was a mixture of in-house and contracted operations. IT systems were owned by Hasbro but were different in each country.

Italy (where the entire operation was contracted out) was the only major country with a single warehousing site. This measured some 5000 m^2 (1 m^2 = 10.76 ft^2), with further space available if required.

In the UK, following the closure of Coalville, stock was held in two owned and one rented warehouse around Newport (south Wales). In total, an area of approximately 18,000 m^2 was available.

In Germany, the largest site was at Soest (7200 m^2). Hasbro had a further eight regional sites, totalling 4200 m^2, to which had been added a Kenner Parker subcontract for up to 14,000 m^2 in Dusseldorf.

For Benelux, Ter Apel performed some storage (4000 m^2) but lack of space meant that an equivalent additional area had been rented in the same vicinity. Kenner Parker had a contract for 3000 m^2 in Utrecht, to serve The Netherlands, and delivered to Belgium from Creutzwald (see below). The Utrecht warehouse was planned to close.

France still retained two operating subsidiaries, each with its own logistics management. Kenner Parker's head office was in Paris but operationally the company was based at the old manufacturing site at Creutzwald (Lorraine). This had 5000 m^2 of warehousing within the facility, not counting the previous manufacturing area (although this was of very limited height), and could double this at peak times by contracting in from local suppliers. Hasbro Milton Bradley was based at Le Bourget du Lac, east of Lyon, where it had an owned warehouse of 10,500 m^2 plus some outside space. In addition, it had two large sub-contractors in the Lyon area with nearly 15,000 m^2 between them. The three main warehouses were allocated specifically to Hasbro, MB and Playskool products, respectively.

In Spain, there was warehousing of 8500 m^2 in Valencia but even that had proved insufficient and a further 3000 m^2 of outside space had been rented.

Despite this large number of sites, storage capacity was under considerable pressure. Across Europe, Hasbro was struggling to reach four stock turns per year (stock turn = annual sales/average stock level). In particular, the German subsidiary was having problems coping with the existing volume (without taking future growth into account) and had put forward plans for a new owned warehouse of a high-tech nature at Soest, where an option on land had been secured at very advantageous terms.

The complexity of transport was at least as great as that of warehousing. It should simply be noted that all transport services were bought in and that each country had made its own contracts with local hauliers.

In total, the consultants found that warehousing costs were between 1.7% and 4.4% of sales, and transport costs between 1.2% and 3.6% of sales, dependent on the country concerned. With one or two exceptions, the total of warehousing and transport lay in the range 4–4.5% of sales. There was some evidence to suggest that Kenner Parker had been less effective than Hasbro at keeping transport costs down, but no consistent evidence as to whether it was better to run warehousing in-house or on a rented or subcontracted basis.

National differences

As the consultants toured the various subsidiaries, they noted many differences. Some of these have already been commented on, and several more are summarized below.

- **France.** The French General Managers (one each for Hasbro Milton Bradley and Kenner Parker) had strong views on the different nature of the French market compared with other European markets. Generally, they felt strongly that it was necessary to have French-language variants of almost all products. Not only were there two subsidiaries, but within Hasbro Milton Bradley there was separation between the three main parts (Hasbro, MB Games and Playskool) each of which delivered separately to the hypermarkets. It was felt that these separate identities increased the sales penetration of the business. Within MB, products were offered in less than full-case quantities and around 40% of order lines required break-case picking (where an outer case is opened in the warehouse and individual sales units are picked from within it for despatch to customers). Normal service to customers was delivery within three days of receipt of the order.

- **Germany.** The two biggest customers in Germany (Toys 'R' Us and Karstadt) were growing strongly and centralizing their own distribution. Already, 10% of volumes were collected by customers (mainly Toys 'R' Us) from Hasbro's warehouses. The German management was looking to develop new ranges of business, such as sports goods, and was mainly concerned with overcoming space constraints.
- **Spain.** A large amount of stock was held by wholesalers, who represented 36% of sales, but this was expected to fall in the future. Partly in consequence of this, and partly as a result of rapid growth in the market, Spain achieved an unusually high stock turn of more than six.
- **Benelux.** A major feature of retailing in the Benelux countries was merchandising the goods in store; that is, filling up the shop's shelves on the customer's behalf. In addition, response to orders had to be fast, as retailers worked to weekly cycles and required their shelves restocked before each weekend.
- **Italy.** As in Spain, wholesalers were important in this market. Service requirements were relatively relaxed, since virtually no customers insisted on delivery to a pre-booked time. There were some contra-cyclical products balancing the Christmas peak: apparently Italians like to buy jigsaws in the spring. The contracted warehouse had direct on-line links to Hasbro's IT system.

Modelling

The consultants developed a standard questionnaire to collect data from each country, backed up with the programme of visits to local subsidiaries. They then set about modelling a range of options for the future shape of the distribution network. The modelling was based on 1996 estimated volumes, converted into cubic metres of product. The total for 1996 was calculated as 727,000 m^3.

Owing to the complexity of the current structure, and the fact that by 1996 many of the existing contracts would have to be renewed or replaced and some of the existing in-house facilities could be modified or expanded, it was decided to compare options on a 'green-field' basis. That is, the team estimated the cost of setting up operations from scratch at chosen locations, rather than using existing facilities. Later in the project the outputs were reviewed against the known costs of the current infrastructure.

For modelling purposes the problem was divided into the following three parts.

- **Transport model.** This was produced on a spreadsheet and based on a grid of regions (consistent with Exhibit 4.4), with distances calculated between the centres of each region. From this, transport costs were estimated by applying a cost function, expressed as:

$$X = a + bY$$

where X is the transport cost per cubic metre, Y is the distance in kilometres, a is the minimum freight cost per cubic metre and b is the incremental cost per cubic metre

Exhibit 4.6 Hasbro Europe: land, labour and building costs

Location	Rent index	Land cost US$/m2	Build cost (9 m) US$/m2	Labour cost US$ per year
Lille	0.55	44	503	22,500
Toulouse	0.84	68	503	23,200
Paris	1.37	110	503	33,000
Lyon	0.84	68	503	24,000
Strasbourg	0.55	44	503	22,500
Le Havre	0.82	66	503	22,500
Cologne	0.64	52	531	31,100
Munster	0.86	69	531	31,100
Munich	1.03	83	531	28,700
Valencia	0.94	76	600	19,000
Ter Apel	0.70	56	460	22,600
Milan	1.05	85	395	30,000
Coventry	1.0	81	659	17,200
Newport	1.0	81	659	17,800

per kilometre of distance. Separate cost functions were used for full-load deliveries, part loads and parcel quantities. Cost functions were obtained from Hasbro's existing tariffs, using regression analysis, on a country-by-country basis. For pan-European operations, an average of the national rates was used (although crude, this was felt to offer sufficient accuracy for the purpose).

- **Warehouse model.** As mentioned above, the warehouse model was based on greenfield development. Costs of land and labour were taken from a variety of sources and are shown for sample locations in Exhibit 4.6. The cost of warehousing is driven by a number of factors, including the mix between the volume of stock and the number of SKUs as well as the technology adopted. The consultants examined a range of options. For holding bulk stock they compared drive-in racking (four pallets high) to an automated double-deep silo (13 pallets high). For picking, the choices included wide-aisle racking, three-level mezzanines and automated sortation. Some of the outputs from the model are summarized in Exhibit 4.7. Automation was found to reduce the footprint of the facility significantly, but was difficult to cost justify.
- **Stock model.** Stock was assessed based on the current level of four stockturns per annum and also at six stock turns. The average purchase price per cubic metre for 1996 was estimated to be approximately $430, and interest rates of 10% per annum were used. An important question was the extent to which the level of stock would vary if it was centralized into fewer locations per country or across Europe. This was assessed pragmatically, without building a detailed model.

National issues

The team first looked at what should be done in Germany and France, which were considered as stand-alone operations. From the models, the costs were estimated as shown in Table 4.2 (for simplicity, stock costs have been omitted, although it should be noted that these are likely to decrease as the number of locations is reduced).

Exhibit 4.7 Sample Hasbro warehouse model outputs.
For three different versions of throughput and number of SKUs and two alternative technologies. Uses cost factors for Lille

	Version 1	Version 2	Version 3	Version 1	Version 2	Version 3
Annual volume (M3)	727,000	200,000	100,000	727,000	200,000	100,000
SKUs	5000	1500	600	5000	1500	600
	Low-bay bulk store with wide aisle picking cell			High-bay automated bulk store wide aisle picking cell		
Areas (square metres)						
Intake/despatch	27,695	7619	3810	31,438	8649	4324
Forward pick	23,000	6900	2760	23,000	6900	2760
Bulk store	68,326	18,492	9613	31,233	8472	4381
Total building	119,021	33,011	16,183	85,671	24,021	11,465
Total site	297,553	82,527	40,457	214,177	60,052	28,663
Manning						
Intake/despatch	115	32	16	131	36	18
Putaway	15	4	2			
Replenishment	23	6	3	26	7	4
Picking/packing	129	36	18	129	36	18
Ancilliary staff	28	8	4	29	8	4
Total Directs	312	86	43	315	87	44
Management	32	9	5	32	9	5
Equipment						
Fork lift trucks	39	11	6	27	8	4
Order picking trucks	130	36	18	130	36	18
Automated cranes				26	8	4
Picking racks	5000	1500	600	5000	1500	600
Bulk racks	97,608	26,417	13,733	113,164	30,696	15,873
Capital costs (US$)						
Land	13,092,318	3,631,179	1,780,114	9,423,806	2,642,280	1,261,179
Building	59,867,599	16,604,389	8,139,977	27,382,232	7,820,970	3,563,415
Static equipment bulk	7,906,275	2,139,750	1,112,400	34,288,545	9,300,872	4,809,511
Static equipment pick	1,000,000	300,000	120,000	1,000,000	300,000	120,000
Mobile equipment	4,030,000	1,126,000	588,000	11,750,000	3,536,000	1,768,000
Systems	1,450,000	1,450,000	1,450,000	1,900,000	1,900,000	1,900,000
Total	87,346,192	25,251,318	13,190,491	85,744,583	25,500,122	13,422,105
Annual costs						
Financing of capital	9,871,069	2,949,739	1,611,193	10,674,654	3,304,210	1,820,340
R&M buildings	598,676	166,044	81,400	273,822	78,210	35,634
R&M equipment	388,088	106,973	54,612	1,411,156	394,106	200,925
R&M systems	72,500	72,500	72,500	95,000	95,000	95,000
Light, power, taxes	4,165,738	1,155,375	566,400	2,998,484	840,726	401,284
Labour directs	7,020,000	1,935,000	967,500	7,087,500	1,957,500	990,000
Labour management	1,080,000	303,750	168,750	1,080,000	303,750	168,750
Total	23,196,071	6,689,381	3,522,355	23,620,616	6,973,501	3,711,933

R&M = repair and maintenance.

What this showed was that, even without stock in the analysis, there were clear advantages in both countries in centralizing the operation at a single location. Re-development of Soest and Creutzwald looked to be the most likely options, although the case for Creutzwald compared to Lyon was marginal in straight financial terms. An

Table 4.2 Estimation of costs

| | Cost per cubic metre of throughput ($) | | | |
	Warehousing	Inbound transport*	Transport to customers	Total
Germany				
One warehouse (Soest)	39	13	18	70
Two regional warehouses	44	14	16	74
Three regional warehouses	48	14	15	77
France				
Current structure (HMB at Creutzwald, KP at Lyon)	36	15	20	71
One warehouse (Creutzwald)	33	14	18	65
One warehouse (Lyon)	34	16	16	66
Two regional warehouses	37	15	15	67
Three regional warehouses	40	15	14	69

*Inbound transport was the cost to the warehouse from the European factories or from the nearest entry port in the case of Chinese imports.

Table 4.3 Model of six-warehouse strategy

Annual throughput (m³, projected to 1996)	727,000
Stock turns	4 per annum
Cost of inbound transport	$10.26 million
Cost of warehousing	$26.47 million
Cost of outbound transport	$10.48 million
Cost of stockholding	$7.78 million
Total cost	$55.00 million

additional factor was that the company already owned the Creutzwald site and it was considered that a buyer for it would be difficult to find, given the depressed nature of the region in which it was sited.

Pan-European issues

The project then moved on to the options for the whole of Europe. On its own, Germany justified having a single warehouse. However, should this also serve Benelux and part of France, or conversely should Creutzwald also cover Germany? Did the outlying countries such as Italy and Spain justify retaining their own facilities?

Still on a green-field basis, the models gave the baseline shown in Table 4.3 for a six-warehouse strategy using Newport, Creutzwald, Valencia, Milan, Ter Apel and Soest. Using this as a basis, the consultants went on to suggest alternative structures for the European network and to estimate their likely cost and benefit.

Case 5 • NIKE Europe

Company background

NIKE is a name that scarcely needs any introduction. It has been one of the business phenomena of the 1980s and 1990s, second perhaps only to Microsoft in its pursuit of global dominance from very humble beginnings. Founder Phil Knight famously made his first shoes using a waffle iron in what he has called 'a tiny operation in my mother's laundry room'. By 1992 it had become a $4.5 billion turnover corporation.

In fact, NIKE's history goes back to 1963, when Knight (still today very much the head of the business) set up Blue Ribbon Sports to import running shoes from Japan to the US, or even to the late 1950s when he ran for the University of Oregon track team and started looking for better footwear. The name (*Nike* was the Greek goddess of victory) did not appear until 1972, and sales grew steadily thereafter on the public's new-found enthusiasm for fitness. Having overtaken Adidas, NIKE was caught napping by Reebok who stole US market share leadership in 1986. Far from admitting defeat, however, NIKE was 'reinvented' and fought back using sponsorship of sports stars such as Michael Jordan, Andre Agassi and (more recently) Eric Cantona to spearhead its positioning as the maker of top-flight performance athletic wear. Today it is the undisputed industry leader.

NIKE's culture is easy to recognize, if hard to define. It prides itself on being a bit different, creative, iconoclastic. The senior team used to meet together for six-monthly strategy reviews that became known as 'buttface' meetings, with no holds barred and plenty of shouting at each other. Inevitably, as the company grew to have 10,000 employees (or associates as they are known), something of the informality had to go. The surprise, perhaps, is that it managed this transformation without coming to grief. One part of the founding philosophy that is still fundamental is the pursuit of athletic performance. To outsiders, NIKE may appear to live in a fashion-dominated sector, but fashion is not a word that NIKE people like to use. They consider it to be a *technology* company and insist that their success stems from performance and quality, not slick salesmanship.

With growth came internationalization. In Europe, NIKE initially worked through distributors, selecting local partners in each country. The success of these led the company to decide that it wanted to own its own distribution, and gradually through the 1980s it bought out its distributors and converted them into wholly owned subsidiaries, each operating largely autonomously. A European headquarters was set up, which migrated several times through different countries before settling at Hilversum (The Netherlands), but it remained small and did not even act as a financial holding company for NIKE in Europe.

Nineteen-ninety-two was the year that NIKE set out to do something about Europe. It had now reached over $1 billion of sales in Europe alone. It owned its distribution in all the major countries but each country still ran its own operations. Roger Tragesser, an experienced logistics professional who had set up NIKE's operations in Memphis, was sent to Europe to take a fresh look at how the business was being run. With the help of consultants, he set about rethinking NIKE's European logistics from scratch. In

November of that year a workshop was called to bring together key NIKE managers from both Europe and the USA. Its purpose was to receive the consultants' recommendations and to determine which way to go.

Sales and markets

The consultancy team collected data for 1992 expected sales and forecasts for 1997. These were prepared in a pre-recessionary climate and reflected a bullish vision of the prospects for Europe over the intervening period. In aggregate, the forecasts represented a doubling of sales to around $2 billion per annum.

While footwear was the origin of NIKE's strength, it had also become a major seller of apparel (clothing), ranging from socks and sweat bands to jackets and complete jogging suits. In Germany and in the UK, by 1992, it was selling more pieces of apparel than pairs of shoes. However, with the average price of footwear being much higher, shoes in aggregate outsold apparel by two to one in sales value terms.

Exhibits 5.1 and 5.2 show the sales by country for footwear and apparel. It can be seen that three markets – France, Germany and the UK – dominated 1992 sales, representing 68% of footwear volumes and 77% of apparel. This situation was expected to change somewhat by 1997, because of strong growth in the south of Europe. By 1997, total sales of footwear were forecast to reach 31 million pairs, of which 62% would be in the three largest countries. Apparel was expected to reach 27 million pieces, with the main countries representing exactly two-thirds of the total. Exhibit 5.3 summarizes the situation for apparel as it was in 1992. (This pattern reflects what economists refer to as the 'hot banana' of demand in Europe, which curves from the middle of the UK down through

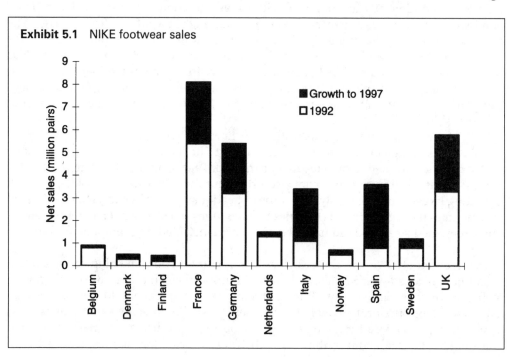

Exhibit 5.1 NIKE footwear sales

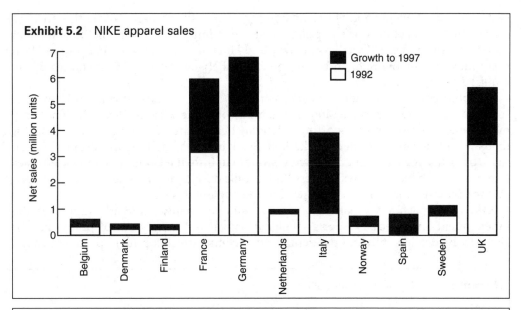

Exhibit 5.2 NIKE apparel sales

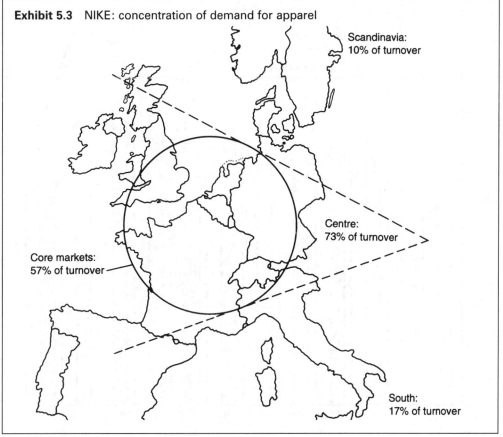

Exhibit 5.3 NIKE: concentration of demand for apparel

eastern France, Benelux and western Germany into northern Italy. Within this area lies a large proportion of Europe's population and spending power.) It should be noted that Scandinavian countries (Sweden, Norway and Finland) were not members of the EU at that time. Goods moving to and from the EU, or between Scandinavian countries, still required customs clearance.

The business was strongly seasonal, with two main seasons (spring and autumn) somewhat alleviated by smaller intermediate seasons. The seasons were driven not only by weather but also by the sporting calendar: demand for tennis shoes in winter, or football boots in summer, was very limited. Stock had to be built up in advance of peak sales, particularly as most products were brought in from the Far East on long lead times (see below). Exhibit 5.4 shows the resulting profile of sales and inventory. It can be seen that the seasons were more pronounced in the apparel business.

NIKE's approach to its markets was a special one. Firstly, it strongly supported the independent and specialist sports retailer. This was not simply out of philosophy or altruism. By dealing with independents, and declining to sell top-flight product to mass

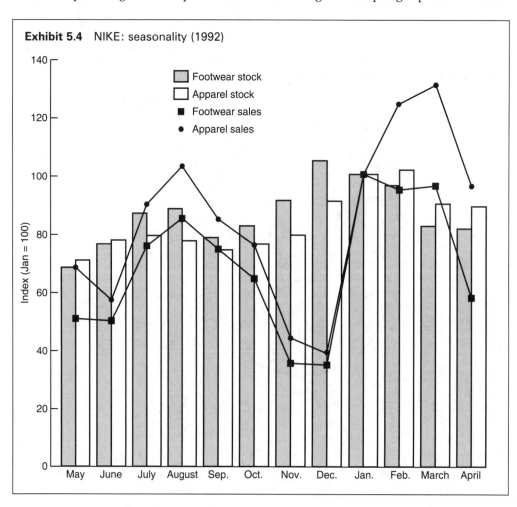

Exhibit 5.4   NIKE: seasonality (1992)

retailers, NIKE maintained the image of its shoes and at the same time avoided price discounting. For example, it did not sell to hypermarkets or discount retailers, with the possible exception of close-outs, i.e. product left unsold at the end of a season. This policy is legitimate provided it can be shown that the product has special needs which require a particular level of advice to the consumer. NIKE argues that performance sportswear cannot be sold in the same way as tins of beans.

Secondly, a large proportion of NIKE's sales were on what it termed the 'futures programme'. Basically, the retailer was expected to place his bulk orders some six months in advance of the selling season. For example, for spring 1993 (products which would reach the retailer from January onwards), samples were shown to the trade in May and June 1992 and their orders were required by the end of July. This enabled NIKE to manufacture at least a proportion of its requirements on the basis of firm orders, thereby reducing its inventory risk. Not surprisingly, retailers had been less than impressed by the introduction of the futures programme. However, the strength of the brand was such that NIKE was able to impose it in most cases. Retailers had to agree to place futures orders in order to earn the right to order replenishments during the course of the season. In aggregate, around 70–80% of NIKE's volumes were shipped under the futures programme, the balance being bought for stock and then sold as replenishments.

Although, as stated, NIKE supported specialist outlets, this did not mean only dealing with 'mom and pop' stores. The customer base included some very large sportswear retailers, including Olympus in the UK and Decathlon in France, both of which were expanding internationally. In addition, the US retailer Foot Locker was starting to enter the European marketplace. NIKE's nationally based organization was poorly positioned to service international retailers who expected the same prices and service in each country. This was one reason why change was necessary.

Larger retailers tend to have their own distribution centres and buy centrally. In the UK, the top 20 delivery addresses accounted for over 50% of NIKE's sales. In France, the equivalent figure was under 40% and in Germany only around 15%. Spanish retailers were much less concentrated and the top 20 addresses accounted for less than 10% of that market.

Logistics

Among the consultants, it became a standing joke that no one could ever work out exactly how many stockholding points NIKE had in Europe. There were almost 20 main warehouses in the 11 countries that the consultants visited, but several others were also used on a seasonal or *ad hoc* basis. In some cases, footwear and apparel were stocked in separate warehouses.

The majority of products were sourced in the Far East and imported in container loads. There was a small function in Hilversum which consolidated the orders raised by national subsidiaries and passed them to NIKE's Hong Kong office which co-ordinated purchase and manufacture. Where necessary, different products destined to a single country would be consolidated together to make up a full load. Consolidation of goods for a number of countries was less common, although not unknown.

While virtually all footwear was imported from the Far East, apparel was more varied. Of this, around 30% was sourced in or near Europe, from low-cost countries including

Ireland, Portugal and Turkey. The precise source tended to vary from year to year, as orders followed the lowest costs or the most favourable exchange rate. Goods from these sources were normally shipped by road in full truck loads.

Exhibit 5.5 shows the main locations used for warehousing. Details on the three largest countries are as follows.

- **UK**. NIKE had an in-house operation at Washington, County Durham, of around 18,600 m^2. The status of the site was somewhat unusual, in that part of it was owned freehold and part was leased. There was some scope for expansion and the possibility of buying the remainder of the freehold. The distribution centre performed a range of value-added services for customers, particularly Olympus, such as relabelling and repackaging of the shoes. Import containers came through the port of Southampton and goods could be held in the warehouse under customs bond, i.e. without paying duties or VAT until they were delivered to customers.
- **France**. NIKE France was based at an owned facility north of Paris, which had itself only been opened some two years before. Although it had an area of around 14,300 m^2,

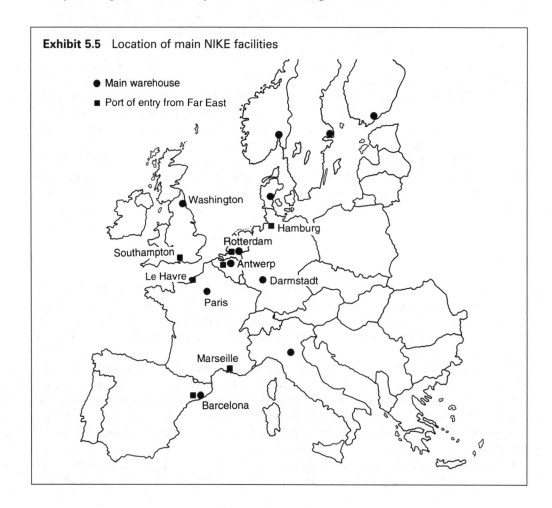

Exhibit 5.5   Location of main NIKE facilities

strong growth in the market meant that the warehouse had been almost too small on the day it opened, and stock was also held in at least two outside warehouses with an area totalling some 10,000 m^2. The building had, however, been designed for easy expansion on to the adjoining plot, which was available for purchase. Le Havre was the main port of importation, but the only bonded storage was at a forwarder's warehouse at the port. Value-added services were not performed on-site but sent out to a subcontractor.

- **Germany**. Stock in Germany was split between three warehouses, a mixture of in-house and contracted operations, totalling 25,000 m^2. The lease on one of these was close to expiry. Like France, Germany was struggling to cope with the volume that it had reached.

A critical difference between countries was the number of SKUs that each was able to offer in its range. It should be understood that, in footwear and apparel, there is a multiplication of SKUs:

$$A \text{ styles} \times B \text{ colours} \times C \text{ sizes} = D \text{ combinations.}$$

From the point of view of the logistician, D is what counts since each of these is a separate reference for picking and packing. Calculating SKUs at the most detailed level (D), NIKE's total catalogue for footwear and apparel ran to over 10,000 SKUs each per season. However, no single country was offering anything like this range. The large countries were selling an average of around 5000 SKUs of each category. In the smaller countries, the figure could be under 2000.

Although the nature of the retail market varied significantly from country to country, there was a similar pattern of deliveries in most countries. An analysis of delivery notes showed that in Belgium, which was reasonably typical, half of all orders delivered were for fewer than ten pairs or pieces and a further third were for between 11 and 50 pairs or pieces.

This pattern of many small orders was created partly by customer demand (frequent replenishment orders during the season) but also by internal company failures. In many cases, although customers placed their orders months in advance, goods were not available in stock by the agreed shipment date. This led to split shipments and the release of a large wave of back-orders when the goods eventually arrived from suppliers. The problem was particularly acute on the apparel side. One particular case was the difficulty that NIKE experienced in the handling of collections. For example, customers might want to buy not only Jordan basketball shoes but also co-ordinating socks, pants and sweatshirt. These three items were often sourced from three different manufacturers and received in Europe at different times. The warehouses found it very difficult to ensure that all items in a collection were shipped to retailers at the same time.

An analysis of order lines showed that the large operations were processing around 10,000–20,000 per day on average, and several times this at peak. Small operations might pick under 2000 order lines per day outside the peak. However, the average number of units (pairs or pieces) per order line was between one and five in all subsidiaries. (An order will typically be for a number of different products. Each of these is usually set out on a separate line of an order form, hence the description order line. For example, if you order six red widgets, three green and three blue, this is an order for three order lines comprising 12 units.)

Generally, footwear and apparel were ordered and delivered separately. This corresponded to the way in which both NIKE and large customers were organized.

Customer service issues

Roger Tragesser and the consultants met with both general and logistic management in all NIKE's subsidiaries, to discuss not only the operation but also the needs of local customers. It became clear from this that, despite (or in some cases because of) the growth in the business, NIKE was far from perfect in the delivery of customer service.

Some of the issues highlighted were as follows.

- There were major problems in getting apparel to the retailer by the due date. Long order lead times and unreliable suppliers were blamed for this.
- There was a lack of information available to local management about the expected arrival date of shipments, and a corresponding failure to keep customers informed of when they might receive their orders.
- There were difficulties, as mentioned, in keeping 'collections' together. If a retailer wished to specify some special collection of their own, ensuring that this was sent as a single delivery often proved impossible.
- There was a lack of availability of consistent value-added services. Relabelling, reboxing and other services were recognized as potentially an important part of the package (summarized as making NIKE 'easy to do business with') but not all countries were equipped to provide these.
- Computer systems had been developed autonomously in each country and most had serious deficiencies. In some cases there was no on-line inventory record to refer to when taking a customer order. In others, there was no scope for prioritizing or batching up orders before passing them for picking. If a customer tried to order a product which he or she was informed was out of stock, this 'lost sale' was not generally recorded. Indeed, there was little measurement of customer service standards in most countries: Belgium suggested that 10% of customer orders were cancelled for one reason or another, but it was impossible to know for certain.

Deficiencies in customer service, delays in production or volatility in the markets tended to lead to goods being left unsold in the warehouse at the end of the season. These were referred to by NIKE as close-outs. There were several options for disposing of these. The first was to reduce the price and sell them through the normal channels: to do this it was desirable to spot as early as possible in the season that there was a developing overstock situation and to start taking action to push the product with a minimum of discount. The second option was to wait until the end of the season and then sell at much larger mark-downs to discounters or other secondary channels. The third option was to keep the goods until the following year and then hope to clear them. Unfortunately, this not only cluttered up the warehouse but risked undermining the sales of the new products for the following year. Close-outs were a headache for management and a symptom of underlying problems.

Analysis of the options

In advance of the November 1992 workshop, the consultants produced a range of options and modelled the costs for each. The modelling was similar to that performed for Hasbro (see Case 4) although the transport model was somewhat more sophisticated.

Modelling was done separately for footwear and apparel. The options included a series of alternatives ranging from the existing national structures to a single European distribution centre to service all countries. Table 5.1 shows some of the outputs from this work. It excludes, however, any analysis of stocks or close-outs. Assessment of these was done mainly by NIKE management, based on their experience from the US. For scenarios involving two or three European distribution centres, it was assumed that the stock-holding would be managed as a single inventory across all sites. For footwear, the consensus was that there would be no further stock savings from complete centralization. For apparel, however, given the considerable difficulty which NIKE was experiencing in managing their inventory, it was felt that a single centre would enable further savings to be made in stock carrying costs and close-outs. Details of the assumptions for stocks and close-outs are shown in Exhibit 5.6.

The figures produced showed that some degree of centralization was financially beneficial in terms of operating costs. They also demonstrated a stronger case for apparel than for footwear. But was this enough?

Table 5.1 Comparison of annual operating costs*

	Cost ($ million per annum)			
	Inbound transport	Warehousing	Transport to customers	Total
Options for footwear				
Base case: national warehouses	13.55	27.90	16.65	58.1
One European distribution centre (Benelux location)	12.83	16.33	24.57	53.7
Two distribution centres (Benelux and southern France)	12.98	19.75	21.80	54.5
Three distribution centres (Benelux, southern France and southern Sweden)	12.96	20.85	20.20	54.0
Options for apparel				
Base case: national warehouses	3.68	20.11	5.14	28.9
One European distribution centre (Benelux location)	2.73	9.56	7.89	20.2
Two distribution centres (Benelux and southern France)	2.75	12.17	6.89	21.8
Three distribution centres (Benelux, northern Spain and southern Sweden)	2.73	14.63	6.93	24.3

*Inbound transport includes the cost from Far East origin to European port, from port to warehouse and from European supplier to warehouse. Warehousing includes annualized capital costs. The indicative capital investment for single warehouse solutions was $51 million for footwear and $33 million for apparel, excluding systems, transition costs, etc. All figures are calculated as green-field development.

Exhibit 5.6 NIKE: basic assumptions used in modelling.
(Figures as at November 1992 workshop. Many revisions were made later)

Total volumes (1997 forecast)

	Pairs/pieces (millions)	$ at full selling price (millions)
Footwear: total	32.1	1411
Excluding Scandinavia	29.7	
Apparel: total	27.9	556
Excluding Scandinavia	25.7	

Product cubes

Footwear	150 pairs per cubic metre
Apparel	600 pieces per cubic metre

Stock turns

	Footwear	Apparel
With national warehouses	4	3.5
Single European DC*	4.5	4
Two European DCs	4.5	3.75
Three European DCs	4.5	3.75

Interest rates

Annual rate assumed	10%

Close-outs

	Footwear		Apparel	
	% unsold†	% discount	% unsold	% discount
With national warehouses	15	30	15	40
Single European DC	10	30	10	30
Two European DCs	10	30	12.50	35
Three European DCs	10	30	12.50	35

Notes
'% unsold' is the percentage of purchases that are left unsold at the end of the season.
'% discount' is the average discount off NIKE's normal full selling price that has to be given in order to clear close-out merchandise.
*DC = distribution centre.
Other assumptions

Cost of stock in warehouses (FOB + freight)	$17 per pair	$10 per piece

The US-based managers at the workshop came with some predisposition in favour of centralizing NIKE's European logistics. One of them commented, 'How can we justify having more than one warehouse in a place no bigger than Texas'. The European managers came in some cases to defend their own turf and in others with a genuine wish to improve their own infrastructure (for example, both Germany and Italy badly needed new distribution facilities). The consultants, however, needed to take a more dispassionate approach and identify what the real advantages of centralization might be and what difficulties would have to be overcome. Was there really a case for investing around $100 million of NIKE's money in a European distribution centre?

Acknowledgements

Martin Ashford would like to acknowledge the assistance received in preparing these cases from Malcolm Major of Hasbro Europe and Roger Tragesser of NIKE Europe. He also wishes to acknowledge the role played in the original projects by other members of the Touche Ross team, including Tony Cotter, Ian Fleming, John Humphries, Sean McMorrow, Ken Porter and Rebeca Ramos.

Global supply chain management*

Professor Philip B. Schary
Oregon State University, USA

and

Daniel F. Carr
Logistics Analyst, Hewlett-Packard Corporation, USA

Introduction

Rob Brown sat at his desk in late 1994 awed by his new assignment as implementation team leader for Valkyrie. Both he and his team members were new to this concept of managing the supply chain, although everyone had come from within the Valkyrie organization. He remembered the comments of Richard Jones, the Director of Operations:

> This is a crucial time for Valkyrie. We know we can't go on the way that we have in the past. This idea of a supply chain is not entirely new to us, but the way that we have to make it work is. That's why I pulled this team together. Every one of you has been here long enough to have a stake in the survival and prosperity of Valkyrie. Each of you brings a particular perspective to the team. This is important in making the supply chain an integral part of the company. It also means that the old ways of doing business are not good enough. We have to rethink the entire process.

Rob thought of the other team members. Marcia Gulick came from corporate finance. He was glad she was aboard the team because she had a good analytical mind. Al Ferrenti had been in sales for the last five years. He had frequently passed on the comments of frustrated customers who could not get the products delivered in the quantities or times that they wanted. John Sherwin had been responsible for production planning at Valkyrie's main plant in Denver and was instrumental in reducing work-in-process

---

*This case is based on a real situation but the names of the companies and individuals concerned have been changed for reasons of commercial confidentiality.

inventory for Valkyrie. George Fuentes represented the information systems group. Sandra Falkner had extensive experience in production procurement. Rob's own experience from logistics was substantial but different from theirs. He had negotiated for transport services and more recently had managed distribution centre operations.

If any group could implement the supply chain, this team was it. However, this task was going to extend everyone's experience. He thought to himself, 'We are at the beginning of a learning curve. We are bound to make some false starts as we go along. The main thing is that we get started. Jones as Director of Operations has charged us with the task of design, implementation and operation of the supply chain. We will have to live with this result and take responsibility for making it work.' At the time, Jones dropped a sheaf of documents and reports on Rob's desk. This was the only information that the team could use to guide their task.

The industry

The technical lighting industry was highly competitive. Until recently, there had been few major innovations and the competing firms had consolidated into a small number who were competing for market share in a slow-growing market. This balance had been recently disturbed by a change in technology, starting with quartz-halogen lamps, but soon exceeding that. Valkyrie had been early to seize on the new trend and gained superiority based on a technical virtuosity. Other competitors soon followed, so a technological lead was only temporary unless it was maintained and supported by other forms of competition such as pricing and customer service.

The market for the most part consisted of large buyers who liked to play off their suppliers against each other. Some of these were contractors who wanted to supply entire buildings at one time. Others were mass merchandisers and retailers who offered large sales volumes but wanted their suppliers to carry inventory for them. The outward sign was an aggressive price rivalry. Customers would ask for and receive 1–2% discounts regularly. While these might appear small, they were taken against small operating margins and high overhead costs. The market was also fragmenting in the sense that standard designs were becoming less desirable and each customer was asking for variations. Each competitor tried to counter this by offering a wider variety of product designs (stock-keeping units or SKUs). At the same time, there was pressure for competitors to supply on short notice with precisely timed delivery service.

The US market was now dominated by Valkyrie and two other large firms, followed by a host of smaller ones that were struggling to stay alive. One competitor was a recent entry, coming with deep financial pockets, and a policy of aggressive technology which was actually ahead of Valkyrie's. They had gained a 24% share of the market through rapid market acceptance. They were hampered, however, by an inability to maintain consistent quality, coupled with an erratic supply. A second competitor had been a long-time rival, and was now roughly equivalent in technology, but providing consistent product quality and delivery. They had gained market share at Valkyrie's expense, from 30 to 32%. Valkyrie's own share had slipped from 35 to 30%.

Competition was taking its toll. Operating margins were declining for all of the surviving firms, an aftermath of the intense price competition now prevailing. Valkyrie's own margins had declined from 23% to 18% within two years, and the established competitor was experiencing a similar decline. The new competitor, however, was actually gaining because their technological advantage gave them some immunity from the price wars that plagued the rest of the industry, while the costs of producing were gradually coming down.

Markets

The North American market was becoming more competitive. It was hard to remain an American producer in the face of low-cost Asian competitors who were just now beginning to enter this technical lighting market. There was increasing pressure for product variety along with good design. Preferences, however, were not stable but changing continually so that while there had to be enough inventory to cover the product range, it was dangerous to carry too much as it would soon be obsolete.

Large customers were in the driver's seat, but they were facing their own competition and margin pressures. They wanted minimal inventory for themselves but with immediate delivery when they needed it. Most customers were using electronic data interchange (EDI) for transactions but appeared to want closer contact than that.

Europe was a different kind of problem. A serious entry move by Valkyrie would require more than exporting from the USA. The product lines were different, and European tastes had evolved in a different direction. Suppliers varied considerably in capability and performance. Could a third party be counted on to perform not only assembly but also to manage the suppliers? Customer service requirements varied considerably from northern to southern Europe and communications were a jumble. The one constant was a lack of interest in EDI. How would the market be serviced?

Valkyrie had already begun to exploit the European market on a small scale, exporting directly from the USA through a Dutch distributor, but this would not be satisfactory for the future. There were several regional competitors who were able to provide better service to customers with roughly equivalent products. The only long-term answer would be to manufacture in Europe. This would make possible faster response to the market while also satisfying the European Union customs rules about local content. This last was a particularly annoying obstacle which was going to take negotiation to determine whether local assembly of components combined with an external casing would be sufficient to qualify Valkyrie's products as locally manufactured.

South-east Asia was also a promising market. The prospect of shipping components to the USA, assembling them and then shipping them back to south-east Asia was discouraging, as Valkyrie products would have to be priced several times higher than local competition. In addition, local content rules would become a problem as in Europe, forcing Valkyrie to assemble in an Asian country.

Valkyrie's strengths and weaknesses

Valkyrie, at one time, had dominated the market through superior products, which were technically advanced and well designed aesthetically. They were featured in decorator and office furnishings trade shows and attracted a wide following. The technical lead was being eroded by Alpha products, leaving only the aesthetic design advantage.

At the same time, the fragmentation of the market required an increasing number of SKUs to maintain market share. Valkyrie's production system was conceived around a push concept, of building to a forecast which was revised every quarter. Even the production people regarded it as hopelessly rigid: as demand changed, Valkyrie was unable to match it. Production planning tried to move toward short production runs and produce to stock. This would require large amounts of finished product inventory. It also turned out to be a costly effort as changeover costs in production were unexpectedly high. The effect on service was not always positive. It was difficult to maintain adequate stocks on each individual item (SKU), resulting in stockouts and a reputation of inflexible service to customers.

In order to meet product demand and service requirements, Valkyrie had experimented with regional distribution centres but had abandoned the idea and moved to single point distribution. Rob remembered negotiating service contracts with carriers to provide national distribution from a single distribution centre at Denver in the middle of the USA. He was surprised how quickly delivery could be made to most major markets even by surface carriers.

Proposed supply chain

The file relating to the proposed supply chain was sparse, including only a verbal description but no data. The task of the implementation team was to outline a course of action to follow. Any additional information would have to come out of their own background knowledge.

One of the documents in the file was an outline of the proposed supply chain. Most of the elements were in place and were a 'given' for the implementation team. How to make it work was something else. The objectives were to become more responsive to the changing market-place and to reduce cost. From a corporate finance perspective, Marcia Gulick saw the new plan as a way to reduce inventory cost; she would be evaluated by her home department on her success in achieving this goal. In contrast, Al Ferrenti remembered sales which had not succeeded because Valkyrie could not deliver on time, and others in which the customer order was suddenly changed and Valkyrie production could not promise an early delivery. These two viewpoints were obviously in collision and Rob wondered how he could create a solution which would satisfy both of them.

The supply chain plan defined the flow from suppliers through product assembly to distribution for both the US and the European markets. Sunshine Products was Valkyrie's most important supplier, with a key proprietary component which was vital to Sunshine's success. Sunshine was an American company using contract manufacturing in Taiwan. Other suppliers were less critical to Valkyrie's success and could be substituted although it might take a while to find replacements.

Product assembly for the US market was a two-stage process, with both stages taking place in the Denver plant. The first stage, technical assembly, produced the functioning core of the product. There were eight different basic assemblies to meet individual customer technical requirements. This assembly process was followed by a second which matched these assemblies to customer style preferences; this was the source of most of the variety in customer demands. Finished products were then placed in stock awaiting orders from customers. Retail customers were willing to accept a three day order cycle, but resisted orders which took longer than one week. In the background was a bargaining point which a few aggressive customers had raised, about selling Valkyrie's full product line but delivering products from their suppliers' stock and only holding floor samples to make the sale.

Contractors placed tentative orders when they prepared their construction bids. Lead times requirements varied from one to six months, but in had to be stretched as construction delays were encountered. Some contractors raised the possibility of just-in-time delivery – vendors of other product lines to these contractors had managed to develop just-in-time delivery systems. Ferrenti in Sales had been an advocate of this and he saw a chance here to bring it to fruition as a major selling tool.

Most shipments were to these large retail customers and contractors. Other orders from smaller customers were less specific in their requirements, and could be taken care of as their orders came in.

The European system was going to be essentially parallel to the US market. Production for this market could also be done initially in Denver, with the same eight technical variations but with 220 V power rather than the 110 V common in the US market. However the plan had eventually to include assembly within Europe.

Marketing in the Single European Market required a high degree of local content if Valkyrie was going to avoid high tariff duties. The plan proposed having a third party to perform final assembly in The Netherlands, drawing on local sources for outer cases. There was a question about how much value had to be added in Europe to avoid tariffs.

Unique, locally originated styling was essential to market success in the European market. Valkyrie had settled on an assembler, but there was uncertainty about how orders were to be co-ordinated. Valkyrie also established contact with several potential suppliers, showed them production drawings and began negotiation about scheduling and production. The assembler would ship finished products to major distributors in regional markets. Service requirements were not clear. Rob remembered conversations with sales people who described the need for short cycle times which were appearing in major markets.

Other markets would be handled outside the USA. Both Latin America and south-east Asia were small but expanding rapidly and could represent significant potential revenue in the future. No plan had been developed for Latin America as yet, but the present thought called for an assembly and distribution centre in Singapore for distribution to Malaysia, Singapore, Thailand, Taiwan, Korea, the Philippines and Indonesia.

Relations with Sunshine Products

Sunshine Products played a significant role in Valkyrie's success because of the former's unique technology. The relationship between the two companies was always informal, literally based on a handshake between the managers of the two firms. As a component supplier, business always took place on an individual transaction basis without the benefit of a formal contract. This worked smoothly in the past. While Sunshine served two other customers in non-competing fields, the relationship with Valkyrie had always been solid, even though all customers were treated equally in production planning.

Sandra Falkner, from her experience in procurement, was more than a little apprehensive about how long this relationship would continue. Sunshine had recently responded erratically because of the infrequent orders with a wide range of order sizes from Valkyrie. She had a sense that Sunshine was operating close to capacity and was reluctant to add more at this time under the same terms as in the past. The Sunshine component was an essential foundation for Valkyrie's designs and would be difficult to replace. The lack of a formal commitment would give new managers an escape if they wanted to deal with Valkyrie's competitors.

Sunshine production system

Sunshine used a sophisticated production planning system that had served them well in the past. Planning was done in the USA and then transmitted electronically to the Taiwan plant. Any change took two weeks to implement in production and then only under protest. Sunshine operated on a two month planning horizon which they felt was necessary to accommodate their own suppliers' lead time. Anything shorter would require accepting inventory and the accompanying risk. Production was run as a job shop, with frequent changeovers to meet specific demands. There were problems in scheduling Valkyrie's components when Sunshine ran out of capacity. The result was obvious in the erratic delivery performance that Sunshine had been providing in recent months.

Sunshine used its customers' forecasts as a basis for its own production planning, thus creating a push production system rather than responding to last-minute demands. To this was attached a two-month lead time for Sunshine to order material. Most of this material was low value, but Sunshine had only limited space to hold any inbound or work-in-process inventory.

Valkyrie's orders were for two different types of components which had little in common. Sunshine used batch scheduling, even building in a sequence of variety, similar to a pattern followed in some older Japanese production systems. It required anticipating which units would be in demand, without direct customer input other than the forecast supplied by Valkyrie and Sunshine's other customers.

Rob saw the impossibility of an accurate forecast, based on his own experience in the market. Large orders suddenly showed up without prior notice. While Valkyrie could create flexibility in its own assembly operations to match this new pattern, he was more concerned about Sunshine and its ability to supply an unpredictable market. Even without this market turbulence, Sunshine components had to be stockpiled in anticipation of orders because they were often on back-order, an unsatisfactory arrangement from both a financial and an operations standpoint. These were high-value items which added inventory holding costs at a time when competition was reducing Valkyrie's margins. Production complained that Sunshine components had to be stored in awkward locations because of the lack of floor space.

There was no way to avoid using Sunshine components. They were a vital part of Valkyrie designs, and to substitute any other supplier would be impossible without rethinking Valkyrie's entire product design programme. Rob recognized that Valkyrie needed Sunshine as a supplier more than Sunshine needed Valkyrie as a customer.

Rob thought that he could manage a combined production system if he could get Sunshine's co-operation. In production planning, John Sherwin was used to dealing with planning emergencies within the Valkyrie planning unit, and Ferrenti and others had begun to treat these emergencies as routine. There were four assembly lines: two were common, providing some flexibility but the other two were dedicated to specific models and could not easily be switched. Scheduling was managed on an MRP system. The system was blind to Sunshine's own production plans, and the level of management could only extend to finished component units already in stock. Some flexibility was possible with a two day production lead time using inventory on hand. Any further flexibility was costly because it was difficult to get Sunshine to respond to emergencies; the result was that Valkyrie had to buy additional stock from Sunshine.

Overseas production

Plans for Europe indicated a rapid expansion to make up for the mature market conditions in North America. Exporting was not satisfactory; freight and duty costs combined with importers' mark-ups consumed the profit margins.

One solution was to license the product to someone else and arrange for Sunshine to supply them. Licensing might be a low cost way to participate, but profits could be lower, and certainly there would be a loss of control which might result in poor market performance.

Another solution was to establish local production under Valkyrie's name, either as a direct investment or by contracting with a third party. Direct investment would require learning about the market unless they took over a firm already in the business, and would also require significant volume to get past break-even and overcome the fixed costs. Furthermore, there was a problem with potential suppliers who would have to be evaluated and recruited into a regional supply chain. Valkyrie would have to establish its own communication and control systems, a task made difficult by the lack of acceptance of EDI within Europe.

On the surface, contracting would have advantages. Almost all costs were variable. The contractor would have to be an experienced operator who could both assemble and distribute, or failing that, be able to work with a third-party logistics provider who could transport and distribute. Valkyrie would have to provide a sales force and marketing effort. The major uncertainty was how this operator would deal with suppliers. Presumably, Valkyrie would still have to seek them out, determine their qualifications and select them. The contractor would have to be able to take action to maintain and operate the system, but with how much freedom to move? How would supplier performance be evaluated? These were questions that the team would have to answer.

Order entry

Orders entered the system from sales representatives by direct transmission to Valkyrie via e-mail. These reps carried laptop computers and could tell customers what was directly available from stock. If it was not in stock, they would have to call the production planning centre to find out when an order could be scheduled and delivered. After the production schedule was confirmed, an EDI or fax order would be placed. This system encouraged the sales force to compete to get their orders in place first. It also encouraged a short-term outlook of individual transaction orders rather than a more sane planned order system.

As Ferrenti described the atmosphere in Sales, it was highly competitive, not only in timing, but also in encouraging special orders and promotions. The reps would promise anything to get an order and then lean on production to build it. Sherwin commented that it was difficult to turn down an order, and that there was a lot of pressure from Richard Jones as General Manager to 'look good' for the quarterly report.

Information system

Fuentes, in his role in information systems, had thought about making the production planning system visible to both sales reps and key customers. Orders could be received and scheduled clear through to the production floor. This would allow them to look ahead in their own ordering and negotiate for better planning for Valkyrie and better terms for customers.

Sherwin, the production manager, pointed out some problems with the procurement system. The system was blind about inbound material. He had little information on what Sunshine was planning to run and how to incorporate daily changes into their production planning system. They were always telling him about material shortages affecting their own production. Planners only knew what stock of Sunshine's components they had on hand, but had no precise information on production or shipments from Sunshine. It would extremely useful to know about Sunshine's production problems as they occurred. This information was even as valuable as Sunshine's advance weekly shipping schedule. Seeing Sunshine's production planning schedules as they were created would be extremely useful. However, there were technical problems to overcome, of identifying part numbers and even database compatibility. All of this was imposed on top of a computer-based management information system that had not been revised in four years.

Sunshine was not in direct electronic communication with Valkyrie on advance shipping notices and schedules. These were always hard-copy documents sent by courier from Taiwan, which took two days in transmission. When Fuentes had raised the issue about EDI, he had been told that Sunshine resisted it, not wishing to change their computer system at this time.

The problem with this communication system was that the goods from Sunshine arrived in Denver almost on the same plane. Normal transit times were three days, with goods precleared through US customs. If production were to be established in The Netherlands, the lead times would be longer, five days, but the problem of delays in hard-copy information would still be there. Valkyrie's carrier, Oryxair, was introducing automated shipment status reporting. Could this be used as a substitute for a Sunshine EDI link?

How would a European assembly operation adapt to these lead times, added to Sunshine's own production delays? Even in south-east Asia, there would be problems. There was a lack of capacity in intra-regional air cargo, so that shipments from Taiwan to an assembly plant in Singapore could often be left waiting for as long as two days for available lift capacity.

The issues

After a preliminary discussion, the team adjourned to consider the problem individually. Rob reconvened the group to discuss how they would approach the task. Sandra Falkner opened it up with a heated discussion about Sunshine. 'They never have enough capacity for our orders. We could order a single unit and they still wouldn't have enough. I don't see why we couldn't put a dedicated production line in their plant. From what I hear, they either have enough room or they could expand the building.' Marcia Gulick raised a question, 'What about the cost? Would they pay for it or do we?'

Rob interrupted, 'Hold on. Are we getting to solutions before we even see what the problems are? That suggestion of Sandra's might be good in context, but it is too early to deal with it. We have to see what the problems are before we arrive at a solution.'

Rob began to make a list of possible problems on the blackboard. The market was becoming if anything more complex: more SKUs of finished products, more need to respond to individual customer requests. Customers were even more reluctant to hold inventory, relying on suppliers like Valkyrie to provide them with faster delivery times.

There were problems in supply chain design, even though the system was supposed to be a given. The Denver facility was new. Should manufacturing and the distribution centre be located next to each other? Manufacturing would always be tempted to make products for stock and hold them at the distribution centre.

There were problems of relationships with both customers and suppliers and particularly with Sunshine Products. There were production and product issues that could affect the rest of the system, such as variety and standardization. There were communication and co-ordination problems.

Al Fuentes commented, 'This is interesting to me. You know that Sunshine's and our computer can't even talk to each other.' This could be partly solved on a technical level but also required co-operation with other parties.

The supply chain raised potential problems of global strategy, starting with Europe. Was it possible to manage supply, including both assembly and distribution, through third-party operators, particularly when they would have to deal with regional suppliers?

The first task would be to decide what was really important, then other problems might fall into line so that he could move towards effective implementation. This was a bigger task than anything he had dealt with in logistics before. It reached out across the company. This task seemed to be at the core of corporate strategy.

PART TWO

Purchasing and supplies management

Procurement and supply management

Peter Hines
Cardiff University Business School, UK

Introduction

In early 1995 John Ramsay, the Procurement Manager of Filton Aerostructures, faced a number of problems. First among these was that the aircraft industry, in which Filton Aerostructures operated, was undergoing major strategic change involving significant downsizing. In addition, the history of relationships with suppliers was not all rosy. The remedies appeared to lie within his own department and partly through closer integration with internal customers and suppliers. But how was this to be achieved in a period of significant change in the company involving John being asked to operate with far fewer staff?

Filton Aerostructures is part of the British Aerospace group of companies and is located in Bristol, UK. The site underwent several reorganizations during the 1990s. In 1993 Filton Aerostructures was created in order to supply parts to sister British Aerospace sites, primarily for the construction of wings for the Airbus programme. This is a co-operative venture between British Aerospace and firms from Germany, France and Spain to build complete aircraft, which are assembled in France. Filton Aerostructures is thus a second-tier supplier to the Airbus project.

The company employed 2300 staff and was split into five manufacturing units: fabrication, machining, bonding, assembly and manufacturing services. Each of these areas required a generally distinct set of parts and raw materials that had to be serviced by the Procurement function.

The industry

In 1990 sales volumes were high for British Aerospace and its competitors, with a booming market for air transport, and projections at this time showed a further rapid growth in sales. To some degree the constraints on the industry were more of a capacity nature rather than of the cost or quality of the products. At this time, being in the industry was easy, with a mentality of cost plus pricing and relatively low levels of competitive pressure.

However, this changed in the following few years. The first reason for this was the worldwide recession in the early 1990s which resulted in fewer flights and lower investment by airlines in new aircraft. This situation was exacerbated by the Gulf War which further cut demand for flights, particularly on the major trans-Atlantic routes. As a result, on aggregate, world airlines have been unprofitable from 1990 onwards, with a few exceptions such as British Airways. Although the severity of this airline recession eased in the 1990s, more airlines were in the red than the black by the middle of the decade. Unfortunately for British Aerospace, the fall-back position of government support was also being removed during this period, resulting in severe internal pressure for change.

The results of this were continued reorganization, disruption, redundancies and closure programmes for British Aerospace and its competitors. Thus, many smaller manufacturers merged or went out of business, and therefore only a few major makers could effectively compete in the final assembly of aircraft. A realization overtook the management of British Aerospace that in the medium-to-large aircraft sector they were unlikely ever to assemble another aircraft. As such their future was as a leading partner within the European Airbus consortium.

Together with this realization came the fact that the remaining assemblers, faced with the same problems as Airbus, were making plans for huge improvements in the design, time to market and cost of aircraft. The leading company in this move was Boeing, which announced that lead times for aircraft would be cut from 24 months to six months by 1998. In addition, they were targeting cost reductions in the order of 30% for their products.

These moves meant that British Aerospace and their Airbus partners would have at least to match these targets in order to continue to gain market share. Although the picture appeared rather bleak, in 1994 Airbus captured over 50% of the world market for large jets for the first time, suggesting that some progress was already being made.

The site

As a response to these pressures, Filton Aerostructures set themselves ambitious improvement targets. These included a 35% reduction in unit costs within two years, stock-turn ratios to be improved from around 4 to 12, production lead time to be reduced by 75% and overhead costs to be slashed by 66% within four years. They also made the following promise to their customers.

> Filton Aerostructures is committed to satisfying its customers through world class standards of quality and delivery. Working in partnership with our customers we aim to continually enhance the value of our products in the market place. We are confident that we can offer technical and manufacturing excellence at highly competitive rates that through the continuing development of our people, our resources and our relationships with our customers, we will ensure a sound base for manufacturing into the 21st century.

In order to achieve these targets the site sought to cut costs, reduce staffing levels through wastage and redundancy programmes and introduce continual improvement programmes. The staff reduction involved a slimming of over one-third in a two year period between 1993 and 1995. These reductions were reasonably evenly targeted between the different departments. Because of this turbulence there was a feeling from many staff that they were not sure who they worked for, what they were supposed to do and indeed whether they would have a job at all in a few months' time. As a result, morale was quite low.

The Procurement function

These pressures were also being felt in Procurement, where the 58 staff employed in 1993 had already been reduced to 45 by early 1995, when they were to be further reduced to 38 with no guarantee that further cuts would not occur. At the start of 1995 the structure within Procurement was fairly traditional, with the Procurement manager, John Ramsay, presiding over four managers controlling purchasing, expediting and scheduling, administration and statistics, and change implementation. Each of these four individuals had between four and 16 staff. In one case this meant that there were four tiers in the Procurement department alone. The situation is shown in Figure 7.1. In 1995 the company made the decision that this structure no longer supported the rest of the business adequately, as a number of problems were being faced by their internal customers.

These problems mainly centred around dissatisfaction with the service offered to internal customers together with difficulties in communication with purchasing. The internal customers, despite having a representative from Procurement within their sections, were facing an unacceptable degree of disruption to their supplies. Many staff within the company were blaming either Procurement, the suppliers or the continual

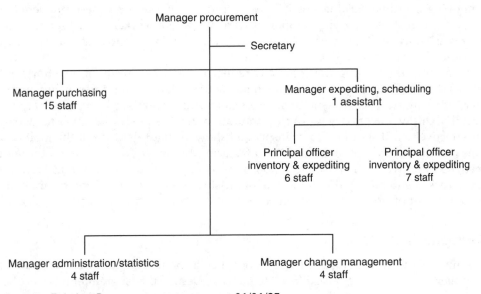

Figure 7.1 Existing Procurement structure at 01/01/95.

reorganizations within the company. Coupled to this were frequent problems encountered by manufacturing in getting hold of the right person in Procurement. The satellite Procurement members in each of the manufacturing units became the brunt of this dissatisifaction and were placed in very difficult situations as it was often not within their power to be able to address the problems directly.

This feeling of isolation was exacerbated by the remote location of Procurement, in some cases separated from their manufacturing customers by half a mile. As such, minor problems were often not passed back to Procurement until it was too late to avoid a serious situation. There were also frustrations within the department as many staff felt that they could cope with either the continual changing nature of their job or with doing their job, but not both.

It was therefore felt that a continual fire-fighting approach was being maintained by manufacturing and Procurement alike. Further changes were suggested to rectify this situation, but these in themselves would result in more change. A co-ordinated and well-planned change in structure and strategy was therefore required.

A case in point was the situation within the metal stores, which had traditionally had a poor reputation for the checking, quality inspection, storage and delivery of metal to the various internal customers. The stores were therefore viewed as a bottleneck, which in some cases caused problems for manufacturing and inevitably resulted in higher stock levels in the stores than were actually required. The backlog at times was as much as seven weeks in this materials management task, representing about 900 individual deliveries waiting for processing.

Working in this environment was inevitably demoralizing for the 30 or so staff involved. They were, in addition, each being asked to undertake more than 40 hours of overtime a month. Part of the approach being taken was to bring in temporary staff to help to reduce the backlog. As a result those staff who did not want to work overtime were not happy and those that did were critical of the temporary staff, seeing them as removing overtime earning possibilities. In order to get around these problems (and remove the cost of employing temporary staff) shop-floor workers were drafted into the stores as and when they were available. This was disruptive and these new staff were in general not trained to work in the stores.

Over time, the backlog was gradually reduced, partly as a result of the efforts of the stores staff and partly as a result of the removal of stock from the stores by Procurement agreeing with suppliers to send back excess stock which had already been delivered. The fact that this was necessary was a clear indication that the total system was not working as effectively as it should. Closer inspection showed that this was not the fault of any one part of Procurement or indeed Manufacturing, but was due to a lack of coordination between the two with consequent poor forecasting, so that raw materials were often overstocked and potentially almost half of the stock was redundant. This meant that the total number of stock turns in the metal stores was consistently under 4 per year.

Suppliers

Because of the wide range of the products being made by Filton Aerostructures the supplier base was diverse and difficult to manage. Despite this, some attempts were being made to co-ordinate the several thousand suppliers and encourage them to improve as they were responsible for over 50% (or £45m) of the value of products sold by the company. This was mainly being done by an on-site quality-based supplier audit system that was introduced about two years before the recent changes. However, this programme was having only a marginal effect on the suppliers, partly because of the large number of suppliers on the current usage list.

Another of the barriers to improving both suppliers and relationships was the past history of poor relationships. An example of this was the destocking system that Filton Aerostructures had previously undertaken, which involved the return of excess stock to suppliers for the latter to store (and depreciate) at their own cost until it was required. In many cases the returned stock was not even required at a later stage by Filton Aerostructures. Such an approach was hardly conducive to close long-term relationships.

Another factor that was difficult for suppliers to cope with was that possible improvements were often not made because of the way that Filton Aerostructures operated. This was typically because Filton Aerostructures made unilateral decisions which caused unintentional problems to the suppliers; for example, last-minute changes to schedules and changes to specification resulting in on-time delivery performances of only between 60% and 70%. These difficulties were often made worse by the fact that the suppliers had to deal with many or all of the subfunctions within Procurement, and staff in one area of Procurement frequently were not aware of what another section had been doing with any particular supplier. Thus suppliers were often dealing with buyers, expediters, schedulers and sometimes even staff from Manufacturing. This created a great deal of frustration on the suppliers' part because often they could not reach the person they wanted and when they did this person could rarely deal with all the issues that needed to be covered.

There was also a high degree of dissatisfaction among the suppliers because their expertise was not being fully utilized and their ideas were not taken seriously. In general, the expertise of the various suppliers was not held by or available to Filton Aerostructure's staff. As a result this expertise could only be used on an *ad hoc* basis and only when recognized by informal channels. Coupled to this was the fact that any suggestions put forward by suppliers were often treated in an off-hand manner, as many of the Filton Aerostructures staff regarded themselves as the experts and suppliers were viewed as being there to do what they were told. On the rare occasions when supplier suggestions were acted on, the supplier was given few or none of the benefits. Consequently, suppliers became rather cynical about the whole process and were reluctant to put forward their ideas.

There was a number of other sources of annoyance among the supplier community. Two, in particular, were common among many suppliers. The first was the frequent changes to the build schedule within Filton Aerostructures and the consequent last-minute changes to orders. The second was the system, or more accurately, lack of system for disputed invoices. As a result of what the suppliers saw as inefficiencies in Filton Aerostructures, they were often paid late or invoices were refused because delivered quantities differed from the order owing to Filton's late schedule changes. The result of this was that suppliers were kept at arms' length.

Future direction

In 1995 Filton Aerostructure's strategic direction was being developed by the senior managers in the company as well as the managers within Procurement. In this respect the mission statement for the company was set by Mike Crabtree, the General Manager:

> To be a mainstream supplier of aircraft components and assemblies that successfully competes in the world market by delivering a high level of customer satisfaction.

This was then deployed to supplier level:

> We have to recognize that the future well being of our companies requires us to share our management and technical skills in such a way that we both add value to each others operation. (Mike Crabtree, General Manager)

> By working in partnership with suppliers and customers, Procurement will guarantee products of highest quality at optimal cost. (John Ramsay, Procurement Manager)

However, although a good foundation was being laid at this senior level, there was no clear view of how a new structure within Procurement might look, what other measures might be necessary to achieve the mission statements and indeed how to go about implementing the change itself.

Acknowledgements

The development of this case would not have been possible without the assistance of John Ramsay and his staff at Filton Aerostructures. Thanks are particularly due in this respect to Jason Bullock and Terry Longstreth.

Flying high – relationship strategy development*

Paul Cousins

Centre for Research in Strategic Purchasing and Supply, University of Bath, UK

Introduction

Westland Helicopters Ltd (WHL) is a UK-based manufacturer of helicopters. In 1995, Martin Porter, the company's newly appointed Director of Materials decided that the company needed to change the way in which it dealt with key strategic suppliers – they were going to develop partnership relationships. In order to achieve this aim Porter enlisted external help in the form of a team of specialist management consultants. A new procurement strategy was to be developed which, in the first instance, would be applied exclusively to the new EH101 helicopter and then, if successful, extended further to other existing and planned helicopter product ranges. The consultant's task was split into two distinct, but related phases: phase one was to analyse the existing WHL purchasing function and determine how it might be improved; phase two, was to advise the company on how they should develop strategic collaborative strategies with their key suppliers.

The company situation in 1995

Westland Helicopters Ltd supplied complete helicopter systems and total customer support to world markets. A major proportion of its business was for export customers, typically foreign governments. Recently, Lynx naval helicopters had been delivered to Korea and major orders were won in Portugal, Quatar, Denmark and Germany.

The company designed, developed and manufactured military helicopters and associated weapons systems. Total systems integration formed a significant element of most of its defence contracts.

*Please note that some facts, dates and individuals' names have been changed in order to ensure personal and commercial confidentiality.

Customer satisfaction was a key element for the company and support operations were focused to respond to the increased emphasis that customers placed on reliability and rapid repair turn-around.

In 18 countries around the world, from Brazil to Australia, more than 1000 Westland helicopters were operational and had accumulated 5.5 million flying hours, a figure which was increasing by 200,000 hours every year.

WHL produced four main helicopter ranges, as follows.

- Sea King. The Sea King was originally (i.e. the early 1960s) produced under licence from Sikorsky Aircraft as the S61. Its main roles include transportation of troops and machinery and air/sea rescue. It was the dominant 'cash cow' within the group.
- Lynx. The Lynx helicopter was designed as a combat aircraft, being small and extremely manoeuvrable. The Lynx also held the record for the world's fastest helicopter. It was the 'Star' of the group.
- Black Hawk. The Black Hawk was built under licence from Sikorsky Aircraft, USA. It was similar in appearance to the Lynx, but was much larger and could therefore be used for troop-carrying work as well as an attack aircraft The main market-place for this aircraft was Saudi Arabia, where a prospective order for over 1000 aircraft was imminent.
- EH101. The EH101 was the latest aircraft to be added to the range of WHL helicopters. It was designed and developed under a joint venture agreement between Augusta of Italy and WHL. All research, development and production work were shared equally. The core competencies of both organizations had been utilized to design a large, manoeuvrable and extremely saleable aircraft. The EH101 looked like becoming a big success, with a large of number of firm orders already received, based on the pre-production aircraft.

Company history

WHL's company history is infamous. They were thrown into turmoil in 1985 when the company became bankrupt. After a good deal of publicity, governmental intervention and the resignation of two government ministers, the company was saved by forging an alliance with the American company Sikorsky Aircraft, part of the United Technologies Corporation. The impact of this crisis on the supply base was substantial. Suppliers were very cautious in dealing with WHL and some even went so far as requiring *pro forma* invoices.

The ensuing years have seen WHL grow from strength to strength with the development and successful launch of the Black Hawk and EH101 helicopters. The company's successful recovery was well documented (e.g. in the *Financial Times*, March 1994). The return to profitability made WHL a desirable commodity and they were taken over in 1995 by the large GKN defence group. This proved very useful for WHL as it extended both their financial base and their market opportunities.

Manufacturing strategy

All helicopters are manufactured and assembled at the WHL site in Yeovil, Somerset, UK At its height (1983) Westland employed close to 7000 people on this one site alone. In

1995 the figure was closer to 3000 employees. The reduction in numbers came from two major areas: (1) the adoption of new technologies and technological equipment and processes; and (2) the realization that the supply base could do a large amount of the previous in-house work. This second point meant that the role of the purchasing function within WHL increased substantially. WHL realized that part of its core competence was in the design and development of key technologies (e.g. composite materials), and not necessarily in assembly and manufacture. They therefore began to move to a process of tiering the supply base, whereby key suppliers would be responsible for producing entire subassemblies and delivering them to WHL for final assembly. This process required significant management time, as well as the development of intra-organizational relationships, as process technologies had to flow from WHL to its key suppliers.

The purchasing function

Up to the early 1990s the Purchasing department at Westland was viewed by management as a service function. Its task was to provide a procurement service to the rest of the organization – value added was seen as minimal.

Like most organizations, WHL had a very structured approach to their supplier qualification, selection and management. It would normally be the responsibility of design to produce the specification and in some cases nominate the supplier (sole source). It was then the responsibility of purchasing to negotiate price and delivery schedules based on the information received against the master production schedule, supplied by the production planning department. In fact, up until 1986, all purchase requisitions were written out manually by the buyers. Monitoring of the supplier once an order had been placed was also the responsibility of the purchasing function.

The other departments within the company that had some impact on or interest in purchasing decisions such as design, quality control, marketing, and finance were all separate functional groups, which tended to work independently and only pass on such information as was necessary to purchasing and other departments. Indeed, there was something of a 'power of information' approach within the company; as one group member put it 'we only tell them what they need to know, anything else would be just plain stupid!'

The buying department was split into the following four distinct areas, each with a separate purchasing manager, who reported to the head of purchasing:

- **Subcontract purchasing**. This area was responsible for the management of all subcontract work, i.e. various treatments and operations conducted out of house, e.g. crack detection, specialized machining work.
- **Raw materials.** This section purchased all of the raw materials for the factory and build operations, e.g. rubber, metals, chemicals.
- **Commercial.** They were responsible for the purchasing of all items associated with the running of the organization, e.g. pens, paper, office machinery and equipment.
- **Bought-out.** This was the largest section, with around 50 buyers. It was split into two distinct areas: low value/high volume and high value/low volume. Expenditure here accounted for approximately 80% of company's total spend. They were responsible for the purchase of all items for the build of all of the aircraft ranges, i.e. nuts, bolts,

rivets, engines, gear boxes, windscreens, etc. – a huge variety of parts, values and quantities. This function also had a subsection, 'expediting', which had its own managers. It was their responsibility to manage the delivery schedules, protracting or expediting deliveries based on changes in the customers' aircraft requirements. To summarize, buyers negotiated for the parts, and agreed a delivery schedule and price. Expediters adjusted deliveries if and when required, by liaison with the production scheduling department.

The majority of buyers were qualified to a very basic level, approximately four 'O' levels (a basic qualification), which in 1986 conformed to the industry norm (Cousins, 1992). The function was positioned in what Reck and Long (1988) term the 'passive' stage of development, Stage I (Table 8.1).

In the 1990s, the perception of purchasing began to change with the appointment of the first commercial director, who had responsibility both for purchasing and for contracts and marketing. The department began retraining its staff with the Chartered Institute of Purchasing and Supply's professional examinations, it introduced new information systems and began a recruitment campaign which specifically targeted graduate and post graduate personnel.

The purchasing department was attempting to form itself into a strategic or integrative function. This transition is succinctly captured by Ellram and Carr (1994) who point out that:

> ... it is critical to understand that there is a difference between *purchasing strategy* and purchasing performing as a *strategic function. When* purchasing is viewed as a strategic function, it is included as a key decision maker and participant in the firms strategic planning process. In addition, purchasing will participate in strategy formulation and suggest ways that the purchasing function can help support and enhance the firm's strategic success.

Table 8.1 Purchasing positioning matrix

Stage	Major characteristics
Stage I	In the *passive stage*, purchasing strategy normally begins as a reactor to requests from the other departments. Many of purchasing's legitimate activities are handled by other functions outside purchasing.
Stage II	In the *independent stage*, purchasing departments spend considerable time attempting to professionalize the purchasing function by introducing such things as computerized information systems, formalized supplier programmes, and communication links with the technical function.
Stage III	In the *supportive stage*, purchasing departments are viewed by top management as essential business functions. Purchasing is expected to support and strengthen the firm's competitive advantage by providing timely information to all departments in the firm about potential changes in the price and availability of materials, which may impact the firm's strategic goals
Stage IV	In the *integrative stage*, the firm's competitive success rests significantly on the capabilities of the purchasing department's personnel. Purchasing's role with the firm changes from facilitator to functional peer. This development process must be implemented and guided by management over a period of time.

In 1995, the commercial director was replaced by a new board level position, Director of Material. Martin Porter was appointed and given direct responsibility for the strategic supply management of the firm's resources. He knew that he had to make changes to the structure and approach of the purchasing function. The department was still functionally organized and predominately monitored on a tactical basis with traditional measures such as purchase order throughput, lead time from receipt of a purchase requisition to placing of purchase order (i.e. requisition age) and cost savings. The structure was not reactive enough for the highly competitive environment in which the firm now found itself. Supplier relationships fell mainly into the traditional or adversarial mode of purchasing. In his judgement the WHL purchasing function was somewhere between stages I and II of the purchasing positioning matrix. This had to be changed as the firm needed to access the technology and goodwill of its supplier base if it was to compete with the new EH101 range.

The problem

Porter had several issues to consider. He was under pressure from the board to show that his new position was justified and sustainable, i.e. he had to show results. The EH101 had to be a success for the company. In order for this to happen, lead times needed to be reduced and new innovations on products needed to be thought through and incorporated very quickly into the design specifications. The EH101 offered massive potential for both Westland and its suppliers – how was he going to capitalize on this? In addition, Westland's relationships with its suppliers were very traditional or adversarial. He needed to shift this way of doing business towards the partnership philosophy. Unfortunately, Westland's suppliers were all too used to the ways in which business has been done in the past, a perception that would have to be changed. Porter had been reviewing a model which he thought might help him to approach the current situation (Figure 8.1).

The model was based on the level of knowledge that the buyer and supplier have of each other, compared to the level of dependency or interdependency within the relationship. The greater the dependency and certainty within the relationship the more

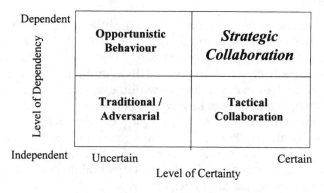

Figure 8.1 Relationship transition model (source: Cousins, 1996b).

likely the parties are to form true collaboration. Unfortunately the majority of the WHL relationships were positioned very clearly in the bottom left box. Porter had quickly decided that this must change and he identified a specific project, known as the colour display generator (CDG) as a pilot exercise in which to develop a new approach. CDG was a very high-value and high-profile project within the company.

Colour display generator project

The CDG project was budgeted at around £4 million. The CDG was a new piece of equipment that allowed the pilot of a helicopter to view instrumentation, e.g. air speed indicators and altimeters, on a computer-enhanced display unit. This had the benefit of one display to emulate a number of instruments (simultaneously if required). By 1995 the WHL design team had written one-third of the specification for the CDG and the intention was to work with the supplier to complete the remaining two-thirds. The design engineers were grappling with two major issues: the weight and the heat output of the unit. The problem was that the instrument panel became very hot because of the amount of electronics contained within the unit. If the heat was not dispersed efficiently the panel would eventually catch fire. Air conditioning packs were therefore necessary, but these were both bulky and heavy. Any increase in weight would reduce fuel efficiency and consequently the distance that the aircraft could travel. With these considerations in mind, it was clear that WHL needed to choose a supplier who was capable of working closely with them to develop the technology so that it would fall within the aircraft's safety parameters. It would also involve the two organizations sharing technological capabilities and possibly developing a new type of CDG that could have future commercial applications in other types of aircraft.

Porter decided that as the potential for this product was so great, it would provide a good opportunity to develop, prove and gain credibility for a new method of supplier selection and management. He said, '… we need to send a clear signal to suppliers that this is not business as usual, we need to convince our partners that we mean business.' He was also conscious that any new approach would be rigorously scrutinized internally in terms of performance, cost and outcomes.

Progress to date

At the time that Porter took up his appointment ten suppliers had quoted for the CDG contract: all were capable of making the equipment, but naturally they all had different skills and strengths: some were cheaper, others better at innovation, and so on. Porter was not sure of the best route by which to proceed. In addition there was a major time-scale problem. The aircraft had to in production within two years.

What should his strategy be? How was he going to choose the preferred supplier? How was he going to develop a partnership relationship with one of the ten possible suppliers? Some of the suppliers he already knew, others were tendering for the first time. How could he calculate payback? How could he ensure that any new purchasing process would work? What he needed was a methodology, a way of thinking about this problem, which had to be fast and show real commercial returns.

It has been suggested to him by an academic colleague that he consider a multi-attribute approach to supplier selection (Cousins, 1995, 1996a). This involved the use of up to ten attributes (Table 8.2), to help with defining the type of relationship required. Research had shown that these attributes were common to many purchasing decisions in many different industries.

Although the multi-attribute model seem to have merit, he felt that he really needed to develop a wider framework with which to approach the whole process of supplier selection and management. He therefore decided to engage a team of specialist purchasing consultants to help in the formulation of a broader policy. The brief given to the consultants was two-fold:

- phase one was to analyse the existing purchasing function at WHL and determine what resources were required; what skills and competencies were needed; what changes in procedures and working practices would have to be initiated?
- phase two was more complex and the most important. The consultants were asked to advise the company on the methodology that should be used to select the most suitable supplier for the current CDG project, and how they should develop a strategic collaborative relationship with their chosen CDG supplier and with their suppliers in general.

Table 8.2 Attribute definition

Attribute	Attribute name	Attribute description
1	Price	The overall cost of the part or project being purchased.
2	Delivery	The lead time for delivery and terms of delivery.
3	Quality	The level of quality expected from the supplier – usually referred to in terms of defect rates.
4	Innovation	How innovative is the supplier? Do they come up with new and original ideas on a regular basis?
5	Level of technology	How technologically competent is the supplier/buyer? Do they have systems that can sufficiently integrate? Are they are market leader, follower, etc.? Do they have a key technology that could be utilized by both parties, i.e. competence in composite technology?
6	Culture	What are they like? Can they be trusted? Is it possible to work closely with these people?
7	Commercial awareness	How good are they at contracting? Are the contractual arrangements going to be stringent or are they looking to move towards more simplified arrangements?
8	Production flexibility	What is the current and foreseeable capacity loading of the supplier/buyer? Will they be able to cope with increased order quantities or changes in delivery scheduling?
9	Ease of communication	Do they have sufficient integration of communication systems both inter- and intra-organizationally to allow for the free flow of information? Do they operate a 'gatekeeper' system for partnering?
10	Current reputation	What is their current reputation in the market- place? Are they financially stable?

References and further reading

Axelrod, R. (1984) *The Evolution of Co-operation,* Penguin Books, Harmondsworth.

Birts, A. and Cousins, P.D. (1994) Purchasing partnership, technology and treasury function. *Logistics Information Management,* **7**(2), 18–24.

Cousins, P.D. (1991) Choosing the right partner. *Purchasing and Supply Management,* November.

Cousins, P.D. (1992) Purchasing, the professional approach. *Purchasing and Supply Management,* September.

Cousins, P.D. (1995) Partnership sourcing a misused concept, in *Strategic Procurement Management in the 1990s: Concepts and Cases* (eds R. Lamming and A. Cox).

Cousins, P.D. (1996a) Supply base rationalization – myth or reality? *European Journal of Purchasing and Supply Management,* **5**(1), forthcoming.

Cousins, P.D. (1996b) *Collaborative Sourcing Strategies for Competitive Advantage,* Prentice-Hall, London

Ellram, L.M. and Carr, A. (1994) Strategic purchasing: a history and review of the literature. *International Journal of Purchasing and Materials Management,* Spring, 10–18.

Farmer, D. (1981b) Seeking strategic involvement, *Journal of Purchasing and Materials Management,* **17**(3), 20–4.

Hines, P. (1994) *Creating World Class Suppliers: Unlocking Mutual Competitive Advantage,* Pitman Publishing, London.

Lamming, R.C. (1993) *Beyond Partnership – Strategies for Innovation and Lean Supply.* Prentice-Hall, London.

Saaty, T. (1980) *The Analytical Hierarchy Process: Planning, Priority Setting, Resource Allocation,* McGraw-Hill, New York.

PART THREE

Manufacturing logistics

Restructuring the logistics system in response to changing customer requirements

Paolo Bianchi
Principal Consultant and Director, A.T. Kearney SpA, Milan, Italy

Background

At the beginning of 1991, Mr Paolo Cantarella, Chief Executive Officer of Fiat Auto SpA, was facing a problem. Fiat Auto was redesigning the whole product range of its three main brands, with an investment of about $25 billion. But, in the opinion of Mr Cantarella, to have an excellent product was not enough to be competitive in the European market; the service to the final customer had to be as good as the product.

At that time, Fiat was (and it still is) one of the six European volume car makers. It had production facilities in Italy, Poland, Brazil and (through a joint venture) Turkey, with a total output of more than 2 million cars, of which about 1.5 million were produced in Italy. Its sales were mainly in Italy (about 1 million cars) and western Europe (about 0.5 million cars), almost all produced in Europe. In 1991, Fiat was at the end of a very favourable cycle, at the peak of which it was a close second to the Volkswagen Audi Group in Europe, with a market share of 15.2%. It operated with three main brands: Fiat, Lancia, Alfa Romeo, covering the volume segments of the market. Its financial position was very good, with small debts and huge liquidity, but some difficulties began to surface:

- the product range was ageing: the most successful model, the Fiat Uno, was nine years old; the Fiat Tipo was not as successful as expected and the remaining models, even if still successful, were, on average, more than five years old
- the Italian market was under attack by the competitors, who were trying to compensate for the downturn in their domestic markets

- in the major European markets, Fiat had the image of a cheap car, with poor quality and poor service
- the integration of the European community was posing new challenges, ranging from increased competition due to the progressive elimination of borders and of different technical standards, to the allowance of increased imports from Far East countries.

To address this deteriorating picture, Fiat initiated a vast turnaround programme. Beside the design of 18 new models (covering some new market segments, such as mini vans and sport cars), it had launched 20 major projects, including:

- Reorganization of the design and engineering departments by platform instead of function (according to the platform concept, a multifunctional team is established, which concurrently develops a family of cars having in common the chassis and a given percentage of components. The advantage of using the platform concept is to avoid the reworking that traditionally takes place when a project is passed from one function, e.g. engineering, to the following, e.g. manufacturing)
- new relationships with the suppliers, aimed at developing a limited number of first-tier suppliers and at reducing the total number of direct suppliers
- new organisation of the plants, adopting the lean production concept (*fabbrica integrata*, in Fiat's definition)
- development of a large new plant at Melfi, in south Italy, capable of producing 700,000 cars/year)
- revision of the sales organization concept, to consider western Europe as the domestic market, to exploit the opportunities given by the development of the European Single Market
- a new logistic concept, to achieve a competitive service level in Europe.

Service targets

Fiat saw outstanding customer service as a key competitive weapon for the future as well as a necessity to support the old models during the transition to the new range. Mr Cantarella believed that a competitive service level had to be reached by the end of 1993, when the first and most important model of the new range, the Fiat Punto, was due for the launch. He declared that the company should attain:

- delivery time for cars sold from inventory: one week
- delivery time for cars made to customer order: six weeks for 90% of cars, eight weeks for 100 % of cars
- reliability of the promised delivery date: 95% within the promised week, 100% one week later
- conformance to final customer requirements: 100 per cent

This would mean a real breakthrough from the 1991 situation, when the cars were delivered in Europe from inventory in two to four weeks and made to dealer order in 10–15 weeks, with no commitment on the promised delivery date. Moreover, the conformance to the initial customer requirements was at about 40%.

The project team

To design and implement a logistics process able to meet the targets, a task force was formed with fully dedicated middle managers from logistics, systems, manufacturing, purchasing, organization, domestic and export sales. Additionally A.T. Kearney, an international management consulting firm, was hired to provide the team with international experience and insights on competitors' best practices. The Fiat team included:

- Mr Giovanni Le Mele, team leader: after a short period in sales, his career developed in production, including plant direction and production planning. He was very skilled in navigating the political waters of a large company
- Mr Matteo Di Mase, who had long experience in sales, ending up as an area manager in Italy, and who knew everything about Italian dealers
- Mr Jorg Muller, a young manager with experience in logistics and sales at a Fiat competitor in Germany
- Mr Antonio Di Giovanni, who was very much a 'no- nonsense' manager from the production department of Alfa Romeo
- Mr Lorenzo Marsili, from the purchasing department.

In briefing the team, Mr Cantarella made clear that he was not concerned about the cost of the solution, because he expected that possible cost increases would be more than offset by the positive impact on sales. Nevertheless, a solution combining competitive service and reduced cost would be greatly appreciated.

The team's findings

The team set out to examine Fiat's current European sales structure, the information systems that underpin the sales and distribution operations and the logistics system. It also initiated a study to benchmark the practices of major European and Japanese competitors.

Sales structure

At the beginning of the project, Mr Di Mase and Mr Muller shared with the rest of the team their knowledge about the sales structure of Fiat in Italy and in the major European markets (Germany, France, Spain and UK). Each brand (Fiat, Alfa Romeo and Lancia) had a sales manager in each market, reporting hierarchically to the general manager of the Fiat subsidiary in the market and functionally to the central sales department in Turin (Italy). The role of the sales manager was to agree the sales objectives with the headquarters (in terms of volume, inventory, profitability and turnover) and to translate them into objectives for the area managers. To reach the objective there were a number of levers, e.g. a mix of incentives to the dealers, special series, i.e. minor modifications to the product, sometimes made at the market inventory holding compounds, and support through advertising and promotions.

To the sales managers reported the area managers, the number of whom was related to the size of the market, varying from 12 for Fiat in Italy, to zero in a small market. Their role was to co-ordinate the zone managers, i.e. translate the objectives of the area into objectives for each zone, and monitor the activity of the zone managers. The zone manager was the interface with the dealer with regard to the sales of new cars (other interfaces existed for the sales of spare parts and for technical assistance).

Each market had an inventory holding compound, to which the cars were sent from the plants. At a given moment, in a typical compound there were both cars in transit, i.e. bought by a dealer and waiting for delivery to the dealer, and cars owned by the market, i.e. produced by Fiat but not yet bought by the dealer.

In a compound a number of activities could take place including:

- receiving of cars from plants
- storage of cars
- shipment of cars to dealers
- preparation of special series
- repair of transportation damages
- periodic maintenance of the stored cars.

In Europe, the three brands were represented by about 3000 dealers, of which about 1000 were in Italy. On average, a zone manager was in charge of ten to 20 dealers, and an area manager in charge of ten to 15 zone managers. The sales volume by dealer varied greatly, from an average of 600 cars/year in Italy to 50 cars/year for many dealers in Germany.

The sales organization is shown in Figure 9.1, and the distribution channels are shown in Figure 9.2.

Information technology structure

In each dealership a personal computer existed, or was planned, to link the dealer with the Fiat information system. The exchange of data was via transfer file. An on-line

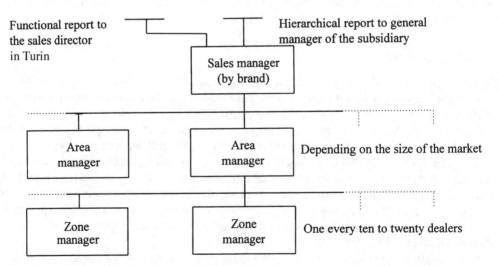

Figure 9.1 Sales organization of a major market.

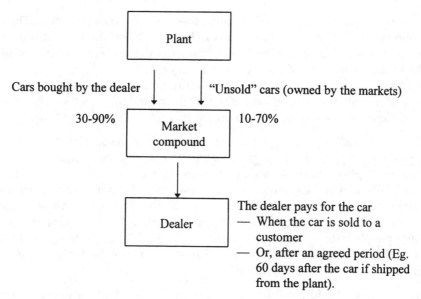

Figure 9.2 Distribution channels.

exchange of data was too expensive to be widely used, but was technically possible. The connection of the personal computer with the information system of the dealer was not standardized and in some dealerships did not exist at all.

Logistics process

The team examined the current logistics process at Fiat and compared it with the processes of the main competitors.

The first step in the process was the Decision Plan. It was described by a manager in the sales department as follows:

> It is the tool we use to manage volumes by market. At the beginning of each month we ask the sales managers of each market for a monthly forecast with a six months' time horizon of deliveries to dealers and to final customers. We use these forecasts as a base to agree with the markets how many cars they will receive during the third to the sixth months and consequently, how many cars the dealers should sell to the customers in order to have, at the end of each month, the 'physiological' inventory of five to six weeks of sales. Of course, we check the feasibility of the decision plan with the production department.

There was a general consensus in Europe that each dealer should have a certain amount of inventory at its premise to satisfy customer demand for prompt delivery and to 'push' the dealer to sell as many cars as possible. What the right level should be varied by OEM and by country, but Fiat believed that five to six weeks of sales was the right one (*livello fisiologico* in Italian). Thus the sales department of Fiat, knowing the actual inventory level and based on the monthly sales forecast, was able to calculate the number of cars (by model/version) that the dealer should buy in each month, to satisfy the demand of its customer and to have, at the end of the month, five to six weeks of inventory. The market, in turn, should receive the sum of the cars to be brought by the relevant dealers. The need for an agreement between the central sales and the markets was due to different forecast and different views of the trends in the market.

This meant, in practice, that Fiat had to try to convince the markets to accept a number of cars consistent with the production capacity of the period (i.e. to sell what is produced). The next step, the Sales Plan, was illustrated to the team by Mr Di Mase:

> Based on the decision plan, a proposal is made to each dealer. The decision plan is detailed by model. To make a proposal to the dealer, we must define every configuration option. To do so, we apply to the decision plan the "weight matrix". It is a matrix in which the relative weight of each body/colour option is statistically stated by model/market based on sales history. The area managers are supposed to update the weight matrix, but this is a typical administrative and cumbersome task that sales people hate. Anyway, as a result, each month a list is produced for each dealer, detailing how many cars and of which specifications the dealer should order to Fiat for delivery in the third month.

The zone managers had the duty of convincing the dealers to 'subscribe to the list'. Mr Muller added that outside Italy the dealers had more bargaining power and often did not subscribe to the list. This difference in bargaining power was due to:

- different regulations: in certain countries some contractual conditions, e.g. regarding the conditions under which a dealership could be revoked by the car producer, were more favourable to the dealer
- the presence of powerful dealer associations, which could support the dealer against the car producer
- the lower market share of Fiat outside Italy (4–7%, as opposite to about 50% in Italy), which made the Fiat dealership less attractive.

The cars that were not subscribed accumulated in the market inventory holding compounds and were sold later using heavy promotions.

The dealer would receive the cars in the second month after the order. A dealer commented: 'When a customer enters my dealership, I always try to sell him a car I have in stock; even if I have to give him some form of discount to compensate for non-conformance, the customer is not usually willing to wait until a made-to-order car is delivered; he prefers to ask another dealer, Fiat or competitor.' Another dealer added: 'I do not know two months in advance which cars I will sell, but often I feel that the sales proposal from Fiat does not fit my needs. It is almost impossible to change it, because of production constraints. But what really upsets me is that some of the proposed cars are in Fiat's inventory, and they are delivered well in advance of schedule, even if I do not need them. Moreover, when I sign the proposal I do not know which these cars are.'

At this point, two walls of the meeting room were covered with flow charts of the process, but the team went bravely on. The signed proposals, the team was told by Mr Vialli, operating logistics manager, were put together and checked against the decision plan. If needed, more unsold cars were added to fulfil the decision plan objectives, and the result checked again with the production department against the production constraints. Finally, in a formal meeting with the participation of senior executives from sales, production and logistics, the production plan was confirmed and the dealers orders were accepted.

Mr Muller, the voice of the foreign markets, pointed out that the unsold cars were mainly sent to the non-Italian markets, since the foreign dealers were not totally subscribing the proposals. The unsold cars went to the market compounds and were owned by the relevant marketing subsidiary (owned by the market, in Fiat terminology).

The confirmed plan was used by the production department to plan the production. The main steps, Mr Vialli said, were:

- monthly check and confirmation of the production volumes for the next three months
- allocate the orders by plant for each week in the next eight weeks and freeze the second week. Changes were allowed in the following weeks, if consistent with the production constraints. In practice, changes involving minor and non-critical options were allowed two weeks ahead of production, and changes involving major and/or critical options (e.g. engines, sunroofs, colour) four weeks ahead of production
- deliver the production orders to the plants
- confirm to the suppliers of components the required weekly delivery for each week of the 'current month plus two' (i.e. month $N + 2$).

The production department believed that its planning and scheduling system was state of the art. It was recently redesigned to this purpose, based on the MRP II concept. A dealer commented: 'I do not understand why, if they have the best production planning process in the industry, I cannot know when a car will be delivered to me until the car leaves the plant'.

At the end of the analysis, the team schematically summarized the process as shown in Annex 9.1.

Benchmarking

In the meantime, the consultants had concluded the benchmarking of the logistics process of the main competitors. The results were presented in a number of meetings, first to the team, and then to the senior management of Fiat (Annex 9.2 contains extracts from the presentation). 'Three main models of logistics process exist', said Mr Neri, A.T. Kearney project leader, each of them has pros and cons:

1. The traditional European model
The first is the traditional model, applied also by Fiat. Your competitors use better information support, or, as Renault does, allow more time to the dealers to specify the cars they want, but from a customer point of view, the cars are still sold from inventory. In its more advanced form, the model works as follows.

- In the first week of the current month (month N), the car producer (known also as the original equipment manufacturer) produces a proposal for each dealer. The proposal is the share of the production capacity of the third month ($N + 2$), that the dealer should buy based on its past performances and its sale potential. The proposal is detailed by 'family'. A family can be a group of models derived by the same platform, or a model, or a version of a model for which severe production constraints exist.

- In the following three weeks the proposals are discussed, modified and agreed with each dealer. This involves a clearing process among areas and markets to compensate for the differences between the initial proposal and the willingness or capability of the dealer to subscribe more or fewer cars than initially proposed.
- Four weeks ahead of production the dealer must specify the number and options of the cars it wants to be delivered in that week, i.e. define for each family the number of cars of a given colour, body type, engine, internal trimming and so on. The specifications are accepted or rejected depending on production constraints. In the case of rejection, the dealer can change the specifications.

This model allows for a minimum order-to-shipment lead time of four weeks, but only within monthly volume availability and production constraints. Otherwise, the order is rejected and the dealer must try to include it in the next monthly cycle. Of course, in this case, the lead time becomes unpredictable. Since the cars are sold from inventory, this model can fit the needs of a customer who wants the car immediately and does not care very much about the conformance to his initial requirements. This model is working pretty well in North America, but appears outdated in Europe.

2. The German model

The second is the model applied by the German 'quality' car makers. It requires a brand/product which is very strong and in high demand, and/or a customer who is very demanding in terms of required specifications. The model works as follows.

- The dealer is committed only on the yearly sales volume.
- The car producer reserves a given weekly volume by family to each dealer, based on the past performances and the sales potential of the dealer. The volume reserved to each dealer can be changed by the car maker with two months' notice.
- Every week the dealer orders the cars he needs, and its orders are always accepted. However, the order-to-delivery lead time is not fixed as in the traditional model. It depends on the number of weeks of production that the former dealer orders have already saturated. There is a minimum, depending on the internal lead times of the car producer and of its suppliers (usually four to five weeks). The maximum lead time can be of several months.
- The car maker accepts every order, but does not make any commitment on the delivery date until four weeks ahead of production.
- The specifications of an ordered car can be changed according to the production constraint. but they are usually frozen two weeks ahead of production.

This model assures the conformance of the car to the initial requirements of the customer at the expense of the lead time. It applies very well to the upper segments of the market, but does not fit the image of Fiat outside Italy or the needs of the average south European customer, since the lead time to get the car is usually too long.

3. *The Japanese model*

The model applied by the major Japanese car makers in Japan seems to combine the production requirements for stable plans and the satisfaction of customer requirements. It works as follows,

- At the end of the current month, the car maker defines a 'frame' plan for the next three months, detailed by model/major options. The volumes are based on forecasts jointly made with the dealers for the Japanese market (dealerships in Japan are very big and their senior management comprises former managers of the car producer), and on the forecasts made by the foreign subsidiaries (NSC, national sales companies) for the export markets. The car producer can decide to add to these forecast some so-called 'political orders', i.e. cars needed to saturate the production capacity that will later be pushed through the sales channels.
- The frame plan is checked for capacity and for production and suppliers constraints. If modifications are needed, they are discussed and agreed with the Japanese dealers and, to a lesser extent, with the NSCs. The output is a three months' production plan, detailed by day/model/engine/colour/major options. Within the plan, the first ten days are frozen, i.e. no change is allowed.
- Every tenth day the plan is revised based on the orders received. However, only minor modifications are allowed (typically, the specifications of five to ten per cent of the volumes can be changed at each revision).
- There is also a monthly revision, but it is normally a 'ceremonial meeting', even if a member of the board attends. The Japanese prefer to adjust the plan through the tenth-day revisions.

You can see that in this process the customer is totally absent. However, the customers perception is of getting a car made to order. The process works as follows.

- There are two types of orders: customer orders (coming from the Japanese market) and other orders (coming from NSCs and from Japanese dealers to replenish their stock).
- If a customer order is entered in the information system of the car maker by the dealer, the system looks for a planned vehicle of the same specification, starting from the first day of production in which there are vehicles not yet customer or dealer tagged. The system scans the production plan until it finds a suitable 'free' vehicle. This vehicle is then reserved to the customer. The process take place every second hour. This means that the dealer knows the delivery day within two hours from the input of the order. Of course, a customer order can be entered at any time.
- The other orders are entered at the beginning of each ten-day period. The system assigns them to suitable production lots considering the predetermined capacity and the customer order forecast. This means that in every production day, a part of the capacity is reserved for customer orders. Dealers and NSCs then receive order confirmation.

This model works very well in the present situation of Japan, but it seems to need the unique conditions of the Japanese market and is not likely to be applicable in Europe without major modifications [Table 9.1].

Table 9.1 Features of the Japanese model

Prerequisites	Actual performances
• Exceptional forecasting capability • Dumping ground for results of forecast errors, e.g. exports • Integrated information systems among dealers, OEM sales department and OEM plants • 'Simple' product range; many models and limited or packaged options	• Immediate confirmation of delivery date (day) for cars from inventory • Conformation within two hours (day) for cars not in inventory • Delivery time: from two weeks to two months • Reliability of the promised delivery date: more than 95% • Inventory level: from three to four weeks
Pros	**Cons**
• Stable production plan; (modifications only within agreed limits) • Very limited inventory of finished cars if the forecast is reliable • Very limited work-in-progress (fits with just-in-time philosophy)	• Slow to adapt to decrease in sales • Reliable forecasts require close relationship between dealers and OEM and deep knowledge of clients by the dealers • Requires accurate planning of product range (packaged options*)

*Packaged options: offering of a predefined combination of options instead of a list of single options that a customer can combine at will. Can satisfy, if well conceived, more than 90% of the initial customer requirements and makes forecasting much simpler.

The key characteristics of the three models are summarized in Annex 9.2. Mr Neri of A.T. Kearney, concluded his benchmarking review by saying: 'I believe that both the German, and the Japanese models have interesting aspects, but Fiat must develop its own model, leveraging on the flexibility of its production and avoiding major redesign of its information systems, since it is incompatible with our time frame.'

Requirements of the new systems for Fiat

After the presentation the team began to discuss the constraints that the organization posed to the development of the new process. They agreed that the new logistics model:

- should be transparent to the production department, since it was politically un-thinkable to ask them to revise a just redesigned process
- should not require major investments in information technology, since the IT systems department was saturated with other high-priority projects
- should be 'bought-in' by the Fiat senior and middle management and by the dealers, since it would have required significant behavioural changes and the dealers are independent entrepreneurs
- should deliver at least the same performances of the best competitor, even if that could mean to going beyond the objectives stated by Mr Cantarella.

The team leader, Giovanni Le Mele, eventually decided to conclude the meeting. He emphasized that within the next nine months the team had not only to develop a new logistics model, but to test it on the Lancia brand in Italy, with a view to full operation throughout Europe by the end of 1993.

Acknowledgements

The author would like to acknowledege the assistance of the Fiat project team and of his colleagues at A.T. Kearney Milano, in particular Marco Bonomi, Francesco Moroni and Piero Rosina.

[*The Appendix follows overleaf*]

Appendix A.9: Glossary of technical terms used

Area   A subdivision of a major market.

Conformance   The ability of a car to satisfy the initial requirements of the customer, i.e. the choice of options that the customer has in its mind on entering the dealership.

Decision plan   A six-month plan, updated monthly, used at Fiat to set sales objectives by market.

Direct supplier   A supplier which sells and delivers directly to the car producer.

First-tier supplier   A direct supplier to a car producer, which usually supplies modules. The first-tier supplier assembles the modules starting from components that are brought directly or delivered by second-tier suppliers under agreement with the car producer.

Frame plan   A three-month plan updated every tenth day, used by Japanese car producers to plan production. It is based on sales forecast made jointly by the car producer with the domestic dealers and the NSCs.

Inventory holding compound   A facility in which unsold cars are stored. Different kinds of compound exist: (i) market compound, in which the cars are owned either by the relevant market or by the dealers of the same market. (ii) Pan-European compound, that serves several markets, up to the whole of western Europe. (iii) Plant compound, holding the cars waiting for delivery to markets, Pan-European compounds, or dealers for storage.

Market   Usually a country (e.g. Germany) or a group of countries (e.g. Scandinavia), in which a NSC operates.

Module   A pre-assembled part of a car which is assembled to the car in the main assembly line, e.g. seats, front-ends, cockpits. Can be supplied already assembled by a first-tier supplier or be assembled on a sideline.

NSC (National Sales Company)   A subsidiary of a car producer responsible for sales and technical assistance in a market.

OEM (Original Equipment Manufacturer)   The car produced, e.g. Fiat, Renault or Nissan.

Option group   A component or a group of components that can be added to the base model at the will of the customer.

Packaged options   The offering of a pre-defined combination of options instead of a list of single options that the customer can combine at will. Used to simplify production and forecasts.

Platform   The structural part of the body of a car (chassis, pillars, roof). Different models or versions (e.g. sedan, estate, hatchback) can be derived from the same platform.

Political order   A production order not corresponding to a dealer or market order. It is used by the Japanese car producers to saturate the capacity of the plant or to smooth seasonal variations.

Proposal   A list of cars that the car producer tries to get signed off every month by the dealer. Ideally, if all the dealers agree on the proposals, the car producer is sure to sell all the cars it can produce.

Respecification   A change in the specifications of an ordered car. The respecification can affect major (engine, ABS) or minor (mirrors, parts of internal trimming) options. Usually the car producer puts some constraints on the freedom for respecification by the dealer.

Sales plan   A planning tool used at Fiat to produce the proposal to dealers.

Special series   A lever to push a model in low demand. Some special colours, or trimming, or attractive options are packaged in a model which is sold at an attractive price and supported by an advertising campaign. Excessive use or this lever can saturate the market and cause lower sales level after the campaign has ended.

Volume car producer   A producer of cars which specializes in high volume models, as opposed to a specialty car producer. In Europe the six volume car producers are Volkswagen, PSA, General Motors, Ford, Fiat and Renault.

Zone   A Group of ten to 20 dealers of the same area, covered by a zone manager.

Annex 9.1: The monthly logistic process at Fiat

Monthly sales objectives by market/family from decision plan

Months

Weeks

N				N + 1				N + 2			
W1	2	3	4	5	6	7	8	9	10	11	12

Customer orders of the previous month

Decision plan finalised

Subscription proposal made by Fiat

Subscription proposals finalised

Zone managers agree proposals with dealers (monthly process)

Subscription proposals completed by markets with orders for unsold cars

Sales plan finalised :
- orders consolidated at Fiat level
- production constraints checked

- Orders transmitted to production
- allocation of orders by week/plant
- production scheduled for weeks 9-12
- suppliers informed

Start of assembly

First possible shipment to dealer

Customer order cycle 10-15 weeks

Annex 9.2: The logistic processes of the main competitors

Annex 9.2.1: The traditional European model (a monthly planning process)

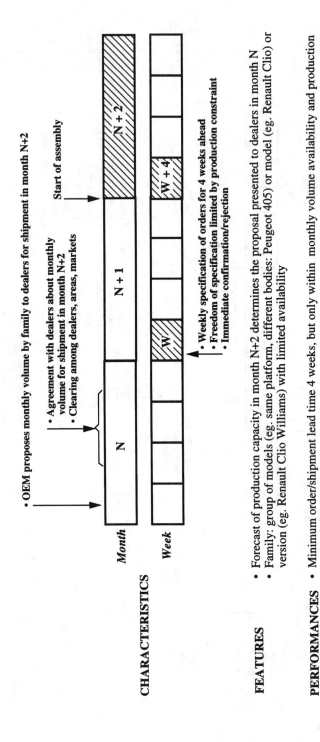

CHARACTERISTICS

- OEM proposes monthly volume by family to dealers for shipment in month N+2
  - Agreement with dealers about monthly volume for shipment in month N+2
  - Clearing among dealers, areas, markets

- Weekly specification of orders for 4 weeks ahead
- Freedom of specification limited by production constraint
- Immediate confirmation/rejection

Start of assembly

Month: N | N + 1 | N + 2

Week: W | W + 4

FEATURES
- Forecast of production capacity in month N+2 determines the proposal presented to dealers in month N
- Family: group of models (eg. same platform, different bodies: Peugeot 405) or model (eg. Renault Clio) or version (eg. Renault Clio Williams) with limited availability

PERFORMANCES
- Minimum order/shipment lead time 4 weeks, but only within monthly volume availability and production constraints
- Otherwise, order not accepted and shipment date unpredictable

Annex 9.2.2: The German model

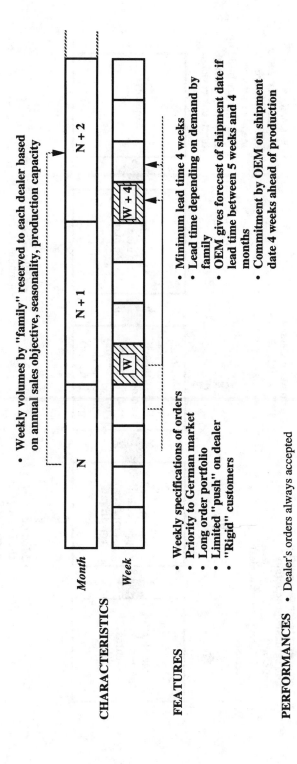

- Weekly volumes by "family" reserved to each dealer based on annual sales objective, seasonality, production capacity

CHARACTERISTICS

- Minimum lead time 4 weeks
- Lead time depending on demand by family
- OEM gives forecast of shipment date if lead time between 5 weeks and 4 months
- Commitment by OEM on shipment date 4 weeks ahead of production

FEATURES

- Weekly specifications of orders
- Priority to German market
- Long order portfolio
- Limited "push" on dealer
- "Rigid" customers

PERFORMANCES

- Dealer's orders always accepted
- Lead time: variable and usually long

Annex 9.2.3: Japanese advanced forecast model

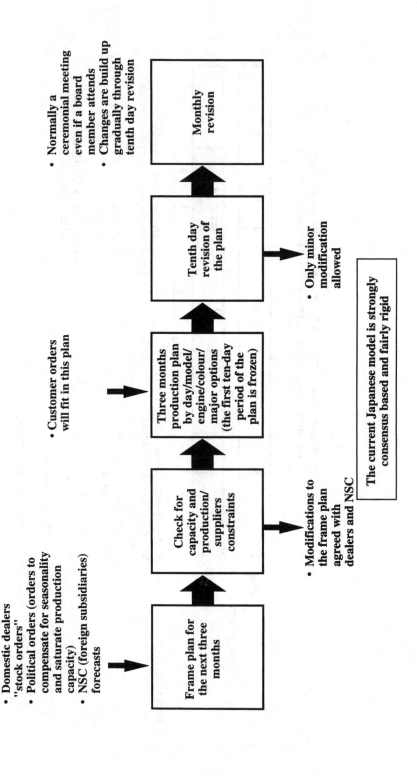

Annex 9.2.4: Japanese model (continued)

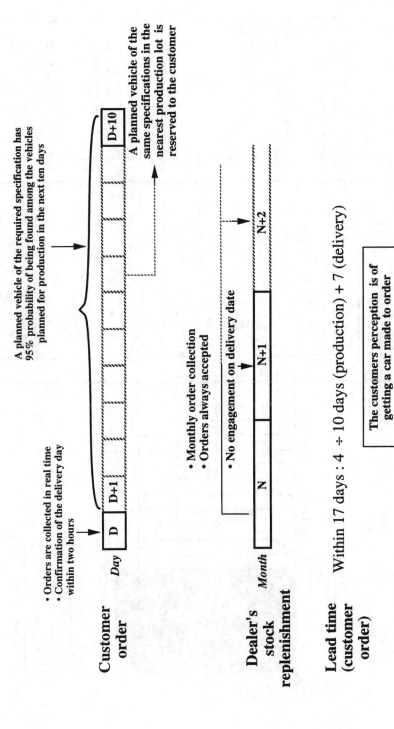

Customer order

Day

| D | D+1 | | | | | | | | | D+10 |

- Orders are collected in real time
- Confirmation of the delivery day within two hours

A planned vehicle of the required specification has 95% probability of being found among the vehicles planned for production in the next ten days

A planned vehicle of the same specifications in the nearest production lot is reserved to the customer

Dealer's stock replenishment

Month

| N | N+1 | N+2 |

- Monthly order collection
- Orders always accepted
- No engagement on delivery date

Lead time (customer order)

Within 17 days : 4 ÷ 10 days (production) + 7 (delivery)

The customers perception is of getting a car made to order

Annex 9.2.5: Japanese model basic planning rules

Hypothetical example:
on the day 1, the new customer order Ⓐ and orders other than customer orders (monthly order) are entered to the system

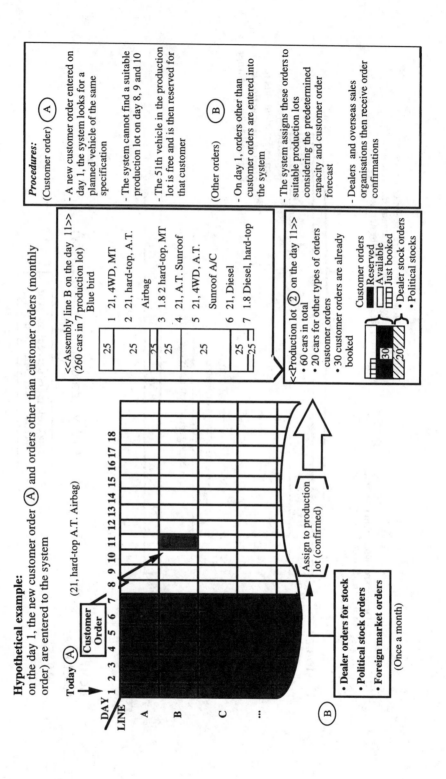

Today Ⓐ

Customer Order — (21, hard-top A.T. Airbag)

DAY 1 2 3 4 5 6 7 8 9 10 11 12 13 14 15 16 17 18

LINE
A
B
C
...

Assign to production lot (confirmed)

Ⓑ
- Dealer orders for stock
- Political stock orders
- Foreign market orders

(Once a month)

<<Assembly line B on the day 11>>
(260 cars in 7 production lot)
Blue bird

25	1	21, 4WD, MT
25	2	21, hard-top, A.T. Airbag
25	3	1.8 2 hard-top, MT
25	4	21, A.T. Sunroof
25	5	21, 4WD, A.T. Sunroof A/C
25	6	21, Diesel
25	7	1.8 Diesel, hard-top

<<Production lot ② on the day 11>>
- 60 cars in total
- 20 cars for other types of orders customer orders
- 30 customer orders are already booked

Customer orders
■ Reserved
□ Available
▨ Just booked
- Dealer stock orders
- Political stocks

30
20

Procedures:

(Customer order) Ⓐ
- A new customer order entered on day 1, the system looks for a planned vehicle of the same specification
- The system cannot find a suitable production lot on day 8, 9 and 10
- The 51th vehicle in the production lot is free and is then reserved for that customer

(Other orders) Ⓑ
- On day 1, orders other than customer orders are entered into the system
- The system assigns these orders to suitable production lots considering the predetermined capacity and customer order forecast
- Dealers and overseas sales organisations then receive order confirmations

Annex 9.2.6: Summary of the key features of the three basic models

"Traditional European"	"Japanese"	"German"
• Central forecast	• Shared forecast by OEM and dealer	• Forecast of annual volume by model
• Cars pushed to dealers	• Adjustments made before pushing cars to dealers	• Cars pulled by dealers
• Hardly any cars made to order	• Cars made to order from customer viewpoint	• Cars made to customer order

	"Traditional European"	"Japanese"	"German"
Lead time	10 - 14 weeks	2.5 - 8 weeks	No less than 4 weeks, often 4-6 months
Reliability of promise	$\simeq 0\%$	95%	$\simeq 100\%$

Strategic logistics management

Tony Whiteing and Paul Corns
Department of Transport and Logistics, University of Huddersfield, UK

Introduction

In the ten years up to summer 1995, Kalon Paints had achieved impressive growth to become one of the major forces and one of the best financial performers in the UK paints industry. Financial analysts attributed this success at least in part to efficient logistics systems which had produced benefits in terms of both costs and customer service. Kalon's other key achievement had been to position itself very well in two key paint market sectors – the professional decorators' market and the production of own-label paints for leading retailers. Depressed trading conditions and strong competition in the mid 1990s reduced the profitability of the company, however. The need in late 1995 was therefore to identify corporate strategies and logistics strategies that would allow the company's rapid growth to resume and continue at low total logistics cost.

Company background

Study of the UK paints industry reveals a number of trends in production, marketing, retailing and distribution which have also affected many other industrial sectors. The industry has experienced a series of take-overs and mergers since the 1960s, exemplified by the emergence of the Berger Paints organization in the late 1960s and early 1970s (Constable and New, 1976). Such take-overs and mergers have turned the major competitors into European rather than national players. Subsequent production rationalizations have led to factory closures and concentration at larger sites where economies of scale can be exploited. Paint retailing has also been transformed, with the decline of the traditional specialist and hardware stores and the growth of the out-of-town, do-it-yourself (DIY) superstore chains. The well-known brands of the market leaders have found themselves facing new competition from the own-label products sold by these modern multiple retailers. Manufacturers of the main brands have had to decide whether to make retailers' own-label products or not.

Against this background Kalon is an undoubted success story. From its roots in West Yorkshire it developed into a major international player from the mid-1980s, achieving substantial growth both by organic means and through acquisition. By 1994 Kalon was achieving group annual profits of nearly £20 million on sales of over £150 million. When compared to others in chemicals manufacturing, Kalon experienced above-average growth in profits and dividends through the late 1980s into the 1990s (Smith New,Court 1993), although its performance dipped in 1994 against the background of the depressed UK property market and the resulting difficult trading conditions in the DIY home improvement market. Kalon's success can be put down to astute acquisitions, a series of well-judged strategic decisions regarding the future direction of the business and efficient management, not least in the area of logistics. To quote Ian Hamilton Fazey of the *Financial Times*, in the paint industry 'independents can survive, but they have to be very good, such as Kalon. ... Its forte is good logistics to ensure just-in-time distribution' (Hamilton Fazey, 1994).

The UK paints industry

Like many other industries, paint manufacturing in the UK has developed into an oligopoly: there are many smaller manufacturers but three or four major players dominate the market. Approximate market shares for 1994 are shown in Table 10.1. Note the key distinction between paints for the retail market – dominated by the major DIY chains – and paints for the trade market, aimed primarily at professional decorators.

By the mid-1990s each of the major manufacturers had developed different strengths, and the absence of major technical innovation in recent years had prevented any company from increasing its market share through such means. ICI Dulux remained the top manufacturers' brand in the market place. Akzo Nobel produced the Crown brand for the retail market, but also produced trade ranges such as Permaglaze as well as retailers' own-label paints. Kalon's retail brands such as Homecharm were less well known but the company was a major producer of trade paints (the Leyland range) and was the largest supplier of retailers' own-label paints in the UK. Own-label products were made by Kalon not only for some of the main DIY superstore chains but also for significant numbers of smaller and regional retailers.

Table 10.1 Leading market shares in the UK paint industry, 1994

Retail market	(%)	Trade market	(%)
ICI (Dulux)	32	Akzo Nobel (Crown)	39
Akzo Nobel (Crown)	30	ICI (Dulux)	20
Kalon	28	Kalon	16
		Manders-Johnstone	14

Source: Kalon plc.

Kalon

Historical development

In the early 1980s Kalon was a relatively small manufacturer, based in Birstall, near Leeds in west Yorkshire. It produced mainly retail paints marketed under the Homecharm brand name. Around that time it took over Leyland Paints. This company was, however, beset by management difficulties, which affected group performance to the extent that losses were made and debts started to mount (Murray, 1995). The turning point was in the mid 1980s with the appointment of a new chief executive, Mike Hennessy, who implemented a range of new strategies.

One such strategy was acquisition, for example, the 1994 acquisition of Vallance, a loss-making manufacturer mainly of sealants, adhesives and putties, based in nearby Morley. Their Morley factory was retained along with the main Birstall factory, allowing future expansion of production.

A second development was the refocusing of the Leyland product range on the trade market. A network of Leyland Decorator Centres was opened throughout the UK, to sell paints and associated decorating products to professional decorators, decorators' merchants and other trade users of paints such as local authorities. The strong technical qualities of Leyland paints and the rapid development of the Decorator Centre network gave Kalon an increased share of the trade market. By 1994 there were 83 centres, with another 12 planned for 1995.

The third important development was the increased production of own-label paints. Kalon had thrived on the growth of the DIY market in the UK property boom of the late 1980s and the associated expansion of DIY superstore operators such as B&Q, Texas Homecare and Sainsbury's Homebase. By the early 1990s the company was the largest UK supplier of such own-label paint products. In 1993 Hennessy built on this experience and launched into Europe with the acquisition of Novodec, France's leading own-label paint manufacturer.

The result of these market developments was that Kalon's UK paint production – 66 million litres in 1994 – was divided more or less equally between trade and retail sectors. Forty-seven million litres of this was produced at Birstall and the remainder at Morley. Table 10.2 shows the approximate breakdown of Kalon's volume by major customer in 1994.

Table 10.2 Kalon customer base, 1994

Customer	Percentage
Leyland Decorator Centres	36
B&Q	32
Texas Homecare	13
Homebase	8
Other DIY retailers, supermarkets, Co-op stores, builders' merchant chains	11

Source: Kalon plc.

Product range

As a manufacturer of several distinct paint ranges, and also putties, sealants and adhesives, Kalon has had to produce a very large number of separate lines or stock-keeping units (SKUs). In addition, it has had to buy in many more SKUs from suppliers for sale in the Leyland Decorator Centres and to other trade customers. Bought-in lines have included many decorating sundries, wallpapers and home insulation products. This problem has been compounded because each paint range is necessarily large, taking into account the different paint types (gloss, vinyl matt, vinyl silk, etc.), the range of colours and the number of can sizes offered. By the mid-1990s the Birstall factory was producing some 3000 SKUs, and nearly 3000 more were either produced at Morley or bought from outside suppliers.

Corporate strategy and logistics efficiency

As its strategy developed, Kalon found contrasting requirements in its two main market segments. The supply of large paint volumes to the major retail multiples enabled Kalon to develop very efficient logistics systems for this part of its business. Operating in this market was not without its risks, however. It was the downturn of the DIY market that slowed growth in Kalon sales and profits in 1994. Superstore operators not only reduced average prices for their own-label paints, but also ran a series of promotions on key items in the brand ranges such as Dulux and Crown, hitting sales of the Kalon-produced own-label products. Another potential problem was that certain DIY chains made strategic decisions not to source own-label products from manufacturers used by their main competitors. This could lead to lost business when chains were taken over. Confirmation of the Sainsbury take-over of Texas Homecare DIY group in January 1995 adversely affected Kalon's share price, because Texas Homecare had been a Kalon customer whilst Sainsbury's Homebase had sourced most own-label paints from Akzo Nobel (Clark, 1995).

In contrast to this experience in the retail market, the success of Leyland in the trade paints market was not without its costs in terms of logistics complexity. A very large product range was offered, and there was a need to service the growing network of Decorator Centres, as well as large numbers of often small deliveries to hundreds of builders' and decorators' merchants, wholesalers and other specialist suppliers.

Customer service in the paints industry

Competition between the main manufacturers in the paints industry in the mid-1990s was both intense and broadly based. Price was an important factor in competition between retailers' own-label products and manufacturers' brands, as explained above. The technical qualities of paint such as durability featured strongly in the marketing of manufacturers' brands. Colour ranges needed regular updating to reflect changing market requirements. Customer service provided yet another element in the manufacturers' marketing mix. Small orders of mixed products were commonplace, and most manufacturers attempted to offer next-day delivery on orders to both the retail and the trade markets. In order to achieve this, both Akzo Nobel and ICI maintained networks of regional depots in the UK (Swords and Meredith, 1988).

Raw materials

The basic ingredients of paint are resins, pigments and solvents (Table 10.3). At Kalon these were purchased from a large range of suppliers. Both oil-based and water-based paints were produced, with the latter constituting just over 70% of total output. Certain materials were common to the production of many different SKUs and were stored in bulk hoppers. Other inbound materials were stored in a 9500 m^2 materials warehouse, with a large proportion of this space allocated to stocks of empty containers waiting to be moved to the filling lines. Kalon tended to use multiple sources of supply for its materials purchases, with the main exception being containers, as explained below.

Production methods

Paint production is basically an operation to blend various liquids and powders. For technical reasons production equipment at Kalon was dedicated to either water-based or oil-based paints. There were four main production lines – two for water-based paints and two for oil-based paints.

For water-based paints various powder ingredients were weighed automatically and dispersed in water. The resins were then added. Batch sizes of up to 12,500 litres could be produced. Once the mixing stage was complete, batches were emptied into one of eight 30,000-litre holding tanks, awaiting the outcome of quality-control tests. If the batch failed a test, corrective action had to be taken which would require extra processing time. Once all tests had been passed, the product proceeded either to canning, to blending operations (certain qualities of paint were created by blending batches together) or to tinting operations to produce various shades.

Oil-based paint production methods were essentially similar. In this operation there was a greater need for production of smaller batches of a large range of colours. Large batches of base colours were produced in the two main blending tanks, and were then passed to one of four 12,500-litre storage tanks for quality-control tests. Low-temperature drying tests at this stage could take up to 24 hours, and could lead to the need for further processing. The tinting stage was undertaken in one of a bank of 24 mixing vessels. These ranged in size between 1000 and 12,000 litres and could handle batch sizes as low as 250 litres. Further tests were necessary before paints could proceed to the filling lines.

Table 10.3 Raw material cost breakdown for oil-based paints

Material	Approximate percentage of total raw material cost
Resin	45
Pigments	25
Solvent	10
Additives	10
Packaging	10

With many relatively small batches, there was a need for frequent changeovers on the ten filling lines. At Kalon, filling lines were dedicated to either water-based or oil-based paints. These operated semi-automatically, with finished product being pumped into containers. Lids were applied by hand and completed containers were assembled on to nearby pallets. Full pallets were then stretchwrapped and a computer-generated barcode was attached. There was no storage space in the filling line areas and pallets were moved immediately to a despatch area to await transfer to the warehouse.

One part of the factory was dedicated to the manufacture of small batches of specialist products. For these, ingredients were weighed and added to vats manually, prior to the mechanized mixing process.

There was also a small stand-alone production area dedicated to the manufacture of wood treatment products, which are relatively simple and cheap to make. Demand for these products was very seasonal with a late summer peak, after which production was closed down for three months or so each year.

Logistics and distribution management at Kalon

Production planning

Historically, demand in the paint industry has proved very difficult to forecast, especially for new or seasonal lines (Constable and New, 1976). Technically speaking, the basis of production planning at Kalon was production for stock rather than production to order or just-in-time. However, the methods in use ensured a relatively high degree of order responsiveness and hence customer service. The on-line computer system contained information on stock levels and the status of each order, and therefore calculated the amount of free or unallocated stock for each SKU. Using demand information from the previous four weeks, this was converted to the number of weeks' cover. Expert knowledge was used to amend such information where necessary. Production runs were scheduled in advance of seasonal peak demand, for example, in order to build up stock levels in the warehouse. At the start of the weekly production planning process, all SKUs with cover below a predetermined threshold were identified automatically. The computer recommended a batch size in order to minimize total production costs. Minimum batch size was 250 litres. Appropriate batches of each SKU required were then entered into the production schedule. The detailed production plan and the allocation of work to particular production facilities were done manually. Once the weekly plan was under way, all SKUs were monitored daily and interventions could be made where necessary. Paint factory capacity utilization in 1994 was approximately 65% (Kalon, 1994).

Processing times varied significantly between SKUs. Standard water-based white paints, for example, had the shortest batch times (three hours), whereas certain oil-based colours took considerably longer (up to three days), sometimes including substantial delays whilst the various quality tests were completed. This information, coupled to the urgency of demand, was also an input into the detailed production plan.

By fine-tuning this production planning system, Kalon had increased stock availability from 94% to over 98% in recent years.

One exception to this system was that export orders were entered into the production plan manually, as and when they were received. Export orders were despatched to many parts of the world and were a growing part of the business, but represented less than 5% of total volume in 1994.

Transport

Despite widespread moves in the UK towards contract distribution, in 1995 Kalon remained a significant 'own-account' transport operator, with a fleet of over 70 vehicles. This fleet was used for outbound product distribution both to the major DIY chains and to the many smaller customers in both the retail and trade markets. Fleet composition was varied, reflecting the mix of customers and order sizes, and ranged from maximum weight articulated vehicles (38 tonnes) through smaller rigid vehicles down to small delivery vans. A range of transport efficiency indicators was used but emphasis was placed on achieving maximum permissible weight per vehicle wherever possible.

Some DIY superstore deliveries such as those to Texas Homecare were made to individual stores. Other chains insisted on deliveries to central or regional warehouses. The most notable case was B&Q, who in 1993 centralized its stockholding in a new depot at Runcorn near Liverpool, operated by contract logistics specialist Tibbett and Britten (Meczes, 1993). This change enabled Kalon to reduce its fleet size by approximately 15 vehicles with commensurate reductions in the numbers of drivers and order pickers, despite doing an increasing amount of business with this retailer. The trunking operation between Birstall and Runcorn became highly efficient. Two vehicles were allocated to this operation, and achieved two round trips each per day, with an average load of nearly 21 tonnes. This represented a load factor of 95% on the outbound journey, compared to 82% for the Kalon business as a whole.

In contrast, many deliveries to trade customers and the smaller retailers involved very small drops, with an average drop size of less than 1 tonne. The order and delivery patterns varied significantly from day to day, and it was not possible to draw up an efficient set of regular delivery routes. As a result, vehicle loading and scheduling operations were performed manually each day, using the mix of vehicle sizes available as efficiently as possible.

The Kalon fleet was also used for trunking products from the factories into the main Birstall warehouse. This operation employed seven trunk vehicles for 12 hours per day. Half the volume inbound to the warehouse was from the Birstall factory. Four schedulers were employed on the manual vehicle routing and scheduling operation and were assigned on a regional basis. All vehicles were serviced at eight-week intervals, regardless of mileage since the last service. At times of peak demand, extra vehicles were hired. Third-party hauliers were used for export loads.

Warehousing and inventory management

Kalon operated centralized warehousing and order processing at Birstall. There was no regional depot network, although stock was held in Northern Ireland and the Republic of Ireland. To provide full range availability in the Birstall warehouse, the own-account transport fleet was used to collect production from the other factories and many other items were bought in from outside suppliers.

In 1994 warehouse stock value reached around £8.5 million at the peak, when paint stock levels reached some 10 million litres. The average stock level was around 8 million litres. The growth in business volume and SKUs put continued pressure on warehousing space. A 14,000 m^2 purpose-built warehouse was built in 1989 on land available at the Birstall site. This replaced the existing inadequate provision, which was in the same building as the production facilities and which was converted for use as the materials store. Subsequent increased business led to one 9500 m^2 warehouse extension, with another similar extension due for completion in 1996. The warehouse operated 24 hours a day for five days per week on a three-shift system.

The warehouse was equipped with single-depth, wide-aisle, adjustable pallet racking 7.5-m (seven pallet locations) high. This racking could accept various pallet sizes, as there were variations in pallet standards across customers and suppliers. A fleet of eight gas-powered-fork lift trucks handled the movement of inbound and outbound pallets, and 20 reach trucks were used in the racking area. Aisles were allocated on a dedicated customer basis, so that the different product ranges for each major retailer were kept separate. In all cases the lowest two pallet locations were used for picking stock and the higher locations were for palletized storage. Reach trucks were also dedicated to each customer.

Some fast-moving SKUs, particularly those packed in large tins and those bulk ordered in full-pallet quantities, were not entered into the racking but were block stacked around the walls.

Picking locations for each SKU were held on computer and printed on picking notes but there was no stock location system in operation for the longer term palletized storage, precluding accurate stock rotation. Manual stocktaking was carried out every three months.

Eight ride-on trucks and numerous unpowered pallet trucks were used for order assembly work.

Much of the B&Q volume was moved as full pallets, but there was a trend towards layering to reduce the volumes moved per SKU. Layers of each SKU were placed on pallets, and these were stacked and stretchwrapped for unitized movement. Kalon offered a special service to B&Q for the many small and slow-moving SKUs. Such items were picked into a separate plastic crate for each B&Q store, and trunked to the central warehouse at Runcorn. This service operated on a one-week lead time, and two order pickers were dedicated to the work. Kalon paid for the hire of the crates. Drivers were responsible for loading their own vehicles.

Order processing

Orders were received in one of three sales offices at Birstall :one for the retail market, one for the trade market and one for the Vallance division (adhesives, sealants and putties). Orders arrived in a number of ways. EDI links had been installed to the Leyland Decorator Centres, to B&Q, Texas Homecare and some of the other major retail and trade customers. Other customers sent orders by phone, fax, letter or through Kalon sales representatives. Once received, order information was fed electronically to the distribution department, where the appropriate paperwork was generated. This documentation was used for load planning, order picking and order assembly. Many orders had to conform to agreed delivery windows and to restrictions on vehicle types and sizes, and these constraints were entered at the order input stage, and printed out on the relevant documents.

For many major customers, ordering was on a routine order cycle with set days and times. For the Leyland Decorator Centres and many other trade customers, order processing ran over three days. For orders received on day one, goods would be picked and orders assembled on day two, with delivery on day three. These customers had the opportunity to submit a top-up order on day two, to be delivered with the original order, a service which was used extensively.

For other customers, orders received before 1 pm would be picked on the same day and despatched on the following day, as long as a vehicle had been scheduled to go to the area concerned and space was available. Otherwise delivery was held over to the third day. Kalon aimed to despatch goods from the warehouse within 48 hours of order receipt. A major exception was B&Q, where Kalon aimed for turnround in six hours.

Picking accuracy in 1995 was over 99%, with a stockout rate per SKU of around 1.5%.

The main peak in ordering was from mid-February to mid-March as sales outlets built stock levels for the spring. A second smaller peak occurred in late summer, particularly in the timber treatment area. Peak order volume reached a maximum of some 4000 orders per week, but the average was around 3000 orders. Many of these were top-up orders on the second day of the cycle, meaning that the number of drops was rather lower – up to 2800 per week in the peak, with an average of 2300. Average weight per drop was around 1 tonne for retail deliveries, but only 0.6 tonnes for the trade market.

Customers could also contact the sales offices to make arrangements for the return of goods for various reasons. This additional work had to be scheduled by the transport and warehouse departments.

Packaging

Metal tins and lids were used for the majority of paint lines, although plastic containers were used for some water-based paints. For each type of container, there was one predominant supplier. Most containers were supplied already labelled, but factory staff were employed to apply the colour identification panels manually before filling. A small number of tins was supplied plain and staff applied paper labels, again before filling.

The 'black-band' service allowed smaller retailers and merchants to have their own company or brand name placed on containers. This service was provided to special order but at no additional charge. The operation was performed manually in the warehouse by adding labels on to a black band on common stock containers before despatch. Over 200 retailers and merchants used this service in 1995.

Products were palletized at the end of filling lines for movement to the warehouse. Corrugated card was placed between layers of containers and the pallet was stretchwrapped. Similar packaging methods were used once orders had been picked for despatch to customers. The main exceptions concerned goods for despatch to UK off-shore islands, Northern Ireland, the Republic of Ireland and most other overseas destinations, when containers were packed in cardboard cases. For some distant exports, products were packed in wooden crates to minimize the risk of damage.

The pallets used by Kalon were owned by the company and were clearly identified.

Distribution costs

Like many other companies, Kalon managed to improve the efficiency of its logistics in the early 1990s. By 1994 distribution costs had been reduced to 5.5% of sales value. The approximate breakdown of distribution costs was as shown in Table 10.4.

Warehousing costs included those elements of packaging and labelling undertaken in the warehouse, but not those undertaken in the factory.

Table 10.4 Distribution costs at Kalon, 1994

	Percentage
Transport	46
Warehouse and inventory	51
Management/administration	3

Future directions for Kalon

Turning to the issue of strategic directions for Kalon from 1995 onwards, growth on the recent scale seemed likely to prove rather more elusive. In the UK retail market, Kalon was already the market leader in the retailers' own-label sector, but its brands lagged behind those of the main competitors. The DIY superstore deliveries in particular provided the company with opportunities for very efficient logistics operations, especially since the B&Q decision to centralize its inventory. There were however strategic risks associated with dependence on a narrow customer base.

Development of the trade paints market had been instrumental in Kalon's growth, but by 1995 the Leyland Decorator Centre network was more or less complete. Increased logistics efficiency would help to improve cost effectiveness in this market characterized by small orders, multidrop work and demands for high levels of customer service.

If chief executive Mike Hennessy wanted the growth rates achieved in the late 1980s and the early 1990s to be maintained in the future he would have to think very carefully about the strategic directions of the business and the importance of logistics costs in the total costs of the product in such a competitive market.

References

Clark, M. (1995) Stock market report. *The Times*, 26 January, p. 26.

Constable, C.J. and New, C.C. (1976) *Operations Management: A Systems Approach Through Text and Cases*, John Wiley, London.

Hamilton Fazey, I. (1994) Survey of paints and the environment (5): moving into sharper focus – markets and suppliers. *Financial Times*, 8 April.

Kalon Group plc (1994) *Report and Accounts 1994.*

Meczes, R. (1993) B&Q opts for three into one. *Materials Handling News*, July, p. 39.

Murray, I. (1995) Painting by profits. *Money Observer*, November, pp. 65–6.

Smith New Court UK (1993) *UK Chemicals Winners and Losers, Winter 1993.*

Swords, M. and Meredith, C. (1988) The distribution of Dulux: a strategic evaluation. Paper presented at the Institute of Logistics and Distribution Management National Conference, June.

Acknowledgements

The authors would like to take this opportunity to thank management and staff at Kalon for their assistance and support, without which this case study could not have been written.

Manufacturing and logistics

Dennis Nettle

Department of Management, Victoria University of Technology, Melbourne, Australia

The start – 1985

As Graeme Boyles, the Production Manager, glanced at the clock on his wall he knew today would be crucial for the whole future of Trico in Australia. Trico was the sole manufacturer of windscreen wiper blades in Australia. A subsidiary of Tricontinental Products (US), it was established in 1959 at a factory in Springvale, Melbourne. Graeme and the Managing Director Frank Sutherland were due to meet with the Vice-President of Trico (US), Richard Wolf, and the subject on the agenda was the nothing less than the future strategic direction of the company. The key question was this: how could the company reverse its current slide? Should it invest heavily in new technology such as FMS (flexible manufacturing systems)? That would be expensive, and it was not clear to Graeme that Trico (US) was either prepared to make such investments or that they would be suitable for the high- volume nature of Trico's business. The second solution was to close down the operation. The site alone was worth $5 million. Was there an alternative?

As Graeme waited for the meeting he pondered how Trico had reached its current situation. Trico like many other auto components producers had followed the major US car companies to Australia in the post-war period. It had benefitted from lavish government protection for the automotive industry – costing around A$1.6 billion per year – but remained dependent on the local car companies and the domestic market. While Trico dominated the original equipment (OEM) market which accounted for 70% of sales in 1984, it had a relatively minor role in the much more competitive replacement market. Exports accounted for only 5% of sales in 1984. To some extent this was due to the policy of Trico (US) which restricted the Australian operation to a role of taking up any excess supply in the US market. For one thing Graeme could not understand why Trico (US) insisted that the south east Asian market should be supplied from the UK rather than Australia. But Graeme knew that like the local passenger vehicle industry Trico was internationally uncompetitive.

Trico's production philosophy emphasized high-volume manufacture. Batch sizes were large – on average eight weeks. Car companies would provide monthly orders on Trico.

When manufactured, the parts were delivered to a warehouse at the car assembly plant. Parts would be supplied from the warehouse to the line by trolley trains. Large buffer stocks were kept on the assembly line. Car companies kept many weeks of inventory. Normally they required only one delivery per week but in widely fluctuating amounts due to the state of inventory stocks. Rush deliveries were also common when production planners found themselves expediting items that were running short. It also didn't help when defective parts were returned despite having passed random sampling by quality inspectors. Trico often found itself obliged to carry much larger finished goods inventories than it would have liked. In fact, car companies obliged Trico to hold at least two weeks of inventory in remote locations, to protect them against loss of supply. Inventory was calculated to be costing the company $2.58 million in 1983 of which $1.5 million was finished goods.

In the early 1980s large batches and long lead times were also required due to the nature of the production process. Wiper manufacture consists of three parts – arm manufacture, linkage assembly and blade assembly. The arms consists of three pieces which are die cast, formed on a 200-tonne press, and then assembled using bought-in springs and rivets. The linkage consists of two parts: the drive and the driven components which are made using a die-cast process in the arm manufacture area and the press shop. The sub-assembled linkages are fed to a final assembly area where bought-in cranks and ball-pins are fitted. The blade consists of four parts formed on the 200-tonne press. A nagging problem had always been the slow set up times on the 200-tonne press, and resultant accumulation of work in progress. Because of the need for large runs and lack of firm long-term forecasts Trico also tended to order large stocks of raw materials and sub-assemblies in advance of actual car company orders.

In 1984, work in progress was calculated as costing $715,000 with $365,000 in raw materials. This high level, relative to a turnover of $6 million, was partially caused by the ordering patterns of the car companies as explained above. Ford, for example, would indicate each year that it required Trico to manufacture wipers for its various models and the approximate volumes involved. Its purchasing department would then place an order on Trico once a month for a number of wipers for each model and variant. Provided there was no major change in sales of cars, this all worked very well. Graeme knew how much equipment capacity, operators and supplies to organize. Unfortunately this did not seem to work at a weekly order-item level. Some of the main problems were as follows.

- Big changes in particular parts occurred because Ford's purchasing department was distant from assembly so that small weekly changes often led to large corrections.
- Changes in the rate of sales of cars in Australia often caused large changes in the quantity of each wiper part ordered each month.
- Ford would frequently require parts on a few days lead time, either due to error in its ordering or due to quality problems in the fitment of the wiper onto the car.

Consequently both Ford and Trico kept considerable stocks of each wiper part, about two months by Ford and one month by Trico.

Another problem, Graeme pondered, was that Trico seemed to lack the capacity to move beyond high-volume manufacture for the OEM sector. In the early 1980s specifications for wiper assemblies were normally issued in detail by the major companies engineers. Trico's role was to quote on these designs. Contracts normally lasted from two to four years. As a result Trico had developed little internal capacity to develop new product designs for the non-OEM market.

As Graeme and other members of the management team filed into the conference room another problem struck him. How often had production lead times and costs blown out because he tended to receive design specifications much too late in the process? Engineers, he thought, grossly under estimated the feasibility or purchasing implications of their specifications. Trico had a traditional functional organization chart. Sales, engineering, purchasing, and production were separate departments. Lack of communication between the managers and the tendency to push department interests and 'pass the buck' made it difficult to address problems (see Figure 11.1). Functional organization, he thought, even extended to the production layout. All press work and die-cast work, even though destined for arm blade and linkage assembly were done in separate 'shops'.

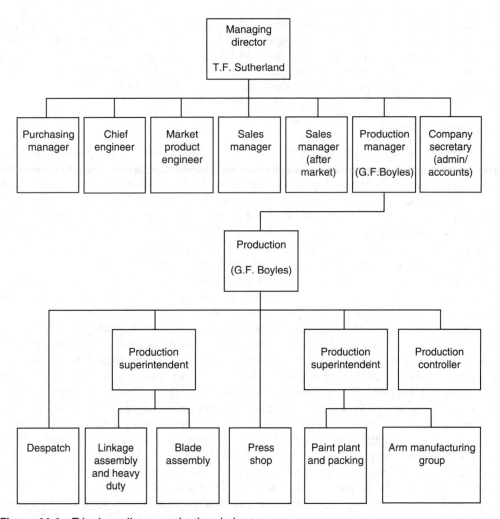

Figure 11.1 Trico's earlier organizational chart.

Production control and material handling problems were rife. Trico's poor performance also meant its 140 employees were concerned about job security.

As Richard Wolf rose to speak, the writing was all too visible on the wall. There had been a steady decline in return on assets. In 1983 a major contract was lost when Toyota moved to import wiper assemblies from Japan. Erosion of Trico's competitive position was also exacerbated by changes in Australian government policy, which in 1985 saw the commencement of a programme of staged reductions in tariff and quota protection, support for mergers and rationalization of car production facilities, and shifts of assistance towards export facilitation (The Button Plan). Meanwhile, responding to this pressure the car companies were requiring much quicker response from their suppliers in terms of greater product diversity, smaller batch sizes and just-in-time (JIT) delivery. Along with JIT delivery the car companies also expected suppliers to qualify under their in-house quality certification schemes to allow for direct delivery to the line without inspection. The question was could Trico meet this pressure and how?

A further blow was when Richard Wolf categorically ruled out the FMS option, since corporate management had already agreed in principle to commit a multimillion dollar investment to a new greenfield plant in south Wales, which was to act as the spearhead for operations within the European Union. Any investment in new technology or skill development by Trico (Australia) would have to be generated internally.

Ten years later

Graeme Boyle had just attended a meeting of the Trico board. As Operations Director he had shared in a major success for the company: achieving a major export contract for supply of wiper assemblies to Isuzu in Japan. There had been a string of such good news since the change of ownership in 1994 when the company had been sold by Trico (US) to Stant Corporation. Exports had increased to 40% of sales by 1992. The company had not sold out or sought a panacea in the introduction of FMS. The reason for success, he thought, lay in a range of internal and external organizational reforms which were allowing the company to become more customer and product focused.

On the one hand, the major car companies had radically changed their purchasing policy. Inwards warehousing was a thing of the past. Toyota, for example, now provided annual forecasts of requirements for each part broken down into monthly requirements. A few months before the period concerned Toyota provides a number of weekly forecasts going out about 16 weeks with the first two to four weeks firm. The extent that Toyota can vary from the estimate is progressively reduced as the time gets closer. Actual orders are now placed by Kanban. Toyota requires four Kanban deliveries per day, General Motors Holden (GMH) one, Mitsubishi one, and Ford once every two to three days. As a wiper assembly point uses a tote box of a particular wiper its Kanban card is placed on a hook. Production planning collects Kanbans off these hooks every two hours and puts them in a pigeon-hole for collection by the Trico driver. When the driver delivers the last lot of parts he takes the Kanbans from the pigeon-hole and conveys them to Trico. Trico now makes exactly the number required by the Kanbans and delivers them to Toyota. Deliveries are on a 6-hour cycle. Parts delivered are taken straight to the correct point on the line.

JIT delivery had secured long-term contracts with the major companies. What was also interesting was how the balance of Trico's business had also changed. Now OEM supply accounted for only 45% of sales. The company now produced a much wider range of products and hence was more competitive in the non-OEM part of the market. Thirty new products were introduced in 1992 and 25 in 1993 against an historical average of ten products per year. Product introduction time had also been cut from 12 to 6 months. The design competence of Trico had improved considerably. The car companies no longer specified the whole wiper assembly, but well in advance gave Trico engineers details of a new design, and the positions for the mounting of the wiper assembly, and basically left the design detail to Trico engineers. Trico engineers have been able to assist GMH in developing design innovations for the new Commodore. Engineering rather than being a separate department was now included along with production within the Operations Director's function.

There had been important changes in the organizational structure. The function of the Operations Director included the coordination of all functions in the conversion process, including sales and purchasing. An important factor was the formation of the design team. The people involved in this team were the Managing Director, Operations Director, Sales Manager, Company Secretary, Purchasing Manager, Product Manager, Quality Manager, as well as leading hands and supervisors in blade manufacture, arm manufacture, linkage assembly and toolroom. It also included the shop steward from the Metal Workers' union. This team had been instrumental in the restructuring programme at Trico.

Allied to these changes in product range and organizational structure, Graeme had made major changes to production control, product quality and purchasing at Trico. Before describing them, some specific manufacture and assembly situations require review.

Pilot project – press shop

The restructuring programme began with the project to reduce set-up times on the 200-tonne press. Exploration of set-up time reduction options involved all press shop production supervisors and tool-room personnel. Fifty per cent of employees were involved. Changes brought about included:

- specifying raw materials to improve ease of handling
- standardization of tools and of guides (location pins) to improve delivery and feed of material
- standardization of dies and provision of better handling devices and supports to facilitate change-over
- modification of components to improve tool changes.

The improvements had been dramatic – reduction of set-up times on the 200-tonne press from 7 hours (1984) to 15 minutes by 1992. With the reduction of set-up times Kanban cards were introduced on all press shop products. Product batch sizes had been eight weeks on average, but were reduced to a Kanban order point quantity of one week. A visible sign of the improvement in work in progress inventory in the press shop was the release of space once occupied by 500 tote pans, 120 $4 \times 4 \times 4$ crates and 100 $3 \times 2 \times 2$ stillages.

Linkage assembly

Success of the pilot project in the press shop resulted in the extension of the JIT project to the linkage assembly line which principally used components manufactured on the 200-tonne press. Again with considerable involvement from shop-floor personnel the linkage area was reorganized into an L-shaped manufacturing cell occupying only 50% of the floor space (Figure 11.2). This allowed reduction of material handling, minimization of lifting and twisting for operators, and greater capacity for group management and multi-skilling. The involvement of the manufacturing cell facilitated smoother new product introduction from off-tool-sample to final production. Release of floor space also

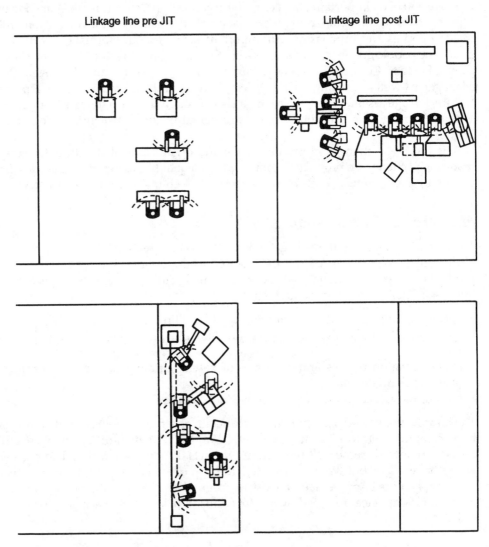

Figure 11.2 Linkage assembly area: before and after JIT.

allowed relocation of all components from a remote storage area (occupying 45 m^2) directly to the assembly area (occupying 30 m^2) giving greater visibility and control, and improving production flow. One aspect of the improvements in production flow had been the elimination of the previous need for batching of pivot sub-assemblies prior to final assembly. The assembly of linkages now occurred on a one-for-one basis through to final assembly.

Arm manufacture

Subsequently the restructuring process was extended further to the arm manufacturing area. The formation of the arm manufacturing cell required tackling the functional layout which saw the location of dedicated arm piece presses and die cast machines in the press shop. These were relocated so as to facilitate complete arm piece manufacture and assembly in the same area (Figure 11.3). Similarly to the linkage area material was moved from the previous components store to the assembly floor. In common with all parts produced on the 200-tonne press and linkage assembly, Kanban batch quantities were reduced to one weeks production requirements.

Recently the process of change had been extended to the blade production area. In conjunction with Toyota, a U-shaped pilot TPS (Toyota Production System) cell had been introduced.

Production control

The restructuring programme had caused major changes to production control. Control was now planned by a three-month forward schedule, in weekly amounts and driven by weekly and daily updates. The load on each manufacturing area, such as the 200-tonne press, was accumulated across each part. This enabled machine and operator capacity to be put in place and then managed as actual manufacture took place. Flexibility was provided by changes in the number of shifts per week in each manufacturing area and mobility of operators between areas.

Purchasing

Finally the advent of the Trico Restructuring Program (TRIP) had also had an important impact on purchasing. With the advent of the new Trico production control and JIT supply to the car companies, Trico had moved from monthly to weekly orders on a Kanban basis from local suppliers. Standard-sized recyclable containers were also provided to suppliers, eliminating much of the wastage which occurred with the use of cardboard. With overseas suppliers Trico was moving towards a two-week logistics cycle with exported product returning on the same ships. A visible sign of improvement was the reduction of the old components store by half.

Quality

Quality improvement had been a key component of the ability of Trico to improve its capacity to supply JIT. At the start of the pilot project managers were generally of the opinion that apart from a few minor areas quality was good because the reject/warranty

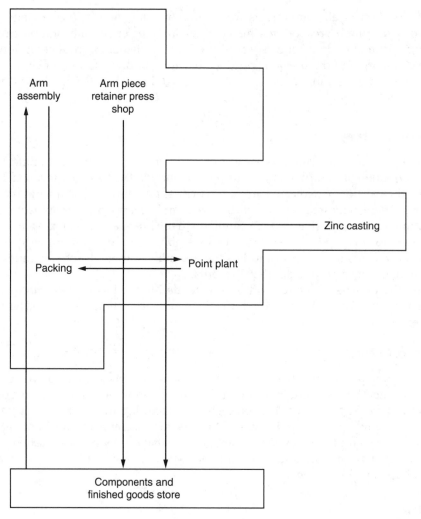

Figure 11.3a Arm manufacture and assembly before JIT.

return rate appeared to be negligible. However, one aspect of the operation of the project teams was addressing and correcting a number of quality problems including:

- porosity in die cast housings
- undersize holes in pivot cranks
- fouling of driven link on motor bracket during functional testing.

Assembled rejects were virtually eliminated. Through operator involvement a Trico 'Operator Caution, Check, Control Sheet' was introduced showing visibly at each station the critical features of the assembly. Non-conformance of any part could be addressed through line stoppage by operators (Figure 11.4). Trico had recently gained ISO 9000 accreditation and was assisting suppliers to do likewise.

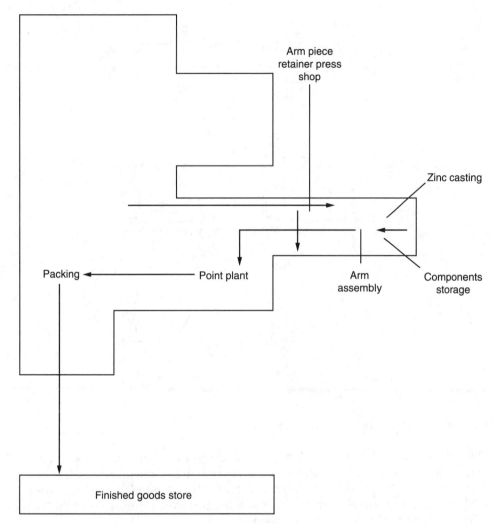

Figure 11.3b Arm manufacture and assembly after JIT.

Teams

Team involvement was a key feature of the Trico restructuring programme. While restructuring is often seen as involving factory closures and retrenchments there were no retrenchments at Trico. Indeed employment increased from 140 in 1984 to 240 in 1992. Job security was an important factor in the greater commitment of employees to products and customers. Since 1991 multi-functional teams linking blade linkage and arm manufacturing groups with support functions such as engineering, sales, and quality had been used in tackling a number of operational issues from the application for Ford Q1 quality certification to the purchase of wire-cutting machines. By 1995 there were 35 groups in operation, with an average of eight persons per group. Trico no longer works with a

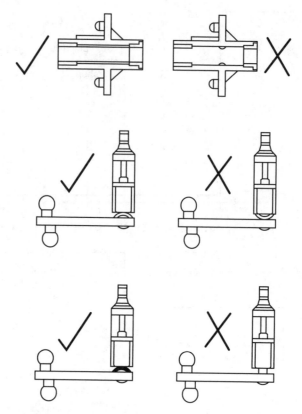

Figure 11.4 'Operator Caution, Check, Control Sheet'.

traditional organizational chart. Managers have responsibilities for cross-functional teams rather than traditional functional areas. According to Graeme Boyles, 'getting out of our boxes' has been one of the main reasons for the turn around at Trico. And the turn around has been considerable: from two inventory turns on a turnover of $6 million in 1984 to six turns on a turnover of $21 million in 1995.

Acknowledgements

The author would like to thank the management and staff of Trico and Ian Sadler of the Department of Management, Victoria University of Technology for their assistance in the preparation of this case.

PART FOUR

Distribution planning and strategy

Delivery vehicles for the Warsaw district

Professor Krzysztof Rutkowski
Warsaw School of Economics, Poland

and

Professor Fred Beier
Carleton School of Management, University of Minnesota, USA

Goman is a Polish import and distribution company which distributes confections, sugar, coffee and tea throughout Poland (see Figure 12.1). In the early 1990s their basic sources of supply were from Israel, Germany and a domestic confection maker in Poznań which supplied approximately 35% of its supplies. Suppliers in Israel and Germany each supplied 20% of Goman's requirements. The balance of the material was imported from wherever the company felt an opportunity existed. In general, the company expected the proportion of Polish products to decline in the future. The company distributed approximately 150 different items to approximately 5000 retailers and a few wholesalers. The company was forecasting continued growth through 1993 and beyond.

In September 1992, Goman, facing increasing competition from other distributors, was looking for new solutions allowing the company to expand its capacity while maintaining or improving customer service. In the opinion of its management, the problem could be solved by increasing the productivity and capacity of the delivery system. In particular, Goman was considering the purchase of new and/or larger vans, but the company was unsure whether the increased cost of purchasing new vehicles could be justified. In addition, a new order assembly ('bucket') technology, which would be feasible with larger vehicles, was under consideration.

Introduction

Prior to 1989, almost the entire system of distribution in Poland was controlled by the state. As an example the Polish Trading Company (PHS) controlled 85% of the market for packaged food. It operated 145 warehouses throughout Poland. The remaining trade

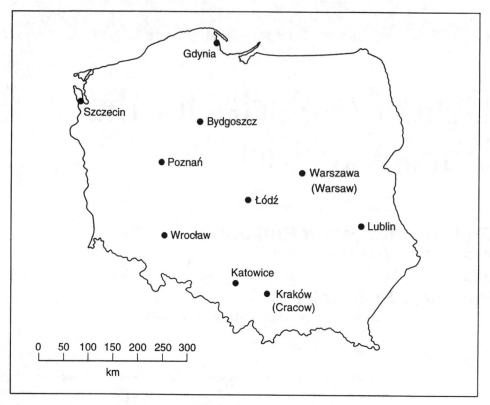

Figure 12.1   Map of Poland with the sites of Goman's warehouses.

was represented by co-operatives and other smaller state-owned companies. The same applied to retailing where, with the exception of privately owned grocery kiosks, the retail shops were controlled by state-owned enterprises or co-operatives. The partial relaxation of policy towards foreign investments in the mid-1980s made some joint ventures possible, but their impact was rather symbolic.

The transportation system in this sector was totally monopolized by the state companies operating trucks and vans servicing centrally assigned markets. The purchase of vans and trucks by individuals was restricted to the second-hand vehicle market. Prices on these markets were substantially higher than the official price set by the state. The official price, however, was only available to state designated monopolies.

Following the changes which took place in 1989, the situation changed drastically. Many of the shops were privatized and thousands of new, privately owned retail shops popped-up within a short period of time. Freedom to enter new markets allowed companies such as Goman to start operations throughout Poland.

An additional change after 1989 was that transportation vehicles became more available on the Polish market.[1]

Company background

Goman Co. was a limited company which was established based on a mixture of Polish and foreign capital. The company operated eight warehouses throughout Poland including Warszawa (Warsaw), Gdynia, Szczecin, Lódz, Katowice, Kraków (Cracow), Wroclaw and Bydgoszcz,. and was planning to add new warehouses in Lublin and Poznań. The original warehouses were 600 m^2 but the company intended the new warehouses to be at least 1000 m^2. The company rented all of its warehouse space and eventually planned to expand all of its facilities. From two to seven sales people were attached to each facility who solicited retailers for orders. One sales manager supervised each group of sales people and also made calls on wholesalers in the district. In addition to soliciting new orders, sales people were also required to make collections from small accounts who had used up their credit period – typically 14 days. Such collections were made in cash and often dictated which districts of Warsaw would be visited by the sales person on any particular day. Approximately 60% of the orders used credit.

The ordering process

The typical retail order consisted of approximately 15–20 items and was valued at 300 PLN^2 and contained 18 separate boxes. While each warehouse had a personal computer which processed these orders and kept track of sales figures, there was no network where this information could be shared with other warehouses or with the central office in Warsaw. Sales people collected orders on a standard preprinted order form which contained only those items which were in-stock or 'available for sale.' This eliminated the problem of selling items which were out of stock. On average, the typical retail shop placed one order per week.

Since the salesperson's efforts to collect orders would often extend past the time when the warehouse was closed, the order forms were physically delivered to the warehouse the following morning. Orders were processed during this day and delivered the next. Goman's customer service target was to deliver the complete order within 48 hours. The company estimated, however, that it was able to achieve this goal only 75% of the time.

The delivery process

On the morning of the second day orders were assembled and loaded into the trucks. This process took approximately 90 minutes. With the exception of Warsaw and Gdynia, each warehouse had one van with which to make deliveries. Warsaw had three vans and Gdynia had two. The vans had a capacity of 10–12 m^3 which would hold 25 average deliveries. On average the driver could accomplish 20–25 deliveries in one day before the shops closed.

Orders were assembled and loaded in the truck according to the route which the van would follow. The cartons in each order were loaded individually in order to utilize all of the space in the truck. This meant that the driver had to search for each carton at the back of the truck and reassemble the order before taking it into the retail shop. Inside the shop the driver compared the delivery with the invoice for the shop manager to verify that everything was being delivered. The process of reassembling the order and then verifying it with the shop manager was often complicated and time consuming because the labelling of the cartons was not standardized and some of the cartons were poorly labelled. This was especially true of the products from Poznań. For example, if a label was difficult to identify the driver and shop owner would have to make an effort to reconcile the order with the invoice.

As noted above, the company was considering buying larger vans for its delivery operation but was unsure about the economics of the situation. It was decided to undertake a pilot study, based on the Warsaw warehouse, of the economics of introducing new vans. A van with 15–20 m³ would cost approximately 46,500 PLN compared to 31,500 PLN for the current size van. There was also a larger van of 30 m³ which could be purchased for 82,500 PLN. The potential benefit of the larger vans was that the orders could be better organized so the driver would not have to 'reassemble' the order and then verify it again for the shop manager. The plan was to assemble the order in a plastic bucket when it was loaded. Then the driver would simply have to bring the bucket into the shop and verify delivery without reassembling it. Using the bucket technology the 20 m³ van held approximately 36 deliveries which also represented the limit of deliveries which could be accomplished in a day.[3] The new bucket technology would allow the truck to be loaded faster in the morning. However, this would be offset by longer time in selecting orders from the warehouse as the orders were assembled in buckets.

The company estimated that it could purchase all of the necessary plastic buckets for 1500 PLN. Operating costs for the vans, for fuel and services, were estimated at 200 PLN per month and the vans were considered fully depreciated after three years. The existing vans in Warsaw were two years old, and there was a three month lead time for new vans. Van drivers and warehouse people worked interchangeably and were paid 650 PLN per month.

Acknowledgement

This case was developed as part of a co-operative programme between the Warsaw School of Economics and the Carlson School of Management, University of Minnesota under the sponsorship of USAID. It was developed during the 1992–3 academic year and was revised and adapted for publication in January 1996 by Grzegorz M. Augustyniak of the Warsaw School of Economics assisted by Professor Beier.

Notes

1. The Polish market, due to its size (a population of 38.6 million) became very attractive for foreign automakers. Due to high import duties and excise taxes (the result of the agreement of association with the European Community giving Poland time to restructure its automobile industry), leading European truck makers eventually began to assemble or even partially manufacture their products in Poland.
2. The rate of exchange: 1 PLN (New Zloty) = US$0.70 (September, 1992). Actually, at that time in Poland the currency used was PLZ (Zloty) which was denominated in 1995 by 1 PLN = 10,000 PLZ. By the end of 1996 both currencies were the legal tender in Poland.
3. The use of the bucket technology with existing 10–12 m³ vans would not be practical, because they would consume a large part of van's capacity, thus reducing the number of deliveries which could be accomplished in a day.

Transport and customer service options for the distribution of small orders†

Professor Colin Bamford
Department of Transport and Logistics, University of Huddersfield, UK

and
Eddie Dennis
Distribution Planning Manager, Palmer & Harvey McLane Ltd, UK

Introduction

Palmer & Harvey (P&H) is a traditional wholesale business in the UK, which was faced with a decreasing customer base due to changed retail structures which had seen the decline of small retail outlets. The company had a small-order problem in so far as there was a relatively high demand for orders from customers wishing to spend small amounts of money. Consequently, in delivering these orders, transport costs were high.

Recognizing these problems, in 1993, the company carried out

- a customer service survey
- a detailed analysis of its transport costs and future strategies based on its largest distribution centre in north-west England at Haydock.

The outcome of these investigations was that the company had to decide what to do to retain the business of such customers whilst providing an acceptable level of customer service in relation to the costs involved.

Company background

In 1993, P&H (the company now trades as Palmer & Harvey McLane Limited) was the largest wholesaler of delivered tobacco and confectionery products in the UK. Its

*Data available on the Internet (see page xxii).

traditional market has been to supply a range of tobacco items (such as cigarettes, cigars and tobaccos) to independent and multiple retailers, public houses and other retail outlets, including petrol forecourt retail shops. P&H's product range in 1992 was wider and included a substantial number of confectionery items (chocolate, sugar sweets and other confections), snack products (potato crisps, nuts and related items), carbonated and still drinks, motor accessories, health and home products and a range of grocery items.

As a traditional wholesaler, it had an extensive regional distribution network broadly consistent with the main centres of population (see Figure 13.1). Each distribution centre stocked the full range of products and delivered to customers within a specified geographical catchment area. Profit margins in the wholesale trade were very low, normally around 1% of sales. In 1988, P&H was bought by its managers in a management buy out.

P&H's mission statement was:

To add value to the operations of customers and suppliers by constantly meeting their changing needs and providing the highest standards of quality, value and service.

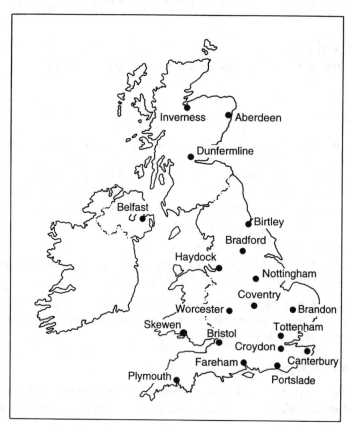

Figure 13.1   Palmer & Harvey Ltd, branch locations.

The external business environment

The external environment in which P&H operated had experienced fundamental change over the past 30 years or so and in 1992 it was one of only a small number of wholesalers to have survived the onslaught from 'cash and carry' (a wholesale warehouse to which small retailers and traders drive to collect and purchase stock items of their choice) outlets. In this respect the company had been highly successful in sustaining its market in the face of the growing power and control of multiple retailers, both in the market place and in the supply chain. The growth of the multiple retailer largely at the expense of independent operators is shown in Table 13.1.

Table 13.1   Market share and number of retail grocery outlets in Great Britain 1979–94

	Market share (%)			Number of outlets		
	Multiples	**Co-op**	**Independent**	**Multiples**	**Co-op**	**Independent**
1979	62.3	12.4	25.3	6000	5550	56,000
1984	68.7	11.9	18.3	4290	3620	40,600
1989	74.5	10.9	14.6	4290	2906	37,500
1994	82.2	8.2	9.6	4787	2379	32,600

Source: Institute of Grocery Distribution, 1995.

Other factors had an important bearing on its operations. Its traditional core business, tobacco products, had experienced long-term decline – cigarette sales, for example, had fallen by around 30% between 1980 and 1993, although the rate of decrease stabilized in the late 1980s. On the demand side, there had been a persistent decline in the number of small shops, in both urban and rural areas (see Table 13.1). The fall in these traditional outlets was in part offset by an increase in the number of non-traditional outlets, particularly petrol stations which often open for long trading periods.

Internal changes 1985–93

Changes in the external market situation described above had necessitated an aggressive response from P&H in order to safeguard as well as develop market share. One strategy had been the diversification of the product range, with the addition of grocery, health and home products and motor accessories to its core business of tobacco

Table 13.2   P&H Haydock customer profile

Customer type	Outlets (%)
Confectioner, tobacconist, newsagent	31.1
Grocer	2.7
Service station	34.3
Schools	13.9
Other (including cinemas, restaurants and public houses)	18.0
Total	100.0

and confectionery products. Second, there had been a need to widen the range and number of sales outlets serviced by the company. In 1993, P&H supplied various types of customer outlet, ranging from hospitals, colleges and leisure centres to small retail shops and petrol service stations (see Table 13.2). This latter market was particularly relevant and accounted for around 34% of P&H's total sales in 1993. Small order customers by value were particularly prevalent in the Schools and Other categories.

The supply chain

The P&H supply chain in theory appears simple (see Figure 13.2) but in practice it is quite complex on account of the extensive product range and the large number of customers. In 1993 the Haydock depot, for example, supplied over 3000 trading outlets per week with a product range of around 5000 different items.

P&H provide a direct, free delivery service to customers from their depot network. Given their highly competitive marketplace, the company promoted a customer benefits package which included credit facilities, business counselling, merchandising, regular deliveries, detailed invoicing and a stated minimum level (98%) of order fulfilment. Figure 13.3 indicates the various stages and related costs which occur when a customer places an order with the company.

Transport

The nature of P&H's business was that transport costs were a relatively high and an increasing proportion of total distribution costs. Deliveries to customers have traditionally been made by a medium-sized goods vehicle of 12,5 tonnes gross vehicle weight (gvw) from the P&H depot to the customer's own retail premises. Within total logistics costs, transport was the largest item by far, accounting for around 45% of such costs. In contrast, inventory and administration costs had been falling and each were about 7% of total logistics costs in 1993. The remaining costs were capital overhead charges, which included the costs of vehicle purchase.

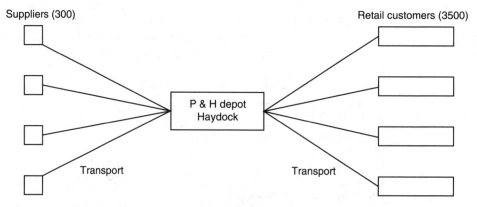

Figure 13.2   The supply chain in P&H: Haydock depot. Note: the company had 19 depots in 1993, each of which had a supply chain like the above representation.

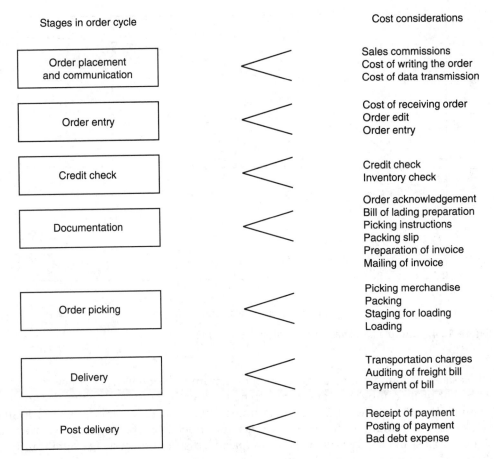

Stages in order cycle | Cost considerations

Stages in order cycle	Cost considerations
Order placement and communication	Sales commissions Cost of writing the order Cost of data transmission
Order entry	Cost of receiving order Order edit Order entry
Credit check	Credit check Inventory check
Documentation	Order acknowledgement Bill of lading preparation Picking instructions Packing slip Preparation of invoice Mailing of invoice
Order picking	Picking merchandise Packing Staging for loading Loading
Delivery	Transportation charges Auditing of freight bill Payment of bill
Post delivery	Receipt of payment Posting of payment Bad debt expense

Figure 13.3 Stages and costs associated with an order.

A major operational worry for P&H was that there were an increasing number of delivery restrictions being introduced in UK urban areas for environmental reasons. Also a growing number of customers required deliveries to be made within a particular time window because of increased efficiency in their logistics management.

The small-order problem

The nature of P&H's customer base was that many of the businesses which it supplied required small orders. P&H even marketed itself as the 'customers' storeroom'; some customers had understandably used this to the full, replenishing stocks on a daily basis. Historically, P&H had been prepared to deliver any size of order, to any one of its customers on any particular working day. This of course raised the whole question of the corporate objectives of P&H and the extent to which the trade-offs related to customer service had been fully identified.

In July 1990, after a careful review of the above issues, P&H introduced a 20 outer ('outer' is a minimum-sized pack of a product which is supplied by the manufacturer for

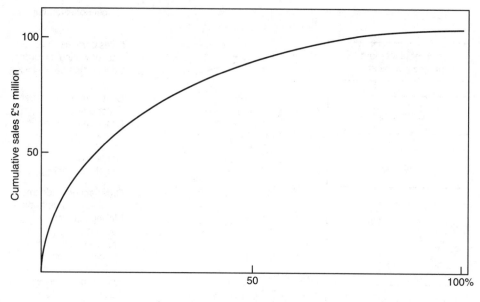

Figure 13.4 Cumulative sales to all customers in 1993.

wholesale distribution to retail customers) minimum order quantity, a policy consistent with that of its competitors and other companies with the same type of distribution channel. The outcome was a 5% loss of customers over and above a more general decline before this minimum order quantity was introduced. Surprisingly, there was no significant loss in total sales value and as expected, distribution costs fell significantly as there were less orders to be delivered.

Figure 13.4 shows the relationship between sales volume and the number of customer outlets. It is a very good example of a Pareto curve and provides some justification for the introduction of a minimum order quantity. The Pareto analysis resulted in two options for P&H:

- the company had to focus its attention on the relatively small number of large customers in order to provide an enhanced level of customer service
- alternative distribution strategies needed to be considered for its smaller customers, i.e. the one-third or so of the customer base which generated just over 13% of P&H's sales volume and which in the main constituted its small-order customers. If the business of this latter group were to be retained, then customer needs had to be assessed and appropriate logistics policies set in place.

Small-order customers: identification of customer needs

A customer service survey of small-order customers supplied from the Haydock depot was carried out in order to assess the probability of retaining such business while servicing them in a profitable manner.

In planning this survey, two methodological issues were addressed: These were:

- how to define small-order customers, in view of the wide range and value of products supplied by P&H
- how best to collect reliable information from them.

For the purposes of this survey an average of £250 per week or less was taken as the threshold for the definition of a small-order customer; for reasons related to statistical response and customer liaison, a personal interview was agreed to be the most appropriate method of data collection.

More specifically the aims of the survey were:

- to identify what factors influence small-order customers in their buying decision
- to ascertain what these customers needed in terms of customer service from their suppliers
- to identify how these customers perceived the customer service provided by P&H.

The final questionnaire which was used, following a pilot investigation, is shown in Appendix 13.1. The nature of the survey meant that the data was collected by means of face to face interviews at the customer's premises by senior management at P&H. Other methods of data collection were not considered, in part due to constraints of time and the commercial sensitivity of the information to be collected.

A sampling frame of the small-order customers was drawn up from the company's records. Respondents were selected on a simple random basis from four main high density urban areas (north Manchester, central/south Manchester, north Liverpool, north Cheshire, south Merseyside and the Wirral). In total, 63 interviews were carried out – this represented just 1% of P&H's total customer base, but 6.2% of its small-order customers.

Ten variables were identified by P&H management as being relevant to the buying decision. These were:

- price
- payment terms
- invoicing accuracy
- product quality
- product availability
- reliability of supply
- delivery lead times
- ease of order placement
- response to problems
- sales and marketing support.

Table 13.3 shows the ranked responses to these variables.

Customer service, both perceived and provided, was assessed by P&H management in terms of:

- ease of order placement
- advice on product non-availability
- merchandising support

Table 13.3 Customer service questionnaire analysis – part 1 the buying decision

Customer name	Price	Payment terms	Invoicing accuracy	Product quality	Product availability	Reliability of supply	Delivery lead times	Ease of order placement	Response to problems	Sales and marketing support
Winwick hosp.	1	3	9	6	5	4	2	7	8	10
McLoughlin	1	2	4	6	5	7	8	3	9	10
Sedgebeer	7	6	9	3	10	5	2	1	8	4
Tansey	3	2	8	7	6	1	9	5	4	10
Ballinger	1	2	3	7	6	4	10	9	8	5
Poplar t/s	9	10	8	2	4	1	3	5	6	7
Rowles	1	4	5	8	2	3	6	7	9	10
O'Hare	1	3	5	6	9	4	2	7	10	8
Garner	1	5	3	4	2	6	9	7	10	8
Williams	1	2	9	10	6	3	4	5	8	7
Daniel	2	7	8	1	5	4	3	6	6	10
Howard	1	9	2	10	4	6	3	7	5	8
Pomfret	2	4	7	8	1	3	5	9	10	6
Mitchell	2	7	10	1	5	9	3	4	6	8
Lamtray	9	1	7	2	8	3	6	5	4	10
Heard	6	7	2	3	8	1	10	4	5	9
Rad	2	1	3	7	4	5	8	9	6	10
Gresty	1	2	10	4	3	5	6	7	9	8
Holt & Son	1	2	6	7	5	8	4	9	3	10
O'Brien	1	9	3	7	2	4	5	8	6	10

Lawler	3	6	10	5	1	2	7	4	9	8
Nicholl	1	5	6	4	2	3	9	8	7	10
Whiteside	1	4	6	8	2	3	7	5	9	10
Smith	1	2	7	4	3	8	9	5	10	6
Cornfield	1	4	10	3	2	6	9	7	5	8
Greaves	2	8	1	6	7	3	9	4	5	10
Roddy	1	8	2	3	4	6	5	9	7	10
Rashid	1	4	2	3	8	7	6	10	9	5
Huxley	3	2	7	5	6	4	1	8	10	9
Jackson	1	10	6	8	7	3	2	4	5	9
NW Gas	1	10	3	2	4	5	9	6	7	8
Preece	1	8	4	5	3	2	7	9	6	10
SUT Danimac	1	9	8	4	5	3	2	7	6	10
GM Gallahers	8	10	3	2	7	1	4	6	5	9
Caine	1	7	9	4	6	2	3	5	8	10
Roscoe	3	4	7	5	1	2	8	9	10	6
Cisco Hyde	1	10	4	2	5	3	6	8	7	9
GM Ciba Geigy	4	9	8	3	1	7	2	6	5	10
Jackson	1	4	8	2	9	7	10	6	5	3
Brit Arkady	4	10	5	1	3	6	8	2	7	9
Sale Moor s/s	1	8	5	4	2	3	7	6	9	10
Thornton	1	5	6	2	3	4	7	8	9	10
Robinson	1	3	5	6	2	4	7	9	8	10
Gibbons	1	8	6	4	2	5	7	3	9	10
Culceth hall	1	5	8	2	3	10	4	6	7	9
GMEX centre	10	9	8	6	7	1	2	3	4	5
Titterington	1	2	3	6	10	4	7	8	5	9
Totals	109	262	278	218	215	200	272	295	336	400

- stock and order systems
- product promotions
- sales person's visit
- invoicing clarity and accuracy
- returns and credit procedures
- completeness of order
- ability to minimize stockholdings
- accuracy of order
- planned delivery day
- planned delivery time
- 24/48-hour product availability
- emergency deliveries
- regular delivery driver.

Table 13.4 shows the customers' responses in terms of their customer service expectations; Table 13.5 shows their assessment of the service performance provided by P&H.

Transport options

Deliveries to all customers to date had been made in vehicles owned by P&H of 12.5 tonnes gvw, carrying a maximum payload of 6 tonnes. An analysis of cost data (Table 13.6) showed that these cost £0.78 per kilometre to operate.

P&H operated thirty-three 12.5-tonne vehicles from the Haydock depot, averaging 17 drops per vehicle day. An average daily requirement was for 29 vehicles to be used. Periods of high volume demand were satisfied by the 'spot hire' (a situation where vehicles and drivers are hired at short notice from hauliers and agencies for work over a relatively short time period and with no particular on-going commitment) of additional vehicles and drivers.

A computerized vehicle routing and scheduling package was used to develop a more efficient and appropriate delivery service for small order customers in response to the customer service survey, whilst retaining 12.5-tonne vehicles. The results of this modelling were

- a reduction in inter-drop distances by 11% to 11.2 km
- a reduction in unit distribution costs to £0.67 per kilometre
- a net saving of two vehicles and drivers from the former 33 vehicle maximum.

The transport options identified were:

(i)   to operate smaller delivery vans (e.g. 3.5 tonnes)
(ii) to service small-order customers from van sales
(iii) to contract out all transport
(iv) to franchise small-order deliveries
(v)   to retain an own-account fleet of 12.5-tonne vehicles.

An assessment of these options was carried out by the company in 1993. The aim was to arrive at the best option in terms of customer service and total logistics costs. Initial views on the options from P&H managers were as follows.

Table 13.4 Customer service expectation responses

How important is this aspect of service to you?	Unimportant	Of little importance	Important	Very important	Essential	Total
Ease of order placement	2.17%	2.17%	45.65%	17.39%	32.62%	100%
Advice on product non-availability	2.17%	10.87%	45.65%	19.57%	21.74%	100%
Merchandising support	19.57%	34.78%	36.96%	4.35%	4.34%	100%
Stock and order systems	26.09%	21.74%	32.61%	8.70%	10.86%	100%
Product promotions	17.39%	28.26%	36.96%	13.04%	4.35%	100%
Sales persons visit	10.87%	15.22%	26.09%	23.91%	23.91%	100%
Invoicing clarity and accuracy			26.09%	41.30%	32.61%	100%
Returns and credit procedures	2.17%	4.35%	28.26%	43.48%	21.74%	100%
Completeness of order		2.17%	28.26%	32.61%	36.96%	100%
Ability to minimize stockholdings	2.22%	13.33%	28.89%	22.22%	33.34%	100%
Accuracy of order			10.87%	56.52%	32.61%	100%
Planned delivery day	4.35%	6.52%	23.91%	28.26%	36.96%	100%
Planned delivery time	7.50%	22.50%	20.00%	27.50%	22.50%	100%
24-hour product availability	15.22%	19.57%	32.61%	26.09%	6.51%	100%
48-hour product availability	13.04%	28.26%	39.13%	10.87%	8.70%	100%
Emergency deliveries	17.39%	15.22%	32.61%	26.09%	8.69%	100%
Regular delivery driver	28.26%	10.87%	28.26%	21.74%	10.87%	100%

Table 13.5 P&H service performance

	Unacceptable	Poor	Satisfactory	Good	Excellent	Total
Ease of order placement		2.13%	17.02%	44.68%	36.17%	100%
Advice on product non-availability		27.66%	34.04%	23.40%	14.90%	100%
Merchandising support	8.51%	19.15%	48.94%	19.15%	4.27%	100%
Stock and order systems	4.26%	8.51%	61.70%	17.02%	8.51%	100%
Product promotions	2.13%	23.40%	29.79%	38.30%	6.38%	100%
Sales persons visit	4.26%	6.38%	21.28%	25.53%	42.55%	100%
Invoicing clarity and accuracy		4.26%	19.15%	34.04%	42.55%	100%
Returns and credit procedures	6.38%	10.64%	27.66%	34.04%	21.28%	100%
Completeness of order	2.13%	8.51%	19.15%	51.06%	19.15%	100%
Ability to minimize stockholdings		10.81%	18.92%	43.24%	27.03%	100%
Accuracy of order		4.26%	27.66%	40.42%	27.66%	100%
Planned delivery day			19.15%	40.43%	40.42%	100%
Planned delivery time	2.13%	10.64%	46.81%	17.02%	23.40%	100%
24-hour product availability	2.13%	2.13%	40.42%	36.17%	19.15%	100%
48-hour product availability	4.26%	2.13%	59.56%	12.77%	21.28%	100%
Emergency deliveries		2.27%	54.55%	15.91%	27.27%	100%
Regular delivery driver	2.13%	12.77%	42.55%	27.66%	14.89	100%

Table 13.6   Haydock depot: distribution costs for 12.5-tonne vehicles (April–December 1992)

Section A. Branch and central costs

	Total cost (£)	Cost per km (£)
Property repairs	8015.60	0.007
Business and water rates	3288.02	0.003
Capital charge (roll cages)	24,562.49	0.021
Branch expenses	27,810.00	0.023
Administration expenses	15,480.00	0.013
Standard expenses	21,660.00	0.018
Established costs (subtotal)	100,816.11	0.085

Section B. Standing costs (based on 34 × 12.5-tonne vehicles)

	Total cost (£)	Cost per km (£)
Licences	11,985.00	0.010
Wages and salaries (transport)	418,191.22	0.353
Wages and salaries (workshop)	31,425.00	0.026
Depreciation	174,420.00	0.147
Insurance	14,280.00	0.012
Workwear	3751.53	0.003
Standing costs (subtotal)	654,052.75	0.551

Section C. Running costs

	Total cost (£)	Cost per km (£)
Fuel	109,909.17	0.093
General running costs	12,292.26	0.010
Maintenance and accident repair	23,451.30	0.020
Vehicle hire	18,265.91	0.015
Running costs subtotal	163,918.64	0.138
Total all costs	**918,787.50**	**0.775**

Standing costs per day/van based on 34 vans = £69.70.
Actual kilometres driven for the period = 1,185,702.
Average vans per vehicle day = 200 km.

Option (i), involving the operation of small delivery vans, had various attractions. In particular, by transferring small orders to small vehicles, delivery requirements could be serviced in a more cost-effective manner and there were likely to be improvements in the level of service provided to small-order-customers. Computer modelling indicated that the total fleet requirement would be for 29 12.5-tonne vehicles and five 3.5-tonne vans. Capital savings were 3%, although operating costs were estimated to increase by over 9%.

Option (ii) was given little consideration, largely on account of the wide product range stocked by P&H. A general van sales service was seen as impractical under these circumstances.

Contracting out, Option (iii), seemed to have attractions from a purely transport standpoint. However, the nature of P&H's business was that it required a quality service to customers, with a quick response to meet customers' needs. Moreover, the driver of the delivery vehicle was invariably the only contact with the customer.

Option (iv) was in certain respects innovative. It was based on the principle that small-order customers would be serviced by self-employed owner drivers, with P&H paying the franchisee a fee for the deliveries which were made. Franchising has many attractions and could provide a means of reducing overall transport and logistics costs, while not reducing the quality of customer service.

To retain own-account operations with the existing fleet, Option (v) was an obvious strategy. However, the increasingly competitive wholesale environment, along with the delivery constraints referred to above, inevitably meant that direct transport costs within total logistics costs would continue to increase.

Concluding remarks

P&H were clear that customer service was essential to the company's well-being; however there was concern that the small order customers might not be profitable because of the cost of servicing them at current service levels.

The management now had to review the outcome of the customer service survey and marry the results with the various transport options that had been generated in order to decide what policy should be adopted in regard to the small-order business.

Appendix 13.1: Customer Service Questionnaire

Part 1 – The buying decision

Please 'rank' in order of importance each of the following categories to reflect how it affects your decision when you are choosing whether or not to buy from a particular supplier or not. In ranking these options it should be on the basis of '1 highest' to '10 lowest'. For those factors Ranked 1 to 5, and given 100 points of value, please indicate their relative importance by allocating points to each.

	Rank	Relative importance
Price	_____	_____
Payment terms	_____	_____
Invoicing accuracy	_____	_____
Product quality	_____	_____
Product availability	_____	_____
Reliability of supply	_____	_____
Delivery lead times	_____	_____
Ease of order placement	_____	_____
Response to problems	_____	_____
Sales and marketing support	_____	_____
Other requirement (please state):	....	

Part 2 – The service decision

	How important is this aspect of service to you?					How do you rate P&H?				
	1. Unimportant 2. Of little importance 3. Important 4. Very important 5. Essential					1. Unacceptable 2. Poor 3. Satisfactory 4. Good 5. Excellent				
Ease of order placement	1	2	3	4	5	1	2	3	4	5
Advice on product non-availability	1	2	3	4	5	1	2	3	4	5
Merchandising support	1	2	3	4	5	1	2	3	4	5
Stock and order systems	1	2	3	4	5	1	2	3	4	5
Product promotions	1	2	3	4	5	1	2	3	4	5
Sales persons visits	1	2	3	4	5	1	2	3	4	5
Invoicing clarity and accuracy	1	2	3	4	5	1	2	3	4	5
Returns and credit procedures	1	2	3	4	5	1	2	3	4	5
Completeness of order	1	2	3	4	5	1	2	3	4	5
Ability to minimize stockholding	1	2	3	4	5	1	2	3	4	5
Accuracy of order	1	2	3	4	5	1	2	3	4	5
Planned delivery day	1	2	3	4	5	1	2	3	4	5
Planned delivery time	1	2	3	4	5	1	2	3	4	5
24-hour product availability	1	2	3	4	5	1	2	3	4	5
48-hour product availability	1	2	3	4	5	1	2	3	4	5
Emergency deliveries	1	2	3	4	5	1	2	3	4	5
Regular delivery driver	1	2	3	4	5	1	2	3	4	5

Other requirements (please state): ....

Part 3 – Customer profile

Circle the following answers:

1. How long have you been trading with Palmer and Harvey?

   less than 1   1–3 years   3–10 years   10 years

2. Which of the following products do you buy from Palmer and Harvey?

Tobacco	Confectionery	Grocery
Snacks	Chemist sundries	Soft drinks

3. Approximately what percentage of each product group is supplied by Palmer and Harvey?

Tobacco ......%	Confectionery ......%	Grocery ......%
Snacks ......%	Chemist sundries ......%	Soft drinks ......%

4. Of the product groups discussed, what are your average weekly purchases?

	£	£	£	£	£
Tobacco	0–250	250–500	500–1000	1000–1500	1500+
Confectionery	0–250	250–500	500–1000	1000–1500	1500+
Grocery	0–250	250–500	500–1000	1000–1500	1500+
Chemist sundries	0–250	250–500	500–1000	1000–1500	1500+
Snacks	0–250	250–500	500–1000	1000–5000	1500+
Soft drinks	0–250	250–500	500–1000	1000–5000	1500+

5. What is the total weekly turnover of your business?

   less than £1500   £1500–3000   £3000–4000   £4000+

Distribution and pricing policy in Ukraine

David A. Menachof
Department of Maritime Business, University of Plymouth, UK

Pepsi Cola has been doing business in the former Soviet Union for over 20 years. Bottling and distribution of their product is done in major cities throughout the Commonwealth of Independent States (CIS) via franchise agreements. This case examines Pepsi Cola International's (PCI) current distribution methods along with resulting product pricing outcomes. As the economic transformation of this part of the world continues, is a change in the distribution methods currently in place advised or warranted?

Introduction

In 1995, a PCI executive team were reviewing the company's Ukrainian distribution and pricing policy. The team was made up of top-level executives from PCI's Vienna office that serves as headquarters for central and eastern Europe, the former Soviet Union and central Asia operations, along with the Vice-President Operations–Moscow and several members from PCI's US headquarters in Valhalla, New York.

The Pepsi generation is now growing up in the former Soviet Union. They have had the opportunity to drink Pepsi since 1973. The problems Pepsi faced in gaining access to this huge market were numerous, but the potential is staggering. Sales of Pepsi in 1993 for Russia totalled 78 million cans (see Table 14.1). However, the typical Russian drinks only seven soft drinks per year, and the typical Ukrainian only 28 soft drinks compared to the 784 consumed by Americans. Currently, PCI has over 85 bottling ventures throughout the former Soviet Union and eastern Europe.

Prior to 1994, several countertrade arrangements were entered into as Soviet law prevented PCI from repatriating earnings to the USA. PCI received Stolichnaya Vodka as one method of payment. In Ukraine, PCI entered into a joint venture with a Crimean shipyard. A simple explanation is that PCI invested its local earnings in the shipyard, then the shipyard built oil tankers which were sold on the world market for hard currency, of which PCI's share of the proceeds were not required to return to Ukraine. Although

Figure 14.1 Pepsi Cola franchise bottling operations located in underlined cities.

such countertrade agreements are no longer required, PCI retains an interest in the Ukrainian shipyard. However, despite all the troubles faced by PCI, Pepsi has become the dominant cola in the former Soviet Union. In fact, they did such a good job, that the Soviet population began to think of Pepsi as a local product; a situation which actually

Table 14.1 Selected soft drink consumption

Country	Population (thousands)	Cans per capita
Ukraine	51,800	28
Russia	148,100	7
USA	248,710	784
Japan	123,612	95
Germany	78,500	380
France	56,556	130
Great Britain	53,926	266
Canada	26,800	434
Australia	17,843	337
Czech Republic	10,400	200

Source: *The Green Sheet*, Beverage Digest.

hurt their image. Pepsi bottles are no longer written with Cyrillic characters, having reverted back to the original in order to emphasis the product's western image shortly after the breakup of the Soviet Union.

In Ukraine, Pepsi is still the cola of choice, but a Coca-Cola bottling plant has recently been built and in Spring 1995 started production in the western Ukrainian city of L'vov. Wishing to maintain its market dominance, PCI was looking at its current business practices and evaluating whether or not change is necessary.

A general word about Ukrainian distribution

Although Ukraine is technically part of Europe, it has not advanced as far as some of its eastern European neighbours with its economic transformation. A standing joke among several expatriates living in Ukraine was that 'You know you are in the east when your western goods come from Poland.' It is generally estimated that Ukraine is where Poland was 7–10 years ago in the transformation process. How fast Ukraine can catch up will be dependent on the success of the first phase of mass privatization that occurred under President Kuchma in the autumn of 1995; however, until those changes actually occur, the current situation is described here.

Transit times are slow. One can drive the 487 km between Kiev and Odessa in just over eight hours (60 kph). Rail service is even slower, with five-day service provided (but not promised). Delays can occur at every step of the movement. One shipper was ecstatic when his airfreight shipment cleared customs in only 10 days.

Distribution is generally carried out by the large state-transport companies, small private firms with only a few trucks and individuals who own their one vehicle, not necessarily a truck. On the streets, one will see trucks being used without regard to the specialized nature of the vehicle. Insulated trucks are used for hauling furniture. Dump trucks are used for hauling produce. The point being that no matter what type of truck one has, that person will use it in order to earn any income possible.

A visit to any of the major Ukrainian ports will amaze the visitor. The ports are full of goods imported to the country but yet to be released because of payment problems. Because of inflation, importers have lost their purchasing power, and many simply cannot afford to pay for the products now that they have arrived. Port operations have been hampered as more and more goods pile up. A Black Sea Shipping Company official explained that the space situation is so desperate that Ukraine-bound cargo that is not pre-paid is being off-loaded in Pireus, Greece because they have literally run out of space. Although no-one will officially verify it, several sources have told of one state-owned customs brokers that informs the port's 'mafia' regarding the identity of individuals and firms importing high-value commodities.

At the same time, there seems to be an increase in theft and banditry. Trucks travelling between cities are being forced at gun point to relinquish their goods. This increase in theft has resulted in several cargo insurance companies refusing to cover cargo for any inland transport beyond the port of entry within the CIS.

'Conventional' warehouse space is virtually unavailable. Warehousing as it currently exists is described as any available space. Spare rooms in buildings, basements and shipping containers are prevalent here. Contracts with landlords are literally only as good as the person that signed it. If a landlord reneges on a contract there is very little that can be done from a practical standpoint, except to try to renegotiate or try and find a new landlord. Laws covering contracts are not fully developed, neither is the entire legal system relating to private property.

The majority of the distribution equipment is over 20 years old. Port facilities are beginning to be upgraded, but are still one or two generations behind the west. Inland facilities are much worse. Containers are hand-loaded as in most instances, forklifts are nowhere. Western investors are increasingly wary of placing equipment in this part of the world because of the high possibility of theft.

Pepsi distribution

With the current channel of distribution, PCI is not in the delivery business as they are in other countries. There are no Pepsi trucks plying the streets. There are no Pepsi drivers who make sure the various stores on the route are well stocked. There aren't even Pepsi machines to provide a drink at any time a consumer wants one (the fact that there are no coins currently in circulation in Ukraine may explain part of the reason, vandalism is the other).

PCI sells and delivers its concentrate to its 12 licensed bottlers throughout Ukraine (see Figure 14.1 and Table 14.2 for locations). The concentrate is shipped by container from PCI's plant in Cork, Ireland to Rotterdam, The Netherlands and St Petersburg, Russia. From the ports it is either trucked or railed to the various bottlers using local transport arrangements. Even Pepsi is subject to all of the general problems described in the previous section, with delays being common once the goods have entered the former Soviet Union. In December 1995, PCI shipped from a facility in India as an alternative source of concentrate supply to the former Soviet Union. The shipment was in transit when this case was written, so the feasibility of long-term use is uncertain at this time.

During the winter months, PCI uses rail transport as roads are poor and are often impassable for days/weeks at a time. Rail service must be secured via negotiation and contracted in advance of the season and always includes armed guards that travel with each section of cars. These cars must also be heated to prevent the product from freezing, but there have been several instances where the fuel has run out causing the product to freeze and become unusable, even after thawing.

After bottling, the bottlers sell the Pepsi ex-works. This means that neither PCI nor its bottlers distribute the finished product. Distributors make their purchases from the factory and are free to distribute the product as they please. The result is regular supplies

Table 14.2   Pepsi franchise bottling plants in Ukraine

Plant location	
Cherkassy	Chernivtsy
Dnepropetrovsk	Donetsk
Yevpatoria	Kharkiv
Khorostkiv	Kiev
Mirgorod	Simferopol
Zaporoshje	Van Pur – Kiev

of Pepsi in Kiev and some of the other major cities in Ukraine. In smaller cities, such as Ternopol, the supply is irregular and stockouts are accepted as normal. When a major distributor arrives in one of these small cities (200,000 is considered small in Ukraine), the supply is immediately bought by local distributors and the product eventually makes its way to the kiosks and stores for sale to the consumer.

In some small villages, the only time Pepsi is available is when an individual makes a trip to a city and brings back a supply for resale.

By the time, a bottle of Pepsi reaches the final consumer, it may have been bought and sold four or more times. Each person in the distribution chain feels entitled to earn a profit, so as the Pepsi changes hands, the price continues to rise.

The result is that the price of Pepsi increases as one travels away from a licensed bottler's location. In March, 1995, the price of a 0.33-litre returnable glass bottle of Pepsi was 30,000 karbovantse (US$1=154,000kbv) in Kiev, where there is a bottling plant. In Odessa, the price was 40,000kbv, while in Ternopil, only 35,000 kbv.

Through other channels, 2-litre bottles of Pepsi arrive from Belarus, St Petersburg, Greece, Austria and Israel. The price of the 2-litre bottle is about 250,000 kbv in Odessa. An interesting observation is that in Odessa, a 0.33-litre aluminium can of Pepsi from Greece sold for 60,000 kbv. Even more interesting is that some Ukrainians consider the Greek, or other western-made Pepsi, to be superior and therefore worth the higher price.

Business realities in Ukraine

Political and fiscal instability is always a concern. At the time of this writing, Ukrainian President Kuchma has kept everything together. It does not seem likely that ethnic Ukrainians and ethnic Russians will fall into armed clashes. Ukraine, unlike Russia, does not have this desire for a 'Greater Russia' (i.e. the former Soviet Union borders run by people in Moscow), and therefore, does not have the level of internal conflict that Russia has with the Chechen crisis among others. However, fiscal problems continue to plague this part of the world. Most of the new entrepreneurs do not want to make substantial capital investments (long-term) because they are not sure of their country's future. Most thoughts are on how to make money the quickest way possible, because there is this feeling among the new élite that the old guard may rise up again.

The 'Soviet' mentality frustrates many westerners attempting to do business here. The western business thought is generally if the law does not explicitly say we cannot do something, we can. The 'Soviet' thought is that if the law does not say we can do something, we cannot (see Exhibit 14.1).

Another major difference in mentality is the time frame for making business decisions. On one hand, Ukrainian business people are very reluctant to make decisions, but those that they do make are basically of a short-term nature. Many decisions are based on no more than 90 days. If there is no profit in it in that time frame, they are not interested. Even if you do have an agreement, it may be renegotiated along the way.

It is also a very difficult process to get any cost/budget information out of your Ukrainian partner. In discussions with several Peace Corps business volunteers, one of their biggest frustrations was trying to assist their Ukrainian business through an examination of their business practices. Usually a business sets up two sets of accounting books; one for the official records and one for actual transactions. With tax rates

Exhibit 14.1 The battle for the Ukraine

'I got my first export licence back in November,' explains one westerner battling to do business in Ukraine.

'The law changed, and I lost it. I got a second licence – lost it; a third, and lost it again. Now I'm on my fourth. To get this far I've had to get permissions from 25 different people. For one meeting, I waited 15 days in a hotel room with fleas in the bed. I'm paying one high up guy's son a salary. Next week another man's two kids are going on a fortnight's holiday to the States – out of my pocket.'

In investment terms, Ukraine has been Central Europe's ugly duckling. The Kiev bourse boasts only a handful of shares, only two of which are traded in any number – Ukraina, a bank and Ukrechflot, a shipping company. Despite a population of 52m, Ukraine attracted only around $200m in foreign capital last year. Hungary and the Czech Republic, both a fifth of Ukraine's size, won $1.4 billion and $7750m respectively. One western-agency official says that foreign investment is still at the 'visit the meat-packing factory and throw up' stage.

This may be changing. Serhiy Oskanich, founder of a small local investment bank, says that over the past three months contacts with foreign investors have increased 'maybe ten times' – and the talk has moved from vague discussions about the country's future to 'real projects'. This is partly due to a new mass privatization programme. Ukraine's reformist president, Leonid Kuchma, aims to auction 8000 big state-owned enterprises this year.

Unfortunately, fewer than half of those firms are likely to be sold off. Many of the plum companies – steel mills, high-tech ex-military establishments, telephone companies – have either been already bought by their own workers, or put on a list of 'strategic' companies that Ukraine's communist-stuffed parliament has decided should not be sold. Even if enough companies are auctioned to revive the Kiev bourse, chaotic securities regulation is likely to mean that Ukraine's stockmarket makes Moscow's market seem orderly by comparison.

Another way for foreigners to invest in Ukraine is through start-ups, but the absence of any functioning commercial law makes this a risky process. Scott Carlson, who is in charge of disbursing $150m of American government money to small businesses, tells his loan officers to visit each of the borrowers in their portfolio 'at least once a week'. Tales abound of foreign businessmen being squeezed out of joint ventures by dishonest local partners, or worn down by regulation.

The result? Western firms in Ukraine fall into two camps. The first is a handful of deep-pocketed multinationals prepared to sit it out. 'You have to come to Ukraine for the long term,' argues Franck Behamou of Johnson Wax, an American household-products firm. Tambrands an American tampon maker, and Tetrapak, a Swedish packaging firm, also own factories in Ukraine. The second camp is a collection of freewheeling individuals who have turned their taste for Ukraine's awfulness into a sort of competitive advantage over less patient rivals. 'The margins are so good,' insists one, 'that even with all delays I will still have made a profit.' He remains in a minority.

formerly up to 90% of sales, it would be impossible by western standards to profitably operate a business; however, if you severely underdeclare sales, it is possible to be very profitable, but it means that you show no one this second set of books, including the Peace Corps volunteer who may be trying to help you or your foreign business partner. It takes a long time to gain the trust of these new entrepreneurs, because some the foreigners who have arrived before you, have taken advantage of these people, leaving no profit for the local partners.

Conclusion

The PCI executive team were responsible for reviewing the company's Ukraine policy. They would have to think carefully about not only what they would like to do in terms of developing the distribution and pricing policy but perhaps more importantly about what would be feasible within the country's macro- and micro-economic climate. Even though the company had been trading in the Soviet Union for over 20 years, the decision team still felt woefully short of information about Ukraine because things were changing so rapidly. However, the policy review became even more critical as it became clear that following investment in the L'vov plant, Coca-Cola were set to make a strong attack on the Ukrainian market.

Bibliography

Adamski, C. (1994) How to stay in the money, internationally. *Financial Executive*, 10, 19–21.

Beverage Digest (1994) 1993 global all channel soft drink corporate shares in 87 countries, 2 September.

Konrad, W. (1992) Cola wars: all noisy on the eastern front. *Business Week*, 27 January, pp. 94–5.

The Economist (1995) The battle for Ukraine, 11 February, p. 62.

New York Times, Business as usual in Kiev: by taunt and bribe, 12 May, p. D3 (1995).

Acknowledgements

The author would like to thank Jay McDowell of Pepsi Cola International for his assistance in reviewing and verifying the information in this case.

The case was developed by the author during 1994–5, whilst teaching through a Fulbright Scholarship at Odessa State University, Ukraine.

Evaluation of contract distribution tenders*

Jane Parkin
University of Huddersfield, Huddersfield, UK

Company background

Rank Hovis McDougall (RHM) is a leading UK food manufacturer. In 1992 RHM Food Services Division was one of five operating divisions within the Rank Hovis McDougall Group plc. Divisional sales in total were £250m and the profit before interest and tax was approximately £25m which constituted approximately 25% of the overall group activity. An organizational chart is shown in Figure 15.1.

The Food Services Division had a small planning team based at the corporate head-quarters in Windsor which was charged with the task of exploring initiatives to reduce divisional costs by using the expertise or facilities in the individual companies for the benefit of the division as a whole.

Distribution costs were highlighted as one of the areas where the consolidation of customers, products, fleets, warehouses or facilities could well reduce the overall costs within the division. After some preliminary analysis of costs three businesses were identified as potentially good candidates for the exercise: McDougalls Catering Foods, RHM Ingredients (RHMI) and Pasta Foods. In 1992 the distribution networks of the three businesses were run completely independently. The businesses had different customer geographic profiles: the majority of the McDougalls and Pasta sales were in the south of Britain, whereas most of the RHMI customer demand was in the north.

The McDougalls business based in Reading and Bristol was primarily serviced by an own-fleet operation supplemented in part by some subcontracted haulage. The RHMI business based mainly in Ossett, but with one distribution depot in Dunstable, was serviced by a fully subcontracted ex-factory distribution operation for warehousing and delivery. Pasta Foods with its main manufacturing and warehousing site at Great Yarmouth and a factory at Ipswich was serviced wholly by subcontracted vehicles whilst

*Data available on the Internet (see page xxii).

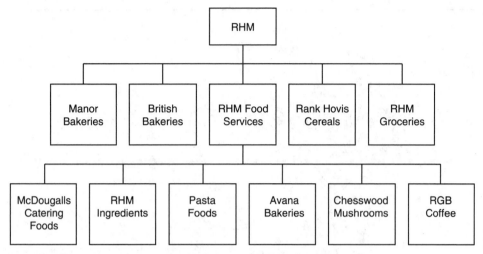

Figure 15.1 Organizational chart of Rank Hovis McDougall (RHM).

the warehouse was operated on an in-house basis (see Figure 15.2 for details of factories and depots for the three businesses).

A working party was formed, consisting of the financial controller of RHM Food Services and the distribution managers from each of the three companies to review, the warehousing and transport operations of the three companies. The objectives of the study were to consider whether a more cost-effective distribution network could be produced through synergies of the three businesses and whether the entire distribution operation should be contracted out. The financial objective was to reduce the total variable cost of distribution (which for the three businesses was some £7 million) by 10%.

An early decision was made by the working party that no major change would be made unless it would result in overall annual savings of at least £500,000.

Activities of the working party

The working party met every two weeks. They first decided what data they would need on the existing operation and decided to work with the annual sales and production volumes for 1991–2. Total annual costs of the current distribution system were ascertained (see Table 15.1). In order to analyse the effects of seasonality they collected information on the monthly throughput for each of the three operations for the complete year (see Table 15.2). Finally they decided they needed details of all deliveries for a typical five-week period and chose to work with Period One 1991–2 (September 1991). This was a time-consuming process as customer lists and addresses plus order details had to be extracted manually from computer databases. A sample of this data can be seen in Table 15.3. The data collection stage took approximately two months.

The next stage consisted of designing an invitation to tender document and contacting various contract distribution companies. The contractors were asked to make detailed proposals for amalgamating the distribution operations of the three divisions and to give the cost of operating their proposed system on a contract basis. Three major UK distribution companies responded with initial proposals which involved possible

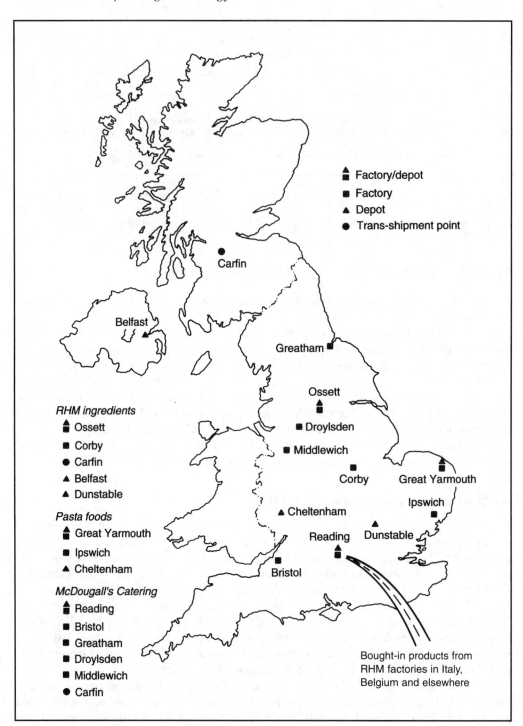

Figure 15.2   Rank Hovis McDougall (RHM) food services existing network.

Table 15.1 RHM existing operations: cost structure by activity (all costs in £ thousands)

By company

	RHMI	McDougall	Pasta	Total
Transport: own account	957	815	26	1798
Transport: subcontract	526	521	1227	2274
Warehouse	1110	1084	337	2531
Total cost	2593	2420	1590	6603

By region. (Assuming north costs = RHMI and south costs = McDougall & Pasta)

	North	South	Total
Transport: own account	957	841	1798
Transport: subcontract	526	1748	2274
Total transport	1483	2589	4072
Warehouse	1110	1421	2531
Total cost	2593	4010	6603

distribution depot sites which had to be visited by the working party. The working party gave their comments to the distribution companies and proposals were refined. This took another four months.

Contract distribution proposals

The three distribution companies were given two months to prepare their final proposals and were requested to make a verbal presentation to the RHM project team as well as submitting a detailed written proposal.

At the presentation meeting, one distribution company presented some general ideas

Table 15.2 RHM throughput (in pallets)

Period	Weeks in period	McDougall	RHMI	Pasta
1	5	6446	4519	4796
2	4	5365	3966	4317
3	4	5426	3897	4317
4	5	4430	4444	3837
5	4	3382	3540	4796
6	4	4132	3701	3837
7	5	5628	4605	4796
8	4	4440	3653	3837
9	4	4866	3606	3837
10	5	5858	4580	3837
11	4	4094	3592	2878
12	4	4539	4307	2878
Total		58,606	48,410	47,963

Table 15.3 Sample of detailed delivery data

Schedule date	Customer number	Town	County	Area	Drop size (kg)
05/09/91	0001	Dublin	S. Ireland	Islands	641
03/09/91	0002	Edinburgh	Strathclyde	Scotland	280
03/09/91	0003	Edinburgh	Lothian	Scotland	40
02/09/91	0004	Bude	Cornwall	South west	44
02/09/91	0005	Birmingham	West midlands	Midlands	385
02/09/91	0006	Cornwall	Cornwall	South west	40
02/09/91	0007	Cullompton	Devon	South west	88
02/09/91	0008	Wimborne	Dorset	South west	461
02/09/91	0009	Newham Truro	Cornwall	South west	12
02/09/91	0010	Bodmin	Cornwall	South west	21
02/09/91	0011	Cornwall	Cornwall	South west	76
02/09/91	0012	Ilfracombe	Devon	South west	205
03/09/91	0013	Fife	Fife	Scotland	12
02/09/91	0014	Spalding	Lincolnshire	Midlands	26
02/09/91	0015	Halesowen	West midlands	Midlands	58
02/09/91	0016	Oswestry	Shropshire	Midlands	38
02/09/91	0017	Shrewsbury	Shropshire	Midlands	15
02/09/91	0018	Leicester	Leicestershire	Midlands	10
03/09/91	0019	Newmarket	Suffolk	South east	199
02/09/91	0020	Leicester	Leicestershire	Midlands	72
03/09/91	0021	Bury	Suffolk	South east	60
03/09/91	0022	Rougham	Suffolk	South east	799
02/09/91	0023	Wellingbro	Wellingbro	South east	1189
03/09/91	0024	Loughbro	Leicestershire	Midlands	809
02/09/91	0025	Walsall	West midlands	Midlands	459
03/09/91	0026	Loughbro	Leicestershire	Midlands	1650
02/09/91	0027	Reading	Berkshire	South east	53
02/09/91	0028	Guildford	Surrey	South east	20
02/09/91	0029	Farnborough	Hampshire	South east	25
02/09/91	0030	Southend	Essex	South east	28
02/09/91	0031	Basingstoke	Hampshire	South east	25
02/09/91	0032	Ramsgate	Kent	South east	1098
02/09/91	0033	Aylesbury	Bucks	South east	153
03/09/91	0034	Witney	Oxfordshire	South east	35
02/09/91	0035	Sidcup	Kent	South east	130
03/09/91	0036	Witney	Oxfordshire	South east	37
02/09/91	0037	Edenbridge	Kent	South east	1092
02/09/91	0038	Bangor	Gwynedd	North west	75
02/09/91	0039	Denbigh	Clwyd	North west	6
02/09/91	0040	Denbigh	Clwyd	North west	25

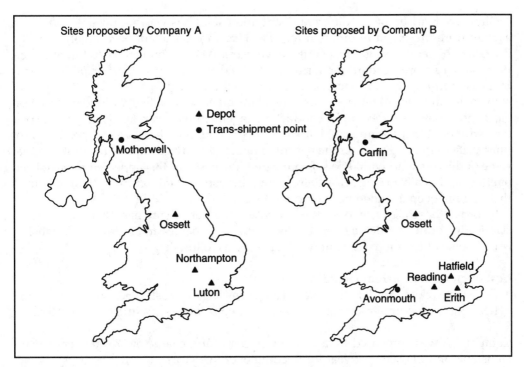

Figure 15.3   Maps showing sites proposed by Companies A and B.

but did not submit a detailed written proposal and was therefore eliminated from further consideration. The remaining two distribution companies presented detailed proposals to the working party having evaluated various scenarios using both distribution planning software (to aid decisions on number and location of depots) and vehicle scheduling software (to aid decisions on number and type of vehicles). Each distribution company put forward more than one solution. Every solution contained both a northern and a southern distribution depot: all solutions agreed that the northern depot should be in Ossett but various different proposals were put forward for the southern depot (see Figure 15.3). Both companies put forward extremely detailed proposals each extending to over 100 pages; a summary of these can be seen in Appendices 15.1 and 15.2.

Evaluation of contract tenders

Because all members of the working party held full-time operational positions within the group, they decided to enlist the aid of an independent consultant in evaluating the contract tenders. The consultant had access to all the documentation, attended meetings of the working party and presentations by the distribution companies.

The consultant's immediate impression from considering the proposed solutions and comparing these with the current RHM distribution operation was that all the proposals offered some cost savings, and that the cheapest alternative (the option from Company B) offered annual savings well in excess of the minimum £500,000 specified by the working party.

Direct comparison of the different distribution solutions was not possible, however, as they were presented in different formats. Had the consultant been involved at the invitation to tender stage, he would have required the contractors to submit their proposals in a more standardized format and would also have been more explicit in terms of the cost and operational factors to be shown within the proposals.

In reviewing the submissions the consultant quickly identified various information gaps and problems for example: contract management fees were unclear; closure costs for redundant depots appeared to have been ignored; there was a possibility of (unspecified) start-up costs for the new operations; although company B had stated that some of the transport would be subcontracted, the costs for this appeared to have been omitted; and finally in every case there were some aspects of the current RHM operation that had not been included in the proposals.

In order to properly analyse the proposals the consultant had therefore to seek clarification or further detail from the distribution companies and RHM on a number of issues, some of the more relevant of which were as follows.

Cost of closure of current facilities
- Dunstable (closed under all proposed solutions) closure cost: £260,000
- Reading (closed under four of the five proposed solutions) closure cost: £400,000.

Company A were prepared to take on these costs for a charge of £73,000 per year for Dunstable and £112,000 per year for Reading over five years.

Company B had included these costs in their first option, but would charge an additional £65,000 per year for Dunstable in the other two options, and an additional £100,000 per year for Reading in their third option, again over a five-year period.

Start-up costs
In their initial proposals, both distribution companies stated that there would be additional start-up costs but these were unspecified. When they were asked to clarify this, Company A detailed start-up costs of £56,000 for the northern depot and £87,000 for the southern depot at Northampton or £101,000 at Luton. Company B would have no start-up costs for the northern depot (as they were already operating the current facility at Ossett) but estimated £24,000 for a southern depot. All these costs were to be amortized annually over a period of five years.

Cost of subcontracted transport for Company B's proposals
This was stated to be £1,092,000 per year.

Distribution operations excluded from the proposals
Finally, each proposal was analysed closely to see which parts of the current operation were excluded from the proposed solutions. It was found that both distribution companies had omitted the costs of operating the existing Pasta Foods warehouses in Yarmouth and Ipswich, and the cost of deliveries to Northern Ireland. In addition, Company A had omitted the direct bulk deliveries from factories to customers. It was estimated that the cost to RHM of these would be £899,000 per year on top of a contract with Company A, or £748,000 with Company B.

Decision making

Once the consultant had gathered this additional information he was in a position to summarize the proposals from both companies, compare them directly with the current RHM operation and make recommendations to the working party.

Appendix 15.1: Proposal submitted by Distribution Company A

1. Summary

- It is proposed that the contract is operated from two distribution centres: in the north from a 60,000 sq. ft. warehouse in the Ossett area, in the south from a 95,000 sq. ft. warehouse either in Northampton (Option 1) or in Luton (Option 2).
- A suitable property has been identified at Northampton and the contract in the south could start within approximately three months of a decision to proceed being made.
- The contract will be for five years.
- The cost for the first year to December 1993 for the lowest cost option will be £5.941 million.
- The warehouse operation will be controlled by a modern warehouse management system with the flexibility to adapt to RHM's future business requirements.

2. Operational overview (Option 1)

- The northern warehouse at Ossett will stockhold and pick all RHMI products.
- The southern warehouse at Northampton will stockhold and pick all McDougall's and Pasta Food products.
- Pasta Foods products for large retailers will continue to be held and picked at Great Yarmouth and Ipswich.
- Ossett will collect stock direct from the factories at Ossett, Corby and Greatham.
- Northampton will collect stock direct from the other factories.
- Ossett will trunk overnight to Northampton picked RHMI orders for radial distribution ex Northampton and for onward trunking to Cheltenham and Reading. Ossett will also trunk overnight with all three companies products to a trans-shipment point at Motherwell in Scotland for onward distribution to customers.
- Cheltenham and Reading depots will use their own vehicles to collect all three companies picked orders from Northampton.
- Northampton will collect stock from Great Yarmouth at the same time as collecting picked orders.
- There will be sufficient spare fleet at night in Northampton (drivers would need to be spot hired) to cover peak trunking and collections both in the north to Ossett and throughout the south.

Option 2 is as Option 1 except that Luton will be the location for the southern warehouse.

3. Warehousing

- Stockholding:

Average week	Northern warehouse	Southern warehouse
Pallets picked	880	1408
Weeks stock cover	4	4
Pallets in stock	3520	5632
+20% spare capacity	880	1408
Storage requirements:		
pallets	4400	7040
sq. ft.	60,500	88,000

No provision has been made at either warehouse for growth in the level of stock-holding.

- A conventional order picking system seems most suitable. In the southern warehouse, Pasta Foods and McDougalls picking locations will be segregated. The reserve stocks for each company will be controlled by the warehouse management system without the need for physical segregation, thus minimizing the number of pallet spaces required.
- The warehouse management system will report the number of pallet spaces used by each company and the number of free pallet spaces.
- Full pallet movements will be carried out by electric reach trucks; case picking will be undertaken by electric-powered pallet trucks. Initially, radio data terminals will not be used; this can be considered further at a later stage.

4. Locations

- A suitable property has been identified for the southern warehouse outside Northampton only 5 minutes from the M1 motorway. It is a modern warehouse unit of approximately 95,500 sq. ft. with ample parking space and is currently unoccupied.
- A search for property in the Luton area has so far not identified a suitable property for the alternative southern warehouse. Therefore for the purpose of providing a costed solution, a theoretical location has been taken using average market rents and rates for warehouses close to the M25 motorway.
- Similarly a search for a property in the Ossett area has failed to identify a suitable location and the northern warehouse has therefore been costed at the prevailing market rates.

5. Management

- Overall day-day-day management will be under the control of a distribution centre manager at each of the two main locations. The northern warehouse manager will also act as contract manager for RHMI; the southern warehouse manager will be the contract manager for McDougalls and Pasta Foods.
- The depots are designed to operate on a five-day, 24-hour basis.

6. Cost summary from Distribution Company A (all costs in £ thousands)

	Option 1			Option 2		
	North (Ossett)	**South (Northampton)**	**Total**	**North (Ossett)**	**South (Luton)**	**Total**
Warehouse						
Warehouse labour	105	363	468	105	363	468
Management	135	154	289	135	154	289
MHE	60	98	158	60	98	158
Trans-shipment	33	52	85	33	52	85
Clerical salaries	65	116	181	65	116	181
Other clerical	46	44	90	46	44	90
Occupancy	437	756	1193	437	918	1355
Other costs	37	67	104	37	67	104
Total warehouse	918	1650	2568	918	1812	2730
Transport						
Drivers	418	699	1117	418	638	1056
Management/clerical	73	91	164	73	91	164
Vehicle standing	256	445	701	256	452	708
Vehicle running	251	441	692	251	449	700
Peak cover	19	32	51	19	30	49
Fuel and oil	261	372	633	261	352	613
Other costs	6	9	15	6	8	14
Total transport	1284	2089	3373	1284	2020	3304
Grand total	2202	3739	5941	2202	3832	6034

7. Financial assumptions

- Costs are based on input prices for the first year of operation.
- Mechanical handling equipment costs are based on contract hire for a period of five years.
- Vehicles for this contract will be purchased by Company A.
- Warehouse personnel and drivers will be paid within an annual hours agreement.
- All stock losses over 0.02% value will be recovered by RHM from Company A.
- Company A will provide all relevant insurances except for stock held within the warehouses which will be covered by RHM.
- Company A will provide for depreciation on a straight line basis as follows:

	Percentage per annum
Buildings	2
Plant and equipment	10
Computers	16.67
Tractors and rigid vehicles	20
Trailers	10

- Company A will make all the financing arrangements to fund the projected capital expenditure at finance charges of 12.5% per year.
- Costs exclude start-up costs. It is assumed that these will be recovered either by amortizing the costs over the length of the contract or by a separate settlement.
- It has been assumed that property will be leased for five years.

8. Terms and conditions of contract

- The proposals assume that the contract will be for a period of five years.
- Costs have been based on values for the year to December 1993. It is assumed that rates will be renegotiated annually to take account of inflation and changes to operating parameters.
- Fuel prices are based on the current fuel price to Company A of 33p per litre. It is assumed that a fuel clause will be included in the terms and conditions contract which will ensure that neither party is penalized as a result of fluctuations in the price of fuel.
- Invoices for the storage, handling and distribution service will be submitted weekly for settlement within 21 days of the date of invoice.

Appendix 15.2: Proposal submitted by Distribution Company B

Company B already own the site at Osset and operate it on behalf of RMH. The initial proposal was for a southern warehouse for McDougalls and Pasta Foods at Hatfield, – an existing site owned by Company B. Following discussions with RHM who were unhappy with the location of Hatfield for the southern depot, two alternatives at Erith and Reading were considered. In each case Company B found a suitable modern, high-specification warehouse with approximately 70,000 sq. ft. of storage space. The detailed proposal discusses the Hatfield site for the southern depot, but the cost summaries include all three options.

1. Introduction

The proposal is for:

- A northern warehouse for RHMI at Ossett – an existing site owned by Company B.
- A southern warehouse for McDougalls and Pasta Foods at Hatfield – an existing site owned by Company B.
- Scottish deliveries via Carfin depot (an existing site owned by Company B) and a third party that will be subcontracted by Company B.
- South-west deliveries via an existing depot in Avonmouth and a third-party transport operator.
- Great Yarmouth factory output direct deliveries from existing warehouse.

2. Hatfield operation

- The Hatfield warehouse of around 125,000 sq. ft. is ideally placed for distributing throughout southern England. It is an existing site which is currently available.
- Three-wheel counterbalance fork trucks are proposed together with ride-on low-level order picking trucks.
- Company B's own warehouse management system will be used. It has been developed specifically for the food industry and offers clients many benefits in stock rotation, full batch traceability, bar-code scanning, electronic data interchange links, etc. For example, a printer at the factory dispatch point can produce barcode labels for each pallet which are then scanned at the warehouse goods-in.
- Hatfield will receive product from Great Yarmouth and Ipswich for small orders in southern England. Direct retail deliveries will continue to be covered from Great Yarmouth primarily using local hauliers as this is considered more cost effective than having dedicated vehicles as there is little opportunity for backloading.
- McDougalls and Pasta food orders for northern England will be trunked to Ossett for consolidation with RHMI orders.

The proposed fleet at Hatfield is four rigid and seven articulated vehicles. Where possible, vehicles will be used for night trunking as well as daytime operations. However, because of the timing of collections from the Bristol factory, a trailer swop is proposed at Avonmouth.

3. Ossett operation

- All RHMI production from Corby will be trunked nightly to Ossett. Ossett-based vehicles will also trunk to Hatfield RHMI orders for the south, plus loads from Droylsden and Middlewich which have been collected during the day, returning with picked orders from Hatfield.
- The proposed fleet at Ossett is three rigid and nine articulated vehicles.
- There will be an overlap in delivery areas: in the Midlands there will be areas covered by both Hatfield and Ossett vehicles since the origin of the product and the minimizing of trunking are important factors.

4. Scottish operations

- The majority of Scottish deliveries will be made through the site at Carfin. The exception would be those orders for the north of Scotland which are most effectively collected from Ossett by a third party. It is proposed to subcontract the Hatfield–Carfin and Ossett–Carfin trunks.

5. South-west deliveries

- Small orders in the South-west will be delivered via Avonmouth by a subsidiary of Company B. Large orders will be delivered direct from Ossett, Hatfield and Great Yarmouth.

6. Cost summary from Distribution Company B

- The estimated annual costs for 1992/93 budgeted volumes are given below. Note that, termination costs for the closure of the Dunstable and Reading warehouses have been excluded.

Option 1

	Warehouse	Distribution	Total
South (Erith)	1,280,043	1,317,001	2,597,044
North (Ossett)	893,412	1,125,017	2,018,429
Combined	2,173,455	2,442,018	4,615,473

Option 2

	Warehouse	Distribution	Total
South (Reading)	1,542,577	1,128,082	2,670,659
North (Ossett)	893,412	1,136,248	2,029,660
Combined	2,435,989	2,264,330	4,700,319

Option 3

	Warehouse	Distribution	Total
South (Hatfield)	1,803,357	1,171,427	2,974,784
North (Ossett)	893,412	1,136,248	2,029,660
Combined	2,696,769	2,307,675	5,004,444

7. Invoicing method

The basis of the contract would be cost plus (a method of charging for contract distribution services whereby the contractor declares all costs to the client on an 'open book' basis and the client is charged these costs plus an agreed percentage management fee). There would be a period cost statement matching actual spend against a phased budget and a short-term forecast based on information provided by RHM. The report would be produced within two working weeks of each period and the actual format of the statement can be jointly decided at a later date.

8. Conclusion

Company B is confident it can provide an efficient, cost-effective warehousing and distribution operation for the three RHM Foodservices companies. In summary the benefits are:

- use of existing sites at Ossett and Hatfield
- cost-effective use of consolidated distribution in peripheral areas through Carfin and Avonmouth
- use of other companies in the same group as Company B as sub-contractors but with overall control with Company B
- night trunking to double shift vehicles for cost-effective utilization
- cost-effective use of subcontractors
- possible phased implementation
- extensive experience of RHMI business at Ossett
- proven benefits of in-house warehouse management system
- the redundant Reading warehouse could be converted to production use, enabling closure of the Bristol factory.

The restructuring of a depot system

Professor Alan McKinnon
School of Management, Heriot-Watt University, UK

Introduction

The restructuring of a firm's distribution system can be precipitated by a host of external and internal pressures. Within the British brewing industry the distribution function has been subject to two major external pressures over the past decade: a steady decline in draught beer sales and an intensification of competition following a liberalization of beer sales through public houses. This case study illustrates how Scottish Brewers, Scotland's largest supplier of draught beer, responded to these pressures by undertaking a fundamental review of its distribution operation in 1991–2.

The company

Scottish Brewers is part of Scottish and Newcastle (S&N), which in late 1995 was the largest brewing group in the UK. It has responsibility for the distribution of beer and other drinks to public houses, clubs and hotels throughout Scotland. These premises, where people can consume as well as purchase alcohol, represent what in brewing circles is called the 'on-trade', to distinguish them from 'off-license' retail outlets where drinks are purchased for consumption elsewhere. Apart from a handful of public houses which have an off-license business on the same site, Scottish Brewers supplies only on-trade premises. Most of the draught beer originates from S&N's large Fountainbridge brewery in Edinburgh and is distributed in kegs and casks. Scottish Brewers also supplies its customers with bottled and canned drinks, many of which are sourced from outside the S&N group. The firm currently has around 5000 customers in Scotland.

Pressures for change

Pattern of consumer demand

The volume of beer sold in the UK peaked in 1979 and since then has been declining.

Sales in 1993 were 15% below the 1979 level. This contraction of the beer market can be attributed to several factors (Economic Intelligence Unit, 1995a):

1. Shift in demand to other alcoholic beverages: particularly by the young male population which has traditionally been the core market for beer in the UK.
2. Demographic trends, particularly the relative ageing of the population. The average consumer's demand for beer declines as they get older.
3. Change in the employment structure. There has been decline in the proportion of the work force in manual occupations typically associated with heavy beer drinking.
4. Relatively high level of price inflation. Between 1979 and 1993 the price of beer rose by 265%, significantly more than wines (148%), spirits (172%) and the general retail price index (148%). Much of the increase in beer prices was the result of a tripling of excise duties over this 14-year period.
5. Decline in the proportion of beer consumed in public houses. The proportion of beer sold through on-licence outlets dropped from 89% to 75% between 1978 and 1993, reflecting a marked shift towards off-licence purchases and home consumption (Economist Intelligence Unite 1995b). This is reckoned to have depressed the total demand for beer as people tend to drink more in the social atmosphere of a pub or club. Road safety campaigns designed to curb drink-driving have also reduced beer drinking in pubs and this has been only partially offset by the substitution of low-alcohol and alcohol-free lagers.

Scottish Brewers' beer sales were, therefore, declining not only as a consequence of the general contraction of the beer market, but also because of the diversion of beer sales from the on-license distribution channel, upon which it was almost totally dependent, to off-licence outlets. Between 1984 and 1994, sales of draught beer in Scotland declined from 2.3 million barrels to 1.6 million (1 barrel = 36 gallons or 165 litres) (Figure 16.1).

Scottish Brewers has tried to compensate for this reduction in draught beer sales by increasing the range of drink products that it handles. Between 1990–1 and 1994 around 50 new products were added to the range, mainly national brands of soft drinks. These brands have been gradually displacing locally-produced soft drinks which were previously delivered directly to pubs by local suppliers. Despite this product diversification, however, net volumes through Scottish Brewers' distribution system have declined. By the early 1990s there had been a significant decline in depot throughput with little prospect of this trend being reversed in the foreseeable future. Company management recognized that there was a need to rationalize depot capacity and as a result undertook a major study of the company's distribution operations.

Competitive environment

Until the early 1990s, the British brewing industry was characterized by a high degree of vertical integration. In addition to producing beer, most brewers tightly controlled their wholesale and retail distribution. Control at the retail level was achieved through the ownership of public houses either on a 'managed' or 'tenanted' basis. In 1989, around three-quarters of all public houses in the UK were owned by breweries. Following a two-year study of the industry, the Monopolies and Mergers Commission (MMC) concluded

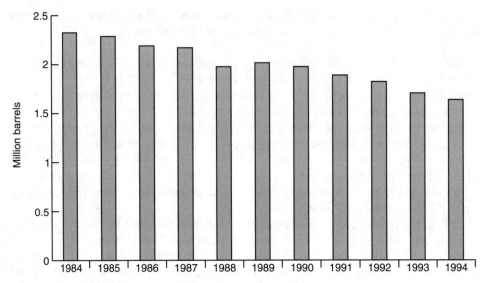

Figure 16.1 Total Scottish draught beer sales, 1984–94.

in 1989 that this created a 'complex monopoly' which restricted competition 'at all levels' and was detrimental to the public interest (MMC, 1989). It argued that:

> Brewers are protected from competition in supplying their managed and tenanted estates because other brewers do not have access to them. Even in the free trade many brewers prefer to compete by offering low-interest loans, which then tie the outlet to them, rather than by offering beer at lower prices. Wholesale prices are higher than they would be in the absence of the tie. This invariably feeds through into high retail prices. (p. 4)

The MMC recommended a series of measures to stimulate competition in the beer market. One of its main proposals, which the government subsequently endorsed in its 'Beer Orders' of 1989, was that no brewer should have more than 2000 'tied' public houses. This meant that most of the larger brewers had to scale down their 'tied estates' by selling off thousands of pubs (Table 16.1). This measure had less of an impact in Scotland, where the proportion of brewery-owned premises was well below the UK

Table 16.1 Numbers of tied public houses operated by national brewers, 1989

Brewer	Managed	Tenanted	Total
Bass	2420	4770	7190
Allied Brewers	2199	4479	6678
Whitbread	1870	4613	6483
Grand Metropolitan	1848	4571	6419
Courage	1329	3673	5002
Scottish and Newcastle	881	1406	2287

Source: MMC (1989).

average; only 49% of on-license outlets in Scotland were tied by comparison with 79% in England and Wales. It also had much less effect on S&N's distribution operations than those of its major rivals as its tied estate was only marginally larger than the limit imposed by the MMC. In Scotland, however, control over free on-trade outlets had been exerted more through the medium of loan-ties. Although this practice has continued, it has declined in importance.

Implementation of the MMC recommendations had major implications for brewers' logistical operations. On the one hand, it gave individual brewers access to a much larger potential market, creating the possibility of supplying many more outlets. On the other hand, those premises which had previously been tied and thereby locked into the delivery network, were now free to source beer and other drinks from elsewhere. Under the new regime, brewers had to compete for more of their business and a key element in this competition was the quality and efficiency of the delivery service. In 1995, tied public houses accounted for only around 200 of Scottish Brewers' 5000 customers.

Managers of premises that were freed from the brewer's control began to exercise more discretion over the nature and scheduling of deliveries. Scottish Brewers had operated a nominated day delivery system for many years, with customers placing orders up to 48 hours ahead of the scheduled delivery day. While this ordering system remained in place, the transport operation had to accommodate a growing number of delivery time restrictions. In the case of the company's Bellshill depot, for example, the proportion of customers specifying delivery time windows increased from 37% to 51% between 1989 and 1993.

This demand for a higher standard of delivery service occurred at a time when brewers were aggressively cutting costs to survive in the post-MMC competitive environment. Many of them, like Scottish Brewers, identified the distribution operation as a major potential source of cost-savings. The company believed that there was considerable scope for economizing on warehousing and inventory costs by rationalizing its depot system.

The depot system

The distribution systems of brewing firms have traditionally been build upon a decentralized pattern of stockholding. The dispersal of inventory to local depots has been justified primarily by two factors:

- the high cost of delivering keg beer, which usually requires specialist vehicles and the services of at least two draymen
- the short order lead time expected by customers, often 48 hours or less.

The development of the larger brewers' depot systems in the post-war period was closely associated with the expansion of their market areas and encroachment on the territories of small local breweries. In the case of Scottish Brewers, the main phase of depot development occurred during the 1970s, reaching a maximum of nine stockholding depots around Scotland. This system remained intact until 1991. Figure 16.2(a) shows the locations of nine stockholding depots in operation at that time and the areas that they served. Each of the stockholding depots had its own management team and sales processing department. Responsibility for delivery operations and stock control was devolved to local level. The Hillington and Ayr depots were supplemented by two 'stockless transit

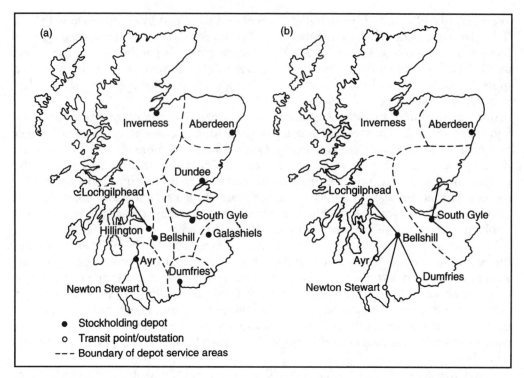

Figure 16.2 Scottish Brewers depot system in Scotland. (a) 1991, pre-rationalization and (b) 1993, post-rationalization.

points' (or 'outstations') at, respectively, Lochgilphead and Newton Stewart. All the stockholding depots worked two daily shifts, closing down overnight.

In late 1991, an in-house review of the distribution system had suggested that the two most southerly depots, at Dumfries and Galashiels, should be downgraded from full stockholding facilities to basic transhipment points. This change took effect from early 1992.

Later that year senior management of Scottish Brewers embarked on a more wide-ranging review of the distribution operation. This was prompted by a combination of declining volumes and a general pressure to cut costs. A preliminary investigation by an operations management team established that there was considerable scope for rationalizing the depot system and raising the productivity of the local delivery fleet. Although expenditure on Scottish Brewers' transport, warehousing and order processing operation accounted for only around 5% of sales revenue, this was one of the few cost elements over which the company had leverage and which offered relatively large potential savings.

In reviewing its distribution function, the firm was able to seek advice from S&N's core logistics planning unit called Centre Logistics. This unit provided an internal consultancy service drawing on greater technical resources than Scottish Brewers itself could muster and on the experience of other group companies that had similarly restructured their distribution operations in the past. Some of the analysis was undertaken in parallel by

Scottish Brewers and Centre Logistics, permitting independent checking of critical values and promoting a healthy discussion on points of disagreement. As Scottish Brewers was an autonomous business unit, however, its senior management had the final say on distribution changes.

The main focus of the distribution review was the opportunity to reduce the number of stockholding depots. Consideration was given at an early stage to the possibility of centralizing all inventory at a single location. Computer modelling indicated that the optimum location for a centralized facility would have been Falkirk, roughly mid-way between Glasgow and Edinburgh. This would have entailed closing down all the existing premises and undertaking a major new greenfield development. Although this option would have maximized inventory savings, it was rejected mainly for two reasons:

- The new facility would have required a large capital investment and diverted resources from other activities likely to earn a higher rate of return. Most of the existing depot premises, on the other hand, were largely depreciated assets
- the firm wished to retain much of its existing workforce and suspected that many employees would not transfer to the new facility.

It was anticipated that, by retaining a network of trans-shipment points around Scotland, the company would have been able both to keep local delivery costs within acceptable limits and to meet customer service requirements within a fully centralized system. There was, nevertheless, a risk that completely reconfiguring the system around a new greenfield development would cause some temporary service disruption.

Subsequent modelling work indicated that concentrating inventory at four of the existing depots, Edinburgh (South Gyle), Bellshill, Aberdeen and Inverness, would prove a much more cost-effective solution. These four stockholding depots were strategically located to serve the Scottish market (Figure 16.2b). Roughly three-quarters of Scotland's population of 5.1 million lives in a 60-mile wide zone, known as the Central Belt, running between the Clyde estuary in the west and the Forth and Tay estuaries in the east. Within this zone there are two major concentrations of population, the Glasgow conurbation and the city of Edinburgh, which have a combined population of around 2 million. Scottish Brewers retained a depot in each of these areas, effectively splitting distribution to the Central Belt into separate east and west operations. These depots, at Bellshill (near Glasgow) and South Gyle (Edinburgh) were centrally located within their expanded hinterlands, though these areas were now too large to be served directly by local delivery vehicles. To maintain the efficiency of the transport system, trans-shipment operations were continued at Ayr, Dumfries, Newton Stewart and Lochgilphead (outstations for Bellshill) and Dundee and Galashiels (outstations for South Gyle). Computer modelling indicated that, with the retention of break-bulk facilities at these places, the locations of the two main stockholding depots would remain optimal within a four-depot configuration. The company also considered the opportunities for rationalizing depot capacity in the north of Scotland, though these were constrained by the standard of the road infrastructure and the low density of population.

Scottish Brewers found that the depot rationalization yielded annual cost savings of around £1.7 million (Table 16.2). It was recognized, however, that concentrating inventory on fewer sites would be likely to carry a local delivery cost penalty, reflecting the longer average distance from depot to customer. The firm investigated various ways of

Table 16.2 Annual cost savings from depot restructuring

Cost element	Saving	Details
Labour	£1.25 million	Elimination of 50 jobs mostly management and supervisory posts
Property-related expenses	£0.4 million	For example, rates, utility and maintenance charges
Inventory	£0.03 million	Approximate 13% reduction in inventory level, also yielding a one-off reduction of £0.4 million in working capital
Trunking	£0.01 million	Mainly from consolidation of brewery–depot flows

improving the efficiency of its delivery operation within the more centralized structure. Prior to the reorganization, for example, the level of vehicle utilization was relatively low, vehicle schedules were drawn up within a framework of rigid depot boundaries and vehicle routes were planned on traditional manual basis. By overhauling its transport operation, the company was able to confine the increase in local delivery costs to roughly £0.25 million per annum.

To assess the full cost-benefit position, it is necessary also to take account of one-off expenditures and savings. The main expenditure in this category was £1.1 million awarded in staff redundancy payments. A further £0.15 million was invested in modifications to buildings, computing equipment and other miscellaneous items. On the credit side, there was a one-off release of £0.4 million in working capital from the reduction in inventory levels across the distribution system.

At the time of the reorganization, serious consideration was given to the option of contracting out the entire distribution function to a third-party operator. Several other British brewers had recently externalized their delivery operations, taking advantage of new contract distribution services specially tailored to the needs of the brewing industry. Indeed, around the same time, S&N, the parent company, decided to contract out its primary distribution to Hays, the fifth largest distribution contractor in the UK in 1993–4. Centre Logistics, which had been closely involved in this externalization decision, was invited to make an independent assessment of the case for Scottish Brewers taking a similar course. It compared the cost and quality of the company's rationalized in-house operation with that available from outside contractors. This analysis established that the most cost-effective option would be to retain the in-house system, building on Scottish Brewers' long experience of distributing beer in Scotland. It was, nevertheless, acknowledged that the company could do more to 'sweat its existing distribution assets'.

As indicated above, around 70% of the gross annual savings were achieved by reducing the numbers of staff and warehouse personnel. Management recognized the possibility that the threat of job losses could create an industrial relations problem. Industrial action could have disrupted operations prior to the restructuring and obstructed the transition to the new system. Senior management attached great importance, therefore, to maintaining the support of the workforce during this period of reorganization.

It can be seen, therefore, that in appraising the new system the management of Scottish Brewers were mainly concerned about four strategic issues:

- the need to maintain customer service
- the scope for reducing logistics costs
- the relative merits of contracting-out the distribution operation
- the consequences for labour relations.

Implementation

By the late summer of 1992 a firm decision had been taken to proceed with the restructuring programme, though its timing remained uncertain. It had been intended to implement the programme over a period of 18 months to allow the human resource and customer service issues to be dealt with adequately. Two unforeseen developments occurred, however, which upset the original plan and resulted in more rapid implementation. First the S&N group as a whole introduced a major restructuring initiative which put subsidiaries under added pressure to rationalize their operations. Second, there was a change of managing director within Scottish Brewers. These two developments resulted in the restructuring being announced in late March 1993 and completed by the end of February 1994.

Note

Since the creation of the Single European Market on the 1 January 1993, there has been a sharp increase in 'personal imports' of beer from other European Union countries. This too has been depressing draught beer sales in the UK. This is not a relevant factor in the present case study, however, partly because the depot rationalization programme pre-dated the growth of the 'import' traffic, but also because Scotland is too far from other European countries for it to have much impact on local beer sales.

Acknowledgement

The author is most grateful to the management of Scottish Brewers and in particular Mr Ken McIntosh, the company's distribution manager, for their support in the preparation of this case study.

References

Economist Intelligence Unit (1995a) market surveys: beer, part 1. *Retail Business*, No. 444.
Economist Intelligence Unit (1995b) Market surveys: beer, part 2. *Retail Business*, No. 447.
Monopolies and Mergers Commission, The supply of beer: report on the supply of beer for retail sale in the United Kingdom. HMSO, London (1989).

Distribution planning in a developing country*

Stephen Errey
Senior Consultant, Distribution Projects Limited, UK

Introduction

It was half-past six in the morning on 23 May 1994 at Harare airport in Zimbabwe. Stephen Errey had just arrived from the UK at the beginning of a nine-week secondment. With him were the other members of the project team with whom he had travelled out; the project leader, an accountant/economist and a mechanical engineer. Stephen was the logistics specialist. Together, their task was to come up with a proposal for a phased vehicle replacement policy for the Zimbabwe Dairy Marketing Board (ZDMB). There was a lot for everyone to do, and not that long to do it in. Still, the first thing to do was freshen up after the flight, and then get down to the offices of the ZDMB to see how the land lay.

The Organization

The ZDMB was responsible for the collection, processing, distribution and sale of milk products throughout Zimbabwe. It was a parastatal organization which meant that, in effect it was a nationalized industry. It had no competition, but the government had a strong influence on the prices paid for raw milk and the prices charged for the finished product. It carried out its work through a network of dairies and depots, spread through-put the country (see Figure 17.1). All raw milk was collected from farms by the nearest dairy, where processing took place. All dairies undertook processing of the principal products, but some specialist products (such as ice cream or cheese) were only manufactured at one or other of these. All the dairies carried out local distribution to retailers or domestic customers, but there was also a network of depots used solely for local distribution. Mostly the local delivery was carried out by various types of diesel trucks, but in the two large urban areas there were also electric milk floats and bicycle rounds-

*Data available on the Internet (see page xxii).

Figure 17.1 ZDMB – location of facilities.

men. These depots were supplied from their nearest dairy, and administratively the ZDMB was split into regions based on these dairies.

The need for the study had arisen because the ZDMB had been operating at a deficit fro a number of years. Although this was partly due to a mismatch between the producer prices and the consumer prices, it had also been identified that there were operational inefficiencies which needed to be addressed. Transport costs formed a large part of the total operating costs, so a project to assist in reducing transport costs had been funded by the UK Overseas Development Administration. A British logistics consultancy company DPL, for which Stephen Errey and the other team members worked, had been engaged to carry out the study.

The resources

Stephen reviewed the resources available to him. He had access to a personal computer (PC), which already had a proprietary spreadsheet installed on it. Knowing that this PC could be used, he had brought with him on disk, a computerized vehicle scheduling system called Routemaster (see Appendix 17.1). He installed and tested this, and was relieved to find that it was working correctly. He had a complete set of 1:50,000 maps for Zimbabwe and some more detailed ones of the main urban areas; these would enable him to match any data he obtained with the digital map used by the scheduling system, once he had annotated the maps with the reference codes used by the system. Finally, he had brought with him some details of work standards for house-to-house milk delivery which had been compiled from studies carried out in the UK. Other than a calculator, and plenty of pencils and paper, that was it.

The team

Before anybody started any work, the project manager called a meeting of the project team to clarify the objectives of the study and define the roles that each member of the team would play.

The task that the team was charged with was to set out the requirements that ZDMB would have for new commercial vehicles over the next five years. This general task was subject to a number of provisos. First, the total expenditure on vehicles should be minimized. That meant that if there were different ways of performing the same task which used fewer vehicles, or used vehicles which were cheaper to operate, then those methods of operation should be built into the plans. Secondly, if there were changes to operating methods which gave large cost savings to the organization, but led to an increase in vehicle costs, then these should be clearly set out in the report, but excluded from the replacement plan.

The project leader explained that he would not take a direct part in the analysis work being carried out. His task was to liaise with the ZDMB, with the sponsor of the study, and with the other organizations providing administrative support. He would also take responsibility for structuring the final report, and ensuring that each member of the team provided the necessary information at the appropriate time during the nine weeks available.

The job of the mechanical engineer was to assess the current fleet. The team would need to know how many vehicles there were, where they were located, and what their expected life was. On the basis of this information, and the forecast requirement, the mechanical engineer would also be responsible for drawing up the five-year plan showing the purchase requirements.

The economist/accountant had the task of providing the other members of the team with any costings they needed to carry out their task, and also with costing the final replacement plan.

The task of the logistics specialist was to define what the ideal vehicle requirement would be over the next five years, so that this could be matched with the actual availability of vehicles. He would also be expected to identify beneficial changes to the method of operations that had impacts beyond the vehicle requirement, so that these could be included in the report.

The available information

The first few days were spent finding out what information was available. It soon became clear that there were some features of working in Africa that were very different from Stephen's previous experience.

First of all, all the information was still paper-based. This affected Stephen in three ways:

- the information was not available in one place; much of the information on physical receipts and despatches was held at the local depots
- the information was sometimes difficult to find, because it was rarely used again once it had been filed; sometimes even when it was found, it had physically deteriorated
- each locality had developed the reporting systems to suit their own circumstances, which meant that it was very difficult to combine and compare information from different parts of the company.

Secondly, there were difficulties caused by the difference in culture. Stephen soon found that it was necessary to spend much more time ensuring that his requirements were understood by the people carrying them out, and that he understood the answers to his questions. It was very important to have face-to-face meetings, so that visual cues could be used to ensure that both sides understood each other. It was also important to avoid time pressure in these meetings so that there was the opportunity to explore the same issue from different angles, to confirm the understanding of answers.

Thirdly, communication was more difficult than Stephen was used to. Telephones were not always reliable, distances were much greater, and some parts of the country could only be accessed by dirt roads that were not always passable. The need for face-to-face meetings made this more significant; it would probably take a week simply to visit the main distribution depots.

By the end of the first week, Stephen was able to summarize for himself the information he had available:

- there were sales forecasts available by product group by region for three years; these were contained in the ZDMB strategic plan, an extract of which is shown in Appendix 17.2
- there was no detailed information on sales per customer or per route held centrally; telephone conversations with some of the depots suggested it was unlikely that there was any consistent information there either
- the ZDMB had no work standards for either driving speeds or the time it took to make deliveries.

The fortunes of the other members of the team were also mixed. The accountant thought that all the information he needed was available, although it would take quite a bit of work to present it in the form that was needed. The engineer, on the other hand, had come to the conclusion that he was going to have to visit all the locations where vehicles were based if he was going to obtain accurate information about the state of the fleet.

The task

At the end of the first week, Stephen had a meeting with the project manager. 'What I want from you by this evening' Stephen was told, 'is a work plan for the next eight weeks, setting out what you are going to do, why you are going to do it, and when it is going to be done. You need to include a clear specification of the information you require and how and where you propose to obtain it. And remember: some of what the other members of the team need to do will depend on your work, so you must allow time for them to pick up where you leave off. In particular the engineer will need four or five days to develop a detailed vehicle purchasing plan once the fleet composition and size have been specified. Also, let me know what information you will need from the other members of the team. I don't want you to start thinking about any solutions or proposals until we have an agreed project plan and know exactly what information we need to collect.'

Appendix 17.1: Details of the Routemaster vehicle scheduling system

Description of system

The computerized vehicle scheduling system is specifically designed to provide solutions to the problem of scheduling multi-drop deliveries from a central depot. It is an optimizing tool, containing an algorithm which minimizes total driving time for any given set of customers.

The system is able to take into account all the variables needed to provide a realistic solution. These include:

- varying vehicle types
- varying shift times and duration
- combination of fixed and variable drop times
- up to 24 different driving speeds, depending on road category
- time windows for deliveries to customers.

Where there is considerable fluctuation in the location and volume of demand, Routemaster can be used as an operational tool to avoid the inefficiencies caused by fixed routes. However, where demand is more consistent, it is more appropriate to use it to set up delivery rounds which will then remain unchanged for a period of time.

Parameters used

The principal parameters which have to be defined as part of the set-up procedure are:

- driving speeds
- drop times
- shift times
- weight delivered to customers
- time restrictions.

The output from the system consists of a listing for each route giving:

- the drop sequence
- the maximum load
- the trip distance
- the trip time.

Appendix 17.2: Extract from the ZDMB strategic plan

Marketing plans

ZDMB's milk intake and production has risen steadily in recent years as is shown in Table 17.1.

- This increase (which is expected to continue over the next few years) poses considerable problems for the marketing department. It is necessary to make plans well in advance in order to be able to dispose of the future production.
- The master plan for the dairy sector produced by Dangroup has been reviewed and discussed with the marketing department. The department has not accepted all the recommendations of the plan, particularly with regard to the doorstep delivery service.
- The department has produced a marketing plan for 1994–5 which contains a five-year programme for eliminating the trading deficit, while ensuring the annual disposal of available milk, and retaining present levels of employment.
- Prominent among the strategies outlined in the plan is the question of reaching an agreement with the farmers to control the volume of milk to be offered to ZDMB and the price to be paid for it. Discussions have recently been held on this topic.
- Product-lines are to be rationalized, with an emphasis on the planned deletion of the products which have reached the end of their life cycles, and the introduction of new ones to replace them. Concerted efforts are to be made to raise the sales of longer-life products in rural areas, and to increase exports.
- The marketing department prepares its plans methodically on a five-year rolling basis. It is at present in the final stages of preparing the 1994–5 plan, which will be completed by June, 1994. The advance results were made available to the Consultant's team during the study and were discussed with the department.
- The emphasis on increased exports is maintained and the question of packaging is under consideration. Due to the shortage of foreign exchange, the packaging materials for sterimilk and yoghurt are in short supply. This has led to the occasional halting of production lines in some dairies. In turn, this has led to suggestions that ZDMB should switch its packaging entirely to glass, which is locally manufactured. However, such strategy would lead to a substantially higher demand on ZDMB's transport: the weight and volume of product to be moved would be greatly increased. This would lead to

Table 17.1 Utilization of milk intake by major product group (million litres)

| Product group | Financial year | | | |
	1990–1	1991–2	1992–3	1993–4
Wholemilk	112	107	93	86
Lacto	6	22	33	39
Industrial users	30	21	20	23
Sterimilk	8	10	14	17
Cheese	15	14	14	12
Skimmed milk	–	–	12	22
Other	2	7	2	3
	173	181	188	202

a need for more vehicles, fuel and spares, with a concomitant rise in the need for foreign exchange. Tentative calculations suggest that the increased requirement for foreign exchange for transport would be greater than the reduction due to the elimination of imported packaging material.

- The proposed change in packaging thus appears to be strategically non-viable. Instead, the marketing department proposes to solve the problem by a major increase in exports, which were Z$1 million last year. A total of Z$5 million/year is needed for the packaging. The department feels that this is an achievable target and therefore proposes to generate its own foreign exchange. A number of large deals are now in the course of negotiation.
- The 1994–5 plan gives forecasts of growth by product for each region and depot in 1998. These have been discussed by the department and the consultant's team. The targets appear reasonable and attainable.
- The forecast growth between 1994 and 1997 for each product by region is summarized in Table 17.2.

Table 17.2   Forecast growth by product group, 1994–7, percentage increase

Product	Harare	Bulawayo	Gweru	Mutare	Kadoma	Chipinge	All regions
Wholemilk	20	14	16	16	16	33	18
Flavoured milk	13	9	6	12	16	16	11
Sterilized milk	14	12	21	20	19	33	16
Skim milk	16	5	–	–	–	–	16
Lacto	24	11	21	21	25	33	19
Cheese	34	38	37	36	36	33	35
Butter	26	52	35	39	33	33	36
Fresh cream	39	52	12	16	16	16	39
Yoghurt	15	52	12	16	16	16	22
Ice cream bulk	9	16	12	16	33	33	14
Ice cream soft	16	10	–	–	–	–	10
Ice cream in-hand	39	52	33	52	52	52	40
Ice cream cones	39	52	33	52	52	52	40
Fruit juice	16	8	16	16	16	16	14
SMP	33	33	33	33	33	33	33
All products	26	29	19	19	20	33	25

The growth rate for 'all products' (the bottom line of Table 17.2) includes an allowance for the introduction of UHT milk in the Harare and Bulawayo regions, and for the opening of a new depot in the Norton area of Harare region.

PART FIVE

Warehouse planning and operations management

The development of an automated storage and retrieval system

Professor David Jessop
The Business School, University of Glamorgan, UK

Introduction and company background

British Airways Avionic Engineering Limited (BAAE) is a subsidiary to the British Airways (BA) Group. Established in December 1993 and operating from a brand-new purpose-designed facility in Llantrisant, south Wales, the company quickly attained a prominent position in the business of servicing, repairing and overhauling avionic equipment for the parent company and other airlines. The company goal was stated as 're-certifying any component on our capability list within three days of receipt'.

A key element in achieving this performance goal was the requirement for a state-of-the-art warehouse to store and supply parts to the maintenance workshops. BAAE were fairly sure from the outset that such a warehouse, dealing with up to 40,000 part numbers would probably have to be based on an automatic storage and retrieval system. What they didn't know was the specific design and operating characteristics that should be incorporated into such a facility. A broad specification for the new warehouse was developed by BAAE and AEG (UK) Ltd and following a competitive tendering process AEG Softwaretechnik GmbH of Berlin were selected as the contractors to design and build the new facility.

The Llantrisant maintenance facility

The design brief for the Llantrisant site was simple: 'design the most efficient and cost-effective avionics maintenance facility in the world'. The company has invested over £22 million in the development of the facility , which occupies an area of 140,000 sq. ft. and features state-of-the-art technology. Production started with the opening of the site in

December 1993, which became fully operational in September 1994. All the resources from the avionic workshops at London's Heathrow airport were relocated to south Wales in phased moves. BAAE now employs approximately 375 staff, some 270 being in direct production areas. Customers contract with BA Engineering who, in effect, subcontract avionic maintenance to BAAE. The process is a seamless operation with both companies using the BA inventory management and component tracking system, known as 'TIME'.

A good indication of the scope of the company's work can be gained from a list of the 12 production units operated at Llantrisant. These are:

- flight recorders
- instrumentation and indicators
- catering equipment
- actuators and motors
- in-flight entertainment and interiors
- inertial navigation systems and gyroscopes
- flight instruments
- radio and radar
- general electrical
- automatic test equipment
- central air data computers
- aircraft control systems.

In addition to the production units there are two support units, a test equipment centre and a mechanical support unit. As will be seen from the site plan (Figure 18.1), the workshops and other resources are laid out in a rather dispersed way, many of the points at which materials and parts are used being some distance from the storage location. The buildings are constructed with two stories, with workshops at both levels.

The space allocated to the storage system is adjacent to the goods receiving area, the storage system itself occupying the full height of the building, with offices situated above the receiving space. Goods are received five days a week during normal working hours. Deliveries are inspected and reconciled with supplier orders through operator interaction with BA's materials management system (MMS) computer.

The current overhaul and repair capability extends to more than 12,000 avionic items from over 300 original equipment manufacturers. The avionics of all current Boeing aircraft can be handled, and capabilities exist in connection with Airbus, Concorde and Tristar aircraft. The average annual throughput is 58,000 items. It is, of course, intended that the scope of BAAE's capability will expand, and the capacity of the workshops and other facilities has, at present, some room for increased activity. It is envisaged that the stores may be required, in due course, to accommodate over 65,000 different lines.

On establishment, the company took the opportunity presented by the green-field site project to develop innovative approaches to its work. BAAE operate cellular working practices and have a policy of continuous improvement, and the multi-skilled workforce enables flexible operation. BAAE has a 'flat' management and support structure, and the staff operate within a single trade union agreement; employees are a mix of new recruits and those relocated from Heathrow.

Central to the success of BAAE is the rapid turnaround of components. Through innovation in the use of systems, and attention to work-flows in the design of the facility, the company has sought to eliminate all unnecessary process time from the repair service.

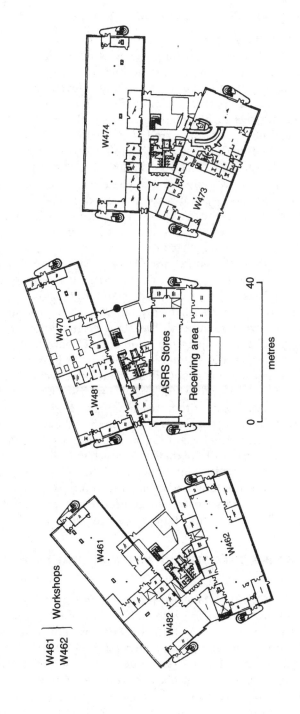

Figure 18.1 BAAE Llantrisant maintenance facility ground floor plan – September 1995.

Planning and spares provisioning

The achievement of the goal of re-certifying any item on the company's capability list within three days of receipt naturally depends on the availability of the necessary components and spare parts. If the competitive advantage arising from the ability to respond rapidly to customer demand is to be fully enjoyed, then a great deal of attention needs to be given to spare parts availability. BAAE has, therefore, been working closely with avionic vendors to ensure immediate access to the spares needed. Many suppliers, including Boeing, Collins, Gables, Garrett, GEC, Delco and Matsushita, have established distribution centres within the UK thereby helping BAAE to meet short lead-time targets. Other vendors have agreed to place consignment stocks at Llantrisant, and all are co-operating towards greater responsiveness. The existence of electronic data interchange links with key suppliers also facilitates automatic ordering and enhances responsiveness.

BA Engineering (of which the avionics facility is a part), have a highly developed level of logistics sophistication. The division as a whole spends more than £100 million each year on inventory, most of which comes from the USA. Locating and shipping that equipment costs a further £4 million. John Osborn, manager material logistics is on record as saying that 'The trick with logistics is not to do the work yourself. It's about managing a network of suppliers to your own set standards'. This is something which BA Engineering seem to do rather well, the organization earns around £2 million per annum supplying logistics services to other airlines. In a recent edition of *World Engineering*, the BA Engineering global bi-monthly publication, John Osborn comments 'We need to work our stock harder, which requires better levels of service. In my opinion, the emphasis in future is not about storage, it is about efficient and effective distribution, and logistics is an essential part of that. The more efficient we are at supplying parts, the more we can reduce our stock levels. And that requires an efficient logistics operation.'

However, notwithstanding the clear recognition that the holding of unnecessary stocks is not, in itself, conducive to efficient logistics operations, there remains a need at the Llantrisant facility to carry stocks of materials which will be called for on an as-and-when required basis for repair and maintenance activities which give rise to 'independent' demands. The economic thinking underlying inventory policy at Llantrisant is, of course, influenced by the fact that the cost of non-performance, perhaps arising as a result of a parts shortage, can in some circumstances be extremely high.

The need for an automated storage and retrieval system (ASRS)

In seeking to reduce the time taken to retrieve a part from the stores and get it to the appropriate repair location BAAE set themselves an ambitious target. They planned to move from the response time of anything between one and seven days which was what was attained at the London facilities, to a target of 3 minutes for 80% of components and a maximum of 15 minutes for the remainder. The 3-minute target time was selected because that is the average time it takes to remove a faulty component from an item under repair. It was obvious to BAAE's management that what they needed was an automated system for the storage and retrieval of avionic parts. A scoping study was undertaken which led to the development of an outline specification, that was used as the basis of an invitation to tender to select a warehouse design and build contractor. Edited extracts from the specification follow.

Operational requirements

- The ASRS shall be capable of being installed and operated within the central storage area as shown on the site plans provided. The space allocated for the storage and retrieval system is 40 m long, 9 m high and 8 m wide.
- The system is required to be capable of being operated 24 hours a day, 365 days a year. The acceptable level of system availability is 97% including downtime for maintenance.
- The minimum operating life of the system shall be 15 years.
- All parts shall be tagged and traceable as required by the Civil Aviation Authority. Traceability of information shall, as a minimum, include manufacturing batch number and date. The history of rotables will be maintained in the material management computer system.
- The ASRS and other stores functions shall be managed and controlled by its stand-alone computer system, which shall also interface to higher level management computers. Any loss of communications, or any failure of the management computers will not affect the stores operation.
- At the failure of major system components, the system will continue to operate at a reduced level of service. Typically parts will be issued from the bin located at the alternate aisle if a stacking crane fails.

System capacity

- The system shall provide sufficient capacity to enable the retrieval of 75 demands per hour.
- The ASRS system shall be designed for 40,000 part numbers.
- The ASRS system will require a minimum of 65,000 bins. There shall be eight types of bins, with 48 of smallest type per tray.
- Generally, different batches of a particular part number will be stored in different bins: (i) *Expendables*. Parts of a particular batch will be kept separately from other batches of the same part number in dedicated bins. Depending on the volume of each part, and quantity stored within a particular batch, it may be necessary to store contents of a particular batch in more than one bin. On average two batches shall be stored at any time. Slow moving parts may be kept in one batch, whilst fast moving parts may be held in three or four batches simultaneously. (ii) *Rotables*. Each part will be tagged individually, hence parts that belong to different batches can be stored within a particular bin.
- For expendable items, the different batches of the same part number shall be stored in dedicated bins located in separate aisles. This will provide system resilience, and at the failure of one stacking crane it should be possible to retrieve parts from alternate aisles.
- The tenderers shall be responsible for the determination of optimum tray dimensions. Trays accommodating more than one part number shall be partitioned. The tenderer

shall confirm: (i) partition details for different tray configurations, (ii) number of aisles – and gross storage volume (including racks and crane area, etc.) and (iii) total effective storage volume.

• Parts, consisting mainly of electrical and electronic components, mechanical components and sub-assemblies, fastenings and other small spare parts will be stored in appropriately sized bins. An appropriate range of bin sizes shall be supplied according to a given schedule, the trays are to be capable of being configured with a variety of combinations of bins.

The internal distribution system

Fast response is a key capability of BAAE, and the response time to an external customer must embody the time it takes to receive parts from the store. A difficulty was posed by the fact that there are a large number of workshops to be served, all of them some distance from the issuing point. There was clearly a need for a fast and continuously available internal transportation system to carry components from the store to point of use.

The project team, given as they were, a clean sheet of paper as the starting point for the specification of the transportation system considered many alternatives, amongst them the following:

• a conveyor system (gravity? powered? overhead? roller? belt? pneumatic? other?)
• robotic automatically guided vehicles
• a messenger service operated from the stores
• a 'customer-collect' provision
• a regular scheduled internal delivery service, visiting each delivery location in turn
• substores (formal or informal) near to point of use.

Following a tendering process, BAAE selected AEG (UK) Ltd and AEG Softwaretechnik GmbH of Berlin, to convert this outline specification into a functioning warehouse that would fully meet the operating needs of the Llantrisant maintenance facility. The first task facing the AEG team was to create a detailed design specification and operational plan on the basis of the information provided by BAAE.

Development of a major distribution centre*

Martin Green
Logistics Consultant, Touche Ross Management Consultants, London, UK

Introduction

Britvic Soft Drinks Ltd (BSD) is a leading manufacturer and supplier of soft drinks to the retail sector in the UK. These include a number of major brands, such as Tango, R. Whites Lemonade, Pepsi, 7-Up and Britvic fruit juices and mixers. In early 1992, Touche Ross Management Consultants issued an invitation to tender on behalf of BSD. This was sent to major UK logistics service providers, inviting them to tender for the setting up of a new dedicated central warehousing operation.

An increasing proportion of BSD's sales was accounted for by supply to major retailers, including Tesco and Sainsbury. These customers were becoming increasingly demanding in terms of their service requirements:

- they now required daily deliveries to each of their regional distribution centres (RDCs), as distinct from the traditional once a week delivery
- they required all their products on a single vehicle (Britvic traditionally sent a number of vehicles to each retailer from each of their production sites)
- they required delivery effectively within 24 hours of an order being placed.

The growth in this part of the market, combined with the retailers' specific requirements, caused Britvic to reassess its overall distribution strategy. Working with consultants from Touche Ross, BSD decided to create a new warehouse to centralize flows from all the company's production sites and enable them to supply major retailers on a 'quick response' basis. This would operate quite separately from the local delivery depots which would then be required to service pubs, confectioners, etc.

*Data available on the Internet (see page xxii).

By 1992 BSD was ready to implement the new strategy. In the invitation to tender it set out the objectives of the move, as follows:

The company's five-year plan has generated a requirement for a facility that will fulfil several purposes:

- service company depot and major take-home customer orders that cannot be sourced from a factory warehouse
- provide a 'quick response' service to major grocery customers involving smaller and more frequent deliveries than currently
- service other take-home customer orders that are of a size that makes it more economic to do so from a centralized facility than from a company depot
- provide strategic storage capacity.

The company wishes a contractor to set up and manage this centralised facility at the most economic cost consistent with quality, safety and service criteria. A system is required which retains operational flexibility and which is capable of being responsive to the needs of the company and its customers.

The main part of the invitation to tender was the requirements specification against which tenderers had to bid. This is reproduced below, with only minor simplifications to the original document.

Requirements specification for a centralised 'quick response' warehouse operation

Contents

1.0 Purpose and scope

1.1 Definitions

'The Company' shall mean Britvic Soft Drinks Ltd. of Britvic House, Broomfield Road, Chelmsford, Essex, CM1 1TU.

'The Contractor' shall mean the company appointed by Britvic to undertake the warehousing operation set out in this specification.

'The Customer' shall mean the customer of Britvic Soft Drinks Ltd.

1.2 General

The purpose of this specification is to set out the requirements for a new centralised warehouse operation through which the Company proposes to:

- provide a 'Quick Response' (QR) service to certain major retail customers involving smaller and more frequent deliveries than currently;
- service other customer orders that are of a size that makes it more economic to do so from a centralised facility than from a Company depot;
- provide strategic storage capacity.

This specification provides information on throughputs, stockholding, etc. to enable a supplier to bid for the construction of the warehouse operation. Start-up is planned for 1st October 1993. The scope of this specification requires the following facilities and services to be provided:

- the provision of a building of a suitable construction, size, specification and layout to warehouse and despatch the forecast throughputs; this is also to include office space suitable to accommodate the Company's order staff (approximately 20 staff in total) and computer hardware;
- the collection of palletised goods from the Company's Rugby factory and transportation to the centralised warehouse;
- the receipt, storage, stock management, assembly and despatch of palletised goods;
- the administration of order processing functions and associated documentation;
- management and staff;
- the provision of delivery services to customers premises.

2.0 General information

Through this new centralised facility, the Company proposes to:

- supply a number of major customers including Tesco, Sainsbury, Asda, Safeway, Somerfield and others for whom the QR service is primarily intended;
- service a number of 'semi-bulk' customers such as cash-and-carrys [a 'cash and carry' is a large warehouse-type outlet where small retailers typically go to buy their supplies in case-quantities and on trade terms]
- transfer stock to the Company depots.

It is planned that palletised goods will normally be delivered on the day following receipt of confirmed order at the warehouse in order quantities up to full truckloads. The effect will be that for these and the smaller customers, order will need to be processed several times per week for subsequent assembly and despatch to Customers' regional distribution centres and Company depots.

The Company will receive all orders for both retail customers and depot transfers and download orders to the Contractor. For guidance it is estimated that, in 1994, 95% of volume will be handled in full pallet quantities and 4–5% will involve mixed pallet/case picking. This is expected to grow to 10% of case volume by 1998. Case picking will be required for smaller customers only. Please indicate cost and operating implications if, in the future, this percentage was increased to 20%.

3.0 Operating statistics

The Company intends to stock a total of between 180/220 SKU's [stock-keeping units] including promotional lines. However, over the course of a year it is anticipated that the total range will be in the order of 300 SKU's. It is planned that this facility will handle the volumes shown in Table 1. The order profile by customer group is shown in Appendix 2.

Table 1 Planned warehouse throughput

Intake	Million cases	
	1993–4	1997–8
Ex Rugby	51.7	60.9
Others	20.8	31.9
Total	72.5	92.8
Despatch	**Sales and transfers**	
	Million cases	
	1993–4	1997–8
Cans	51.7	67.7
PET [plastic bottles]	13.4	16.7
Others	7.4	8.4
Total	72.5	92.8

4.0 Operating methods

4.1 Collections

A basic requirement is to collect palletised goods from the Company's Rugby factory and to transport them to the centralised warehouse. A profile of this requirement is included in Appendix 1.

In order to optimise efficiency, maximum (38 tonne) gross weight articulated road vehicles will be required to carry out this task and it should be assumed that a sufficient number of full pallets will always be available at the factory to constitute full (38 tonne GCW) truck loads.

Automatic loading equipment will be in operation on the despatch dock but this may be assumed to operate with standard road vehicles.

The vehicle and driver resource for the collection operation should be estimated using the following assumptions:

• the factory will load on the following basis:

From 1993–4   Evenly spread over 16 hours per day Monday–Friday, except for 8 weeks (weeks 41–48 inclusive) in Summer when it will be over 24 hours per day, 7 days per week;

From 1998–9   Evenly spread over 16 hours per day Monday–Friday, except for 12 weeks (weeks 37–48 inclusive) in the Summer when it will be over 24 hours per day, 7 days per week;

- vehicles will be loaded by Company staff using automatic equipment;
- the resources for maintaining the integrity of the operation must be provided to cover for holidays, sickness, and vehicle scheduled and non-scheduled maintenance, in order to ensure that the specified stockholding levels are maintained at the centralised warehouse.

4.2 Receiving

An automated loading will be in use at the Rugby factory, consideration should be given to the automated un-loading of these vehicles at the centralised warehouse. A supply profile is included in Appendix 1.

Turnaround time of the vehicle at the unloading dock must not exceed 30 minutes whether it is manually or automatically unloaded. In 1994, 60% of incoming stock will come from the Rugby factory. By 1998, this will be approximately 55%.

These are overall figures. The figures may change on a daily basis, so flexibility must be built in.

Warehouse staff will receive a schedule of receipts which they will use to plan resources and to check against arrivals. The Company will incorporate into this schedule those collections from Rugby factory for which the Contractor is responsible.

Receipts will therefore be of three types:

- product collected from the Rugby factory;
- stock transfers from other factories or Company depots;
- product delivered by suppliers.

The latter two methods will be by curtain-sided vehicles.

It is a required performance standard that stock will be updated on the Company computer system no later than two hours after arrival on the un-loading dock. The Company will require confirmation of goods received to be input via computer terminals into the Company's Total Logistics System (TLS).

If product is to be directly loaded without being put away into stock (trans-shipped) then it should be possible to turn round the supplying vehicle and load the outward vehicle within two hours, including stock management and pick list generation.

On presentation of delivery notes from the driver, receiving staff are required to check that the purchase order number on those documents agrees with that supplied by the Company on the receiving schedule. Pallets will have bar codes containing day lot number, product code and best-before date for identification purposes, and will have the following additional man-readable annotation:

- 8 numeric number (including 4 numeric product code), for example: 92092740 = 33cl Cola (2740) with best before date of September 1992 (9209).

All goods are received on Chep 1000 × 1200 mm pallets with the exception of cans of fruit juice which are received on a non-returnable pallet. [GKN-Chep is the major supplier of rented or 'pool' pallets to the UK grocery trade.]
Products on non-returnable pallets will need to be re-palletised onto Chep pallets and new pallet labels attached. These account for less than 1% of product throughput.

4.3 Storage

Products are required to be stored at ambient temperature and in conditions which are not extreme.
Pallets are to be stored in such a way that fast retrieval is possible in order to provide the quick response demanded by this new operation.
The strength of the racking should be sufficient to support an average weight per pallet of 1.1 tonne, up to a maximum of 1.3 tonne.
There may be up to 300 SKU's, including promotional lines, although a maximum of only 180–220 will be 'live' at any one time. Provision must be made in the Warehouse Management System to identify pallets by day lot number as well as product code and best before date.
Every SKU is subject to case picking; therefore, appropriate provision is required.
It should be noted that product from Rugby manufacture will not be stretch-wrapped. If pallets require stretch-wrapping for safe storage then provision must be made for its removal prior to despatch.
  Stockholding requirements are summarised in Appendix 3.

4.4 Stock control

The Company requires that modern stock control systems and techniques are applied, with the following principles of operation:

- stock is to be rotated under the principle of strict date/batch order;
- every SKU is to be counted once every two weeks on a rolling Perpetual Inventory basis;
- a full annual physical stocktake must be undertaken in conjunction with Company staff.

The contractor should provide experienced stock control management and staff to carry out the following functions:

- accurate stock accounting, including stock adjustments, stock movements and replenishments;
- control of damages;
- maintenance of warehouse management systems;
- adherence to Company guidelines on stock control;
- layout design, including the provision of temporary locations for promotional lines. Most promotional activity occurs during the pre-Christmas and early summer periods. These normally take the form of on-pack promotions, with such products identified as unique SKU's. A typical effect of this is the generation of additional SKU's on the database but not an increase in the number of 'live' SKU's.

4.5 Order processing

Movements through the facility will be generated through three methods:

- the Company's Central Order Office will deal direct with Top End Grocery (TEG) Customers [TEGs are the major food retail groups such as Sainsbury, Tesco, Asda];
- the Company's Distribution Resource Planning (DRP) Office will deal with stock movements to Company depots;
- the Company's Telesales office will continue to look after local 'semi-bulk' customer deliveries;

These orders and movements will be communicated to the centralised warehouse via the Company's TLS and SOP [sales order processing] systems. Order lead times for delivery will be as follows:

- stock transfers to other depots: Previous day;
- customer: Previous day, up to 7 days ahead.

'Previous day' shall mean;

- Day 1 order received by the Company;
- Day 2 Contractor receives confirmation, normally by 18.00 hours, but there may be occasions when this could be up to 22.00 hours;
- Day 3 order delivered.

It is intended that the Contractor will have the facility to view provisional orders on the computer system up to seven days before the required delivery date. This will enable the Contractor to plan for any additional resources, if appropriate.

Within week seasonality should be assumed to be typically as shown in Table 2.

Table 2 Within-week demand seasonality. TEG and smaller customers

	Mon	Tues	Wed	Thurs	Fri	Sat
% wks demand	13	9	14	21	22	21

Depots					
% wks demand	21.3	21.3	16.7	19.1	21.5

Whilst the above illustrates the current profile for design purposes, the company anticipates an overall smoothing of the weekly despatch profile over the next few years.

4.6 Case picking

Case Picking will be carried out manually in a forward pick area. There must be a minimum of 400 pick locations, each with at least one reserve pallet location.

For planning purposes, you should assume that the average number of cases on a full pallet is 90. However, a picked pallet holding mixed product will hold only 60 cases.

Picking instructions will be given to the operators via Radio Data Terminals mounted on picking trucks. The order profiles are shown in Appendix 2.

Communications between the Warehouse Management System and the picker will allow on-line control of the operation, instant correction of stock discrepancies, adjustment to pick instructions, printing of accurate despatch notes and invoices, etc. Empty pallets (non-returnable) will be required for the picking operation and provision must be made for handling these as well as the stock pallets which become empty.

4.7 Despatch

The Contractor is required to assemble and despatch palletised goods up to the point of loading them on to the road vehicles. It is not envisaged that automatic equipment will be required for outward loading. However, it may be considered if so desired. Customers will require confirmation of despatch. The WMS shall produce despatch documentation.

Despatch is likely to be on to a mixture of box and curtain-sided vehicles. Flexibility needs to be provided within the design to accommodate changes in this mix.

Some loads, particularly TEG Customers, will be collected by the Customer's own vehicles. In this case the time of despatch cannot be guaranteed. It is therefore essential that sufficient space is allowed in despatch area for at least 1.5 hours worth of stock, i.e. 20 vehicle loads at peak periods.

4.8 Returns

Returns from customers are an infrequent occurrence, of the order of 0.10% of throughput. In the event of returns due to over-ordering, goods will normally be returned to stock. Returns due to quality issues will be held waiting the instructions of the Company. There will be no requirement for re-packing.

5.0 Organisation and staffing

5.1 Before start of operation

5.1.1 The Contractor will set up a project team, with a nominated team leader, to oversee the design, construction, manufacture, installation, commissioning, acceptance testing and completion of the Centralised QR Warehouse. The project team leader will represent the Contractor on the Working Group to be set up by the Company. The Company will require to approve management staff nominated by the Contractor. Appropriate CV's and/or job descriptions to be provided.

All Contractors must provide a project organisation chart indicating key personnel and areas of responsibility.

5.1.2 All designs and layouts will be submitted to the Company for comment before construction or manufacture has commenced. Reasonable notice shall be given to the Company of 'In-House' Tests prior to despatch to site to allow attendance if so desired.

5.1.3 Immediately after the instruction to proceed has been issued a detailed Project Plan including expenditure associated with the project must be submitted and this will be monitored throughout the duration of the project.

5.1.4 The Company reserves the right to visit the construction site at any time during the construction installation programme and to be present at any tests.

5.1.5 The Contractor and/or the Supplier shall provide all necessary training of operational and maintenance personnel to the satisfaction of the Company, including provision of manuals.

5.2 *After start of operation*

5.2.1 The Contractor shall provide resources to carry out the following management functions:

- management of the contract and liaison with the Company;
- management of the warehouse operation including receiving, stock control, order processing, assembly and despatch;
- management of systems and administration.

The Company will require to approve management staff nominated by the Contractor and will schedule regular review meetings to monitor progress. Additionally, the Company's Contract Manager will maintain daily liaison with operational staff. The Contractor will be required to provide cost and performance data on a period basis.
5.2.2 The Contractor will be expected to appoint a nominated Contract Manager, who will advise on and monitor all aspects of the contract concerning the distribution of the Company's products.
5.2.3 The Contractor's management will be required to ensure that warehouse staff are adequately trained to meet the performance and quality standards laid down by the Company.

6.0 Systems and procedures

6.1 *Introduction*

The purpose of this section is to outline the requirement for systems and procedures within the operation to be provided by the Contractor and/or the Supplier. In this context 'Systems' means any computer hardware or software supplied by the Contractor and/or the Supplier to fulfil the requirement of the Company. 'Procedures' means the manual operations required to operate and work with the System.

6.2 *Purpose and scope*

The Systems and Procedures will support the operation of the centralised warehouse. Nothing within the Systems and Procedures shall constrain the operation or performance of the centralised warehouse to the extent that the requirements stated in this document can not be or are not met. In particular, this requirement applies to, but is not limited to, the requirements stated in this section.
The scope of the Systems and Procedures covers all the software, hardware and associated manual procedures necessary to operate the warehouse in compliance with the requirements stated in this document. This includes the Warehouse Management System (WMS) and any control systems for automated equipment such as Automated Storage and Retrieval Systems (ASRS) and conveyors. The Radio Data Terminal (RDT) system is included within the WMS.

6.3   *Functionality*

The functionality of the Systems and Procedures is outlined and referred to elsewhere in this document. It is accepted that the detail of the functionality will need to be specified during the project, for example, to resolve the precise interfacing needs between the company TSL system and WMS. It is the Contractor's responsibility to ensure that the functionality is adequate for the purpose for which the Systems and Procedures are required.

6.4   *Performance*

The response time and throughput of the Systems and Procedures must be at least sufficient to support the peak operation of the warehouse on a sustained basis. When WMS is communicating with TLS there must be no significant degradation of performance of either system. Please indicate the basis of the assumptions made.

6.5   *Availability*

There should be no interruption to warehouse operations for hardware preventative maintenance. The System should be immune to the failure of a single processor. The Contractor should state what disaster recovery facilities can be made available and what precautions will be taken to prevent loss of data both under disaster conditions and in normal operation.

6.6   *Company access to WMS*

The Company will require access to WMS in order to transmit order details and other information via an interface with TLS. The Company will also require access to other systems facilities.

6.7   *Systems support*

The Contractor should state what support is available for the Systems in the event of software or hardware failure, the period for which this is available and the escalation procedures.

6.8   *Documentation and training*

The Company will require up-to-date copies of all documentation for the Systems and Procedures and that this documentation be kept up-to-date. The Contractor should state whether copies of the source code of all the software can be made available.

6.9 Company involvement

The Company requires to be involved in the process of specification and development of the Systems and Procedures. The Contractor should take this into account in planning the project.

Appendix 1: Profile of collections from Rugby factory (1993–4)

Week No.	Pallets	Week No.	Pallets
1	7679	27	6282
2	7366	28	8016
3	8273	29	9072
4	7621	30	10,247
5	7698	31	9820
6	7661	32	7641
7	9418	33	13,944
8	8555	34	12,947
9	7957	35	8828
10	8790	36	9696
11	8712	37	9156
12	7151	38	7216
13	1556	39	7519
14	2170	40	9584
15	4332	41	15,840
16	4871	42	15,840
17	4391	43	15,840
18	5156	44	15,840
19	6081	45	15,840
20	7146	46	15,154
21	8117	47	11,468
22	9634	48	9049
23	7051	49	11,978
24	8603	50	12,127
25	8066	51	10,458
26	8257	52	8301

Annual total 470,014 pallets

Appendix 2: Order profile by customer group (based on the average order during the average and peak weeks)

	1993–4		1997–8	
	Average	Peak	Average	Peak
TEG				
Pallets/line	1.5	3.2	1.0	2.1
Lines/order	40	40	40	40
Pallets/order	60	128	39	85
No. of orders	80	90	180	200
Pallets (100 cases/pallet)	4800	11,500	7,000	16,900
Depots				
Pallets/line	3.1	3.6	3.5	4.3
Lines/order	50	70	50	70
Pallets/order	154	254	177	300
No. of orders	65	65	65	65
Pallets (80 cases/pallet)	10,000	16,500	11,500	19,500
Total				
Pallets/line	3.7	7.6	2.6	5.5
Lines/order	28	24	29	25
Pallets/order	102	181	76	137
No. of orders	145	155	245	265
Pallets	14,800	28,000	18,500	36,400
Semi-bulk				
Cases/line	62	110	62	120
Lines/order	10	10	10	10
Cases/order	620	1100	620	1200
No. of orders	90	90	90	90

Notes: Depots and TEG – delivered in whole pallet units only.
Semi-bulk – delivered in case units on non-returnable pallets.

Appendix 3: Outline stockholding requirements
Peak stock holding will be 45,000 pallets in 1993–4.
All pallets are 1200 × 1000 mm.
Maximum pallet height = 1.6 metres.
Maximum pallet weight = 1300 kg.

Acknowledgements

The author wishes to thank Bitvic Soft Drinks Ltd and Touche Ross Management Consultants for assistance with and permission to use this case. Thanks are also due to Martin Ashford for assistance in preparing the case for publication.

Warehouse planning and operations*

John Beaty
Department of Marketing, Logistics and Property, Royal Melbourne Institute of Technology, Australia

Introduction

In March 1995, for the second time in 12 months, logistics and warehousing consultant John Beaty had been called into the Melbourne-based retail group The Discount Shop. He had just come out of a two-hour meeting with the company's managing director and was contemplating the various options for improving the warehousing and distribution-to-stores operation.

Company background

In 1987, John Potts started a chain of discount stores with a home base in Melbourne, Australia. He had a simple concept: 'everybody loves a bargain, so let's give them a store that is at the high end of the discount market'. It was called 'The Discount Shop' and it was an overnight success story. The chain had won the prestigious 'Business of the Year' award from *Business Week*, a major national business magazine. It was a privately owned company, with three directors, John Potts, the Chairman, Richard Taylor, the Managing Director and Alan Mason, Buying Director.

The Discount Shop occupied a niche market in the discount retail zone in that it appealed to discount shoppers as well as people of all income profiles who 'just appreciate a bargain'. The average sale per customer was in the region of $8 to $10. The Discount Shop concept was not new to Australia. About 40 years before, Coles and Woolworths had both established discount stores, following on from the American '5 and 10' stores where nothing was over a dime (10 cents). Over the years, Coles and Woolworth had developed into large national chains, moving away from the small discount

*This case is based on a real situation but for reasons of commercial confidentiality the name of the company, its personnel and some data have been disguide.

Note: all currency values are in Australian dollars.

shop concept. John and Richard realized that a gap in the market existed, hence their gambit into The Discount Shop. They established shops of about 5000 m^2 in major shopping centres.

By 1995 The Discount Shop employed about 500 people and had 52 stores in cities throughout Victoria, New South Wales and South Australia. The turnover had grown to about $40 million annually with the Christmas period (October to December) accounting for 30% of the volume. In 1992 the company had had just 10 stores and focused on cost-effective houseware lines with 400 stock-keeping units (SKUs). By 1995 there were 6000 SKUs with an expanded range into confectionery, clothing and car accessories. There was at least one catalogue per month, containing new lines and promoting old favourites. New stores were opening at the rate of about one per month, a rate which was planned to continue throughout 1996 and 1997. The target was 100 stores by the end of 1997.

The three directors were each specialists in their areas, John Potts was a lawyer and property expert and was responsible for the selection and development of the retail properties that the company acquired. Richard Taylor, had considerable experience in store operations and merchandising, while Alan Mason was an experienced retail buyer with over 20 years experience in the retail industry. Together, the directors of The Discount Shop were a formidable and dynamic team with a strategic focus on merchandising and buying that had delivered a winning combination across Australia.

The business philosophy of the group was to offer consumers excellent bargains in housewares, confectionery, clothing and car accessories. A great deal of their success was based on a constant stream of new lines. This could amount to 60 new product lines each week, so that customers always had a reason for coming into the shops to browse through the new bargains. In order to achieve the keen prices that attracted shoppers, the buying director needed to purchase large quantities from suppliers so as to obtain the best possible discounts.

Distribution

Up to mid-1994 the company head office and warehouse was located in Brunswick, in Melbourne's northern suburbs. However there was a shortage of office space, and the warehouse was congested and obviously was not going to cope with the continual expansion in store numbers and merchandise volume. All receipts from suppliers, both Australian and overseas, were processed through this central warehouse as were deliveries to all stores.

In July 1994 the company retained a warehouse consultant, John Beaty, to advise on the selection of a new warehouse and the design of an appropriate warehouse storage and operational system.

Beaty started the project by carrying out an audit of the existing Brunswick warehouse. An extract of his report is given in Appendix 20.1. A short time later an office and warehouse complex in Kensington, on Melbourne's inner west became available, and the management and the consultant were impressed with it's facilities. In fact the only concern was that the warehouse might initially be too large until the store expansion was more advanced. However it was decided to go ahead and a five-year lease was negotiated. A summary of Beaty's initial recommendations for the operation of the new warehouse are given Appendix 20.2 and his proposed layout is shown in Figure 20.1.

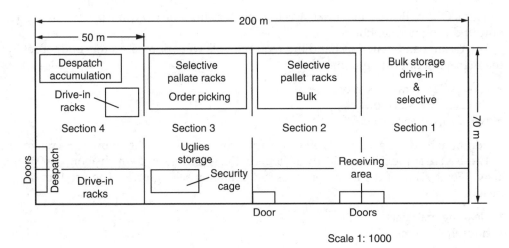

Figure 20.1 The layout of the new Kensington warehouse.

The Kensington warehouse

The new warehouse was divided into four interlinked sections, each contained by fire walls and automatic self-closing fire doors. Sections 1 and 2 contained loading docks and dock levellers, and section 4 contained two large loading doors. Section 3 had no external doors apart from emergency exits.

Beaty decided that the best configuration was to use sections 1 and 2 for receiving and storing bulk, section 3 for order picking and section 4 for despatch processing. In planning the operation he obtained confirmation from the management that the distribution concept was to be based on full cartons or 'inners', i.e. there was to be no split-case distribution. There were a few exceptions to this including jewellery, cosmetics, cane-ware and a few other non-packaged items. As a result the storage and order processing system was based on pallet racking and order picking from multi-level pallets using stock pickers.

Figure 20.1 illustrates the storage layout. There were 4000 pallet storage locations, including selective pallet racking in sections 2 and 3 and drive in racking in section 4 for despatch accumulation storage. Section 1 was left unracked and was intended for emergency block stacking. In general the intention was to limit block stacking so as to avoid product damage and ensure safety. Pallet racking was either four or five levels high, depending on the varying roof height and the pallet slot heights.

Stock was located randomly and an individual item could have multiple locations. Store orders (pull system) were picked by use of a 'man-up' crown stock-picker, the operator picking from pallet rack to the pallet on the stock picker. Each order was picked individually. Central allocations (push system) were sorted in section 4, bulk pallets were broken down by allocating to a store pallet in a sorting area. As far as possible this was a 'cross-docking' operation.

The warehouse staff consisted of 30 people. There was a warehouse manager, two shift managers, four teams on the day shift and one team on the evening shift. The warehouse labour cost was about $1 million in 1994. Overtime had been worked extensively up to this time and the warehouse labour cost was causing the managing director some concern. One of Beaty's first tasks was to rapidly reduce the overtime by improving the output during normal hours.

The racking and materials handling requirements were purchased to a budget set by the managing director and included

- 4000 pallet storage locations
- three Crown stock pickers
- two Crown reach truck.

In addition the two existing fork-lift trucks from the Brunswick warehouse were retained.

There were approximately 6000 line items in the warehouse, of which about 3000 were active. Total value of the inventory was $18 million at selling price. The product range included

- cleaning materials
- household items
- confectionery
- clothing
- car accessories
- jewellery
- cosmetics
- garden equipment.

Each of the 52 stores received two deliveries per week, which included store ordered items, new item allocations, catalogue and seasonal allocations. An average delivery to a store would be between four and eight pallets. The lead-time for processing orders and allocations was two days.

The move into the new warehouse took place in October 1994, and the Christmas 1994 distribution took place with relative success, considering the inevitable problems that occur in a new warehouse layout.

The Discount Shop was a very successful company, but like many such companies its commercial expertise far exceeded its logistics performance. Despite the new larger warehouse and improved storage and materials handling facilities, there were still some serious problems

- There was a limited warehouse information management system, based on facilities available in the business management system. Stock control was fairly simplistic, and there was no internal warehouse management system apart from a stock location record. Stock location information was manually entered into the computer after individual fork lift operators made decisions about storage location based on where they could find an empty space.
- The merchandise buying process, while successfully stocking the stores, had little concern for stock turn, or stock level, or delivery timing. The emphasis was on unit price and if this meant buying 3, 6 or 12 months stock at a time, that is what happened.
- Planning was not coordinated; catalogues, new store openings, stock takes, seasonal promotions all occurred without evaluation of the warehouse's ability to handle the workloads

By March 1995, these influences were having an obvious adverse effect on the warehouse operations. The number of pallets to be stored had risen to 6000 which meant that 2000 pallets had to be block-stacked, with all the attendant problems of damage and lack of safety. Even more important, the warehouse was rapidly approaching saturation, as the volume of receipts continued to exceed the volume being dispatched to stores. There were also signs that service levels to stores were beginning to deteriorate.

In March 1995 Richard Taylor the managing director again approached John Beaty and asked him to recommend what should be done to solve the warehouse problem.

It was clear to Beaty that the immediate priority was to increase the storage capacity to 6000 pallet positions, and reduce block-stacking to a minimum. But Beaty also considered what he should suggest to the managing director regarding warehouse policy in the light of the company's strategic plan for opening new stores. The plan called for 100 stores by the end of 1997, and clearly the current inventory levels and projected number of stores would limit the operational life of the warehouse, on which the company had a lease up to 1999. He knew there was a large piece of open ground adjacent to section 4 of the warehouse on which an extension could be built. This would increase total space by at least 25% and possibly up to 30%. However it would require an extension of the lease, possibly up to the year 2005.

[The Appendix follows overleaf]

Appendix 20.1
Evaluation of The Discount Shop Brunswick warehouse
Report from: J. Beaty, warehouse consultant
To: Richard Taylor, managing director, The Discount Shop
Dated: 1 August 1994

In general I have been impressed that the warehouse achieves its current level of store support despite all the disadvantages of lack of space equipment, systems, information, procedures, standards and forward planning. The degree of success achieved is due in the main to the resilience and determination of the warehouse staff.

It is however important to identify the deficiencies in the current operation to ensure that they are not continued in the new warehouse operation.

The major problems/deficiencies

- the almost total lack of planning and control information about receipts, locations, store orders, work in progress, and performance levels
- the storage system in that most stock is block stacked, resulting in very difficult access and I suspect an unnecessary level of damage
- the manually controlled random location system which leads to an unnecessary degree of internal travel, very low picking productivity and a total lack of information about available space
- a lack of safety in the warehouse, which is covered in more detail later in the report
- congested receipt processing, resulting from the restricted space, slowness in processing and putting receipts to stock
- a high level of paperwork and manual data input in the receipt process and in the allocation of stock to stores
- a lack of coordination between the buying department and the warehouse, which makes the speed of processing merchandise slower and more complicated than it should be
- a lack of effective control of stock rotation. With a significant proportion of short shelf-life items, it is essential to have effective control on a first in–first out (FIFO) basis
- poor house-keeping standards, including open cartons, collapsed stacks and rubbish laying around the warehouse
- the allocation decision process for new stock to be centrally allocated to stores. This must be a head office decision and the allocation information must be electronically communicated to the warehouse, as far as possible prior to the receipt of the stock.

Safety

The company, its directors and executives have a legal obligation to provide their employees with a safe working environment. In the case of the warehouse, the working environment is not safe enough. The fact that there have not been any injuries up to now is due to a combination of good luck and the athletic ability of the warehouse staff.

This situation must not be allowed to continue in the new warehouse and the following action is recommended:

- block stacking should be discontinued apart from short-term requirements and then not more than two pallets high. The majority of stock should be stored in pallet racking. This will ensure good access, will reduce damage and provide a safer working system
- safety procedures for the use of all equipment, such as stock pickers should be documented, explained to all staff and strictly enforced
- proper safety training should be introduced as soon as the move to Kensington is completed
- a company safety officer should be appointed with responsibility for safety policy, procedures and training. The warehouse manager is the logical choice for this responsibility
- safety procedures and training should include manual handling training to avoid strain injuries.

Warehouse process notes

Receipt process
- no receipts scheduling, work loads vary, considerable receipt congestion
- on arrival storeman collects delivery documentation
- receipt is unloaded, packages counted and compared with data on invoice/consignment note
- sample of cartons opened to check content and quantity correct
- receipt quantity variations noted on documentation
- receipt documentation passed to warehouse office and entered into Goods Inwards Book (GIB)
- receipt documentation passed to head office for processing (what does this consist of?)
- warehouse office identifies new products which are taken to central allocation area
- standard lines are located in the main warehouse area
- stock put away by storeman-controlled random allocation.

Store orders
- store completes store order by code, sell price and quantity required and faxes to head office
- warehouse office enters data from store into computer, stock code and quantity
- computer produces packing list showing bin location, stock code, description, quantity and price, list is printed in travel sequence
- storeman uses pick slip to pick items from locations to pallet, storeman amends pick slip if inner/outer quantities have changes from stock list, or if quantity ordered is not realistic (note this is a subjective decision, which may not always satisfy the store)
- picked order taken directly to despatch area for loading, orders are picked in accordance with the loading program
- picking slip is returned to warehouse office, data in computer re-order is amended as per changes made by storeman, invoice is printed
- pink copy of the packing slip is sent to the store with the order, also the invoice, if printed in time
- seal number is entered on packing slip.

Central allocation

• allocation sheet prepared for all stores. Quantities are notified by buyer for some lines, but if not, allocation is done by store persons based on experience and information from area managers and store managers (note this allocation process is not very scientific and can lead to some stores being over allocated and others not getting enough stock)
• items are picked as per allocation sheet, and taken to store allocation areas
• on completion of items on sheet, balances are checked and completed sheet taken to warehouse office
• photocopy of allocation sheets goes with delivery to stores
• details from allocation sheets entered into the computer to generate the store invoice
• store is sent blue copy of invoice.

Appendix 20.2
Recommendations for the layout and operation of the new Kensington warehouse
Report from: J. Beaty, warehouse consultant
To: Richard Taylor, managing director, The Discount Shop
Dated: 15 August 1994

The recommended layout of the new warehouse is shown on a separate drawing (Figure 20.1). The warehouse has the capacity to store 7000 pallets in pallet racking. I am proposing to establish racking for 5000 pallets in the first instance with expansion room for a further 2000 pallets. The basics of the proposal are as follows.

Layout

Section 1 (adjacent to the head office) is primarily the receipt processing area utilizing the two dock levellers. About 40% of this warehouse next to the receiving door will be used for receipt processing. 620 pallet spaces in a drive in configuration (5 high × 4 deep × 31 long) will be used for storage of large single-item receipts. The balance of space in this warehouse will be for future storage capacity expansion.

Section 2 will be fully pallet racked in selective pallet racking with a capacity of 1680 pallets. This is 5 pallets high × 14 rows × 10 pallets, 12 double bays. The two dock levellers in this warehouse can also be used for receipt processing, 40% of the storage space will be unused and can be an additional receipt processing area.

Section 3 will be similar to section 2 and contain 1560 pallet spaces, 5 pallets high × 13 rows of 10 pallets × 12 double bays. The lower levels will be for the fast moving items for store order picking. Again about 40% of the total space will be unused and will provide for future expansion. Some of this spare space will be used for stationary storage, store fittings, and the jewellery storage area.

Section 4 will be the despatch building. The three doors at the end of the warehouse will be the despatch doors. On the internal wall there will be a drive in rack configuration of 620 pallet positions. This will be used for the accumulation of store orders and allocations prior to vehicle loading, and for the storage of new order receipts for direct allocation to stores. There is also a requirement to have individual store allocation areas and the company concept is to have 50 caged areas each holding two pallets on the ground. I am not convinced that this is the best solution and I am proposing to rack this area with two or even three high racking providing two pallet spaces for each store. I believe this will provide better access, and better space utilization as the number of stores increases. I am assuming that the number of stores will continue to increase and could reach 100 within two to three years.

Materials handling equipment

As soon as you have agreed the warehouse layout and storage equipment mix, it will be necessary to review the current materials handling equipment to identify what additional equipment is required.

[Note: the managing director decided for cost reasons, that 4000 pallet spaces should initially be created, rather than 5000 as recommended by Beaty.]

PART SIX

Inventory management

A review of stockholding policy*†

Ian Black
Centre for Logisitcs and Transportation, Cranfield University, UK

Introduction

Following a radical review of the UK National Health Service (NHS) in 1988 the government introduced an internal market with the intention of injecting into the framework of a public service the stimulus of competition. The introduction of an internal market separated the purchase of healthcare from its provision, by making hospital and other community services dependent on patient choice for funds. An important component of the reorganization that accompanied this change was the opportunity for major providers of healthcare services – including the hospitals – to become autonomous trusts (NHS Trusts) with more freedom to pay staff, dispose of assets and purchase supplies as they saw fit. Whilst being providers of healthcare the NHS Trusts, general practitioners and community services are also purchasers of supplies necessary for their services.

Following the introduction of the internal market for healthcare and critical reports by the Audit Commission and the National Audit Office, there was a reorganization of the various fragmented supplies organizations in the NHS. In October 1991 the NHS Supplies Authority was set up to provide a total supplies service for the NHS with responsibility to not only manage the supply, storage and distribution of goods for the purchasers in the NHS but, if requested, also to negotiate contracts on their behalf.

In the financial year 1992–3 the potential market for NHS Supplies was almost £3000 million. This market included such items as stationery, cars and energy; but the major components were medical equipment (£900 million) and drugs (£500 million). Of the former about £670 million was provided by NHS Supplies. The remainder was supplied by direct purchase or independent wholesalers, who were usually closely connected to manufacturers and had always played a small but significant part in the market. One

*This case is based on an actual company but the company name and some of the data have been disguised for reasons of commercial confidentiality.
†Data available on the Internet (see page xxii).

such company was Medisupply with a turnover of £25 million through five warehouses in 1993. With the introduction of the internal market the NHS Trusts were not required to use NHS Supplies; they could choose how and where to spend their money on supplies and how much of the supply chain they wanted to manage. This apparent opportunity for the independent wholesalers was at the same time threatened by a radical reorganization in structure and, according to management, the philosophy of NHS Supplies. 'Putting the customer first', 'proactive and flexible rather than reactive and restrictive', 'a reliable, responsive and forward looking service' were phrases that were accompanied by a streamlining of the warehousing and logistics operation into a more efficient and integrated system. Savings in operating costs of over £50 million were claimed in the first two years.

The changes in the market and the opportunities available prompted a wide interest in the market for supplying medical equipment and a number of take-over attempts were initiated. A successful one in 1994 was for Medisupply by a large multinational company with strong interests in the medical and surgical equipment market. Following the take-over a major review of the Medisupply's operating practices was initiated. One of the key elements in this review focused on the company's stockholding policy which on cursory examination was considered by the new owner to be '... naive, lacking any appreciation of fundamental inventory control methods and, most important, excessively costly'.

Medisupply's products

The company's total list of products was 20,000 supplied from 300 European manufacturers. A maximum of 5000 of these products was held in stock at any one time. From this long list of products the main categories and their contribution to total sales were sutures (35%), gloves (20%), needles and syringes (9%) and dressings (6%). Each of these categories contained within it a large number of individual products. These individual products were classified by the frequency of recent orders into four bands; A: fast movers ordered at least 24 times in the last three months; B: medium movers ordered at least six times and less than 24 times; C: slow movers ordered less than six times; and Z: no order in the last three months. The number of products at that time in categories A, B and C was 752, 687 and 1240, respectively. Category A accounted for 63% of sales by value.

The main customers were Trust hospitals which generated approximately 55% of the company's revenue, the second and third largest customers were NHS Supplies (25%) and private hospitals (15%).

The initial review

In order to assess the current strength of the stockholding policy and provide a guide to the implications of any change in policy an analysis of current costs was undertaken, accompanied by an examination of the methods used to determine orders for products. The review focused on one of the company's warehouses where data were collected on the ten products that contributed most to sales. In the previous year these products had contributed 11.1% of total case throughput. These data, it was thought, could then provide an illustration of the impact of different policies and by extrapolation some

Table 21.1 Total sales for two years – ten major products (units = cases)

					Products					
month	SU15	GP07	GP09	NS42	NS44	SU09	SU05	NS22	SU17	NS08
Jan	92	43	207	68	169	198	78	190	227	20
Feb	101	41	201	101	120	161	89	164	202	20
Mar	94	38	177	131	132	169	76	269	216	17
Apr	100	49	176	94	70	139	80	182	187	39
May	97	32	197	51	113	125	79	253	214	50
Jun	105	42	185	115	140	132	74	198	222	33
Jul	100	39	176	99	117	87	141	311	234	47
Aug	98	52	171	139	152	94	99	387	217	57
Sep	104	42	191	65	148	112	94	234	221	64
Oct	96	87	177	116	190	130	85	339	212	56
Nov	93	74	185	105	155	132	133	157	198	54
Dec	90	66	175	106	175	167	82	244	235	33
Jan	103	75	174	118	139	130	90	129	231	52
Feb	103	61	167	91	193	162	101	175	226	70
Mar	95	60	165	91	210	168	89	48	233	77
Apr	104	70	134	105	173	124	102	176	236	56
May	97	68	142	104	134	124	102	184	236	68
Jun	102	71	164	122	131	111	110	231	243	59
Jul	102	64	157	148	273	62	145	283	232	68
Aug	91	74	150	93	182	80	87	310	230	65
Sep	107	64	132	103	215	64	104	218	216	57
Oct	105	71	129	112	210	118	104	331	244	53
Nov	91	63	137	89	214	117	103	185	231	76
Dec	90	53	127	60	145	137	113	149	252	77

tentative estimates of the overall impact on the company's costs and resource requirements. A list of the products and the sales over the last 24 months is given in Table 21.1. A longer data series was not possible (or only at excessive cost) owing to a changeover in the computer system used. The units of demand used (Table 21.1) were 'cases' or 'cartons'. The weight and volume of these cases for different products are rather different but this is taken into account when calculating storage requirements and costs.

The current ordering method

For categories A, B and C the system in operation at the time used the sales data for the previous six months. Average demand for this period was calculated and the second highest peak identified. The 'minimum balance' was defined as the estimated demand in the lead time for the order plus the difference between the average demand and the second-highest peak. Mathematically this is given by

$$\text{minimum balance} = L \cdot D + (D_h - D),$$

where D is the average demand, D_h is the demand at the second highest peak and L is the average lead time all defined in terms of monthly units. This minimum balance provided the trigger for a new order. The order size was one month's demand based on the average sales over the last six months.

This ordering policy was heavily criticized by some members of the review panel. The forecast of demand implicit in the calculation of average demand was thought to be too limited in the number of factors taken into account. The relevant demand, it was argued, was the expected demand in the immediate future and estimates should take into account any trend in sales and seasonal patterns that might occur. It was suggested that the company should use one of the numerous computer packages available for forecasting using techniques such as exponential weighting. The existing method was defended on the basis of its simplicity, its modest requirement in terms of data and its good track record in keeping the number of orders that could not be met immediately at an acceptable level. The percentage of unfilled orders was generally below 1% except for four products, two of which experienced quite exceptional changes in demand (Table 21.2). These large jumps in demand appear to have been due to changes in a competitor's marketing practices and could not have been forecast with any method based on analysis of trends in sales.

Table 21.2 Unfulfilled orders for two years: ten major products (percentage of total orders)

Product	SU15	GP07	GP09	NS42	NS44	SU09	SU05	NS22	SU17	NS08
Per cent	0.12	2.04	0.01	0.54	1.73	0.62	1.92	0.82	1.88	0.17

A level of less than 1% was considered acceptable as some unfulfilled orders were not cancelled but merely delivered a few days later. The net revenue loss of an unfilled order was also examined. The ratio of net profit to sales for the previous financial year was 1.7%. It was argued, however, that when considering whether to hold additional stock to avoid potential lost sales then the profit margin was much higher because the marginal, or additional cost, of holding a unit of stock was much lower than the average cost. If just the handling cost of the stock was taken into account (i.e. excluding fixed costs such as depreciation and rates) then the profit margin was estimated to increase to 5.1%. These estimates of profit provided a basis on which it was possible to examine whether the costs of extra stockholding might outweigh the revenue loss from not having items in stock. The member of the review panel closely concerned with marketing argued that with a more competitive market emerging, there was an increasing danger that lack of availability of products or late delivery of orders may lead to customers moving the entire order to another distributor.

Another technical concern with the formula used to calculate the minimum balance was the role of lead time. The formula used to estimate minimum balance did not take account of any variance in the lead times which in some cases was quite significant. The estimates of variance were highest (see Table 21.3 for figures rounded to the nearest day) where deliveries were only on one specified day a week. The main conclusion by members of the review panel critical of the existing policy was that stock levels should be increased in order to improve the service offered by the company.

Table 21.3 Costs and lead times: ten major products

Product	SU15	GP07	GP09	NS42	NS44	SU09	SU05	NS22	SU17	NS08
Storage cost (£/case/month)	0.7	0.7	0.7	1.5	1.5	1.1	1.2	0.4	1.1	0.9
Lead time (days)										
Mean	5	7	8	5	5	8	15	10	20	5
Standard deviation	2	2	2	1	1	2	4	1	4	1
Purchase cost per case (£)	71	101	66	211	29	43	129	50	21	179

The issue of the order size was also subject to some criticism. The practice of making all orders equal to one month's demand failed to take account of the difference between products. Furthermore it could lead to significantly higher stocks being held than necessary. The level of stocks was critical, as another purpose of the review was to examine the warehouse space needed for future operations; the intention being to use any spare capacity as a storage location for products of the parent company. The existing policy was defended on the grounds of its administrative simplicity and the absence of the computations and data necessary for such formulae as the economic order quantity.

Costs

An examination of the costs of holding stock and the costs of ordering posed considerable problems given the breakdown of expenditure included in the accounting framework. Examination of the all the administrative costs of placing orders, checking orders, queries and payment amounted to £25 per order. This included all office-related costs and labour costs. A study of the time and resources used for a small sample of orders (50) handled in one week tentatively suggested that of the total figure of £25, about £17 was constant regardless of order size.

When it came to the issue of the cost of holding stock the allocation of costs attempted to identify those cost elements that were dependent on the level of stock held and whether they would vary in the short or long term. The calculation of long-run warehouse holding costs included the depreciation of part of the warehouse and part of the office space (Table 21.4). Only 80% of the warehouse and 20% of the office space was included as the remainder was assumed to be used for handling orders rather than the storage function. The same percentages were used to allocate the cost of maintenance and heating of the warehouse and offices. The cost of materials handling equipment and nearly all the warehouse labour force was assumed to be related to the consolidation of orders and the movement of stock into and out of the warehouse rather than its storage. The (modest) cost of pilferage was included with maintenance of the warehouse. Any difference in the storage volume used by a product was taken into account in estimating the *per case* storage costs which are shown in Table 21.3. Given the difficulties of allocating certain costs it was reckoned that these costs were accurate to within 20% of the true figure. Turning to short-run storage costs it appeared that none of the warehouse and office costs was very sensitive to the level of stocks held.

Table 21.4 Warehouse costs in last financial year

Costs		£ (thousands)
Rates		23.5
Utilities		14.7
Labour		135.4
Administration		9.1
Maintenance		8.7
General expenses		7.2
Depreciation		57.7
Insurance		1.5
		257.8
Inventory value		423.0
Finance	0.15	63.5
Throughput (cases/year)		143,158
Cases in stock		15,747

Examination of the financial accounts also showed that the company had quite high current liabilities and was running an overdraft facility with the bank, paying an average rate of interest over the last year of 15%.

Outcome of the initial review

The initial review posed more problems than it answered. Strong arguments were put forward by one side to adopt an approach that was based on classic stock control methods. The other viewpoint was that a change of policy would be costly, requiring more data collection and a resort to methods heavy in computational complexity and based in many cases on dubious estimates of cost. The need to decide on the appropriate size of warehouse for the future gave considerable urgency to the next phase of decision making.

Collaboration in business process re-engineering: purchasing and supplies

Valerie Bence
Centre for Logistics and Transportation, Cranfield University, UK

Introduction

St James's University Hospital in Leeds is one of the biggest teaching hospitals in Europe and one of the largest acute service units in the UK National Health Service (NHS). Granted 'trust status' in April 1991, it employs over 5000 people and sees 450,000 patients a year (see Industry Note in Appendix 22.1). Operating income from the internal market totalled £125.8 million (1993–4) with 70% of the income coming from the contract with Leeds Healthcare. For 1994–5 the Trust has negotiated contracts with 12 health authorities and 130 general practitioner (GP) fundholders.

St James's provides services both locally and to the wider Yorkshire community against the background of national, regional and local objectives and priorities required to meet the ever-changing demand on services. In spite of increases in activity by the hospital, admissions and waiting lists are increasing, reflecting this increasing demand (Table 22.1).

Table 22.1 Admissions

	1991–2	1992–3	1993–4
In-patient	17,444	17,198	15,641
Day cases	16,136	21,893	27,237
Acute	36,459	37,793	39,490
Waiting list		8723	8820
Total	70,039	76,884	82,368

In 1993–4 acute admissions increased by 4.5%; day cases increased by 24.5%.

Health authorities want the best value for money service, best use of resources and high patient throughput. In addition, the government wanted 2% more activity in the financial year 1994–5 plus a 1% cost-improvement programme.

In view of the constraints and demands placed on the hospital and their commitment to improving both quality and value for money, St James's began an innovative collaboration in 1991 with Lucas Engineering Systems Ltd (LES), the aerospace and automotive group. Initial contact between the two organizations was made during a working party on electronic data interchange and the NHS. A member of St James's supplies staff encountered work done by LES, who were keen to investigate the transferability to the public sector of some of the techniques that have led to increased efficiency in car manufacturing plants. Lucas, a leader in such systems, had developed their methodologies during their restructuring in the late 1980s and were now looking beyond the manufacturing sector.

After an initial meeting, good working relations were established and possibilities were discussed of transferring the methods used in industry to within the hospital organization in order to improve the efficiency of working processes.

LES gave a presentation to St James's at board level. This overview was not project specific, but did interest the board enough for LES to be invited back to hold a two-day workshop for senior hospital managers. This would investigate possible areas for collaboration using the Lucas approach to the management of change, involving business process redesign (BPR). The aims were:

- to review LES redesign methodologies
- to discuss whether and how these principles could be applied to specific change projects at St James's and/or compliment current initiatives
- to discuss relevant case examples of the application of the methodologies in order to identify tangible benefits
- to make specific decisions on how to progress the change programme.

Following the workshop, the board gave the go-ahead for work with LES and proposals for possible projects were invited from within the hospital. Careful selection was necessary since there had to be an element of cost saving to pay for the project, which would hopefully go on to generate revenue for St James's. There were also issues surrounding trust status (management changes); the Patient's Charter (performance measurement); and customer care (quality) to consider.

Selection criteria were developed based around the need to choose something with a good chance of success, which would test the thesis that these systems could be transferred from industry, and which was health related and financially viable.

It did not take long for a number of potential projects meeting the required criteria to be identified. Both partners were learning from each other and whilst in most areas it appeared that manufacturing techniques for process change could be transferred, it was becoming apparent that there were to some extent a 'separate set of rules' for the NHS. This was because of the nature of the organization, internal and external constraints and the pace, extent and speed of change. Two projects were identified with different objectives. A reorganization of the purchasing and supplies function would hopefully meet the cost-saving requirement, whilst a reappraisal of the admission procedure was more of a cross-functional experiment, but both involved systems investigation and a process approach. Thus the final decision was:

- Project A: elective admissions
- Project B: non-pharmaceutical supplies – purchasing and supplies.

This case will examine the design and implementation of Project B.

Two groups of hospital staff were selected (on voluntary secondment) to work full-time on both projects. It was made clear early on what the starting base was, what the aims were and why they were doing it. The projects began with one week's off-site training, in order for LES to familiarize St James's staff with the theories and methodologies to be used and for the teams to look at time scales and deadlines. Both teams would have weekly progress meetings with their managers, plus presentations on findings and monthly meetings with the hospital's director of organizational development.

Producing the hospital's application for trust status acted as a catalyst for many changes and part of this involved spelling out how much and how far medical staff would become involved in hospital management. The 15 clinical directorates (similar to business units) evolved from this and covered all aspects of clinical activity at the hospital. They are headed by clinicians with day-to-day management undertaken by full-time operations managers (see the organizational chart in Appendix 22.2.)

Following project selection and staff training, specific process issues were refined in discussion with clinical directors. However, it is important to remember that St James's went into the exercise knowing what the particular process problems were but not knowing what the outcomes would be or how the process of change would evolve. Both projects represented a potential risk with large investments committed in time, money and people – and the hard work was just beginning.

Project B: non-pharmaceutical supplies

The objectives for the purchasing and supplies project were quite clear – they were to repeat the success that LES had achieved elsewhere in similar circumstances. It was felt that the methods used in this area were more easily transferable from the manufacturing sector.

Objectives

Although the aims were defined, the team did not know what the end result would be. They had, however, identified objectives and a structure to work within in order to look at the purchasing process:

- to reduce the costs of operating the purchasing system
- to improve the availability and response of the delivery of materials to the point of use (wards, etc.)
- to decrease lead times within the system (and therefore stocks held)
- to reduce the number of suppliers and product costs
- to rationalize product variety
- to make enough money to pay for the project and eventually make cost savings.

Background

Historically St James's supplies function had evolved with little planned growth; things continued to be done in the way that they had always been done and were geared to-wards saving money. In 1991 supplies was devolved down to operating units, essentially three supply teams, to cover St James, Seacroft and the Community Hospital. This arrangement was confirmed by the Audit Commission Report in 1991, which set up the NHS Supplies Authority (NHSSA). The NHSSA was able to buy in bulk at the lowest prices and it operated on three levels: national, divisional and local. St James's supplies were on the local level.

In 1991 St James's took the option open to first-wave trusts to retain the right to have their supplies staff employed directly by the trust, instead of by the NHSSA, but they could still use the NHSSA as a supplier and warehousing facility. The benefits of this were that:

- St James could retain and pay their own supplies staff
- it allowed them to purchase direct from the best supplier
- it gave them the ability to gain on economies of scale (as NHSSA gave no reductions for bulk purchases which gave St James no advantage for size)
- they had identified high on-costs with the NHSSA service (some items were on national contract to the health service and they would pay the NHS contract price plus approximately 10% on-costs, with no room for negotiation).

The supplies manager had a fairly new supplies team consisting of 24 people and he already wanted to implement changes to the system, to improve the quality of the service provided and reduce costs if possible, but not at the expense of quality. He wanted to concentrate on value for money and was looking for a way to do this, but he had to make changes whilst keeping everything running, which was a very difficult task. Collabora-tion with LES would facilitate this but with the advantage of it being on a structured basis, within a formal project and with the benefit of advice and support from Lucas.

A project team was set up in a separate room, physically remote from the supplies department and consisting of the supplies manager, a charge nurse from coronary care (who wanted to move into management), and two Lucas engineers.

These four people were taken out of their full-time posts for a period of three months, a considerable investment in time and resources. The supplies manager brought expertise from the department itself and a background in finance whilst the charge nurse had technical knowledge from the customers' perspective (customers being departments, wards, clinicians and nurses – the end users of the purchases). The LES engineers brought project management knowledge and methodologies plus the enthusiasm to transfer what were essentially manufacturing techniques into the public sector.

Following their off-site training they worked within a three-phase process: diagnosis, design and implementation. Phase One was to identify workable objectives, outline proposals and, in the case of the supplies project, work on areas for savings. Phase Two was analysing and proving that it could be done and Phase Three was implementing the necessary systems. At the end of each phase, board approval was necessary before the team could move on.

Phase One: diagnosis

The fully computerized order system showed that St James's currently purchased over 14,000 product lines from more than 1600 different suppliers. Problems soon became apparent:

- too many products – they were not buying effectively
- too many suppliers
- too many people interfering in the purchasing system
- too much information in the system
- too much inventory.

LES's expertise helped to isolate possible areas to tackle. They initially looked at high-spend areas and identified selected product ranges for further investigation. Within the 15 clinical directorates each ward or department had its own budget. Previously, each one ordered whatever they wanted from supplies as it was needed. Storage was on an *ad hoc* basis in individual wards, with stock being spread over many areas, leading to duplicate orders and overstocking for many items. This decentralized purchasing system had simply evolved over time and every budget holder had the freedom to spend within their budgets, i.e. medical representatives would sell to individual ward sisters. As a result, single items (e.g. syringes) had many different suppliers and the main function of Supplies had been to process all orders raised by all budget holders, on as many as 10–12 different requisition systems (depending on what was being ordered). Thus, the main problem to be addressed was how to stop people having the freedom to choose which products and which suppliers to use.

At this stage the team had a problem. Having done the analysis and identified the problem, they had to look for a mechanism which would take into account the needs of directorates, individual budget holders and the supplies function and at the same time be transferable for all purchases (old and new). That would be the task of Phase Two.

At the end of Phase One the recommendations were:

- to reduce the product range and the supplier base, therefore ultimately reducing purchasing costs
- to alter the system of providing goods to wards and departments (storage, delivery, etc.)
- to review the ordering system and processes within the supplies function itself.

These recommendations were accepted and the team moved on to Phase Two – verifying the benefits and designing solutions.

Phase Two: design; Phase Three: implementation

These two phases will be considered together, as once the recommendations were proven to be necessary and/or desirable, implementation was the next logical step and followed quickly. The following three areas had been identified as requiring new systems, and process design and the next task was to set about proving the need to change the *status quo*, e.g.

(a)   Reducing the product range and supplier base would reduce costs.

(b) That altering the system of ordering, delivery and storage of goods for wards and departments was desirable and/or necessary.

(c) Following on from (b), a review of processes was needed within the supplies function in order to implement these changes – a move to materials management.

A. Reducing products and suppliers

The team began by choosing four or five different product ranges and concentrating on a few high-spend departments, e.g. X-ray, renal unit, anaesthetics. Main products and suppliers were analysed and data gathered, e.g. the hospital was purchasing 18 kinds of disposable gloves, from disposable plastic costing 50p per 100 to surgeons' gloves costing several pounds per pair. A member of the team did a breakdown of where and when the different types were used, spoke to different departments and users, looked at suppliers and arranged trials. The need for some variety was accepted and in the end three types of gloves were decided on: sterile examination gloves, non-sterile and surgeons'. None of these was the cheapest on the market but they were thought to be the best value for money.

Thus, the link between reducing suppliers and costs was shown by looking at such specific examples. The team also investigated possible savings gained by rationalizing suppliers, e.g. anaesthetics bought six perishable items for anaesthetics machines (tubing, etc.) from six different suppliers at a cost of £45,000 per year. In Lucas's manufacturing experience if all products could be sourced from a single supplier, then considerable discounts could be negotiated, but was this transferable to the hospital? The team visited all six suppliers and found that each one could provide all six items! One was chosen, discounts were negotiated and all the items were delivered at the same time in a single-drop operation with a saving of £13,000 per year.

The director of pharmacy and supplies used a drug audit group for the selection of pharmaceutical supplies and this model became one of the recommendations of the project team for the selection of non-pharmaceutical products. The chief executive officer (CEO) and the board accepted this and authorized the formation of a product selection group (PSG). This would be chaired by a consultant and include representatives invited from the clinical directorates, technical specialities (e.g. physics, pathology) and finance, with a total of 10–15 members. Meeting monthly, their brief was to examine the whole range of non-pharmaceutical supplies (the 14,000-plus products currently in use), group them together and rationalize, giving recommendations on the best value for money items. They would then have the mandate to impose their recommendations hospital-wide. For example, they decided that only three types of gloves identified during project analysis could be ordered, although exceptions could be made if a purchaser could demonstrate a special or even one-off need for a product, which would in turn be examined by the PSG.

B. Storage and delivery system to wards and departments

The team examined what was actually being ordered and put the products into three categories (again borrowed from manufacturing): runners (stock items used all the time), repeaters (items used occasionally, with known suppliers), strangers (new items, which could be one-offs).

All items ordered by budget holders were put into these three categories (using the computer order data) and patterns for each ward or department were analysed. The existing system was that each ward would decide what it needed and place a requisition through to supplies. If it was a stock item, an order would be placed accordingly and the items obtained mainly from NHSSA; if not, an individual order would be raised to a specific supplier: how it was ordered depended on what it was.

A procurement system was needed which should be designed around the three groups, runners, repeaters and strangers, and which would eliminate the ward sister's involvement with stock levels. The recommendation was for a materials management system to be introduced, which would eventually be hospital-wide, controlled by the supplies function. The old order system had resulted in fragmented stockholding, vast overstocking and bad use of storage space on wards. The need was for purpose-built, high-density storage and LES recommended a Kanban system of continual replenishment; this is based on the Japanese storage-bin replenishment system, where stock is ordered as it is used.

The team found haphazard storage on wards and £200,000 worth of overstocking, this was money tied up in inventory. Once identified, the solution was to stop orders being placed for the next three months to use up the overstocking. With the money freed in this way, each ward invested in high-density shelving and converted the main store-room to an effective storage system. A major problem was to prevent people wanting to hold large quantities of inventory 'just in case'. The materials management system was first introduced to one floor of Gledhow wing; this proved very effective and soon afterwards all wards in this wing had their stock managed by supplies.

C. Reorganization of the supplies function itself

There had been 24 people in the existing supplies function, seven or eight of whom were buyers processing orders from budget holders, supported by the computer system.

The purchasing department itself was reorganized to accommodate the changes necessary to move to a materials management system (but they too had their own budget constraints). Fewer requisitions and orders should reduce the buyers' workload; all staff were interviewed and some became materials managers with different responsibilities.

New roles entailed close liaison with budget holders on the wards and departments to set appropriate initial stock and reorder levels for all items. In addition, weekly visits were made to the wards to check stock levels and reorder as necessary around the three category groups; runners were ordered weekly; repeaters, with known sources, were ordered less often, possibly three or six monthly; and strangers were slightly different. Since these are non-stock items (e.g. furniture or items for special patients) they were ordered only when required, and this could still be done by the budget holders.

Within the supplies function, buyers had previously been organized around budget holders, e.g. one dealing with X-ray purchases. Following rationalization of the product range and suppliers, LES recommended that after the move to materials management the remaining buyers should develop their expertise around product groups. This was implemented and is shown in Appendix 22.3.

The new system was quite a change for personnel. Budget holders no longer placed orders (except for one-offs); they could still see the sales representative and request the purchase of new items but this would go before the PSG. They no longer had responsibility for overseeing stock levels on wards and money was not tied up in inventory as before. Staff could always be sure where to find stock, and goods should be in the store room bins as required and replaced as used. Some saw this as a freedom from tiresome administration, others as a loss of power.

Supplies staff were given new responsibilities, and materials managers took direct responsibility for ordering, stocking and delivering to wards as and when needed, as well as the initial negotiating of stock levels.

Buyers soon developed expertise in specific product areas and built relationships with fewer suppliers. NHSSA and suppliers became the central stores function, with stores at the hospital responsible only for the receipt of goods and distribution to wards and departments on arrival, usually in ward boxes.

This BPR project was a success for the hospital and has resulted in considerable cost savings. The CEO required that this project should ultimately pay for the BPR project collaboration with LES, and this has been done. Future savings on product rationalization will benefit the hospital directly. The project team and the PSG continue to monitor all product orders and the emphasis is on value for money with the most appropriate product, not necessarily the cheapest, being used for quality, safety and customer satisfaction.

Summary of achievements from supplies project

The supplies project team met its aims and achieved the following.

- It established mechanisms to review current suppliers and product range.
- It removed some suppliers and products from use.
- It reduced stockholding inventory at ward level and transferred funds to buy a 'custom' storage system.
- It created materials managers within the supplies and purchasing department, who developed improved relationships with their suppliers.
- It established mechanisms for assessing new products and controlling the introduction of new products – PSG.
- It established 'technical' support for supplies.

At the time of writing, the new materials management system was almost hospital-wide and continuing to make savings.

Acknowledgements

The author gratefully acknowledges the help given by staff at St James's Hospital, Leeds, during the research for this case.

This case was written with the help of The Harold Burmeister Scholarship 1995, created by the Centre for Organizational Studies, Barcelona, and is available from European Case Clearing House, Cranfield, Beds, UK.

Appendix 22.1: Industry note

The 1979 election victory by the Conservative Party in the UK has had a profound impact on the structure and culture of public sector organizations. Many profitable state industries were privatized whilst a new strategy was adopted for public sector services (previously run around the welfare ethos) based on the creation of 'internal markets'; budgetary devolution and competitive tendering (internal and external). These new markets are best illustrated by the health and education sectors and the UK public sector is now characterized by a competitive contract system and devolved responsibility for performance at individual business unit level (e.g. hospital, health authority, school).

The State remains the primary source of funding, thus the UK government gives local/regional health authorities funds to purchase or commission health care on behalf of their population. Health authorities then commission hospitals or Trusts to fulfil a series of contracts, delivering set amounts of operations and admissions over a given time, e.g. in 1993 St James's was contracted by Leeds Health Authority to provide 4695 in-patient episodes of general surgery, a set number of maternity deliveries, etc.

Local health authorities (LHAs) are the customers, and patients are seen both as customers and as the 'products' of the system. The waiting list represents the order book and the objective is 'order fulfilment', a successful admission and operation for patients, giving customer satisfaction and fulfilling contractual obligations for the LHA. Therefore, since processes influence the order book, if they are not carried out correctly or efficiently, people could buy the 'product' elsewhere. The hospital needs to ensure that its processes are as effective as possible so that all customers (general practitioners, health authorities and patients) are happy with the product.

It is important to remember this background, especially the funding implications (which are fairly new to the NHS) when considering this case. The modern NHS, like all other businesses, has many financial constraints including income generation, budget performance, and return on assets and contract targets (Appendix 22.2). It must also strike a balance between its customers and other stakeholders. Over the past four years the organization has had to undergo major changes in moving towards market orientation. The project outlined in this case fits more easily into this culture, since the hospital still needs to be able to gather and collate information for contracts and costs, which would be impossible if the central functions were dismantled. Projects such as A, if it were extended, would fragment the organization and information for purchasers, patients and LHAs would be spread over as many as 15 directorates. This was not a potential problem for Project B and may have contributed to its success.

Appendix 22.2: St James's University Hospital Trust – corporate management structure, July 1994

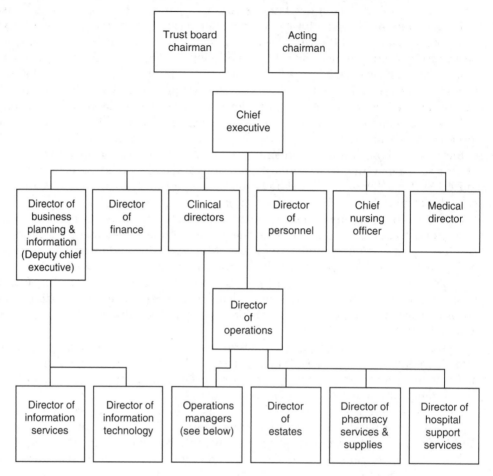

Clinical directors

Accident & emergency
Anaesthetics
Children's services
Elderly services
General medicine
General surgery
Intensive care
Orthopaedic surgery
Pathology
Radiology
Renal services
Plastic surgery
Special surgery
Theatres
Women's services

Operations managers

Children's services
Elderly services
General surgery
Medical services
Operating theatres
Renal services
Special surgical services
Women's services

Appendix 22.3: Reorganization of purchasing and supplies department

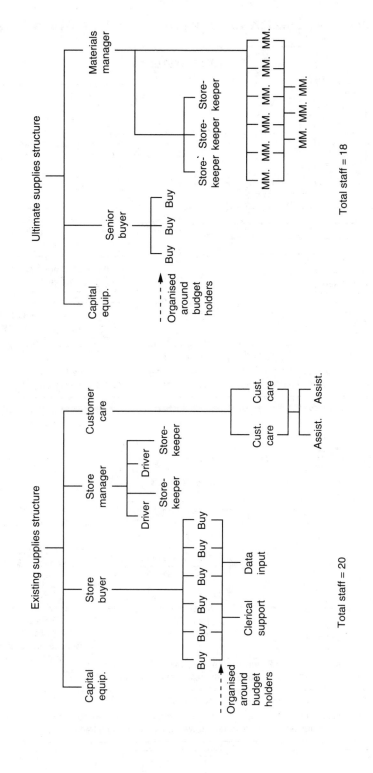

Existing supplies structure

Capital equip. — Store buyer — Store manager — Customer care

Store buyer: Buy Buy Buy Buy Buy Buy Buy Buy — Clerical support — Data input

Organised around budget holders

Store manager: Driver, Driver, Store-keeper, Store-keeper

Customer care: Cust. care, Cust. care — Assist. Assist. Assist.

Total staff = 20

Ultimate supplies structure

Capital equip. — Senior buyer — Materials manager

Senior buyer: Buy Buy Buy

Organised around budget holders

Materials manager: Store-keeper, Store-keeper, Store-keeper

MM. MM. MM. MM. MM. MM. MM. MM. MM. MM. MM. MM.

Total staff = 18

Appendix 22.4: Health care supply at St James's Hospital

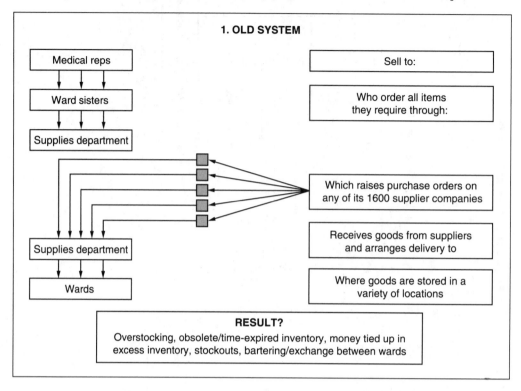

1. OLD SYSTEM

Medical reps

Ward sisters

Supplies department

Supplies department

Wards

Sell to:

Who order all items they require through:

Which raises purchase orders on any of its 1600 supplier companies

Receives goods from suppliers and arranges delivery to

Where goods are stored in a variety of locations

RESULT?
Overstocking, obsolete/time-expired inventory, money tied up in excess inventory, stockouts, bartering/exchange between wards

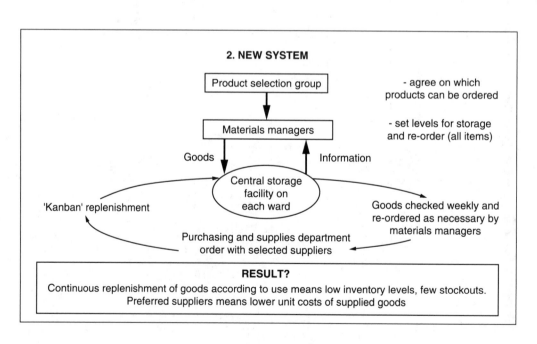

2. NEW SYSTEM

Product selection group

Materials managers

Goods   Information

Central storage facility on each ward

'Kanban' replenishment

Goods checked weekly and re-ordered as necessary by materials managers

Purchasing and supplies department order with selected suppliers

- agree on which products can be ordered

- set levels for storage and re-order (all items)

RESULT?
Continuous replenishment of goods according to use means low inventory levels, few stockouts. Preferred suppliers means lower unit costs of supplied goods

PART SEVEN

Transport management

Camels in the desert night: transport safety analysis

Will Murray
Department of Transport and Logistics, University of Huddersfield, UK
and
Adrian Grey
Personnel Manager, Almarai Ltd, Saudi Arabia

Introduction

Almarai is the Middle East's leading dairy foods processing company. Adrian Grey, Almarai's Operations Division Personnel Manager, had just completed his July 1993 meeting with the company's Transport Safety Group. He was concerned that despite the many safety measures that the company had introduced into its long-haul transport fleet over the past few years, the number of accidents involving the company's vehicles had continued to increase.

In 1992 an in-house transport safety group had been formed to examine the operations of the long-haul fleet, analyse international best practice and make recommendations appropriate to the environment. The outcome was an Almarai transport safety policy that was adopted by the company in October 1992. The policy covered the regulation of drivers' operating hours and rest times, the use of tachograph control and the introduction of company speed limits. In essence the policy was a start – the introduction of an imposed structure into a culture that had no regulation or legislation imposed by national authorities.

In an attempt to build on the initial successes, Grey decided that action was required on the following three fronts.

- **Driver selection**: a more structured approach to driver recruitment was required, with stringent testing regimes as the underpinning requirement.
- **Driver training**: a comprehensive analysis of training needs needed to be conducted and a structured approach to driver induction and training to be undertaken as a matter of urgency. The emphasis on existing driver training was to be on attitude, defensive driving and accident avoidance.

- **Causes of accidents**: a detailed analysis of accidents was required to establish the root causes of accidents and to develop an accident database to establish trends and provide structure for additional focus.

The driver selection issue could be tackled on an in-house basis in conjunction with the recruitment agencies, but both the training and the fleet safety analysis required appropriate expertise. Accordingly, Almarai requested the assistance of a specialist driver training agency and a transport safety consultant. To give the chosen consultant a greater understanding of the Saudi Arabian environment, the company's operations and the issues at hand, Grey prepared the following brief.

The Kingdom of Saudi Arabia and its environment

The Kingdom of Saudi Arabia (KSA) controls over 25% of the world's oil reserves, and is a religious centre for over 1 billion people world-wide. Islam is the official religion of the country and Arabic the major and official government language. However, until the 1970s few people knew much about the country or where it was in the world. Those who did, associated it with camels, Bedouin tents, sultans, sheikhs and harems.

The global demand for oil to fuel the growth in the use of motor cars in Europe and the USA changed all that. Almost overnight KSA became a world power, and obtained the finances to develop huge education, agriculture, construction, technology, transport, telecommunications and military infrastructures (Al-Farsy, 1990). Despite this diversification of the economy, in 1994 oil production still accounted for about 80% of gross domestic product. Much of the growth and development was undertaken using expert expatriate skills and labour from all over the world. Price Waterhouse (1991) provide a comprehensive guide to 'doing business in Saudi Arabia'.

Despite its rapid development Saudi Arabia remains an absolute monarchy, in which all legal and social processes are based on Islamic principles and Bedouin traditions. The five daily prayer times of Islam are respected and most Muslim holy days, pilgrimages and festivals observed. Foreign visitors and residents are expected to respect the social and religious customs and conventions, including a total ban on alcohol.

The population of Saudi Arabia is estimated at between 9 and 14 million, about two-thirds of which now lives in urban areas, compared to a third in the mid-1970s. This change has seen urban migration from rural areas, and a large influx of foreign workers. The increase in the population of the capital Riyadh (Figure 23.1) from less than 10,000 in 1975 to over 700,000 today gives a good indication of the pace of urban growth. Jeddah, the Red Sea-based commercial capital and largest port, has grown from a walled city of under 50,000 in 1945 to about 600,000 today. Other major cities are Mecca, the holy city, which is closed to non-Muslims, and hosts about 2 million religious pilgrims annually; Taif, Medina (also a religious pilgrimage site closed to non-Muslims), Yanbu, Jizan and Khamis. The major oil regions are in the east of the country, based around Al Khobar, Dammam and Dhahran.

The KSA weather, although varied, can be summed up as desertic, dry and hot. During the months between May and September average monthly temperatures rise above 35–40°C. Inland the desert heat is fierce and dry, in the coastal regions it is hot and damp. Only in some mountainous areas are temperatures moderate. December through to March sees average monthly temperatures drop to 15–20°C. Average rainfall in the

Figure 23.1 The Kingdom of Saudi Arabia.

kingdom is about 120 mm per annum. Strong winds often cause desert sandstorms. The topography of the kingdom varies widely from the coastal plains of the Red Sea, focusing on Jeddah in the west; through mountain ranges to the vast desert of Rub al Khali (the empty quarter) in the south of the country. The culture, climate and geography of Saudi Arabia are totally different to anything experienced in the 'western' countries of Europe and America.

The Saudi Arabian road network

The roads throughout the kingdom are generally of a high standard. Most inter-urban routes are expressway (motorway) and urban areas make extensive use of flyover facilities and American-style traffic control systems.

Driving standards, however, are low. The country has a high accident rate. A lot of road accidents are speed related, with consequential effects in terms of injury, disability and death. While no accident statistics are available, the number of deaths attributable to road accidents is much higher than in European countries. The problem is compounded by a number of unique issues.

* Large herds of camels and goats wander across most areas unhindered. Camels in particular, weighing an average 1000 kg, pose a serious hazard to motorists. This is particularly the case at night, or in times of poor visibility. A camel meeting a truck travelling at 110 km/h yields no winners!
* The large mix of cultures in KSA has resulted in varying levels of driving standards. In particular, African and Asian expatriate contract workers transfer poor driving standards from their countries of origin into Saudi Arabia.
* There is a low rate of prequalification and driver skill development within the indigenous population.
* The policy of not allowing females to drive encourages the use of under-age, inexperienced, male drivers.

Unlike regions such as Europe, USA and Australia, KSA has no statutory regulations and safety requirements relating to the operation of commercial vehicles. Issues such as permitted driving hours, speed, tachographs and the general operation of commercial vehicles, that are strictly adhered to in Europe, are not followed.

The company

Almarai is the largest dairy operation in the Middle East, employing over 2500 people, drawn from 29 different countries. The company was originally established in the mid-1970s by the Irish dairy farming company Mastock. Although it is now substantially owned by a number of Saudi interests, the strong influence of Irish expertise and management can still be seen through the company's many expatriate Irish managers.

The activities of the group are highly vertically integrated, from 'crop to shop'. The company's arable farms provide fodder for the cows at their dairy farms. Herds are maintained in controlled, air-conditioned, environments and fed using a computerized food-mixing and preparation system. The raw milk is processed at four large state-of-the-art processing facilities located at Jeddah, Khamis, Al Kharj and Judah. It is distributed via Almarai's in-house long-haul transport fleet to 20 sales depots throughout the Middle East for onward distribution to customers. Almarai's range of dairy products (including milk, laban, cheese and yoghurt) is distributed by the company's local delivery vehicles and sold through 13,000 outlets across KSA and the other Gulf countries.

The management structure of the company is relatively decentralized. The operations division is responsible for farm collections of raw milk, processing and bulk distribution. Local delivery is the responsibility of the sales and retail division. Adrian Grey was particularly concerned about the long-haul transport fleet. However, many of the issues discussed are equally relevant to the company's smaller local distribution vehicles and company cars.

Long-haul transport fleet

The operations division has four processing plants located in different regions of KSA. It operates a long-haul transport fleet of about 80 vehicles to collect milk from the farms, transfer products and raw materials interplant and deliver finished product to the company's depots. The long-haul fleet is based at the three sites shown in Figure 23.1: Al Kharj, Jeddah and Khamis. From each of these depots, vehicles operate on a 24-hour basis.

The farms, plants and depots are spread across the Arabian Peninsular, which is bigger than western Europe. In the words of one of the company's transport managers, the operation is the equivalent of 'collecting milk from a farm in Berlin, processing it in Dublin and then placing it for sale as a packaged product in Madrid. Considering the short shelf life and temperature control requirements of the product, this is a massive and complex operation.'

Almarai's long-haul transport fleet consists of 80 high-specification tractor units, mainly Scania and Man vehicles which are sourced in Europe. In addition, there are 45 bulk tankers and 70 refrigerated trailer units (reefers). Each tractor unit averages approximately 1000 km per day, or 300,000 km per year. In 1994 the fleet was on average one year old, with no vehicles over three years old. The typical replacement life is up to four years or 1,000,000 km. The fleet undertakes in excess of 25 million km per annum.

The drivers employed by the company comprise Saudi nationals and expatriate Thais and Filipinos. Typically, the Saudi drivers work on the longest haul international routes, as unlike the non-Saudis, they do not have problems obtaining multiple-exit visas from KSA. The Thai and Filipino drivers work almost solely within KSA.

The accident problem

In response to a rising awareness and concern about the problems and costs of accidents in the long-haul fleet, Almarai set up a transport safety group in 1992. The group included the personnel manager, the transport managers, the fleet engineer, and a representative from Almarai's insurers. As well as the financial implications of accidents (particularly rising maintenance and insurance costs) they were particularly concerned about the moral implications of people being killed in accidents involving Almarai vehicles. However, as the transport operation and management was decentralized to the processing sites, the level and quality of management information and emphasis given to safety procedures varied substantially with location. Much of the information relating to safety and insurance, which is required in Europe, was not actually kept or considered important in KSA.

Despite this problem, the transport safety group took many positive steps, including looking closely at legislation in other countries, evaluating Almarai's existing long-haul routes from a safety point of view, setting up driver awards for safe driving in conjunction with their insurers and undertaking some analysis and discussion of the previously reported accidents.

In 1992 managers on the safety group accompanied drivers on a series of routes and reported their findings back to the group. Exhibits 23.1(a–c) shows three examples of their reports.

Exhibit 23.1(a)   Safety group report on the Jeddah to Khamis route

MEMO
To: Transport safety group
From: AR, Training Officer
Subject: Reefer route investigation report, Jeddah – Khamis – Jeddah
A Information
Reefer number: x; trailer number: x
Driver name: AB; Nationality: Thai; Number of years as Almarai driver: 2.5
The road condition is good, with a 2 way lane highway and well equipped road reflectors for night time vision. The environment is mountainous and the road going from Mujayil very 'zigzag'. Approximately 11 tunnels are built as passages through the mountains, along with bridges along the side of the mountains. Slopes range from 30–45 degrees. Police check points are very common along this stretch of road.
B Observations
Route 1: Jeddah – Khamis
Time left Jeddah: 1500 hr
Date: 16/2
Time arrived Khamis: 0300 hr
Date: 17/2
 1. The driver stopped for 1 hour to take his dinner, after about 5 hours' driving.
 2. Heating of food and coffee is being done inside the truck cab using a portable LPG stove.
 3. The driver does not use the seatbelt provided.
 4. The driver does body stretching while the vehicle is in motion due to physical fatigue.
 5. Driving speed did not reach 100 kph, average was about 85.
 6. Second stop after another 2 hours drive to take rest and sleep for 2 hours.
 7. Third stop, at Mujayil Town, after another 1 hours drive. Half an hour rest, driver taking coffee and some outdoor exercises to keep himself awake in preparation to drive up the 'zigzag' road to Abha. Average speed on this road is 20 kph.
 8. Upon reaching Khamis the driver sleeps in the truck sleeping compartment while waiting for transport people to report for work (0800). The average sleeping time whilst waiting at Khamis is 4 hours.
 9. The driver also has to drive the vehicle to the unloading area so that it can be unloaded.
 10. The driver checked the tyres of the vehicle at every stop.
Route 2: Khamis – Jeddah
Time left Khamis: 1200 hrs
Date: 17/2
Time arrived Jeddah: 0300 hrs
Date: 18/02
About 1.5 hours going down the mountainous 'zigzag' road in Abha. Average speed is 20 kph.
After 7 hours' drive from Khamis, 1 hour stop for dinner.
Second stop after another 3 hours' drive, takes 3 hours' sleep.
C Recommendations
 1. Provide sleeping quarters or transit room, with food and drinks, for drivers to relax and rest properly after arrival at destination.

Exhibit 23.1(a) (Continued)

2. Rest times and provision for permanent stops can be established, however I believe the drivers know when to stop and rest – as it depends on their physical feelings. Stops and rests should be up to the drivers, as long as they reach their destination in the time specified.
3. On this route, after 6–7 hours' driving is a reasonable time for the driver to stop and take a rest.
4. Provide shunting personnel to manoeuvre vehicles at destinations. This will allow drivers who have driven long journeys to sleep and prepare themselves for their next trip. The number of stops *en route* would be lessened and travel time reduced.

Is it allowed to cook or heat food inside the cab using an LPG stove?

Exhibit 23.1(b) Safety group report on the Al Kharj to Khamis route

MEMO: Trip report
To: Transport safety group
From: RT, Personnel and Insurance Officer
Route: Al Kharj – Khamis – Al Kharj
Date: 26/2
Driver: D; Driver nationality: Thai
Vehicle: x1
Trip survey
We left Al Kharj at 12:30 pm loaded with empty crates.
From Al Kharj to Dilam Town the road is 3 lanes on each side. After Dilam the roads are mainly 2 lane.
The average speed of the tractor was 110 km/h. We encountered 3 police checkpoints on the way. We ate at around 5 pm, and again at Khamis. Each meal break took about an hour.
Approximately 150 km before Khamis is a mountainous area with a 'zigzag' road. As the elevation increases, so the average speed reduces.
We arrived at Khamis at 1:30 am on 27/2, after a total trip of about 13 hours.
Going back to Al Kharj we had a load of UHT milk. The trip back took 13 hours along the same route.
Recommendations
1. We should allocate approximately 15 hours for the trip from Al Kharj to Khamis, to allow ample time for driving and rests.
2. It is advisable to create a transit room for drivers to get proper rest and have a place to clean themselves before travelling the following day.

Allocate 1 rest day per week per driver; and if a driver has just completed a long trip, the next should be a short one.

Exhibit 23.1(c) Safety group report on the Al Kharj to Buraidah route

MEMO: Trip report
To: Transport safety group
From: PP, Site QA Manager
Route: Buraidah
Date: 10/6
Driver: TM; Driver nationality: Thai; Driver age: 51
Vehicle: x2

A visit was paid to Buraidah Depot with a reefer vehicle on 9/6. The following observations were made.

1. Buraidah Depot is located about 25 km from Buraidah Town and is approximately 500 km away from Al Kharj plant.
2. Every week six trips are made to Buraidah from Al Kharj by a single driver.
3. The driver leaves Al Kharj at 8:30 am and reaches Buraidah at 2:30 to 3 pm.
4. The Buraidah unloading bay is an open one (with no shade or covering) so unloading starts only after 6 pm (to avoid product exposure to heat). Unloading takes 3 hours.
5. The driver leaves Buraidah at about 10 pm and reaches Riyadh at about 2 am, where he sleeps for 4 hours only. He then starts again for Al Kharj to lift the next load for Buraidah.
6. During his stay at Buraidah depot (3 pm to 10 pm) the driver cooks his meal and takes a few hours' sleep inside his cab. It looks unlikely that he gets a sound sleep, due to the continuous disturbance of the unloading/loading (of empty crates) work going on.
7. There is no provision for any rest-room at the depot. The driver cooks his food in the cab of his vehicle, which is undoubtedly a safety hazard.
8. There was no speed limiter on this vehicle, and speeds well over 120 km/h were noticed. However, the condition of the road was excellent with very few instances of broken camel fences along the side of the road. The driving was found to be very stable with no jerks or rushing by the driver.

Recommendations
1. There is a definite need to rework the schedule, as it looks too much for a single driver to make 6 round trips of 1000 km each week.
2. It would be better if timings are reworked. The start from Al Kharj could be delayed by 2 hours to enable the driver to get a few more hours' sleep.
3. There should be provision of a rest-room at Buraidah where drivers can take a rest and cook food.
4. Cooking in the driver's cab should be stopped immediately, as it is a safety hazard.
5. There is a need to relook at the speed limit of 110 km/h. In my view, looking at excellent roads, and the heavy stable loads of reefer vehicles, perhaps it could be increased to 120 km/h.

Transport safety policy

In October 1992 Almarai developed a safety policy (introduced by the company, but not a statutory requirement in KSA), the main points of which were:

• maximum speed set at 110 km/h
• drivers' hours and rest periods
• tachograph use
• driver recruitment, induction, training, assessment, incentives and disciplines
• fleet maintenance and replacement guidelines
• accident reporting.

More details of the policy are shown below.

Drivers' hours and rest periods

Even though KSA has no statutory control on drivers' hours Almarai has developed its own driving regulation policy as an internal safety measure. Table 23.1 shows the drivers' hours policy that the company put in place, compared with the statutory regulations for Europe and the State of Victoria in Australia. (For a fuller description of EU regulations see Exhibit 25.7, page 282.)

Tachograph use

Tachographs are not required by law in Saudi Arabia. However, they are fitted into all Almarai long-haul vehicles, so that the recommended speed limits and rest periods can be controlled. In 1993 the company had decided to establish two tachograph analysis centres at Al Kharj and Jeddah, to allow analysis and interpretation of tachograph charts. However, no deadline was set for the implementation of the centres, and the company suspected a high level of tampering with the tachograph equipment and charts by drivers.

Systematic driver recruitment, induction, training, assessment and discipline

Almarai's safety policy document stated that all new drivers should preferably have experience in driving in the Middle East and be recruited and trade tested in KSA. The test would be a short practical driving test in a large goods vehicle. This was not always

Table 23.1 Comparison of Almarai's drivers' hours policy with the statutory regulations in Europe and Australia

	Almarai	Europe	Victoria State, Australia
Maximum uninterrupted driving	6 h	4.5 h	5 h
Maximum total driving time in 24 h	15 h	9/10 h	12 h
Minimum rest after 6 h driving	1 h	–	–
Minimum rest after 4.5 h driving	–	45 minutes	–
Maximum driving time in 7 days	90 h	45 h	approx. 72 h
Maximum distance in 7 days	6500 km	–	–
Minimum rest period in 7 days	24 h	45 h	–

h: hours; – indicates no similar regulation exists.

adhered to, and often several drivers were recruited *en mass* from Thailand or the Philippines. In some cases no vehicle or time was available for the tests. Other criteria for new drivers include fluency in oral and written English (Arabic for Saudi nationals), age range 30–45 years and a thorough medical investigation. The nationality mix is confined to Saudi, Filipino and Thai nationals.

Almarai's induction process for new drivers included briefings on:

- the company organization and product range
- detailed information on transport equipment and costs
- Saudi law and work practices
- general personnel and administration policy
- safety.

All new drivers had a probationary period of three months, a period which included initial training. The training programme set out in the safety policy document covered: basic and advanced driving skills, equipment use, yard work (where new drivers typically start working for Almarai), product handling and temperature requirements, documentation and Saudi traffic regulations and customs. A new driver training manual based on all these areas was drawn up for use during induction training. Where necessary, the needs of the business dictated the extent and depth of the induction and training programme. In other words, during very busy periods it may not have been strictly adhered to, and drivers may have been expected to operate without completing all of the training and induction process.

A 'carrot and stick' approach was taken to driver management. The 'carrot' included trip allowances as well as the basic salary, a formally presented annual safety certificate for accident-free drivers and an annual depot and company-wide driver of the year award sponsored by Almarai's insurers. The 'stick' was a very strong disciplinary procedure, where drivers faced dismissal for failing to comply with speed, compulsory rest periods and any other company guidelines, or interfering with vehicle tachographs or speed limiters.

Fleet maintenance and replacement guidelines

Table 23.2 compares the maintenance and tyre replacement schedules between Almarai and a similar UK-based company.

Table 23.2 Vehicle maintenance and tyre replacement schedules

	Almarai	Typical UK company
Service periods		
Tractors	10,000 km	10,000 km or 4–6 weeks
Tankers	6 months	10,000 km or 4–6 weeks
Running gear	6 months	10,000 km or 4–6 weeks
Tyre replacement		
Tractors front	110,000 km	60–110,000 km
Tractors rear	250,000 km	110,000 km
Tankers/trailer	220–300,000 km	80,000 km

Accident reporting

After each accident the company completed an Interim Accident Report Form (Exhibit 23.2) and an accident sketch. This information was aggregated for insurance and cost purposes. However, uninsured accidents (those under the insurance excess of US$2000) were not generally included. The forms were stored in files at head office by the operations division's accountant and no further use was made of them.

The transport safety group's summary report of the nine major accidents involving Al Kharj vehicles from January to September 1993 is shown in Exhibit 23.3. Many theories and viewpoints within the company were put forward for the causes of such accidents, including:

* speeding
* tiredness
* driver incompetence, particularly use of brakes and driving too close
* milk tanker instability (especially when only part full)
* the lack of experience of many of the drivers in KSA road and climatic conditions
* tyre blow-outs
* camels straying on to the road at night
* poor driver recruitment and training
* too short or unrealistic time allowances for vehicle runs
* poor facilities and working conditions for drivers
* the nature of the Saudi road environment.

Exhibit 23.2 An interim accident report form

Almarai Company Ltd – Interim Accident Report
Ref.
Attention
Cc

Date & time of accident
Place of accident
Name & staff number of driver
Tractor involved
Trailer involved
Tanker involved
Private car involved
Commercial sales van involved
Loaded product at time of accident
Other vehicle involved
Injuries to our driver
Any known injuries to third party
State how accident happened

Reported by   Manager
Date

Exhibit 23.3 Reported accidents involving Al Kharj vehicles, January–September 1993

1. January 5. Tractor and tanker. Khamis to Al Kharj. Approx. 100 km from Khamis. No cause specified. Driver said third party at fault. Police report said Almarai 100% at fault.

2. January 7. Tractor and tanker. Hofuf to Al Kharj. Approx. 80 km from Hofuf. Third party 100% at fault in head-on crash. Third party killed.

3. January 26. Tractor and tanker. Hofuf to Al Kharj. Approx. 100 km from Al Kharj. Night-time collision with camel on road. Truck caught fire and completely burnt out.

4. February 21. Tractor and trailer. Abu Dhabi to Al Kharj. Approx. 30 km from Abu Dhabi. No cause specified. Almarai 100% at fault.

5. May 1. Tractor and trailer. Jeddah to Al Kharj. Approx. 400 km from Al Kharj. Night-time collision with camel on road.

6. June 26. Tanker. Khamis road. Tractor broke down. Tanker fell over when uncoupling it to replace tractor. Almarai 100% at fault (maintenance and driver error).

7. August 23. Vehicle not specified. Dubai to Al Kharj, midpoint of journey. Front tyre blow-out.

8. September 3. Tractor and tanker. Fahad Bin Saad Farm. Driver turning into farm as third party overtaking. Almarai 100% at fault.

9. September 9. Tractor and trailer. Dubai to Al Kharj, in Al Kharj area. Almarai driver overtaking hit third party head on. Almarai 100% at fault.

At the end of the first meeting with the transport safety consultant Adrian Grey said, 'we are conscious of improving our safety procedures in an environment that does not have a safety culture and where driving is considered a dangerous activity. The safety policy limits the distances and hours that drivers can undertake, imposes realistic speed and traffic regulations and stipulates minimum rest periods. However, the company's safety record has not improved. During the previous 18 months we have had about 20 recorded traffic accidents. In some cases there was no third-party involvement, and the relatively new age profile of the fleet means that repairs have become increasingly costly. What we need, I guess, is an expert analysis of the situation and a clear indication of what actions are necessary to minimize accidents and reduce the risks of injuries to employees and third parties'.

References

Al-Farsy, F. (1990) *Modernity and Tradition – the Saudi Equation.* Kegan Paul International, London.

Price Waterhouse Information Guide (1991) *Doing Business in Saudi Arabia.* Price Waterhouse, London.

Further reading

McCorry, B. and Murray, W. (1993) Reducing commercial vehicle road accidents. *International Journal of Physical Distribution and Logistics Management*, **23**(4), 35–41.

Moses, L. and Savage, I. (1994) The effect of firm characteristics on truck accidents. *Accident Analysis and Prevention*, **26**(2), 173–9.

Murray, W. and Whiteing, A. (1995) Reducing commercial vehicle accidents through accident databases. *Logistics Information Management*, **8**(3), 22–9.

Road transport operations in Papua New Guinea

George Wilson
Transport Superintendent, Ok Tedi Mining Limited, Papua New Guinea

and

Adrian Murray
Department of Marketing, Logistics and Property, Royal Melbourne Institute of Technology, Melbourne, Australia

Introduction

'George, I'd like you to think about all we've discussed and come back to me with your thoughts. We need to meet the demands placed upon us but bear in mind the safety factors. Let's meet in about a week from now, say the 10th of April. I'll make a start on defining the major issues we need to consider and will try to come up with some suggestions and George, can you start to analyse the transport requirement for the next year, the resources we have and what you think we might need. I guess we ought to also bear in mind any longer term issues and requirements.' The speaker was Peter Bergmann, manager of transport for Ok Tedi Mining Ltd, the date was 3 April 1995 and the audience of one was his superintendent of road transport, George Wilson.

The Ok Tedi Tabubil project

The Ok Tedi project is an open cut copper mine in the north-west of Papua New Guinea (PNG). It is centred on Mount Fubilan, a peak in the southern reaches of the Star Mountains in the Western Province about 18 km from the border with Irian Jaya (Figures 24.1 and 24.2).

The region is characterized by rugged vertical cliffs and dense tropical rain forest and with an annual average rainfall of 8000 mm is one of the wettest areas on earth. Rain usually falls 339 days of the year.

Mt Fubilan's core is a disseminated copper porphyry ore body which was capped with a substantial gold deposit. Gold mining per se ceased in 1986 and the principal operations

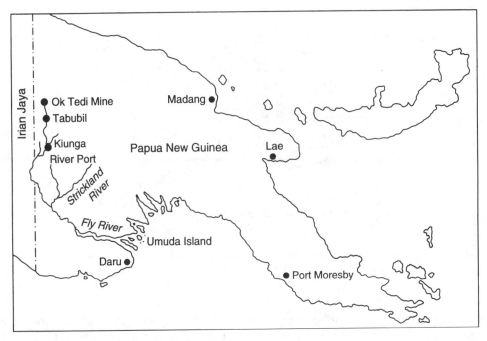

Figure 24.1 Location of the Ok Tedi mine.

Figure 24.2 The Ok Tedi mine pit.

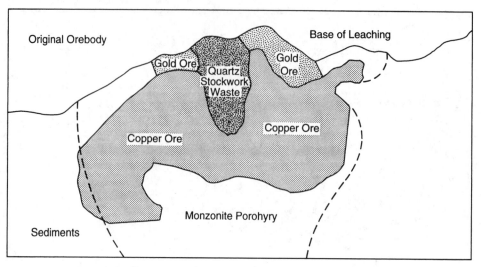

Figure 24.3 Original orebody.

are based around the recovery of copper, although there are still traces of gold and silver (Figure 24.3). The mine in 1992 accounted for all of PNG's copper exports and 14% of its gold exports. The local currency is PNG Kina (K) which after a 1994 devaluation was worth around US$0.78.

The township of Tabubil has been built and developed to house and cater to the needs of the mine employees and families. The shopping facilities are also utilized by a wide range of contractors employed in various areas of the mine. In 1994 the population of the town was estimated at 10,000. This does not include a large squatter settlement, attracted from outlying areas by the activity generated by the mine operations. The mine itself lies 22 km to the north-west and while Tabubil is at 1500 ft the mine altitude is 6000 ft (Figure 24.4). Ambient daytime temperature is 27°C, dropping to 20°C overnight.

The project lies 137 km north of its only port, Kiunga on the Fly River, to which it is connected by a graded road built by the project during its construction phase. Because of the nature of the country this highway is extremely torturous and narrow, and daily supply convoys employ escort vehicles to warn road users that large trucks are on the way.

Orders for every item required to support the project ('from tin-tacks to toilet rolls' is a much-used purchasing department expression) are placed on suppliers with instructions to deliver, packed for sea-freight to the nearest Ok Tedi Mining Limited. (OTML) depot. Airfreight is used in extreme cases only. The company have consolidation depots in all major Australian ports and also in Port Moresby, the capital of PNG. All supplies are hauled by truck from Kiunga to Tabubil, and there are very few backloads apart from empty containers.

A complaint often voiced by drivers is that it is uncomfortable to drive the road as the trucks are not air-conditioned and driving with open windows allows a great deal of dust into the cab. In 1993 The Broken Hill Proprietary Company Ltd (BHP), a major Australian company, announced that it was increasing its shareholdings in OTML to greater than

50%. Later, the PNG government holdings would be increased to 30%. The remainder of the equity is taken up by Metall Mining Corporation.

Mining

Ore reserves at mid-1993 were estimated at:

- 429 million tonnes of sulphide ore averaging 0.56% copper and 0.48 grams per tonne (g/t) gold
- 4 million tonnes of oxide ore averaging 0.31% copper and 0.83 g/t gold
- 77 million tonnes of skarn ore averaging 1.56% copper and 1.46 g/t gold giving an average overall of 0.69% copper and 0.63 g/t gold.

With current recovery methods mine life is estimated to end in 2010.

Using a fleet of Marion Dresser 26 m³ shovels (electrically powered) and 135- and 178-tonne dump trucks an average of 80,000 tonnes of ore and 100,000 tonnes of overburden is moved daily. The mine and mill work two 12-hour shifts seven days a week.

The material is blasted using an ammonium nitrate based explosive. This chemical is stable until mixed with diesel fuel. Normal usage of ammonium nitrate is approximately 30 tonnes per day, although this can increase depending on the type of material to be shifted.

The ammonium nitrate (nitropril) is supplied in 20-ft shipping containers with a 20-tonne capacity and blended by a contractor, currently ICI, at their facility on the southern edge of the mine lease. It is delivered to the blast site by the contractor.

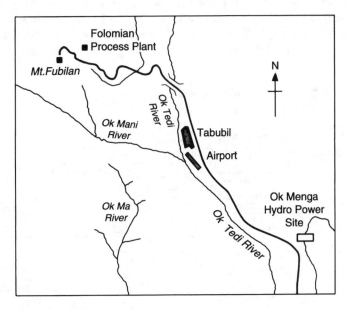

Figure 24.4 The Tabulil region

Milling

Folomian process plant (the mill), situated near the open cut, receives the ore via conveyor belt from the crusher. Here copper recovery (Figure 24.5) is effected by grinding the ore in sag (semi-autogenous grinding, i.e. using the material's own weight) mills followed by further refining in ball mills.

The steel balls used in these mills are of various sizes up to 120 mm in diameter and are sourced from two different Australian suppliers. They are delivered in half-height 20-ft containers, the net weight of which is 20 tonnes.

Following this procedure the ore goes through several flotation processes to separate the copper, gold and silver. Ok Tedi concentrate is recognized as particularly high grade and this grade is kept consistent by homogenization.

In spite of the potential for accidents in its heavily industrial environment, in March 1995 the mill achieved a landmark one million accident-free working hours. Senior management marked this by throwing a party for all mill personnel.

Transport

The concentrate is formed into a slurry and delivered to Kiunga by pipeline. It moves by gravity from the mill to a pump station 59 km north of its destination. At Kiunga it is dried and stockpiled awaiting shipment to a silo ship based 435 river miles down the Fly River off Umuda Island in the Gulf of Papua (Figure 24.1).

A fleet of shallow draft vessels of 2500 tonne capacity is used to transport the concentrate to the permanently anchored silo ship, which has a 50,000 tonne capacity. From there it is trans-shipped to customers vessels. The ore ships also transport supplies, including fuel, as return cargoes from Port Moresby. Sailing time from to Kiunga is approximately four days providing the Fly River level at the bar (about 60 river miles south of Kiunga) is sufficient to allow access. The wet season, June to September, is utilized to maximize supplies of chemicals, spare parts, mine and mill vital materials and fuel. The chemicals and other vital materials are imported from Australia, with a ship

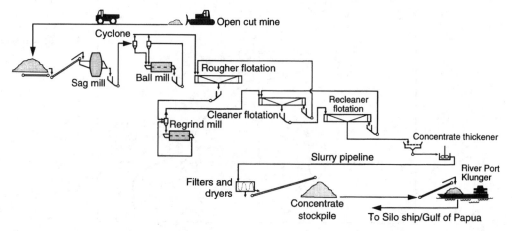

Figure 24.5 Copper recovery flow diagram.

leaving Townsville or Brisbane every two weeks. Sailing time is about seven days depending on conditions. Fuel is supplied from Port Moresby by sea, a normal load being around 1.8 million litres.

Fuel usage

The accounting year runs from June to May and at May 1995, OTML transport department had hauled 60 million litres of fuel for the year. For current production levels this is a normal usage rate. The project employs a hydroelectric scheme, situated on the river Ok Menga, to supply its own power. In times of high demand or low river levels this is complemented by ten diesel-driven turbines; if all ten are being used, daily fuel use can be in the order of 300,000 litres.

During the conversation with George Wilson, Peter Bergmann had noted that the annual usage was forecast to rise by 10 m litres in the financial year ending May 1996. His other main concern was that in previous years the operation had been threatened by a lack of fuel due to unexpected dry conditions. To overcome this, during the three months June to August he would schedule additional fuel supplies. Storage capacity at Kiunga and Tabubil, offset by normal usage, would allow for a total of 24 million litres to be brought in over this period.

Supplies requirements

All supplies are freighted to Kiunga, containerized where possible, then hauled by road to Tabubil. These include contractors' goods such as building materials, supermarket supplies, frozen food and dry goods. Dry chemicals are supplied in 20-ft containers, whilst fluids, including Jet A1 for the three helicopters which are on permanent contract, comes in 20,000 litre tanktainers. The latter cost US$25.00 per day rental and are readily available out of Australia. Usually the maximum weight of any one container is in the order of 22 tonnes. Average weekly cargo moved is 1650 tonnes in addition to fuel.

Transport operations

The trip time from Tabubil to Kiunga, barring breakdowns or flat tyres (a problem given road conditions), is three-and-a-half hours and loading and lunch break account for another two hours. Convoy procedures are in place to maintain a high safety level. Each convoy packet comprises a lead escort vehicle, a maximum of six linehaul trucks and a tyre truck. The escort is a 4×4 utility with green flashing lights and a large notice board displaying the total number of following vehicles (see Figure 24.9). Upon meeting the escort, oncoming drivers are required to move off the road and park until the convoy has passed. There have been incidents where private vehicles have entered from a side road after the escort has passed and have proceeded unaware that a convoy is on its way.

The prime-movers (tractor units) are either Pacific (a now-defunct Canadian company) or Kenworth, fitted with 400 hp Caterpillar engines driving an Eaton Fuller direct 15-speed Road Ranger gearbox. The drivers, all PNG nationals, are used to and are comfortable with this rig. The tyre trucks support the convoy with a supply of tyres for trucks and trailers in the event of flats, which are a regular occurrence. This is a

Figure 24.6 The Tabubil to Kiunga Road at km 126.

contentious issue as warehousing supply retreads for trailers and drive axles on the trucks. Concerns have been raised by the transport department over the potential for increased downtime and the possibility of complementary damage to running gear in the event of retread failure and periodically there are heated discussions between warehousing and transport over the tyre issue, which are usually based on opinion rather than fact.

The trailer fleet consists of six 40,000 litre fuel tankers, all of which are between six and eight years old, 15 dropdeck 48-tonne, six flat-bed 38-tonne, three pipe trailers, one 100-tonne and two 50-tonne low loaders. Pulling these are 28 prime-movers.

Dropdecks can accommodate two containers or one tanktainer plus breakbulk. Flatbed trailers usually carry breakbulk but have been used to haul one container only. Due to their high centre of gravity, tanktainers are loaded on the rear (lower) deck of a dropdeck and are never transported by flatbed trailer. In the past OTML have hired two 40,000 litre tanker trailers from a local contractor, however this has been in emergency situations only, e.g. non-availability of OTML tankers owing to breakdown. The rate for this is considered prohibitive at K1350.00 per week (Figures 24.7 and 24.8).

Maintenance workshop

Repair, maintenance and servicing on the fleet is carried out by the Tabubil-based OTML Workshop 1, which also provides maintenance services to other parts of the OTML operation. The trucks are inspected and repaired after each convoy run by night-shift staff. Current availability runs at between 80% and 86%, at which level it is difficult for the transport department to meet the normal haulage task. The transport department has no control over the maintenance area and is treated as a normal customer with no ability to prioritize work, despite being the workshop's biggest user. The workshop maintains a two-pump fuel supply bowser to service local needs. The trucks are fitted with 400 litre fuel tanks which allow them to make one return Tabubil–Kiunga trip. Kiunga wharf area also has a fuel facility but under normal circumstances the trucks are refuelled overnight at Tabubil.

Figure 24.7 A 20,000 litre 'tanktainer' on a dropdeck trailer.

Convoys

For transport, a division within the OTML logistics department (Figure 24.10), the day starts at 6.30 am with drivers arriving at Workshop 1 to pick up their trucks. Available trucks are driven with their trailer to the transport lay-down area, where they are loaded with empty containers to move back to Kiunga. Drivers hauling fuel tanks also assemble here.

The convoy packets, usually three, are assembled and move to the first regrouping area, known as Six Mile. Load security and vehicle checks take place here before departure. Escorts are in two-way radio contact with tyre trucks, other escorts, transport supervisors and the OTML security channel, but no prime-movers are radio equipped.

Figure 24.8 A 40,000 litre tanker at km 100.

Reception is usually of a high level owing to the repeater network employed between Tabubil and Kiunga. An average convoy comprises five tankers plus nine trailers. Local work, e.g. deliveries around Tabubil, or to the mine or mill, can involve up to five trucks. Driver availability is often a limiting factor as at any one time three drivers may be absent on rest days or annual leave. In addition there is a relatively high incidence of sick leave, in the order of 10 worker days per week.

Normal practice is to work a 13-day fortnight, and because drivers are paid fortnightly this allows them one paid Sunday off. Convoys are run only during daylight hours, which are nominally 6 am–6 pm. Maximum recommended payloads are 38 tonnes, since experience has shown that loads greater than this result in increased clutch and driveline problems.

The day ends when the last load is back in Tabubil.

An occasional source of frustration to other road users is the length of a convoy packet. In dry conditions the dust raised by the passage of a truck/trailer combination necessitates a gap in excess of 1 km. During wet (non-dusty) conditions it is a standing instruction that the convoy should close up, which is difficult to monitor. As a safety issue, road users often miscount the number of trucks and proceed unaware that there may be more heavy traffic. This was another point raised by Peter Bergmann. George estimated that on average there was about one accident or incident per month, which in some respects was not bad, in that the fleet ran approximately 1.6 million km per annum. However, the managers felt that the possibility of accidents was very high, given the educational level of the local inhabitants, hence the company was continually striving to improve levels of safety.

Figure 24.9 Seven-truck convoy packet and escort vehicle.

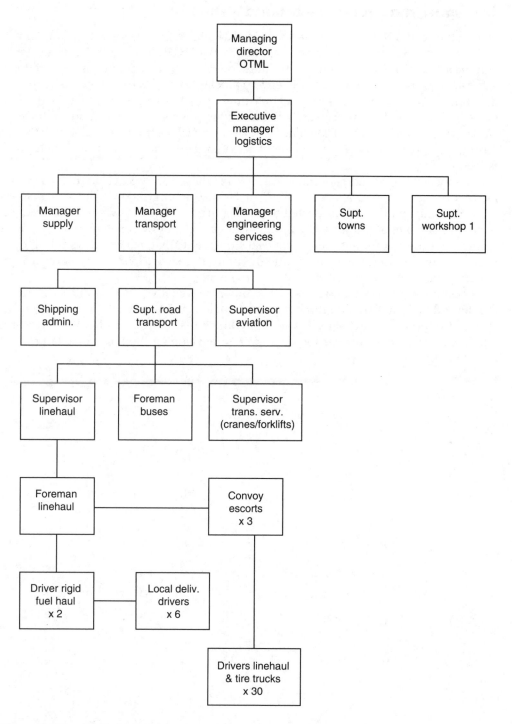

Figure 24.10 Ok Tedi Mining Limited: company structure.

Transport requirements around Tabubil

During the year 1994–5, the mine and mill used 24 million litres of fuel which was hauled up the mountain from the fuel farm in Tabubil by two 18,000 litre rigid fuel trucks. Topographical factors and slow pumping facilities meant that one trip could take up to four-and-a-half hours. An incomplete fuel delivery pipeline existed between the fuel farm and the mine. Together with this, 4500 local deliveries of general cargo and other goods were made in Tabubil to the various warehouse locations, town supermarket and contractors' yards. Of these, 85% involved container off-loading which necessitated a 25-tonne forklift accompanying the truck. Local deliveries used either a prime-mover and trailer or a flatbed truck.

Delivery of nitropril and grinding balls to ICI and the mill, respectively, require a prime-mover/dropdeck configuration. In 1994–5, 10,000 tonnes of grinding balls were delivered to the mill, and this was expected to rise by 10% in 1995–6. Owing to the gradient only one container of nitropril or grinding balls can be moved at one time. No escort is required for these trips, but there have been complaints that vehicles descending from the area of the mill and mine have suddenly confronted such a load, particularly at 5 pm when operational day-shift staff are on their way home.

As George drove back to the transport laydown he went over in his mind the meeting that he had just left. Based on those discussions it looked like it would be a busy year in the road transport department. He certainly knew that both he and Peter Bergmann would be extremely busy over the next week in developing the transport plan for the forthcoming year and beyond.

Improving transport productivity – the introduction of a new driver incentive scheme*

Marion Court
Department of Transport and Logistics, The University of Huddersfield, UK
and
Mark Harrison
Logistics Director, Perfecta Beds, UK

Introduction

In 1994 Perfecta Beds engaged Damar, a firm of transport consultants, to review the scheme for rewarding and providing incentives for the drivers of the company's fleet of delivery vehicles. The existing scheme had been in place for a number of years and had evolved in such a way that it allowed drivers to earn reasonable or good wages, but did not achieve the level of productivity in distribution that the company increasingly required. Perfecta's newly appointed distribution manager felt that it might be more acceptable if impartial, external experts were responsible for recommending changes to the drivers' pay system, an issue which he knew would be highly sensitive and potentially disruptive within the company.

The company

Perfecta Beds has been in business since 1970 and is a member of the Silentnight Beds Group. It is a leading manufacturer of beds which are marketed in the UK through high-

*Data available on the Internet (see page xxii).

street retailers and mail-order houses. The company is based in Barnsley, South Yorkshire and serves approximately 900 independent retail accounts, a number of large multiple retailers and the UK's largest mail-order houses.

The Silentnight Group is structured so that each bed manufacturing company serves a particular market segment or sector. Perfecta's role is to be the lowest cost producer whilst at the same time providing a service at least equal to the competition in its particular market sector. Perfecta's strategic position within the Silentnight Group is primarily to create a competitive barrier to entry at the lower end of the bed market, and therefore deter new low-price entrants who might eventually grow to threaten the more attractive markets within the group's portfolio.

In the early 1990s, recession within the UK economy intensified competitive pressure on Perfecta and forced the company to explore opportunities for cost saving. In 1993 a new distribution manager was appointed and one of the first areas he targeted for improvement was transport, particularly in relation to the labour costs involved.

Sales

Historically Perfecta Beds had been a sales-led company. The sales function was performed by a team of sales representatives who regularly visited retailers, supported by a telesales department. Competition on price was intense and it was difficult to match the service offered by some smaller, local manufacturers based in different parts of the country. Perfecta's normal order cycle was for product ordered one week to be delivered the next week, but there was increasing pressure from the sales representatives to provide a same-week service to match one of the major competitors.

Production

Manufacture was to order, with a maximum lead time from receipt of order to delivery of up to 14 days. Manufacture was on a 'just-in-time' output system, primarily because the company had an inadequate warehouse facility for finished product storage. As volumes had increased over the years, the production plant had been extended into the original warehouse area because there was no other space on site for expansion. As a result the only warehousing space that remained was a transit area between the end of the production lines and the vehicle loading bays. In consequence, it was not at all uncommon for delivery vehicles to be delayed by bottlenecks in production, particularly during busy periods.

Distribution

Initially the company had only serviced the high-street retail sector but it entered the mail-order sector in 1978. Distribution of high-street deliveries was effected through a core resource of owned vehicles supported by short-term hire of third-party contractors to meet peaks in demand. In 1989 approximately 20% of high-street deliveries were carried out by outside contractors but this figure had been steadily rising and had reached 30% by 1993.

As the warehouse was too small to use as a buffer between production and the loading bay, flexibility of loading was achieved through the use of 52 demountable boxes and 22 semi-trailers. The owned fleet consisted of 12 rigid vehicles with drawbar trailers for use with the demountable boxes and three articulated tractor units for use with the semi-trailers.

The introduction of direct home deliveries for mail-order initially provided insufficient volume for operating owned vehicles and drivers and these deliveries were executed via a sister company. In 1993 transfer of responsibility for mail-order deliveries was passed to Perfecta Beds who decided to effect these deliveries via a number of third-party carriers that offered national home delivery services.

As with many companies the growing need to improve customer service and the increasing cost of providing that service created a situation where distribution costs represented an increasing percentage of sales value.

The existing driver payment scheme

In 1989 the then distribution manager identified that distribution costs were rising at a rate above inflation and that the best way to tackle this would be by achieving an increase in driver productivity. He believed that rewarding the drivers on a basic rate of pay plus overtime would cause them to enhance their earnings by working long hours and claiming payments for 'nights out', i.e. nights spent away from base. He had devised a scheme which rewarded drivers on a 'stepped measured day work' basis which was calculated over a two-week period. Performance under this scheme was measured by totalling 'standard' hours calculated from a total of driving time and time for other work. Standard hours were based on notional journey times together with notional time allowances for unloading, taking vehicles for service and other activities. The allowances for both journey times and unloading time were generous in relation to actual times incurred. 'Input' hours were calculated by totalling the number of hours worked based on the contracted 11-hour day. Input hours were measured in terms of the actual hours that drivers worked each day. Drivers then received a bonus if standard hours exceeded input hours. For example, a driver working a normal five-day week at 11 hours per day would have 55 input hours. If the standard hours for the journeys undertaken totalled 65 a bonus would be given for 10 hours. There was, however, a cap on the total permitted bonus earnings. As well as the bonus received through the above scheme, drivers were paid 'night-out' expenses on an allocated basis. This meant that, for example, a driver with a journey or load value of 23 standard hours would receive two night-out payments for that journey even if he returned to base early on the second day, the second payment being termed a 'non-incurred' night-out payment.

The problem

When the new distribution manager was appointed in 1993 he encountered the following situation.

All drivers were union members. An agreement had been signed where the drivers were paid for an 11-hour working day, irrespective of the amount of driving or other work carried out. The contracted working day was 7 am to 6 pm, beyond which overtime could be worked with the drivers' agreement and was paid at 1.5 times normal pay. Productivity was low, with drivers working close to their contracted hours. An analysis was undertaken whereby a direct comparison was made between the Perfecta in-house performance and the delivery and journey times achieved by the subcontract carriers used by the company. This clearly demonstrated that the carriers achieved greater productivity, often by as much as 20%, even though they were delivering to the same customer base. Equally within the Perfecta fleet, different drivers were achieving very different levels of productivity (i.e. overall trip and turnaround time) which was not accounted for by the differing length of journeys. However, most drivers seemed to be reasonably content with their level of earnings.

It was apparent that the capital equipment was not being fully utilized. The transport fleet schedulers had been with the company for a long time and were keen to maintain the *status quo*. They had become accustomed to working with the bonus scheme and their planning of schedules appeared to be aimed at ensuring that drivers achieved maximum bonus, rather than focusing on how productivity could be enhanced.

A further factor was that when drivers were delayed by production bottlenecks their earnings were rarely affected as they would normally recover lost time by performing non-productive but rewarded tasks (see below). There was consequently little pressure coming up through the drivers or the distribution department to ensure better work flow from production.

It was clear that the driver productivity scheme was not yielding the results for which it had been created and was not proving to be effective for a number of reasons.

- Drivers' potential earnings were capped at an easily achievable level.
- Standard hours payments had been introduced for non-productive, non-delivery work such as presenting vehicles at off-site workshops for repair, or waiting whilst the vehicle was loaded. Drivers seemed to spend a significant amount of their time undertaking such non-productive activities and many hours were spent waiting around in the canteen for the next load to be ready. The scheme required no 'pushing' by the drivers to ensure that either the load or the vehicle was ready in time.
- The non-incurred nights out payments were paid whenever the driver's contracted 6 pm finish time was exceeded. Under this system a driver starting work at 7 am with a journey of a value of ten standard hours would not be paid a night out, but if the start time were delayed until 9 am, for example, a non-incurred night out would be paid.
- The capping of the potential earnings level and the fact that it was calculated over a two-week period meant that a driver who had over-achieved in the first week had little incentive to work hard in week two.
- The earnings were not directly related to productivity in terms of product delivered, but appeared to focus on measures of transport activity such as miles run and nights out.
- Under the scheme the drivers often earned more through the non-incurred nights out than through the bonus payments for hours achieved.

Overall it was not clear to the new distribution manager how the original scheme was meant to increase driver productivity. However it was vital that productivity be improved so that Perfecta Beds could retain their position as lowest cost producer. The product was of high volume and low value, with the consequence that it was essential to keep distribution costs to a minimum.

Possible solutions

During several exploratory discussions with the workforce it became apparent that the scheme had been in operation for too long to be easily adjusted. The targets which had been set in 1989 were being achieved and the drivers' stance was that they were exceeding the targets set in the productivity scheme. Those areas where anomalies had evolved were deemed to have been agreed and were now seen as 'custom and practice'.

Following discussions with the managing director and fellow functional managers the distribution manager identified the following possible solutions.

- To invite a third-party contractor to tender for delivery of all high-street deliveries. There was resistance to this option because of the previous experience of other functional directors.
- To consider a unilateral variation of the terms of the drivers' employment. It was felt that this could result in unnecessary confrontation.
- To remove the cap on the present productivity scheme. This would motivate some drivers to do more but the existing anomalies were likely to lead to yet more abuse of the scheme.
- To evolve a new productivity scheme.

The study

After much discussion the distribution manager decided that the best solution would be to develop a completely new productivity scheme and that such a scheme would be best developed by an outside consultancy. A number of potential consultants was approached and eventually Damar, a specialist transport consultancy, was selected to carry out a detailed study to design a new scheme. Following an initial review of the existing payment scheme, Damar agreed with Perfecta that the new scheme should have the following objectives.

- To increase the proportion of work done by the owned fleet.
- To provide an open-ended earning capacity for drivers within the legal constraints of regulations on drivers' hours.
- To provide a visible scheme based on a weekly performance.
- To develop a scheme which would only reward the driver for real productivity.
- To raise the level of productivity achieved by all drivers.
- To produce a scheme that would induce the drivers actively to seek work and to push whenever held up either at delivery points or at base when waiting for their next load.
- To create a situation where transport schedulers would plan work more effectively to achieve the company's productivity aims.

As required by law this was to be achieved within a framework that would not encourage drivers to break either the regulations on drivers' hours or the legal speed limits, or indeed to disregard safe or professional driving practice.

To understand the requirements and realities of the Perfecta distribution system, Damar used a number of approaches, including:

- exploratory discussions with management and drivers
- tachograph analysis over a representative ten-week period

- 'observer's study' by accompanying drivers (four working weeks)
- benchmarking with sister company (Layeezee Beds) which had its production plant located in the north of England, fairly close to Perfecta, and had a broadly similar geographic spread of customers
- use of a computerized routing system
- regular meetings with the drivers throughout the study.

The study produced a great deal of detailed information, the most relevant of which is reproduced in Exhibits 25.1–25.7. One of the early problems identified in considering a new productivity scheme was the geographic spread of retail customers throughout the UK, all of which were supplied from the Barnsley base. Some routes involved long trunking or *stem* journeys to a delivery area, e.g. to the London area, whilst other delivery areas such as Manchester were much closer to Barnsley.

Once the data had been analysed and considered, Damar were in a position to formulate recommendations for the structure and implementation of the new driver productivity scheme.

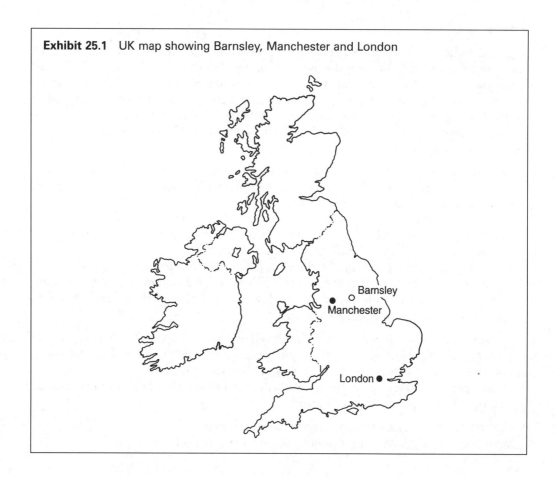

Exhibit 25.1   UK map showing Barnsley, Manchester and London

Exhibit 25.2 Results of benchmarking exercise with sister company, Layeezee Beds

Perfecta	Feature	Layeezee
397	Total drops/week	657
310	Drops/week own fleet	507
87	Drops/week contractor	150
22	Percentage total drops by contractor	23
23	Drops/driver/week	28
1204	Miles/driver/week	1604
53	Miles/drop own fleet	57
19	Pieces/drop own fleet	18
	Pieces/drop contractor	13
	Pieces/drop total	17
48	Miles/drop contractor	
2.74	Number of loads/week/driver	4.04

Drop: one delivery to one customer.
Trip: journey out from and return to base.

Exhibit 25.3 Perfecta Beds vehicle fleet and capacities

Vehicle	Capacity (cubic ft)
DB1	3000
DB2	3000
DB3	3000
DB4	3000
DB5	3000
DB6	3000
DB7	3000
DB8	3000
DB9	3000
DB10	3000
DB11	3000
DB12	3000
A1	2800
A2	2800
A3	2800

DB: drawbar; A: artic.
One bed = approx. 40 cubic feet.

Exhibit 25.4 Trips and drops by area over a nine-week period in 1994

Area	Main town destination	Total trips over nine weeks	Drops per trip per week								
			wk 6	wk 7	wk 8	wk 9	wk 10	wk 11	wk 12	wk 13	wk 14
1. N. Scotland	Inverness	13	12	9.5	7	18	9	7	16	9	0
2. Glasgow	Glasgow	22	7.5	5	2	4.5	4.5	11.5	13	6.5	13
3. Edinburgh	Edinburgh	7	10	16	0	9	19	0	17	0	12
5. Cumbria	Carlisle	6	4	0	0	8	6	0	0	0	13
6. North-east	Washington	17	8.5	6.5	3	8	24	24	13.5	11	5
7. N. Yorks	Middlesboro.	11	10	13	0	0	3	9	12	0	11
8. N. Lancs	Blackpool	8	6	8	10	6.5	0	11	19	8	16
9. Humberside	Hull	12	7.5	6.5	17	8	11	0	10	10	5
10. W. Yorks	Harrogate	20	3.5	0	22	8	0	15	15.5	1	7
11. Liverpool	Liverpool	17	10	7.5	17	6	5.5	12	16	7	5.5
12. Manchester	Bolton	19	6.5	10.5	5.5	21	19	13	18	3	3.5
13. S. Manchester	Knutsford	8	11	14	10	7	10	11	10	0	9
14. S. Yorks	Sheffield	16	13	11.5	9	18	19	0	16	0	13
15. Nottingham	Loughboro.	3	0	11	0	0	0	0	0	0	0
16. Lincoln	Kings Lynn	4	7	0	0	0	0	0	12	0	0
17. Staffordshire	Shrewsbury	9	14	11	17	14	19	15	12	13	6
18. N. Wales	Porthmadog	9	6	7	13	18	6	8	19	0	5
19. Midlands	Kidderminster	17	15.5	9.5	34	0	27	0	19	11	4
21. Leicester	Northampton	8	10	16	12	23	0	0	0	9.5	0
22. Norfolk	Ipswich	14	27	0	16.5	11	17	0	19	15	0
24. Bedford	St Albans	18	8	4.5	17	8.5	13	11	6.5	0	10
25. Oxford	Marlboro.	10	8	0	11	11	13	7	15	12	11
26. Gloucester	Gloucester	5	0	7	0	0	0	0	0	0	13
27. S. Wales	Cardiff	7	14	0	0	0	5	16	14	24	15
28. W. Wales	Swansea	9	11	0	0	2	0	1	4	0	7
29. Essex	Southend	7	7	18	0	22	0	18	15.5	28	0
30. N. London	Slough	25	13.5	0	8.5	10.5	0	0	11.5	11	1
31. S. London	Reigate	14	6.5	6	17	32	0	0	15.5	11.5	0
32. N. Ireland	N/A	0	0	0	0	0	0	0	0	0	0
33. Bristol	Glastonbury	3	0		16	14	0	0	23	0	0
34. Cornwall	St Austell	11	14	11.5	14	0	19	10	17.5	16	0
35. Hampshire	Bournemth.	21	9	11.5	5.5	27	10.5	0	1.5	9	0
36. Sussex	Brighton	3	0	0	0	0	0	15	0	0	0
37. Kent	Hastings	9	19	12	6.5	17	0	12	33	14.5	0

On arrival in the target area (following the stem journey) drops can be effected at a rate of two per hour on average (i.e. the local delivery time plus the unloading time).

Sample weeks were selected to give a representative survey of the workload.

Exhibit 25.5 Comparison of drops achieved by drivers over a ten-week period

Week Driver	46 Drops	43 Drops	41 Drops	40 Drops	28 Drops	27 Drops	26 Drops	16 Drops	14 Drops	13 Drops	Total drops	Average drops/ driver/week
DB1	27	19	20	27	29	30	37	32	19	30	270	27
DB2	20	32	6	21	15	24	39	30	13	41	241	24.1
DB3	23	18	9	11	30	18	20	0	22	31	182	18.2
DB4	28	0	18	26	4	30	19	23	23	14	185	18.5
DB5	31	0	20	8	30	10	25	32	22	32	210	21
DB6	10	20	22	32	25	18	29	18	17	25	216	21.6
DB7	22	34	17	25	12	31	31	17	21	21	231	23.1
DB8	17	32	11	30	22	29	16	30	12	29	228	22.8
DB9	31	22	29	25	29	28	28	18	10	19	239	23.9
DB10	29	0	0	13	20	32	22	22	26	28	192	19.2
DB11	22	11	22	17	37	19	22	23	21	0	194	19.4
DB12	0	36	0	16	15	21	23	0	16	9	136	13.6
A13	12	25	20	16	9	8	4	19	23	29	165	16.5
A14	26	15	25	12	33	14	22	0	0	0	147	14.7
A15	24	32	12	31	29	38	26	38	10	26	266	26.6
Total	322	296	231	310	339	350	363	302	255	334	3102	23
Aver. drops/ veh.	23	25	20	22	23	23	25	25	18	24		
No. of veh's	14	12	11	14	15	15	14	12	14	14	135.6	

All vehicles were exclusively allocated to drivers, so vehicle and driver numbers are the same.

Exhibit 25.6   Comparison of trips achieved by drivers over an eight-week period

Driver	Week 41 Trips	Week 40 Trips	Week 28 Trips	Week 27 Trips	Week 26 Trips	Week 16 Trips	Week 14 Trips	Week 13 Trips	Totals
DB1	3	3	3	3	3	3	3	3	24
DB2	1	3	3	2	3	4	2	3	21
DB3	2	2	2	2	3	0	3	2	16
DB4	2	3	3	2	4	3	2	3	22
DB5	3	4	3	3	4	2	2	2	23
DB6	3	3	2	3	2	4	2	3	22
DB7	1	3	2	3	2	3	2	3	19
DB8	2	2	3	2	3	3	4	3	22
DB9	2	2	3	3	2	4	4	2	22
DB10	0	1	3	2	2	2	2	2	14
DB11	4	3	3	3	3	2	3	0	21
DB12	0	2	2	3	2	0	2	1	12
A13	3	3	4	4	3	3	3	3	26
A14	4	3	3	4	3	0	0	0	17
A15	3	2	2	3	3	2	2	3	20
Totals	33	39	41	42	42	35	36	33	301
Average/ driver	2.54	2.60	2.73	2.80	2.80	2.92	2.57	2.34	2.69
No. of drivers available	13	15	15	15	15	12	14	14	112

Exhibit 25.7   Summary of EU Drivers' Hours Rules (1995)

Activity	Limitations
Aggregate driving time	4.5 hours
Breaks	45 minutes (or combination of 3 × 15 minutes during 4.5 hours)
Daily driving	Nine hours extendible to ten hours twice per week
Weekly driving	No limit but weekly rest must be taken after no more than six daily driving periods
Fortnightly driving	90 hours
Daily rest	11 hours in any 24-hour period, reducible to nine hours not more than three times in any one week
Split daily rest	12 hours in total: can be two or three separate periods as long as each is at least one hour, one is at least eight hours and the total is 12 hours
Weekly rest	45 hours reducible to 36 hours if at the vehicle or driver's base or 24 hours if taken elsewhere

Planning port capacity

David Wilson
Faculty of Computing and Information Technology, Monash University, Melbourne, Australia

Introduction

The Port of Melbourne is Australia's leading container and general cargo port. In 1990 it handled 25.9 million revenue tonnes of cargo of which 15.36 million tonnes was container traffic. The port handled 709,840 TEUs (20-ft equivalent units), 4.5 million tonnes of bulk cargo and 6 million tonnes of break-bulk cargo. Although traffic at the port has been growing at 6% per annum since 1990, it is facing a period of operational and physical changes. Competition between Australian ports has been increasing as ports such as Brisbane, Botany near Sydney and Fremantle expand their container terminals and integrate with the national rail system to create land-bridges.

The port has learnt that it will lose berths 6–11 and 13–17 at Victoria Dock owing to Melbourne's new Western Ring Road (freeway) project (Figure 26.1). The ring road will cut off the mouth of Victoria Dock with a low-level bridge so that ships will not be able to access the berths. This came as a surprise to the planners at the port because they had been part of the working group recommending the alignment of the freeway since 1992 and felt sure that it would pass through the rail yards to the east. In 1994 the Premier of Victoria had announced that construction work would begin before Christmas 1995.

Management at the port was concerned that they might have serious congestion problems on both the land and sea unless new facilities were made available within 12 months. In the longer term, they predicted the need to develop further container terminal facilities downstream of the river Yarra. Planners at the port had to decide where to relocate the cargo from Victoria Dock to other docks. With third- and fourth-generation container ship running costs estimated at AUS$40,000 per day any increases in ship delays could easily result in ship owners avoiding Melbourne in favour of Brisbane or Botany (Sydney). Melbourne-bound cargo could easily be landbridged.

Layout of the Port of Melbourne (see Figure 26.1)

The Port of Melbourne has four main container terminal berths, Webb, East Swanson, West Swanson, and Victoria Docks. Each of these docks is capable of handling third- and fourth-generation containerships. Appleton dock is used as a back-up container terminal and handles smaller containers and general cargo. Table 26.1 gives the 1991 distribution of cargo through these terminals and transport modes associated with each dock. Road–rail refers to those containers that enter or leave the port using road and rail modes. There is a major rail container yard adjacent to the port (north of Swanson Dock). This rail terminal (South Dynon) is the largest intermodal rail container facility in Australia and connects Melbourne to all Australian States as part of an integrated national system. Some containers destined for the port arrive by rail and then are transported by road the short distance to one of the docks. Rail–rail refers to those containers that enter and leave the port using only rail. There are rail lines running into West Swanson Dock and Webb Dock. Note that Victoria Dock had no containers using the rail only transport mode.

The port system currently provides for 50 berths for commercial shipping at seven docks, Victoria, Appleton, Swanson, Holden (which is used for bulk liquids), Webb Dock, North and South wharves (used for bulk cargo, cement, timber, cars and paper). However, container traffic is fed through Webb, Swanson, Victoria and Appleton Docks. Some 76% of Melbourne's total trade is containerized and the bulk of this goes through Swanson and Webb docks. Victoria has been developed as a multipurpose dock serving coastal vessels and overseas Ro-Ro (roll on roll off) and Lo-Lo (load on load off) cargo vessels. Table 26.2 outlines the area and number of cranes at each berth.

Table 26.1   Container traffic (TEUs) 1991

Dock area	No. of containers (TEUs)	Transport mode Road–Rail	Rail–Rail	Road only
West Swanson Dock	166,000	24,209	13,986	127,805
East Swanson Dock	271,000	39,520	20,239	211,240
Victoria Dock	93,000	13,563		79,437
Appleton Dock	28,000	4083	2249	21,668
Webb Dock	166,000	24,209	13,986	127,805

Table 26.2   Container berth details

Terminal	Number of berths	Wharf length (metres)	Area (hectares)*	Container cranes
Webb	5	1012	26	6
W. Swanson	4	942	13	4
E. Swanson	4	942	13	5
Victoria	4	649	7	1
Appleton	3	636	12	1

*The area refers to container storage and marshalling area including the berth face.

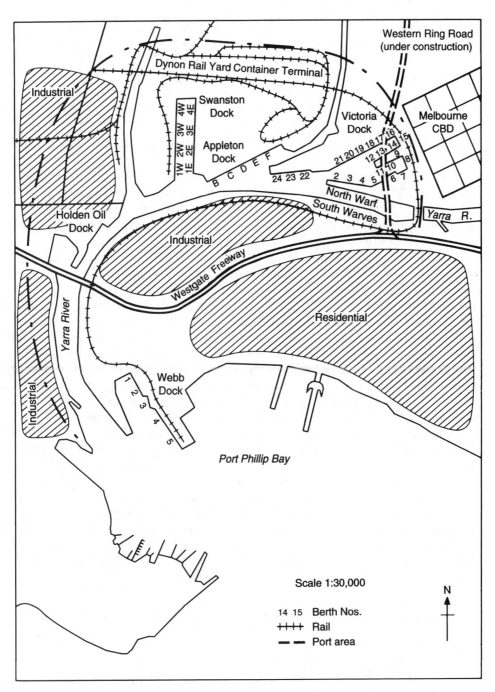

Figure 26.1 The Port of Melbourne.

Table 26.3   Dimensions of container ships

Generation	Capacity (TEU)	Length × width × draft (metres)
First	<1000	85 × 13 × 5
Second	1500	210 × 30.5 × 10.5
Third	3000	285 × 32.2 × 11.5
Fourth	4250	290 × 32.2 × 11.6

Modern container ships of the 1990s (third generation) are about 290 m in length and can carry over 3000 containers. The newer fourth-generation ships are known as post-Panamax because they are too wide to use the Panama canal and can only move between major ports, continent to continent. Table 26.3 gives the capacities and lengths of the various generations of container ships.

Based on 1992–3 productivity rates, container cranes in Melbourne on average moved 14 TEUs per hour (but Victoria Dock, Melbourne, has worked at 20 TEUs per hour). Train turnaround times are about six hours for a train loaded with 240 containers. This means that a train can be stripped of its export containers and loaded with import containers within six hours. Truck turnaround times average two hours. Most of this time (90%) is spent queuing outside the terminal. Once inside the terminal processing time for trucks is measured in minutes. Landside delays are causing concern to customers because transport companies charge AUS$60 per hour demurrage. Planners at the port are concerned because port charges are the highest in Australia. A new truck vehicle booking system for the terminals indicates that queue time outside the terminals can be reduced to an average of half an hour. This is planned for immediate implementation.

In total about 72% of the freight moving through the port does so by road. Rail accommodates 13%, pipeline 13% and 2% is transhipped by sea. Rail use tends to fluctuate as it can be tied to specific contracts, e.g. for cars or to seasonal products, e.g. fruits and rice. Mitsubishi has a car plant in Adelaide and cars are made there and then put on a train to Melbourne where they are exported. Rice and fruit growers along the Murray River containerize their produce and send block trains to Melbourne for export. It is important to note that much of the port's traffic is generated in the Melbourne area (53% of exports and 88% of imports), i.e. most of the containers originate or terminate their journeys within 30 km of the port. About 550,000 full TEUs and 100,000 empty TEUs were either imported or exported through the port in 1991–2.

Transport at Swanson Dock

A study during a six-month period in 1989–90 revealed that Swanson dock handled 192,000 TEUs from 314 ships. Figures 26.2 and 26.3 show the pattern of arrivals and the number of ships and containers for import and export. Each container can generate one truck movement unless it is moved directly on to rail. Direct rail exchanges occur at Webb dock and West Swanson dock. There were significant truck delays at Swanson dock, with average waiting times for a container running at two hours.

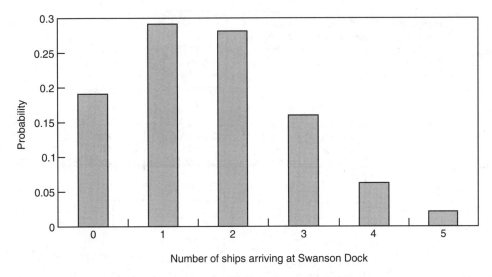

Figure 26.2 Probability of ships arriving at Swanson Dock (based on 314 ship arrivals over six months in 1989–90).

Planning a modern container terminal

Figure 26.4 shows the processes involved in moving containers through a port. Essentially, a container terminal is a large open air warehouse which unloads containers from

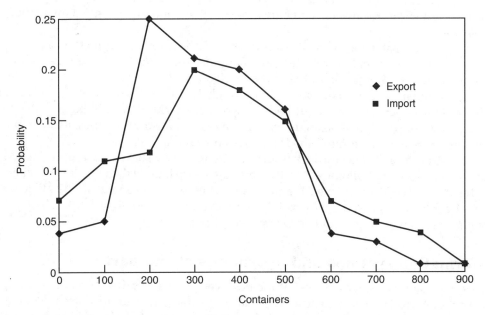

Figure 26.3 Probability distribution of import and export containers.

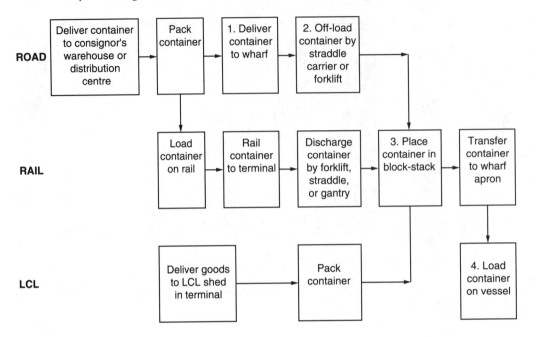

Figure 26.4 Flow of export container cargo.

a ship when it arrives and stores them for pick-up by customers. It also receives containers for export and marshals them so that they can be quickly loaded on to a ship immediately after its import cargo has been discharged. Modern container terminals need space to co-ordinate and control inwards and outwards containers and provide rapid turn-around for ships.

It is estimated that for an efficient terminal about 20 hectares are required. The capacity of a container terminal is dictated by many factors, but the materials-handling equipment plays a key factor. At the Port of Melbourne, terminals use straddle carriers that allow containers to be block stacked three high. It is therefore possible to store about 1400 containers per hectare. About half the space in a terminal would be available for storage, with the other half taken up by roadways and transport facilities, maintenance facilities, container 'de-stuffing' sheds and administration.

To construct a flat 20-hectare deck from a coast-line or river shore costs around AUS$50 million, not including buildings. Post-Panamax cranes (to handle the wide-berth container ships) cost AUS$12 million each and a straddle carrier costs about AUS$1 million. A typical berth face is about 1 km with at least five cranes and 20 straddle carriers. A terminal takes in the region of two years to construct.

Information systems and operations at the port

All of the major container wharves at the port were leased to private operators, except for part of Victoria Dock which was managed by the Port Authority itself. The Port Authority was responsible for channel and wharf maintenance, navigation and construction. The private operators used their own information systems to plan the loads of ships and the placement of containers on the wharf apron. However, their systems were not integrated and a considerable amount of manual location of containers was necessary. Terminal operators did not use container tracking systems to book in containers and were only beginning to explore the use of electronic data interchange links with customers. Consequently the management of containers still involved a large amount of time-consuming paperwork. In 1994 the Port Authority developed a vehicle booking system to help to reduce the long truck queues. This system was being implemented with the help of the terminal operators.

The planning problem

In January 1995 the port planners needed to decide where to relocate the cargo from Victoria Dock which was to be closed within the next year. They had only a short time and had to act quickly. However, they had several options open to them that needed to be considered. Should they begin planning for a new wharf? If so, where should it be located? Should they upgrade Appleton Dock and move all of the Victoria Dock cargo through Appleton? Appleton would need the Victoria Dock crane but this could easily be moved. Alternatively, should the planners ask the other terminal operators at Webb and Swanson Docks to handle the additional load? A more fundamental logistics issue was the capacity of these container terminals to handle the extra load. Would this result in longer land delays or shipping delays, or both?

As a starting point in the planning process the planners formulated the following questions which they felt should be answered.

- What were the wider logistics issues that needed to considered in planning a modern port?
- What time horizon should be considered and what forecasts of traffic volumes should be used? They eventually decided to plan to the year 2010 and assumed a 6% annual growth in trade (and container movements) from 1991–2.
- To what extent might greater use be made of the rail option?
- What options were available to improve the logistics systems in other parts of the port in order to cope with the closure of Victoria Dock?
- Was it necessary to embark on the construction of a new terminal ? They knew that a detailed cost–benefit analysis would be necessary to answer this question adequately.

Oil recovery by truck or pipeline?*

Ian Sadler

Department of Management, Victoria University of Technology, Australia

Introduction

It was October 1995 and Gary Anderson had all the information required to decide how the Bilgola and Narooma oil wells in the Cooper Basin in South Australia should be developed. The main choice was between building a pipeline to conduct oil to the nearest oil handling centre at Wakanui and the use of trucks for transport direct to the centre of oil handling at Moomba. A pipeline was the safe, conventional method, but Santos had pioneered the use of trucks for small oil bodies as a method of recovering oil more quickly with less capital cost. The downside of using trucks was the higher operating cost due to the expense of maintaining more employees in a remote location.

The previous week, Norbert Schwartz, Gary's project manager, had indicated that drilling and testing flow from the new wells was finished, so they were ready for recovery. Now Gary had to put all the information together so that the Santos Executive Committee could make a decision. It would then be his task to buy the equipment, hire the people and develop the well into a production facility. If they got the decision wrong now, his task would be much harder and the renewal of his contract next year would be very unlikely.

Company background

Gary Anderson was the engineering manager of the Cooper Basin area of Santos Ltd, a company of international oil and gas producers. Santos is active in exploration, development and production of oil in the Cooper Basin, located in the north-east corner of South Australia (Figure 27.1). Moomba, the centre of oil handling operations for Santos,

*Certain data have been disguised to protect commercial interests without affecting their relative values, otherwise this case is a true representation of the situations faced by Santos Ltd.

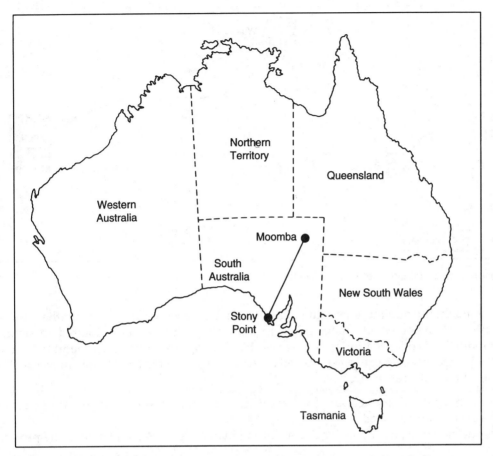

Figure 27.1 Location of Santos oil wells at Moomba.

is the head of the 700 km pipeline which transfers all crude oil to Stony Point, on the coast. Distribution to the Australian market is by crude oil tanker vessels. Besides the Cooper Basin, Santos has licences to explore for oil and gas in six Australian oilfields, plus fields in Malaysia, Papua New Guinea and the USA.

Santos has brought into production eight oilfields in the Cooper Basin since 1991. Five of these fields have involved the installation at Wakanui of crude oil gathering, treatment and storage facilities (Figure 27.2). Wakanui is connected by pipeline to Moomba, 26 km away. The two new fields are fairly close to Wakanui, to which they are connected by unmade roads.

Sale of the crude oil to the Australian market is immediate and is assured at the world price of US$15.05 per barrel or whatever that price may be in the future.

Santos's Cooper Basin development strategy is to phase in the installation of facilities, and to minimize initial capital expenditure (Exhibit 27.1). The primary goal is to commence early oil production using temporary facilities and road tankers. This generates early cash flow and makes a contribution to subsequent development.

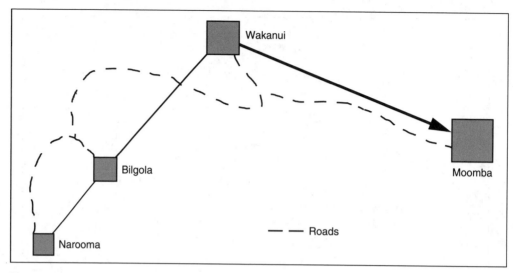

Figure 27.2 Location of new oil wells.

Initially, the minimum permanent facilities are installed to produce oil to the desired specification for either trucking or pipeline. All equipment not required for initial production is deferred for as long as possible. This approach has been found to lead to the best selection of equipment, based on actual operating history. Disadvantages of this development strategy are:

- higher risk of product out of specification and extra staffing requirements, until full facilities are installed
- additional requirements for engineers and managers to plan and control the project.

Santos's prime objective is to maximize the net present value (NPV) of the project. This

---

Exhibit 27.1 Santos's Cooper Basin strategy and policies

Strategic goal
Santos wishes to maximize the return on its exploration and oil production. Santos prefers to keep expenditure to a minimum and obtain cash contributions from each well as soon as possible.

Development policies
Santos achieves its goal by maximizing the net present value* of the project, over its full life. Policies are required to:
- identify the development options
- select the preferred development
- control the project.

*Net present value is a single value which represents the current value of cash outflows and inflows that are forecast to occur during the life of the project. This is achieved by reducing or discounting future flows by a factor which allows for their utility compared to a current cash flow.

requires identification and definition of the development option which optimizes the cost of the project over its full life. NPV is the present equivalent of the future estimated cash flows, discounted back to the present at a rate which allows for the cost of capital to the operator.

In a remote area such as the Cooper Basin, operating costs are high because of the absence of normal infrastructure and the desert conditions. Maximizing NPV often places more emphasis on the effects of operating and maintenance costs than on minimizing capital costs. Lost opportunity costs due to a delay in start up are also an important consideration.

Current decision

Recent exploration has resulted in finding two more wells, at Bilgola and Naroma which, although close together, are 20 km distant from the treatment and distribution facilities at Wakanui. It has been decided to develop the two wells but Gary, on behalf of Santos, has to choose whether to install a new pipeline or truck the oil to the existing facility.

The oil reserves and rate of production have been estimated for each well. For example Bilgola has reserves of 1.04 million barrels and a production rate of 2660 barrels per day (Table 27.1). A small amount of oil has been recovered from each well by truck. Capital costs have been estimated for the pipeline and trucking alternatives, with pipeline requiring considerably greater capital investments. Trucking would involve extra handling, increased numbers of employees and the risk of supply being disrupted by rain, since the roads are not sealed.

The first option, which Gary was considering, was to install a surface pipeline from Narooma to facilities at Bilgola and truck the output of both wells from Bilgola to Moomba. It was also possible to truck separately from each well to Wakanui. Gary has ruled out this latter alternative because, although it gives a similar return, it is less attractive if further wells are found in that same area.

Gary's second option was to install a surface pipeline from Narooma to Bilgola and a

Table 27.1 Reserves and development costs of Bilgola and Narooma wells

	Bilgola	Narooma
Oil reserves, current estimate (million barrels)	1.04	1.12
Production rate (barrels per day)*	2660	850
Pipeline distance from Wakanui (km)	16	22
Road distance from Moomba (km)	26	36
Capital cost – Trucking	$1.4 m	–
– Pipeline	$3.2 m	$0.7 m
Oil recovered to date (million barrels†)	0.426	0.028
Operating cost of trucks:	$1.65 per barrel	
Down time:	Trucking option 15%	
	Pipeline option 5%	

*This is the current production rate which decreases throughout the life of the well.
†A barrel is 35 gallons or 160 litres.

buried pipeline from Bilgola to Wakanui. This would require centralized gathering facilities at Bilgola and a separator and transfer metering at Wakanui for immediate piping to Moomba. A variant on this option would add storage tanks and a gauging system at Wakanui which would cater for differences in pipeline flow. This variant increases costs considerably for no regular return, so Gary has ruled it out.

Oil geology

In the Cooper Basin, oil is located in underground reservoirs trapped under high pressure between layers of permeable rock (Figure 27.3). The operator taps into the underground reservoir by drilling into the permeable rock. Underneath the oil is water, which will rise to fill the void caused as the oil is pumped to the surface. Eventually the water swamps the recovery of oil. The operator has seismic data, rock samples from the well bore and production data from the commencement of the well. Geologists interpret these data to predict the oil recovery rate and the economic productive life of the well, which can be significantly different from early estimates. Also, the recovery rate and production quantity may be affected by the method of recovery. Figure 27.4 shows how the rate of recovery of oil, and contaminating water, changed very rapidly over a period of eight weeks at 'Sybil', a previous well. However, similar information for other wells generally shows a very slow change over extended periods.

The Cooper Basin is a very inhospitable place to work. A very low rainfall and very high summer temperatures, up to 55°C, cause desert conditions. There is limited scrub vegetation without trees or surface water. A great diurnal change in temperature breaks up the surface into deep beds of dust whenever vehicles drive across it.

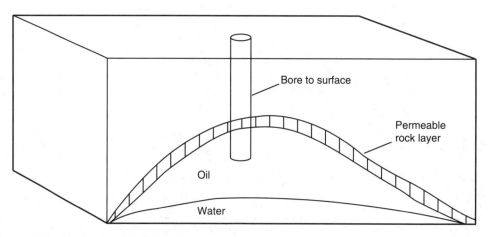

Figure 27.3 Underground oil location.

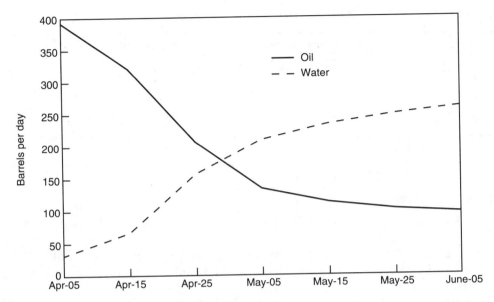

Figure 27.4 Sybil: rapid change in recovery.

Table 27.2 Capital costs of both options

	Option 1: pipeline $ thousands	Option 2: trucking $ thousands
Tanks and heating*	94	134
Pumps and separators	80	34
In-plant pipework	235	92
Electrical and instrumentation	240	56
Roads†	280	427
Accommodation and transport‡	200	95
Commissioning and testing	45	20
Total direct	2094	858
Total indirect	510	252
Subtotal	2604	1110
Contingency at 25%	596	290
Total Bilgola	3200	1400
Narooma	700	0
Total capital	3900	1400

*Storage tanks are at the well head. Heating is required because of low temperatures at night in winter.
†To provide formed dirt roads for access of construction and operating crews in all weathers. A higher standard of roads, including aggregate reinforcement on some sections, is required in the trucking option.
‡This item comprises the lodgings of construction crews and the cost of moving them into the Cooper Basin and from lodgings to place of work. It is greater for the pipeline option because much more construction is required.

Table 27.3 Example of net cash flow calculations ($ thousands)

| | Pipeline option | | Trucking option | |
	1995	1996	1995	1996
Revenue	2090	5770	2340	5650
Operating cost	(370)	(870)	(1390)	(1900)
Capital cost	(3300)	(600)	(1400)	0
Net cash flow	(1580)	4300	(450)	3750

Well development options

Option 1: Pipeline

Under this option, capital costs of US$3.2 million are incurred (Table 27.2) and production is estimated to be 2.16 million barrels over a nine-year period. A free-flowing pipeline joins Narooma to Bilgola so that their joint output can be brought to specification and further piped to Wakanui without storage. From Wakanui the oil is piped in the existing pipeline to Moomba.

Norbert, the project manager, has estimated the costs and revenues accruing each year under this option. Table 27.3 shows examples of his calculations for the first two years.

The net cash flow for each option is shown as a cumulative figure without discounting to current values in Figure 27.5. It is clear that, in absolute terms, trucking provides an earlier payback but less cumulative revenue, over the whole life of the project. The pipeline option involves a considerable extra investment at the start, but its cumulative return overtakes that of trucking after three years. The exhibit also shows the effect of

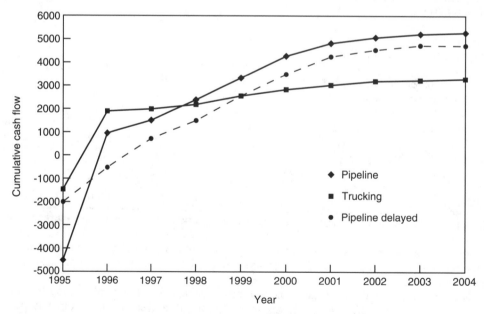

Figure 27.5 Cumulative present values of cash flows for each option.

Table 27.4 Derivation of net present value of option ($m) (after tax)

Year	Pipeline			Trucking		
	Net cash flow	Discount factor	NPV	Net cash flow	Discount factor	NPV
1995	−1.58	1	−1.58	−0.45	−0.45	−0.45
1996	4.4	0.75	3.30	3.75	0.75	2.81
1997	1.95	0.56	1.10	1.35	0.56	0.76
1998	0.75	0.42	0.32	0.45	0.42	0.19
1999	0.75	0.32	0.24	0.45	0.32	0.14
2000	0.85	0.24	0.20	0.40	0.18	0.07
2002	0.85	0.13	0.11	0.40	0.13	0.05
2003	0.85	0.10	0.09	0.40	0.10	0.04
2004	0.85	0.08	0.06	0.40	0.08	0.03
		Total NPV	3.99		Total NPV	3.74

Table 27.5 Estimated returns from each option

	Option 1: pipeline	Option 2: trucking
NPV at 25% after tax (US$ thousands)	3990	3736
Production (million barrels)	2.160	2.065
Payback period (years after tax)	1.4	1.2
Last year of production	2004	2003

delaying the pipeline for six months. This restricts the negative cash flow in the early stages at the cost of a reduced ultimate cash surplus. Norbert's next step was to calculate the (NPV) of the annual net cash flows (Table 27.4); e.g. the pipeline cash flow of $1.95 million in 1997 is discounted by 25% twice (factor 0.56) to give the 1995 equivalent value of $1.10 million. The estimated returns from each option are given in Table 27.5. The NPV with a 25% per annum discount rate is US$3.99 million with a payback period of 1.4 years.

Option 2: Trucking

Under this option, capital costs of US$1.4 million are incurred (Table 27.2) and production is estimated to be 2.06 million barrels over an eight-year period. A free-flowing pipeline joins Narooma to Bilgola and their joint output is trucked direct to Moomba.

In a similar manner to the pipeline option, Norbert has estimated costs and revenues for the trucking option (Table 27.3) and calculated the NPV of the annual cash flows (Table 27.4). He then summarized the cash flows in a NPV calculation (Table 27.5). The NPV with a 25% discount rate is US$3.74 million with a payback period of 1.2 years.

Additional imponderables

Being an experienced manager, Gary set aside some time to think about the 'imponderables' or non-quantifiable factors before he sent his development proposal to the executive committee.

The biggest concern in his mind was the risks involved, whichever way the decision should go. He had a lot of figures on paper and a neat net present value summary of each surviving option, but these figures were only best guesses. The amount of oil coming from each well, and the proportion of water contaminating it, could change quite dramatically over a period of several months, as shown by recent experience at Sybil, one of the other Cooper Basin wells (Figure 27.4). The price Santos would receive for each barrel sold could vary greatly from the US$15 assumed – variations of 20% above and below the mean had occurred during the last five years. Who knew what changes would happen over the next nine years?

He also needed to consider the effect of rain which may seem irrelevant when all the earth around was as dry as dust. It had not rained at Moomba for over a year. But several rainfalls were likely over the next nine years and any fall over 6 mm was sufficient to interrupt the trucking option for several weeks and, probably, affect the total amount of oil recovered because of the need to cap the oil well temporarily.

Decision day

It was Friday, 20 October when Gary sat down with Norbert, his project manager and Jim Gleeson, his cost and planning engineer, to put the finishing touches on his recommendations to the Santos Executive Committee meeting, which was due in two weeks' time in Adelaide. Jim took the view that trucking was the way to extract oil from the two new wells because it offered a faster payback.

Norbert strongly favoured Option 1, the pipeline. This option offered a higher NPV on future cash flows, fewer operating problems and reduced down time, leading to greater expected overall oil production. Gary listened to all Jim and Norbert had to say. He reminded them how flexible the figures were – the actual result could be quite different from the numbers currently in the proposal. He mentioned that he was strongly influenced by the ability of the pipeline option to lower the cost of development of other reserves which might be found near Bilgola and Narooma.

Acknowledgements

The assistance of Santos Ltd in supplying the information for the case and Mr Michael Hannell for checking and approval is gratefully acknowledged.

The transport of nuclear waste: logistics organization in a government department*†

Martin Dresner
College of Business and Management, University of Maryland, USA

Introduction

Samuel Hall, the newly appointed logistics division staff director in the US Department of the Environment, sat in his office with his boss's request in hand. Sharon Green, the deputy secretary for nuclear management, had asked Hall for a report on the efficiency and effectiveness of logistics and transportation operations within the Department of the Environment, and to provide recommendations as to any reorganization that should take place. After receiving the request the previous month, Hall had engaged in a number of interviews with departmental and private sector personnel and toured several of the department's field facilities. The report was due within the week and Hall still had not made up his mind as to its contents.

Overview of the Department's logistics operations

The Department of the Environment is a relatively new federal department, formally established in 1965. The Department operates 73 field sites throughout the USA and has its head office in downtown Washington, DC. Each of the field sites has specific functions to undertake within the organization, including scientific research into the environment, the disposal of hazardous industrial waste, and the handling, storage and transportation

*This case is based on a real situation but for reasons of confidentiality all individuals, companies and organizations cited in the case are disguised.
†Data available on the Internet (see page xxii).

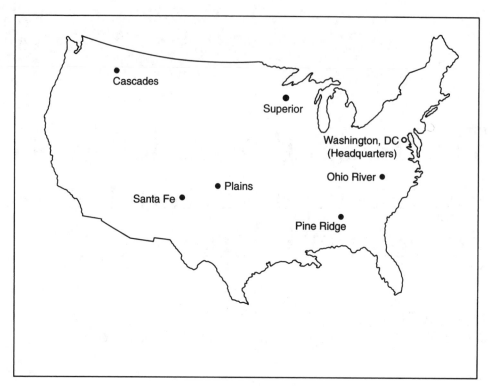

Figure 28.1 Department of the Environment headquarters and major field sites.

of nuclear materials and waste. Of the department's 73 field offices, six of the sites account for 80% of the department's shipments and 90% of the department's shipments of hazardous materials (Figure 28.1). During the 1993 fiscal year, the department was responsible for over 575,000 for-hire commercial shipments totalling 495,000 tons of materials. The department paid the freight bill for 374,000 of these shipments totalling 342,000 tons. Table 28.1 provides a summary of the department's for-hire shipment activity for fiscal year 1993.

Ninety-one per cent of the department's domestic shipments travelled by air, commercial motor carrier or rail. The remainder of the shipments were by water or parcel carrier or were handled by a freight forwarder. Of the 575,000 shipments in fiscal year 1993, 74% were by air, 17% by for-hire truck and less than 1% by rail. However, rail carriers moved 48% of the tonnage, trucking firms, 35%, and air carriers, less than 1%. A breakdown of the department's transportation shipment costs by mode is given in Table 28.2. The top commodities moved by each of the modes are listed in Table 28.3. Although coal made up less than 1% percent of the department's shipments, it accounted for over 60 percent of shipment tonnage.

Hazardous materials were defined as substances 'capable of posing an unreasonable risk to health, safety, and property when transported', according to US Department of Transportation guidelines, and constituted 18,000 departmental shipments – 3% of total shipments, but 30% of shipments by weight. Approximately half of the hazardous

Table 28.1 Summary of Department of the Environment shipment activity, fiscal year 1993

Shipment type	Number of shipments	Weight (thousands of tons)	Transportation cost to department (thousands of Dollars)
Inbound–collect	87,229	298	18,996
Outbound–prepaid	286,595	44	10,219
Inbound–prepaid	190,268	111	–
Outbound–collect	11,121	42	–
Total	575,213	495	29,215

Table 28.2 Summary of shipments, tonnage, and costs by mode for fiscal year 1993 (inbound–collect and outbound–prepaid only)

Mode	Number of shipments	Weight (tons)	Departmental cost ($)	Average cost per ton ($)
Air	332,256	2678	5,660,256	2114
Motor	40,816	63,296	17,914,894	283
Rail	752	276,221	5,639,980	20
Total	373,824	342,195	29,215,130	85

Table 28.3 Top commodities moved by air, truck and rail, fiscal year 1993

Mode / Commodity	Number of shipments	Weight (tons)	Shipments (% of mode)	Tonnage (% of mode)
Air				
Miscellaneous freight	368,211	1968	78	45
Paper products	33,960	179	7	4
Electronic equipment	33,221	640	7	15
Truck–LTL				
Miscellaneous freight	20,250	7375	27	27
Electronic equipment	8925	1917	12	7
Fabricated metal products	7490	2619	10	9
Truck–TL				
Hazardous material	6470	121,533	71	72
Miscellaneous freight	590	7329	7	4
Coal	362	12,525	4	7
Rail				
Coal	1584	292,335	96	98

Note: Hazardous materials accounted for 4800 air shipments, 6900 LTL shipments and 12 rail shipments.

Table 28.4 Projected radioactive materials shipments, 1994–2003

Year	Shipments	Weight (tons)
1994	10,000	100,000
1995	12,000	120,000
1996	15,000	150,000
1997	25,000	250,000
1998	35,000	350,000
1999	45,000	450,000
2000	55,000	550,000
2001	65,000	650,000
2002	75,000	750,000
2003	85,000	850,000

materials shipments contained radioactive materials. It was the responsibility of the Department of the Environment to transport and store spent nuclear materials from public power plants, medical facilities, research installations, and Department of Defense installations. Nuclear materials were currently stored at 22 of the department's field sites and were mainly transported to and from the sites by truck. The department projected a ten-fold increase in shipments containing radioactive materials within the next ten years, owing to a governmental mandate to transfer the radioactive materials from temporary storage at the field sites to a permanent storage facility at a yet to be determined site. Table 28.4 shows the department's projected radioactive shipments from 1994 to 2003.

Logistics organization

Figure 28.2 provides an organizational chart for the department's logistics operations. The Department of the Environment is organized on the basis of programmes. Each deputy secretary is responsible for a functional area, so, for example, there is a deputy secretary for industrial waste management, a deputy secretary for air quality, and a deputy secretary for water quality. In total, there are six deputy secretaries. Reporting to each deputy secretary are a number of programme directors. These programme directors are typically located at field offices and are responsible for overseeing programmes within the functional area of the deputy secretary. The programme director has a small staff of specialists including a logistics manager. The programmatic activities are not undertaken by Department of the Environment staff but by contracting and subcontracting companies. Contractors submit bids on a periodic basis (five to ten years is typical) to operate a field facility for the Department of the Environment. At the six largest Department of the Environment facilities, contractors have from 10,000 to 20,000 employees engaged in environmental research, clean-up activities, the warehousing of nuclear materials or other activities. Contractors also employ subcontractors to undertake specific activities. For example, it is typical of contractors themselves to subcontract the transport of materials to and from the field sites.

Programme funding follows the lines of the organizational chart (Figure 28.2) For

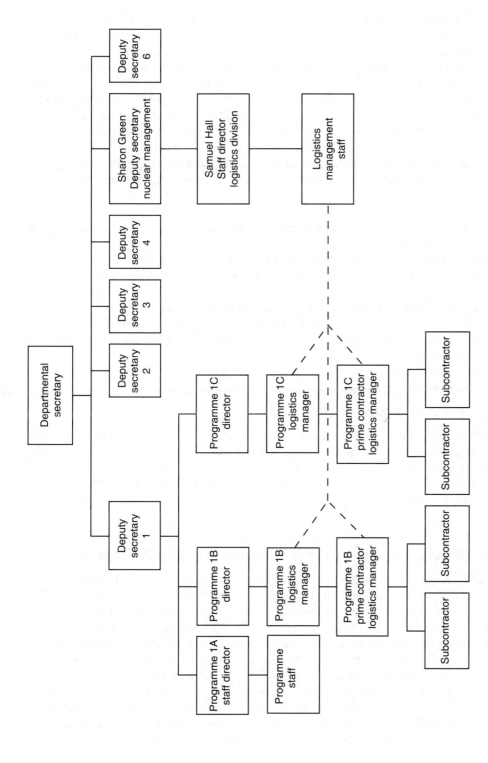

Figure 28.1 Department of the Environment organizational chart.

example, Congress may allocate $50 million to clean up an abandoned nuclear facility. The programme will be placed under the jurisdiction of the appropriate deputy secretary and assigned a director and small staff. Contractors will bid on the rights to undertake the clean-up, and the winning contractor will hire subcontractors when appropriate.

Programme funding is also available for research and development, data collection and analysis, and other specialized projects. These programmes are headed by staff directors who report to a deputy secretary. The logistics division, headed by Samuel Hall with a total of 30 staff members, is one such programme. The logistics division is housed in an office building in suburban Washington, DC and, although under the purview of the deputy secretary for nuclear management, serves as a logistics head office staff agency for all of the department's field programmes. The activities performed by the logistics division include:

- Conducting research into package design for the safe storage and transportation of hazardous materials.
- Providing policy guidelines and technical assistance to field personnel.
- Acting as a liaison with public interest groups regarding the safe transportation of hazardous materials.
- Monitoring regulatory compliance by the department and its contractors.
- Negotiating contract freight rates with national trucking and rail firms.
- Qualifying transportation carriers for departmental use on the basis of driver and vehicle safety records.
- Collecting and disseminating transportation cost data.

Background to Samuel Hall's report

As part of the preparation for his report to Sharon Green, Samuel Hall toured a number of field locations and interviewed departmental and contract personnel. He was especially interested in how logistics functions were divided between the logistics division in Washington, the Department of the Environment field personnel, and the contractors hired by the Department of the Environment. The following are some of his observations.

Visit to the Department of the Environment's Ohio River site

The Ohio River site is a Department of the Environment facility managed under contract by Mega Corporation since 1989. The contract, initially for five years, has been extended for another two years, at which time it will come up for re-bid. Eighty-five per cent of the transportation requirements at Ohio River are inbound. Transportation management functions are split, with inbound transportation under Mega's Ohio River purchasing department and outbound transportation under Mega's Ohio River transportation department. The vast majority of the inbound material is FOB delivered, the transportation costs being prepaid. Suppliers prefer to ship under these terms because they can add up to a 20% profit component to their transportation costs. Currently, the purchasing specialists do very little checking on the reasonableness of the transportation charges embedded in the price of the purchases. Part of the reason for this is that there is no automated computer system that could easily be accessed by the purchasing people that would show transportation rates for the purchases. If such a system existed, the purchasing specialists could easily determine whether or not it was cost effective for the contractor to arrange for its own inbound transportation. Although not directly involved with inbound shipments, transportation department personnel believe that this type of system should be a top priority at Ohio River and is the type of activity in which the logistics division in Washington, DC should be involved in implementing.

The transportation department ships both hazardous and non-hazardous material. As might be expected, the hazardous shipments take a disproportionate amount of the department's time. The transportation personnel claim to have an excellent record with respect to shipment safety, having received positive US Transportation Safety Administration audits over the last few years. Each individual piece of a hazardous materials shipment is double checked with respect to packaging, markings, and paperwork. The Ohio River transportation department measures its success in large part in terms of paperwork, packaging or other errors, all of which have occurred at a zero rate over the past five years.

The Ohio River transportation department collects little or no information on carrier performance and has developed no metrics to measure carrier performance, but uses the logistics division carrier evaluation forms to qualify carriers. On a number of occasions during the visit, the Mega personnel spoke highly of the logistics division. The transportation department looks to the logistics division for carrier evaluations, negotiated rates, and overall direction. Although Mega's transportation department personnel are aware of a Department of the Environment logistics field officer in the area, they do not interact with him, nor do they even know his name.

Interview with Rita Mackay, Department of the Environment logistics manager at the Pine Ridge field site

As logistics manager, Mackay is responsible for overseeing the logistics management functions of the contractor and subcontractors at the Pine Ridge field site. She also conducts rate negotiations with regional and some national carriers and qualifies carriers to ship Pine Ridge goods using the evaluation form developed by the logistics division. Contractors are encouraged to use carriers from her approved list, and one of Mackay's jobs is to audit contractors' shipments. Mackay has access to the logistics division list of qualified contractors but believes that she can get 25–30% lower prices herself, sometimes from the same carrier with which the logistics division has negotiated. She, therefore, rarely uses the rates negotiated by the logistics division even if she uses one of the carriers on the logistics division list of qualified carriers. Mackay says that she likes to see completed logistics division carrier evaluation forms before she adds a carrier to her own list, but claims that these reports are often not forwarded to the field.

Mackay conducts rate negotiations with railroads as well as trucking companies, given that the majority of the freight that she ships moves by rail. Even though there is only track from one railroad at Pine Ridge, there are two competing freight railroads serving the site. The competition resulted from an agreement between the two carriers, where one railroad granted the other railroad the right to use its tracks in return for offsetting concessions. The rail carriers are required to bid for Pine Ridge work. Once a tender is accepted, the carrier is added to the approved list. If the contractor at Pine Ridge uses the tendered rates and shipment terms, the contractor is, at least in theory, relieved of some of the potential liability that could arise from accidents or spills. The alternative would be for the contractor to use its own corporate carriers, who may or may not be on the Pine Ridge approved list.

A possible impediment to achieving lower transportation costs or greater efficiencies is that Pine Ridge is directed by federal government rules to spread business around. Contractors are required not to concentrate transportation business with any one firm but to ensure that a number of firms, including local firms, firms classified as small businesses, and firms owned by women and disadvantaged minority members, receive part of the government business. Although no quotas for each of these types of firms are set, Mackay is aware that federal audits will compare the performance of Pine Ridge to that of other government units and that Pine Ridge's commitment to using firms from the designated categories will be reflected in her performance appraisal. Mackay audits the contractors to ensure that each of the designated categories of firms receives a share of Pine Ridge business.

Mackay believes that the logistics division currently is not focusing on the types of problems on which a head office staff organization should be working. According to Mackay, the last thing that the Department of the Environment should do is to centralize logistical operational responsibilities within the logistics division. The logistics division already spends too much time on specific operational issues, rather than on providing policy and direction to the field. As an example, the logistics division spends a lot of resources developing packages for the transportation of hazardous materials. Mackay does not believe that package development is an appropriate role for a head office staff function. The logistics division should serve as a clearing-house for package development information, not develop the packages itself; however, it provides little or no direction on the type of package that should be used for particular shipments, and provides little co-ordination between field sites regarding packaging or transportation activities. Mackay mentioned that in her eight years of involvement with the Department of the Environment, she has only been aware of one meeting which was attended by more than two contractors.

Interview with Steven Jameson, transportation officer, logistics division

Jameson's position is with the logistics division, with primary responsibility for providing technical support to transportation and logistics field office personnel. He has worked in the transportation industry for 40 years, including eight years in a field office for the Department of the Environment and the last two years at the logistics division.

In addition to providing technical support to the field, Jameson qualifies national carriers and negotiates rates with them. The carriers are approved based on a number of criteria, most of which are concerned with driver and vehicle safety. Safety criteria include a carrier's traffic accident record (traffic accidents per 100,000 vehicle-miles), roadside safety inspection record (safety citations per 100,000 vehicle-miles); driver citation record (moving violations per 100,000 vehicle-miles), and insurance premiums (vehicle insurance payments per 100,000 vehicle-miles). Performance criteria used to evaluate carriers include on-time delivery record (on-time deliveries per 100 shipments) and damage claims record (number of damage claims per 100 shipments). The safety and performance records are self-reported by the carriers and are not independently verified by Jameson. The field offices are sent a list of approved carriers and negotiated rates, although the field offices are under no obligation to use the approved carriers or the logistics division rates.

The major weakness that Jameson sees with the current set-up at the Department of the Environment is a diffusion of responsibility. Since head office control is only advisory, and the field personnel control the programme budgets, money can be spent without central control or accounting. Jameson believes that the Department could save money by having a central logistics organization, which would also reduce the probability of a serious spill of hazardous material, as field personnel would need central office approval for packaging and carrier decisions. The central office would combine all staff logistics personnel from the various agency and programme offices within the Department. A central office would eliminate much of the duplication that currently exists between the various logistics specialists at the logistics division and in the field.

Interview with Keith Awbrawer, packaging development officer at the logistics division

Awbrawer has been employed by the Department of the Environment for three years; two of those with the logistics division. His background is a master's of science in systems engineering and 13 years' work experience with private contractors in systems engieering and transportation.

An important component of the logistics function at the Department of the Environment is the packaging of hazardous materials. Hazardous materials must be packaged during transit to minimize the possibility of environmental damage, especially in the event of the carrier being involved in a traffic accident. There is no standard package for hazardous material – different packages are used depending on the danger posed by a leak and the mode of transportation. For example, a highly radioactive material such as plutonium requires a stronger and more secure package than mildly contaminated nuclear material. The Department of the Environment uses approximately 200 different package designs for its shipments.

Awbrawer would like the logistics division to become more involved in co-ordinating policies among field offices, and his suggested initiatives included: co-ordinating packaging procurement, developing standard packaging, centralizing inventory data-bases for packages, and co-ordinating certification requirements. With respect to this third point, Awbrawer discussed a centralized database, the package management tracking system, which was being developed. The system would contain information on all the packages at the various field warehouses. Awbrawer was concerned that the field offices may not co-operate in implementing the system, given that there would be a considerable data entry requirement by the field. Awbrawer also stated that several departmental contractors had plans to increase co-ordination among themselves by establishing a contractor packaging group.

Awbrawer defined two types of customers to whom he must answer: the field sites and the public. Each customer group is concerned with different aspects of the logistic division's operations. The field sites would generally like to be left alone, while the public is interested in the safe movement of hazardous materials.*

Hall's dilemma

In reviewing his interviews with Department of the Environment logistics personnel and with personnel from Department of the Environment contractors, Hall was troubled by a number of organizational issues. For example, why were the Mega Corporation transportation department personnel at the Ohio River field site not aware of the activities of the Department of the Environment field personnel? If the Department of the Environment field personnel were not supervising contractor operations, then who was? Why did Rita Mackay at the Pine Ridge field site not obtain copies of the logistics division carrier qualification forms when Steven Jameson at the logistics division claimed they were sent to the field offices? Who should be responsible for package development, the logistics division, Department of the Environment field personnel, or the contractors? Can a system be put into place to track packages effectively? Why do the contractors receive inbound material FOB delivered and freight prepaid, and how much does this cost the Department? Do current procedures adequately protect the Department of the Environment from the possibility of a spill of radioactive materials? How well will the Department cope with hazardous materials transportation in the future, given the projected increase in hazardous materials shipments? Hall felt that many of these problems were related to the separation of logistics authority in the Department of the Environment between the logistics division and the field offices. At what level of the Department should logistics responsibilities rest?

In an effort to gather additional information on the organization of logistics activities, Hall conducted a quick review of the practices of leading logistics firms. He found that some of these firms had recently centralized certain logistics activities such as purchasing and traffic management within a headquarters department. Hall, however, was not sure that centralization was the right way to organize logistics in the Department of the Environment. He was concerned that centralization may not be suitable for a government department that makes extensive use of contracting companies. He also thought that an allowance should be made for the type of material transported by the department, and that the centralized structure may not fit a company with a high level of hazardous waste transportation. Hall knew that any attempt to centralize logistics functions would meet with strong opposition from field personnel, e.g. Mackay from Pine Ridge. Finally, given that the logistics division had no direct control over programme budgets, he was not certain how he could effectively manage field logistics operations under a centralized structure.

---

*The US Department of Transportation estimates that 4000 million tons of regulated hazardous materials are transported annually within the USA. In 1990, the Department of Transportation received reports of over 8500 safety 'incidents' (US General Accounting Office, 1991), which included all accidents and safety violations involving vehicles transporting hazardous materials.

Acknowledgements

Special acknowledgements are due to Alan Salton, who accompanied the author on most of his interviews, the author's colleagues at the University of Maryland involved in the 'Best Logistics Practices' study, from which this case material originated, and to Phil Evers, Jane Feitler and Michael Mejza for commenting on earlier drafts of the case.

Reference

US General Accounting Office (1991) *Transportation Safety: Information Strategy Needed for Hazardous Materials*, GAO/IMTEC-91-50, General Accounting Office, Washington, DC.

PART EIGHT

International logistics and international market-entry strategies

Managing international logistics*†

Professor Peter Gilmour
Graduate School of Management, Macquarie University, Australia

Introduction

During the 1980s the Eastman Kodak Company established a network of regional distribution centres throughout the world. These were located in Rochester (New York), Windsor (Colorado), Chalon (France) and in Singapore. In 1994 another one was set up in Brazil. In June of that year Steve Leong, the General Manager of the Central Distribution Centre (CDC) Asia, was called to a meeting in Tokyo with his boss, Pete Zimmerman, the Director of Logistics for the Asia Pacific Region, to consider some alternative logistics options. He explained:

> We discuss service levels with individual countries [Kodak marketing operations in the countries of the region] once a year. We are not tied to the idea of a network of CDCs. Our aim is to have a system which will deliver the service levels required by our marketing companies in the most effective way.

The central distribution centre concept

Eastman Kodak is comprised of six business units: consumer products, office imaging, professional and printing, motion picture and television, health sciences, and clinical diagnostics. Not all Kodak plants in the various parts of the world produce a complete range of these products. The basic idea of the CDC concept is that the entire product range will be consolidated in a number of regions. Then these regional CDCs can supply the local Kodak marketing companies with all their requirements in single consolidated shipments. In practice some variation from this ideal concept does occur.

The CDC–Asia services the Kodak marketing operations in: Singapore, Malaysia,

*Certain data in this case have been disguised to protect the interests of the company.
†Data available on the Internet (see page xxii).

Thailand, the Philippines, Taiwan, Hong Kong, which in turn supplies the People's Republic of China, Korea, Australia, and Japan, which has a limited product range.

The CDC–Asia also supplies to appointed Kodak distributors in India, Sri Lanka, Nepal, Myanmar (Burma), Indo-China (Laos, Cambodia and Vietnam) and the Maldives. The largest of these customers are Thailand ('growing very rapidly'), Korea, Australia and Taiwan ('quite substantial').

Inbound shipments come from Kodak manufacturing plants in the USA (the Rochester and Windsor plants generate together about 40% of the total inbound shipments for CDC–Asia), Australia (about 25% from the Coburg plant in Melbourne) and Brazil (also 25%). The remaining 10% comes from plants in Mexico, Germany, France and the UK.

The CDC–Asia operates as a branch of Eastman Kodak in the USA and is a separate legal entity from the local Singapore Kodak marketing operation. Therefore the CDC–Asia accepts orders from the Asia Pacific Region (APR) and bills these operations on behalf of the Eastman Kodak Company. The stock held at the CDC–Asia is consigned from Eastman Kodak and forms part of the US inventory holding.

Order fulfilment

Each Kodak marketing company in the Asia Pacific region generates a weekly replenishment order on the CDC–Asia. These are sent electronically on Friday night and result in the CDC–Asia receiving between 6000 and 8000 order lines each month. Orders vary in size by location. Typical orders from Australia are between 80 and 100 lines. Those from Korea, Hong Kong, Taiwan and Thailand are about 50–60 lines. The other locations place smaller orders of around ten lines.

In addition to these regular replenishment orders the CDC–Asia receives orders for non-stock items. These are also sent electronically and arrive every day. Emergency orders or 'exceptions' are received by e-mail. These are processed on a one-off basis and are 'quite manageable' in volume.

Picking of the replenishment orders begins on Monday. Depending on the particular requirements of the marketing companies, orders are shipped the same week or 'this week plus one'. As a rule the CDC–Asia will not ship additional product to make up a full container load unless the permission of the destination marketing company is asked.

A number of different customer service measures are used by Kodak for the marketing companies and for the end customers. See, for example, the customer service measures compiled by Kodak Australasia for the years 1992–4 listed in Table 29.1. Key measures are order fill rate (orders filled in full), on-time delivery and error-free order fulfilment. Gold film, for example, has an order fill rate target of 95%. On-time delivery in Singapore means an order placed before 5 pm being delivered the next working day. Error-free means no adjustments or reverses in the order process. For sensitized film and paper the shipment mode is sea. For a marketing company the customer service measure 'on-time' varies from two-and-a-half to seven weeks from order entry to receipt.[1] For an end customer in Hong Kong on-time for these products is next-day delivery from the Hong Kong warehouse.

Table 29.1 Kodak Australasia's customer service performance measures

		Jan.	Feb.	Mar.	Apr.	May	Jun.	Jul.	Aug.	Sep.	Oct.	Nov.	Dec.
					CDC–Asia performance 1992								
Lead-time (weeks)													
Ocean	Stock	5.4	5.4	5.1	5	4.9	4.6	4.7	4.7	5.5	5.2	5.7	5.7
	Non-stock	12.0	12.2	12.1	10.9	11.7	11.7	10.9	11.6	12.0	11.7	11.6	12.1
US shipment direct to Melbourne		14.7	12.4	14.5	12.8	11.7	16.8	11.7	10.2	9.4	10.5	12.1	6.7
Air	Stock	2	1.4	1.7	2.1	2.1	1.7	3.7	2.7	2.7	1.8	1.9	3
	Non-stock	9.5	6	9.3	12	10.3	11.2	6	8.6	6.2	5.2	7.6	8.4
Fulfilment rate (%)		94.30	96.00	96.30	95.00	97.00	96.30	95.50	95.40	94.60	93.20	92.50	94.50
					CDC–Asia performance 1993								
Lead-time (weeks)													
Ocean	Stock	5.5	5.6	5.6	5.1	5	5.2	4.9	5.5	5.8	5.9	5.5	5.5
	Non-stock	12.3	12.3	11.8	11.5	11.8	12.1	12.0	12.7	13.0	12.8	12.8	12.7
US shipment direct to Melbourne		None	11.1	10.7	9.3	7.5	8.2	10.2	10.4	11.4	11	18.3	8.2
Air	Stock	3	1.6	2.4	2.7	1.6	2.2	1.5	3.4	1.6	1.9	1.8	2.2
	Non-stock	10	7.3	7.1	10.3	8.5	9.1	7.9	7.7	8.8	9.5	9.8	8.9
Fulfilment rate (%)		96.50	96.50	96.70	96.70	95.20	95.70	97.50	95.90	95.00	95.40	96.20	91.20
					CDC–Asia performance 1994								
Lead-time (weeks)													
Ocean	Stock	6.1	5.1	5.9	5.3	4.2	4.3						
	Non-stock	14.3	12.0	13.3	12.4	11.8	13						
US shipment direct to Melbourne		10.6	9.4	10.1	9.1	8.5	7.9						
Air	Stock	1.6	1.9	1.8	1.9	1.5	1.8						
	Non-stock	9.1	9.7	9	9.9	9	8.5						
Fulfilment rate (%)		95.60	98.20	97.80	97.50	98.20	97.70						

Fulfilment rate applies only to CDC–Asia, i.e. excludes direct to Melbourne.

Distribution resources planning

Replenishment orders are generated by distribution resources planning (DRP). This is a time-phased planning mechanism to help manage the demand-driven requirements of regional warehouses (the Kodak marketing companies in the Asia Pacific region) on a central distribution centre.

Each marketing company prepares monthly forecasts for product families or key products rolling out for 18 months.[2] DRP helps with this task as it has eight different forecasting algorithms embedded in it. Unless these are overridden the program will itself pick the best of these eight or a combination of them which can most accurately 'forecast' the historical data provided. These methods are shown in Table 29.2. Managerial input is provided to this process by the product sales managers for each business unit in each regional marketing location and the region's demand planners. The result of the monthly meeting of these people is that they either provide the forecast or decide that the DRP program can automatically generate it for them. In either case DRP breaks these monthly figures into weekly requirements over a 52-week planning horizon. The first of these 52 weeks represents the placed order and is fixed. The next week plus the number of following weeks that represent the lead time (e.g. three weeks to Hong Kong) are also considered fixed. The marketing companies can change any of the remaining estimates. These forward estimated requirements, together with a factor derived from the 'safety stock aim' of each marketing company for each product group and the lead

Table 29.2 DRP forecasting algorithms

Forecast method summary			
No.	Method	National parameter(s)	LI?
0	Zero forecast	None	No
1	Moving average	P1	Moving average periods	Yes
2	Single smoothing	P3	Demand smoothing constant	Yes
		P24	Exponential smoothing periods	
3	Double smoothing	P2	Double smoothing periods	No
		P3	Demand smoothing constant	
		P20	Trend percentage	
		P24	Exponential smoothing periods	
5	Manual forecast	None		No
6	Weighted average	P5	Current smoothing periods	Yes
		P6	Prior smoothing periods	
		P7	Current period weighting (%)	
		P8	Prior period weighting (%)	
7	Straight leading indicator	None		Yes
8	Linear regression	None		No
9	Winter's seasonal	P31	Winter's level smoothing constant	
		P32	Winter's trend smoothing constant	
		P33	Winter's index smoothing constant	
		P34	Winter's minimum cycles of demand	

times from CDC–Asia, are the inputs needed for the DRP package to generate scheduled deliveries.

Safety stock levels or the safety stock aim is established for each product group by the CDC–Asia planners. This has been done mainly by judgement after considering supplier lead time reliability, variability of demand and desired service levels. In 1994 simulation tools were developed in-house at CDC–Asia to perform exchange curve analyses (examining the balance between customer service and safety stock) to help set safety stock levels. For Kodak products there are some peculiarities which complicate this process. For example some customers may require a consistent emulsion batch over a given period of several months so that they do not have to recalibrate their equipment. This has an obvious impact on safety stock levels.

DRP at CDC–Asia is linked into the materials resource planning (MRPII) software that is used by the plants. Lam Kit Ying, the inventory planning manager at CDC–Asia, explained that the 'suppliers [Kodak manufacturing plants] keep us on a longer fixed zone.' Australia, for example, operates on a fixed period of four weeks which is equivalent to the finishing lead time.[3] This means that the current month plus one is fixed. For the current month plus two it is acceptable to be within plus or minus 20%, and from there on change of any magnitude is accepted.

Exceptions to these arrangements are flagged and a tele-conference is normally held between CDC–Asia and the marketing companies and the plants to sort it out. For example, a large order may come unexpectedly and Kodak would not want to lose the sale. Possible solutions may be to try and convince the customer to receive staggered deliveries or to source the order from another location on a one-off basis.

Lam Kit Ying described the basic purpose of DRP to be 'to bring the sales forecast as close to the customer as possible.'

Central distribution centre–Asia

Sixty people work in logistics at CDC–Asia. The way in which this CDC is organized is shown in Figure 29.1. Planning, finance, customer service and information systems staff are located, together with the local Kodak Singapore staff, in an office building on Alexandra Road, about 3 km from the port. Staff reporting to Andrew Chng, the CDC–Asia physical distribution manager, are situated at the CDC which is located on a free-trade zone of the Port of Singapore's (PSA) Pasir Panjang port.

Warehouse layout

The CDC is 11,500 m^2 in area and contains 10,000 pallet spaces. Racking is provided for the 48 by 40-inch pallets with each space 1.8 m high and the building accommodating racks five high. The warehouse is divided roughly equally into three sections (Figure 29.2). The first section (shown at the left of the diagram in Figure 29.2) is temperature controlled at 13°C and the second section (the top-right area of the diagram) is another racked area kept at 21°C. (These facilities are required as different types of products require different temperature controlled storage.) The remainder of the warehouse is used for receipt, order assembly and despatch.

In Figure 29.2 the number of rack positions in each row is shown preceded by two

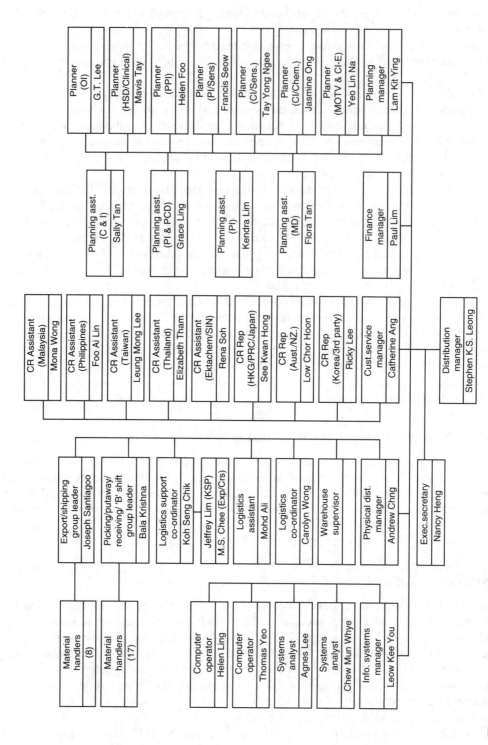

Figure 29.1 Organizational structure of the CDC–Asia.

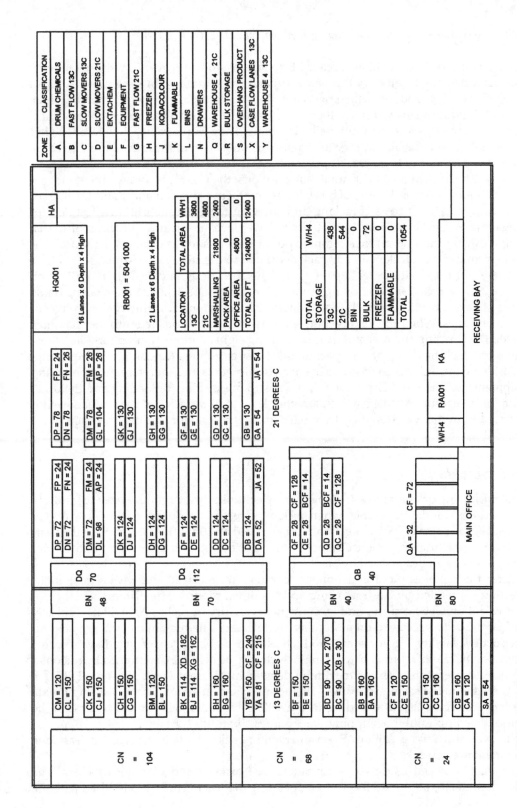

Figure 29.2 CDC–Asia warehouse layout.

alpha characters. For the chilled area the B zone is fast movers (over 50 visits per months for each catalogue number in this category) and the C zone is for slow movers. Racks labelled S are for products which overhang the standard pallet, typically film or paper. X and Y indicate shelving for small products, X for CDC and Y for Singapore domestic. These are the only 'less than full' pallet locations. They were gravity-flow locations but are being converted to flat storage to increase the utilization of these positions. There are 4500 rack positions in this area.

In the 21°C racked area (5500 total rack positions) the G zone is for fast movers (again over 50 visits per months for each catalogue number in this category) and D zone for slow movers. The Q zone is racking and shelving for domestic product destined for Singapore. A third letter F indicates that the lower level of this row of racks is of special height (higher than 1.8 m) to accommodate equipment such as cabinets. The letter A is for a ground-level standard-height rack dedicated to the storage of drums.

There is also a small freezer kept at −17°C. The areas designated RA001 and RB001 on Figure 29.2 are areas for fast-moving product which is block stacked. A marshalling frame is used to assemble 12 containers. Each container has two 6-m long gravity-flow conveyor assembly lanes. When the load is completely assembled it is pushed into the container. Unloading, loading and assembling is done using eight counterbalanced fork-lift trucks, three of which have slip sheet attachments. Most customers (Kodak marketing companies) have the facilities to unload slip sheeted shipments and therefore most outbound shipments go this way.[4] The receiving bay has 18 docks, nine for loading and the other nine for unloading. As this bay is at a higher level than the floor of the warehouse it is serviced from the warehouse by two roller conveyors, one for loading and another for unloading.

Order picking

Replenishment orders arrive in Singapore electronically over the weekend and are released on Monday mornings when picking slips are produced. Exceptions (urgent orders) are all received by phone. If they are received by 10 am they are shipped the same day. Andrew Chng's experience is that 'most countries place these orders almost every day'. They are all despatched by air.

After the replenishment and non-stock orders are received the weekly operations meeting – attended by Andrew Chng and his direct reports – determines TEUs (20-ft equivalent units) by country and by container type (dry or reefer; 20 or 40 ft). Typically 80% of the orders received on a Monday are released. The remaining 20% are held for product availability, e.g. for some products all of a particular order may have to come from a single manufacturing batch. Lines which may be held are determined by customer service requirements with the maximum delay being current week plus one. TEUs are then related to the sailing schedule. 'There is no question about air; we just ship it out.' Orders are accumulated according to the sailing schedule. Subsequent orders can be consolidated up until the shipping date, but less than full container orders will not be held over and miss a sailing. Every marketing region usually receives at least one shipment every week.

Product is picked using six 'reach riders' or 'stackers' and two stock pickers. The operator remains at ground level when operating the reach trucks, but is raised with the boom when operating the stock pickers. Most lines picked (70%) are by the carton or case, with the remaining 30% being full pallets.

Picking is done on a container level. Each container has a shipment number and each picking list is generated for a particular container. The picking list is ordered by location level in the warehouse. As products are randomly located within each of the zones it is possible that a single catalogue number may be in as many as four different locations.

After picking, orders are accumulated in the container frame or on the warehouse floor. Some packing is required for the smaller orders and shipments. When the shipment is due to go to the port the containers are loaded at the receiving bay by fork-lift truck.

Throughput

In 1993 the CDC–Asia handled 4400 TEUs, 2222 in and 2092 out,[5] with the difference being for local Singapore consumption. Each of these averaged 22 tonnes.

From the manufacturing plants the CDC–Asia received the following TEUs: Australia, 771; Brazil, 652; France, 33; Germany, 80; UK, 53; USA, 707; miscellaneous (OEMs), 34.

In addition to these shipments the CDC–Asia received 992,128 kg by air. Of this 50% came from Australia and 40% from the USA. In most cases these air shipments were caused by problems at the manufacturing sites and the cost of the air freight was paid by the supplying country. Air shipments from Australia were Kodak colour film where a study had established that inventory savings justified the freight differential.

Outbound sea and air shipments for 1993 are shown in Table 29.3. For the local Singapore market two 12-ft truck shipments are made each week.[6] (A 3% GST payment is made before this product can leave the duty-free zone.) Three 'lorry size' shipments per week are also made to Malaysia over the causeway from Singapore. In 1993 supply

Table 29.3 Outbound sea and air shipments from CDC–Asia 1993

Destination marketing area	Sea (TEUs)	Air (kg)
Australia	257	76,127
Korea	443	28,929
Hong Kong	357	57,538
Taiwan	353	49,926
Thailand	344	87,885
Philippines	252	11,105
Malaysia		6428
Indonesia	73	
New Zealand		25,600
Japan	198	15,578
India		24,749
Singapore export		
Dubai		21,605
Cambodia		3754
Laos		4768
Total	2277	405,857

of the New Zealand market was moved from CDC–Asia to Australia. Emergency shipments to the marketing companies are made by air with the freight paid by the customer. Normal sea shipments incur no freight costs to the marketing companies. The cost is absorbed by Eastman Kodak into the price of the product.

Sea rates are shown in Table 29.4. In the headings of this table 20D refers to a 20-tonne dry container and 20R to a 20-tonne reefer, or refrigerated, container. The split of dry and reefer containers to particular destinations varies. India, for example, receives all its shipments in reefers whereas Australia receives 40% of its shipments in dry containers and only 60% in reefers. All amounts in Table 29.4 are shown in US dollars. Air rates are given in Table 29.5. These amounts are listed in Singapore dollars.

Customer service

Once a month a quality council meeting is held. Steve Leong is of the view that this meeting is actually an operations planning and review meeting. It takes the form of a conference telephone call between the CDC–Asia planners and the regional business managers. Measures of CDC–Asia's performance are discussed, e.g. inventory levels, customer service: lead times and fill rates and on time shipments, and operations costs. Also discussed are any unusual situations coming up, such as manufacturing delays.

Once a year CDC–Asia discusses service levels with each individual country. The results of these discussions are formalized into a supply agreement. This specifies, among other things, lead times, the percentage of orders shipped within schedule, the percentage of orders shipped within schedule plus one week and the 'commitments the marketing companies provide to us' such as the two-week frozen zone.

The customer: Kodak (Australasia) Pty Ltd

John Fox is the manager–supply chain management for Kodak Australasia. He is located at the Australian plant in Coburg, a northern Melbourne suburb. He reports to Dr Gerry Johnson, the deputy managing director of the company. At the same organizational level are Ron Bade, the manager of distribution, and Ron Muscat, the manager of customer relations. Together these three are responsible for logistics. The Coburg plant provides the Australian operation with 20% of its stock-keeping units (SKUs) and 49% of its volume. The CDC in Singapore supplies 70% of the SKUs and 49% of the throughput. Other Kodak plants and OEMs supply the remaining 10% of the SKUs and 2% of the throughput.

John Fox described the relationship of Kodak Australasia with the CDC in Singapore:

> CDC–A is our best supplier – including our own factory. They are flexible. They have customer minded people. Any problem we have we can work out with one person in Singapore – Choor Hoon – communication is dead straightforward. She comes down to visit us once or twice a year. They are not a manufacturing site. They can buffer a whole load of demands for their customers.
>
> We are a big customer of Singapore. We are not a big customer of Rochester [Rochester, New York, the head office of the parent company Eastman Kodak Company]. It is also easier dealing with Singapore – there is only a two-hour time difference. It is much better than making phone calls in the middle of the night.

Table 29.4 Freight rates from Singapore by sea (US$)

Destination	Carrier	Non-hazardous 20D US$	20R US$	40D US$	40R US$	Hazardous 20D US$	20R US$	40D US$	40R US$	INC THC CHG	Sailing time (days)	Days in port	Fixed sail (Y/N)	Free week
Australia (Melbourne)	POCL	950	1500			950	1800				18	TH	1	
	MYN	950	1500			950	1500				16			
	NEDLLOYD	950	1500			950	1500				16	FRI	YES	1
	MOL	950	1300			950	1300				16-18		NO	14 days
	ABC	800 +	1600 +			850	1300				12			
		58150	58150								14			
India (Bombay)	MYK	700	1700		3200	700	1900		3300	YES				
	MITSUI		1600		2900		1600		2900	YES				
Hong Kong	MAERSK	300	1100			300	1100		1700	YES		M	YES	1
	POCL	300	1100	500	2000	300	1400	650	1700		3			
	HAPAG	300	950	650	1700	300	950							
	MOL	250	1200	350	2200	250	1200	350	2200	YES	3	TU, WE	YES	2
	NEDLLOYD	550	1590	900		390	1200	570	1800		4	TU, WE	YES	2
	TSK					550				YES	3 to 4	WE, SA	YES	2
Japan (Tokyo)	MAERSK	650	1700			650	1200							
	MOL	420		620			1700	900		YES				
	TSK					600	1500	900	2500		10	TU, FR	YES	2
Indonesia (Jakarta)	NEDDLOYD	400	1250			750	1700							
S Korea (Musak)	KAERSK			1600	2550	750	1700	1000	2550	YES	6	TH	YES	1
	POCL			550	2200			700	2500					
	NEDLLOYD							1300	2200					
Philippines (Manila)	TSK					575	1350	950	2350		4	FR	YES	1
	POCL			900					2200		6	TU, FR	YES	2
	MOL			900	2400	500		900	2400					
Sri Lanka (Colombo)	NEDLLOYD		2100								10 to 18			
	MYK		1600											
Thailand (Bangkok)	MAERSK	200	875	350	1100	200	875	350	1100	YES	3	WE, SU	YES	2
	POCL	220	800	550	1200	220	1175	550	1500	YES	3	TU	YES	1
	MOL	180	1200	300	1700	180	1200	300	1700					
Taiwan (Keelung)	ISK					250	800	480	1250		8			
	RTW	300	1250	400	1850	350	1300	500	1950		6	TU	NO	3
	TSK			400		400	1250	580	2280	NO	6	SU, TU	YES	1
	WAN HAI	320	950	400	1750	420	1250	500	2200	YES	4	SU	YES	2
	MOL	350	1500	550	2150	350	1500	550	2150		4	SU	YES	1
Vietnam (Haipong)	NCC TPT	1350	3100								4	MO, FR	YES	2
(Hochi Minh)	LICORN	340	1500			680	3000							
	(38% surcharge for class cargo)													
	POCL	1100												
(K Kimabalu)	T SOON	2550												

A formal contract of supply is renegotiated with CDC Asia each calendar year. This is done through discussions with Steve Leong based on a joint improvement plan.

Kodak Australasia formally monitors the service that they provide to their customers. A customer survey of 13 questions was sent to 300 customers per month during 1994.[7] For each question the respondents were asked to indicate:

- how important the item was to them
- how well Kodak performed on the item.

Table 29.5   Freight rates from Singapore by air (Singapore $)

Airfreight rates: volume ratio 6000 cubic cm = 1 kg

Destination	MIN $	(<45K)	(+45K)	(+100K)	(+300K)	(+500K)	(+1000K)	SVC	Carrier
Auckland		4.5	FLAT						SQ,NZ
Bandar Seri (Begawan)	30	3.14	2.35						BI
Bangalore	80.5	10.72	6	5.5		5.4	5.2		SQ
Bangkok		0.8	Flat						QF
Bombay		2.4	Flat						SQ VIA Consol
Brisbane	75	4.5	Flat						QF
Brunei		2.35	FLAT						SQ, BI
Calcutta	75	6.31	4.74	3.7		3.55	3.25		AI
Delhi	75	8.51	3.4		3.1	2.9			SQ
Dhaka	75	6.56	4.92						BG
Dubai	81	5.35	FLAT						BI/EK
Hanoi (Vietnam)	99	4.53	3.8					Consol	Via BKK
Hochi Minh	99	4.53	3.22					Consol	Via BKK
Columbo			Flat					Consol	GS/UL
Hong Kong		0.85	Flat						
Kathmandu	75	7.07	5.31					IATA	RA
KUL		0.87	Flat						SQ, MH
Los Angeles		4.29	Flat						KE
Madras	75	7.44	3.4		3.1	2.9			SQ
Malé		5	Flat						SQ
Manila		2.5	Flat						PR
Melbourne		3.5	Flat						QF, SQ
Perth	75	4.82	Flat						QF
Phnom Pehn	50	4.5	3.5					IATA	SILKAIR
	99	4.29	3.3					Consol	Via BKK
Rochester (NY)		5	Flat						CLEK
Seoul		3.15	Flat						SQ
Taipei		2.2	Flat					Consol	CX, CL, BR
Tokyo		2.1	Flat						CX
Vientiane	50	6.61	5					IATA	TG
(Laos)	99	3.25	2.64					Consol	Via BKK
Yangon	50	4.28	3.21					IATA	TG
(Myamma)	99	3.96	3.08					Consol	Via bkk
Gvanna Khet	99	3.91	3.33					Consol	
IATA rate:		3.3	2.35						
Brunei	30								

Priority was then given to the items with the biggest gap. In July 1994 the biggest gap was on the item 'order lines filled from stock'. John Fox considered this to be the 'driver of customer service'. Next was 'invoice accuracy'. Kodak only tracked 'very good' and 'excellent responses', not 'satisfactory'. A score of 95% 'very good' and 'excellent' was considered as the objective on the basis that the remaining 5% was likely to reflect 'noise'.

In order to meet these domestic objectives the service provided by the CDC must be good. When Australia places a regular weekly order they are notified whether the order is to be supplied in full and on time. If this is not the case the status of any back-ordered lines is provided. On error-free shipments Singapore is achieving 99.8% performance against a 99.5% objective. For their part Australia provides the CDC each week with their requirements for the next 52 weeks. The first week is a firm order and an order number is supplied. The next 3–13-week period is also fixed. This number of weeks is dependent on the stock status of the particular line in Singapore. If an item is 'a single stock item', e.g. if Australia is the only customer for the item, the number of fixed weeks is equal to the manufacturing lead time, often 16 weeks. If the item is a 'high stock ratio' item, e.g. Australia, being more than 60% of the CDC's total demand, six weeks may be fixed.

For emergency items there are two channels: expedited shipment and air freight. With an expedited shipment the order is identified and given priority, but it is still shipped by sea. This channel is not used much – only to locations close to Singapore such as Hong Kong and the Philippines. An emergency air freight order is changed in status from sea freight to air and is shipped the same night it is received. There are, however, some items that are always sent by air. Control strips of film, for example, have a short-shelf life and need to be frozen when transported. They are always shipped by air. This decision is made by the marketing division and is typically applied to small-volume, high-value items such as electronic equipment. Australia is the only plant that sends other items regularly by air. Each year the plant sends 3000 tonnes of Kodak colour film, X-ray film and graphic film by air. Australia pays half of these air freight costs and the customer the other half. This action is justified by the resultant inventory savings. However, 'Kodak has a mentality that air freight is bad'. This view is exacerbated by the fact that inventory holding costs are not included in the performance measures for Kodak management. Air freight costs are included in earnings from operations – a key performance measure – but inventory holding costs are not.[8] At Kodak, however, as Ron Bade pointed out, while 'inventory objectives change, service objectives seldom do.'

Kodak Australia receives product from any supply point at the same price. For example, if Australia chose to source product from the Windsor, Colorado, plant instead of the Singapore CDC it would cost an additional $2000 per 40-ft container. This is the freight differential between Singapore–Melbourne and Colorado–Melbourne. More recently the real costs (unit cost ex-factory and transport costs) have been provided to the business units in Australia and world-wide. Any sourcing decisions must also consider the impact on the supply source (CDC) losing the business.

Managing the Australian logistics operation presents challenges because of its place in a global network. As Ron Bade explained, 'the direction we receive from world-wide distribution [in Rochester] and the expectations of our business units are not always the same.'

The future

Because of the location of the CDC–Asia on the free trade-zone at Singapore's Pasir Panjang port, no import duties are paid. There is no payment of other Singapore charges or the recently introduced Singapore GST of 3%; but as Steve Leong noted:

> Most of our products are duty free into Singapore anyway. In fact I can't think of any that we would have to pay duty on! The only advantage I can think of in being located where we are is that we avoid a lot of paperwork. Hong Kong would also offer the same environment.

John Fox also indicated a down side to the Singapore operation:

> Conceptually Singapore is wrong from a stock holding and inventory view point. Product has been through three or four warehouses before the customer gets it. It is old. As far as product dating goes we are getting rats and mice rather than blocks of product. This makes it difficult for us to utilise our warehouse space here at Coburg efficiently. Using inventories is an expensive way of doing business.

There are a couple of issues facing Steve Leong. The first is the possibility of supplying Australia directly from the USA. The second is the extension of the lease with the PSA which is up for renewal at the end of 1997.

> We have a pretty good rate now. But we are not sure what the PSA will want to renew the lease. Fully air-conditioned warehouses are not that common in the typical Singapore industrial park. If we moved out we would probably have to upgrade the facility which would be expensive.

Notes

1. This varies according to the transport mode used and the distance from Singapore.
2. This results in the CDC–Asia receiving weekly order estimates for 1500 'catalogue numbers' or stock-keeping units, SKUs.
3. This finishing lead time of four weeks is much shorter than the lead time for the manufacture of the base material.
4. Only a few of the smaller destinations have no facilities to handle slip sheets.
5. In 1992 2027 TEUs were shipped into the CDC–Asia and 1882 TEUs were shipped out.
6. Singapore exports directly to Indonesia, Brunei, Sri Lanka and Myanmar (Burma).
7. Kodak Australasia in 1994 had a customer base of about 12,000 of which about 7000 were considered active.
8. John Fox's performance is evaluated 50% on the basis of stock availability, 25% on meeting inventory goals in terms of weeks supply, not dollars, and 25% on communication and people-handling abilities. Ron Bade's performance is evaluated on the basis of order accuracy, cost – not including inventory costs, and lead time from the port or airport into the Coburg DC. These are the same items as have been included in the enterprise agreement with the DC's weekly staff.

Internationalizing a distribution brand

Valerie Bence
Centre for Logistics and Transportation, Cranfield University, UK

Introduction

In the four years from 1989 to 1993 Exel Logistics grew to be a market leader in distribution and supply chain services. It became the major operating division of National Freight Corporation (NFC) plc and is a *Financial Times* Share Index (FTSE)-100 company listed on the London and US stock exchanges. With a turnover of almost £600 million in 1992, Exel Logistics were operating 3700 vehicles, 1.6 million m^2 of warehousing and almost a million m^3 of cold storage capacity. Its companies employed over 14,600 staff and operated out of 220 distribution centres across the UK, mainland Europe and North America. Independent research carried out in 1991 confirmed that Exel Logistics was UK market leader for contract distribution services, a goal reached well within the three-year target set at launch in 1989, when the company described itself as 'a successful business that has grown out of a previously unsuccessful state owned parent company'.

Exel Logistics must now decide how far it wants to go in becoming a truly global brand and what strategies to pursue to achieve its aims.

Background and buyout

NFC, Exel Logistics' parent company, had its origins in post-war Labour government policies aimed at nationalizing transport in the UK. In 1979 the Conservative government began its privatization programme with NFC. The sale was scheduled for 1981 with an anticipated capital price of £50–55 million but, owing to the recession, postponement was advised. However, an alternative plan was put forward by management and employees, who with the backing of multinational investors secured an employee buyout. NFC was sold into private ownership for £53.5 million in February 1982 and some would say it was the UK government's most successful privatization.

Before 1982, NFC's financial performance was poor, but after the buyout it quickly became very successful, partly because it was the old road transport part of British Rail, and had property to sell or redevelop (stations and land close to the railways). The charismatic leadership of Sir Peter Thompson was another important advantage. He created the possibility and then reality of broad employee ownership and went on to instil a unique employee participative company culture which was integral to the success of the company.

After 1982, NFC experienced rapid growth and in preparation for its flotation on the Stock Exchange in 1989 was restructured into four divisions; distribution, transport, home services and property and travel. This enabled all previous elements of the distribution business to come together within NFC's distribution division under Robbie Burns (managing director) and followed a decision to refocus the previously separate distribution functions based on a stronger single brand image world-wide.

In January 1989 the sales and marketing director and managing director were faced with the difficult task of reorganizing, pruning and bringing marketing input to an assortment of companies, acquired after this restructuring. This mixed bag of 12 brands consisted of the seven companies they already had, those transferred on 1 January from NFC's Special Services Group and one overseas acquisition, Dauphin in North America. NFC's aim was to launch 'a new distribution company' on the back of the high-profile Stock Exchange flotation in February 1989. After much research, it was decided that Exel Logistics was to be the umbrella name for all NFC's distribution, warehousing and transport interests and would emphasize the importance of the strategic management of the whole supply chain, including:

- the transfer of information between interdependent but separate parties within it
- the flow and storage of raw materials, parts and finished inventory
- transfer to and from manufacturing plants
- finished goods storage
- delivery to customers, including home delivery if required.

Contracts with customers would include all or part of the above from the provision of warehousing – even design and building – through all operational aspects, to final delivery.

Changes in the UK distribution market

Since the mid-1980s the UK retail market-place has undergone huge changes. Manufacturers' volumes and fleets have been decimated because of the reduction in numbers of smaller town centre retail outlets and growth in size of the larger multiple, edge of town retailers. Other trends such as retailers centralizing distribution operations and taking control of their own supply chains had the same effect – a fall in demand for shared-use distribution. This meant a radical rethink of distribution activities and many operators set up specific divisions to cope with growing and changing retail industry demands.

Road haulage had been perceived as a low-profile industry but these changes imposed a higher status, with logistics moving from being an operational necessity to a strategic means by which companies could gain competitive advantage. It has become a key area in which manufacturers and retailers have to be good, to drive down costs and improve service. Consequently, the required investment for a company to run its own distribution operation is often enormous. Fleets, warehouses, depots, maintenance and information technology (IT) all tie up a high level of capital expenditure, and thus it is no longer feasible for many companies to retain their in-house operations.

One solution has been the increased use of third party or outsourced distribution. This replaces customers' fleets and/or warehouses with a separate operational framework managed and owned by a third party, often providing a more efficient and cost-effective service than shippers were able to provide for themselves. Third-party distributors had to refine their marketing approach as the market-place grew and became more demanding, and ultimately had to design and manage logistics solutions to meet customers' changing needs. The use of third-party distribution provides tailored, often dedicated, contractual solutions and can encompass transport, warehousing or other contract services, such as labelling and packaging. Operators must be flexible enough to keep fully abreast of new technology, support customers and apply strategic, tactical and operational reviews – in effect continuously strengthening and managing the whole supply chain. Customers quickly realized that buying in this expertise allowed them to concentrate on their core businesses of manufacturing or retail selling and increasingly expect their distribution networks to provide all or part of their supply chain management.

Structure of Exel Logistics (UK)

When Exel Logistics was launched, the constituent companies were being asked to change into something that did not exist, thus there was a certain amount of internal resistance. They had to work on establishing group and team identities within the company, and implemented a three-way organizational split:

- *Exel Logistics Grocery and Leisure* – where the business focus was on serving the grocery, catering and drinks market sectors and the customers were mainly food and drink producers and retailers
- *Exel Logistics Consumer and Industrial* – customers ranged from consumer product retailers and manufacturers to a cross-section of industrial product manufacturers and distributors such as Vauxhall, BMW, Woolworth and Argos
- *Exel Logistics Temperature Controlled Services* – this division worked closely with (and generated specialist business from) the food and grocery divisions within the company. It soon became market leader in the distribution of chilled and frozen food with a fleet of 500 vehicles, 27 depots and 2300 staff. With the expansion of the UK chill food market they turned a number of existing cold storage facilities into chilled distribution centres for short-life products. This improved the financial performance of TCS and the division was back in profit by 1991.

These three business groups were in force until mid-1992 when, after further growth, they were reorganized and split into four management teams, the main change occurring with the amalgamating of grocery and leisure into Exel Logistics Grocery. With total revenue exceeding £300 million per annum, retail and manufacturer grocery distribution was split between two internal management teams but with one external sales and marketing team. This new business unit now controlled all food distribution; retailers and manufacturers, ambient and temperature controlled, including Exel Logistics

Chillflow (dedicated to one client) and was felt to be consistent with market-place requirements (Figure 30.1).

Exel Logistics Industrial now encompassed Exel Logistics Newsflow (distributing 70% of UK national newspapers) and DMS (rebranded Exel Logistics Media Services), the UK's largest independent book distribution company with a £54 million turnover. Operating alongside Newsflow it built on the base of newspaper distribution and worked towards market leadership in all print-media distribution. To some extent Exel Logistics Industrial was a catch-all, with a series of subsectors and targeted marketing, directed at ensuring that potential customers in those subsectors, such as electronics or automotive, were aware of Exel Logistics' presence.

Exel Logistics Consumer was the non-food retail division and included Fashionflow and Storeflow. Major contracts were with do-it-yourself outlets and department stores such as Comet, Woolworths, Superdrug, Boots, BHS, Habitat, Marks and Spencer, and Mothercare.

Marketing for the whole company however, was done as if there were still just three main sectors: grocery, industrial and consumer, with all new business development effort contained within three sales teams.

Strategic directions for Exel Logistics

By 1990 NFC/Exel Logistics had reached a point where the options were either to seek greater penetration in the home market via new market segments or to look for expansion overseas. In the home market they could either:

- seek to develop new market sectors. As Exel Logistics' new businesses were previously predominantly food and retailer based, they could try to open up new sectors where they were not strong, e.g. petrochemicals or pharmaceuticals, or
- develop new services within the food sector. Their existing strength lay with ambient and frozen food distribution (a static market) whilst the chill food sector was growing.

This second option seemed to provide a potential opportunity. More and more outlets were selling fresh dairy produce, yoghurts and short-life products. By effectively altering

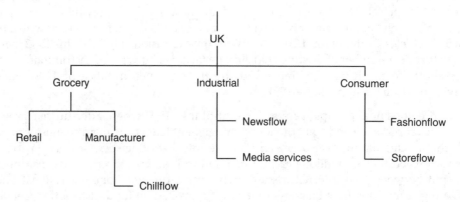

Figure 30.1   Structure of Exel Logistics after mid-1992.

the temperature control systems in existing cold stores, Exel Logistics could easily facilitate a move into this sector.

Background to the frozen food market

The easiest distribution area for market sector monitoring is the frozen market because cold storage capacity is registered (Lloyd's Register) and can be easily measured. In 1992 additional market-place capacity was added as Tesco and Asda (two large supermarket groups) built their own distribution composites (multitemperature warehouses) which included chilled and frozen storage. They were thereby removing products which had previously been in other peoples storage capacity and putting them into their own, thus adding to available capacity even though the frozen food market had stopped growing. Total frozen storage capacity had been approximately 200 million ft^3 per annum, and increased capacity in these new cold stores took it to 220 million ft^3. At this time manufacturer distribution was usually either direct to store or to distributor's stores. Recently, cold stores had been built or added to the market specifically to meet demand for EC intervention stocks. This boom time for the industry had increased capacity from 160 to 200 million ft^3, but after 1986 changes in the EU's Common Agricultural Policy meant that intervention stocks were being withdrawn from the beef and butter mountains and overall market demand for storage fell to around 180 million ft^3. With demand down by 10% and capacity up by 10%, the result was severe overcapacity in the market and fierce price competition. This was tackled by cold-storage providers moving to reduce storage rates to attract new business and to seek alternative types of contract, making it a very competitive sector.

In the past NFC companies such as Tempco Union and Alpine had profited by freezing and storing these intervention stocks but because of external market-place changes they suddenly had to shift and become more involved in stock movement – distribution rather than storage. Other major operators tried to stabilize the market by selling off their older, less efficient cold stores and moving over to the chill sector. This is an example of external market factors created by government (EU) legislative change and European policy changing a market-place.

With an expanding chilled food market in the UK, there were opportunities to build market share even though competitors already existed, e.g. Unigate (UCD) and Express Dairies/Coldstream were manufacturer driven distribution systems and others such as Northern Food Transport (NFT) were already strong in this sector. In the late 1980s companies including Christian Salvesen, Tempco Union and Alpine dealt with predominantly frozen produce and wanted to move into this high value-added area (with chilled produce being perishable, time becomes a saleable commodity). Exel Logistics wanted a share of this growing market.

However, after examining the options, the company returned to their initial vision, of being a truly international company; the problem was how to get there.

The move to North America

By the late 1980s NFC recognized that they were still very dependent on domestic UK earnings and began to encourage all its companies to seek new business overseas. It was decided to expand via Exel Logistics in the USA first, partly because of the size and type of market but also as their only overseas acquisition so far was American (Dauphin in 1986). Expansion in the USA was a key element in the strategy to develop Exel Logistics' brand internationally. The aim was to become the USA market leader in warehousing and logistics via services to global clients. In 1990, 25% of NFC's profits were generated in the USA – the new target was to achieve a 40–50% overseas contribution by 1995.

The market for the storage and distribution of goods in the USA was in essence very different from the UK market and took two forms:

- short-term provision of public warehousing on 30-day terms with no contracts, in effect a shared-user system
- contract warehousing, a dedicated system with one to five year contracts, which was less common.

The existing shared-user acquisition, Dauphin, was profitable and offered a convenient, high-margin service. This was opposite to that offered in the UK, where shared transport and storage was often a low-margin service. Dedicated warehousing in the States was not widespread and was perceived as low margin for low risk. This cultural difference is important: it was wrong to assume that the UK system would be interchangeable, and the strategy needed to be different and adapted to local conditions.

Within the distribution industry, contract work provides greater security (linking customers into long-term contracts) and in the UK Exel Logistics and NFC had formed disciplines of tight financial management and risk control, thus developing real strengths in this area. By moving to the USA they sought to enhance the level of dedicated work but at the same time they continued to offer what the American market traditionally wanted – shared usage with five or six manufacturer's loads being delivered into individual wholesaler's or retailer's stores or regional distribution centres with the ability to buy transport in from local full truck load (FTL) movers on overnight long distance runs.

Exel Logistics had inherited NFC's first overseas acquisition, Dauphin Distribution Services. This was one of the largest warehousing and distribution businesses serving the food and grocery trades in the mid-Atlantic region (clients included Procter and Gamble). The company had 3 million ft^2 of warehousing at 12 locations with 600 employees. This family-owned company was seen as a natural partner for the employee-owned NFC. Its successful acquisition encouraged further expansion and thus there evolved a multiphased strategy for a conscious move to develop in the USA. Dauphin gave Exel Logistics a foothold in the US market-place by delivering a range of consumer and manufacturers' products into one of the largest population centres (about 80 million people on the north-east seaboard). Based 150 miles inland from New York, with relatively cheap labour and land costs, Dauphin's complex of large-scale warehouses was only an overnight trip from this highly populated area. They offered a consolidation service to manufacturers, with goods being stored, picked and moved from Dauphin's warehouses directly to New York. Manufacturers were able to buy transport movements at FTL prices even though they may not have had a full load to be dropped at each delivery destination; again this was effectively shared distribution – exactly what the UK market was moving away from.

Even though Exel Logistics did not ideally want to be acquisition led it was decided that to expand geographically, acquisition was the strategy most likely to succeed in generating critical operating mass in a number of other regions. Thus, it was first necessary to decide which other major population centres it was essential to be in and then determine which companies with at least 1 million ft² of warehousing (preferably more) with several large clients were potential acquisitions. It was not always easy to get a match between what was available to acquire and what suited both the company culture and local market conditions.

In 1989 Distribution Centres Inc. (DCI) based in Columbus, Ohio, was bought. This second acquisition was closer to the UK formula of a dedicated contract business. It was an entrepreneur-led company which distributed medical and office supplies, pharmaceuticals and consumer products almost nation-wide and shared similar values with its new parent. There were 18 locations (some on the west coast and in the south), 5 million ft² of warehousing and 700 staff. DCI gave Exel Logistics the opportunity to expand its dedicated business in the North American market and brought important key customers such as Du Pont, Lever and again Procter and Gamble. This acquisition provided an excellent complement to the operations of Dauphin and was a well-run company where, like many American companies, quality of service was important. Post-acquisition, transport was still being bought in and the main difference for customers was that whereas before they dealt with a family-owned company, they now had to deal with a British-owned company with a bias towards five-year dedicated contracts. Like Dauphin, DCI was a successful acquisition.

Exel Logistics pursued its geographical strategy and concentrated on five main centres: the north-east, the mid-west and Chicago, the south-east and Atlanta, the south (Texas and Dallas), and the west coast (San Francisco and Los Angeles). With five primary regional targets and perhaps 12 subtargets (Denver, St Louis, Kansas, etc.) it was becoming very clear where they needed to be and what they wanted to buy. With dominance in the grocery and consumer manufacturing sectors, they could now either begin to look at new sectors or diversify within logistics services and investigate what other products or services could be beneficial complements, e.g. warehousing, road transport or trucking.

The next acquisition followed this line of thinking, a move into transport, with Minute Man Delivery Systems (1990). This Boston-based company undertook dedicated distribution across the USA, but mainly in the north-east and was 90% contract backed. It had a turnover of $30 million and gave Exel Logistics a different industrial client base with Toyota, Nissan and Chrysler. This sector was felt to be attractive and facilitated a move into new areas with automotive and business service clients (Minute Man also provided a dedicated paper moving service for, among others, several north-east local banks); even so, Minute Man was a low margin company.

In 1991 the fourth American acquisition was Universal Terminal Warehouse Company (UTW), a Texas-based local warehouse operation, mainly shared use, in Dallas, Houston and San Antonio. With five warehouses, 670,000 ft² of storage capacity and 150 staff, it distributed grocery, paper and health products as well as industrial and chemical products. It brought additional major client names to the international customer base, e.g. Philip Morris, Nestlé and Colgate. This acquisition continued the strategic plan to develop from an already well-established and profitable base in the north east across the USA through the southern states into the west.

In 1992 there were two more acquisitions. J.H. Coffman & Son Inc. was a distribution and warehousing company based in Los Angeles. It was acquired to extend coverage to the west coast and the mid-west and Chicago. It had over 40 years' experience in the health care, grocery and consumer product market, with 375,000 ft^2 of warehousing and 40 staff.

In July Trammell Crow Distribution Corporation (TCDC), based in Dallas, was bought. This contract warehousing business had 6 million ft^2 of warehousing, 44 distribution centres, 600 employees and a turnover in 1991 of £27.6 million. As well as warehousing, the company was also involved in value added services, including the management of interstate transportation and packaging operations. With business divided between consumer and industrial sectors, it gave access to the petrochemical sector, with clients including Exxon and Shell.

James Watson, chairman of NFC commented:

This is a further important step in becoming the acknowledged leader in the provision of logistics services in N. America. It virtually completes our acquisition programme in the USA and sets the stage for a period of strong organic growth.

These acquisitions may have been driven by geography but they also facilitated entry to new market sectors. Exel Logistics now had a presence in four out of the five main regions, missing out in Atlanta (south-east); here, as no acquisition target matched the criteria, a green-field operation was set up by building warehousing for a core client (Reckitt and Coleman) with extra capacity for use by others on a contract basis.

Apart from Dauphin, all acquisitions (DCI, Minute Man, UTW, Coffman, TCDC) fell within a three-year period. Exel Logistics' US headquarters was initially in Chicago, but regional offices soon opened in Harrisburg, Atlanta and Dallas and the headquarters subsequently moved to Columbus, Ohio.

In 1991 the resultant organization from the US acquisitions was divided into three operational units:

- *Exel Logistics–Grocery Services Inc.* (was Dauphin) – with its main focus on warehouse management for grocery, health and beauty products, it operated from three complexes in Pennsylvania with total storage capacity of 460,000 m^2. Major customers include some of the US top brand suppliers: General Mills, Nabisco, Procter and Gamble.
- *Exel Logistics–Dedicated Distribution* (was Distribution Centres Inc.) – also warehouse management based in Columbus, Ohio, with 18 locations on the south, west and east coasts of the USA. They mostly dealt with non-food products and multinational customers, e.g. Lever Bros, Du Pont, Sharp Electronics
- *Exel Logistics–Dedicated Delivery Systems* (was Minute Man) – provided a portfolio of products and services based on the physical transport side of the business, such as traffic management, vehicle supply and maintenance and out of hours delivery. There were 500 vehicles which served 43 states, and customers include Nissan, Toyota and Chrysler.

These acquisitions created an organization which probably became the leading logistics business in the USA, with a turnover in excess of £100 million, 18.5 million ft^2 of storage, over 3000 employees, and 600 vehicles working from 40 depots nation-wide. It provided a range of services to many market sectors and customers included several *Fortune 500* companies. The process was strategically logical, it evolved through acquisition on a geographical basis and sometimes available companies were fitted into the strategy rather than being strategy led, e.g. Minute Man was made to fit because it was available for sale; although it broadened their product offer, it was not ideal at that stage of their strategic development.

By the end of 1992 Exel Logistics' strategic acquisition programme in the USA was virtually complete, with a presence in over 30 states. They were now able to offer warehousing and/or transport in each of their five major target regions. In addition, by following contacts with important existing USA clients, Exel Logistics developed initial small operations in Mexico and Canada.

The Single European Market

To meet increasing demand and customers changing needs from the creation, in 1993, of the Single European Market (SEM), many distribution contractors felt that they had to expand geographically and broaden their range of services along with, or preferably before, their customers. Operators targeted their efforts at the market sectors that they were best equipped to serve, which for Exel Logistics offered the prospect of exporting to the Continent the concept of dedicated distribution which they had developed so successfully in the UK retail sector. There appeared to be a market opportunity: whilst the UK grocery market was already contracting out 70% of its distribution needs, in Germany and France the figure was only 15% (*Director*, August 1990).

Whilst some manufacturers set up pan-European production and distribution facilities, retailers were more cautious. The UK's leading retailers were preoccupied with the battle for national market share and really only Marks and Spencer and Iceland took the bold step of opening stores under their own fascia; in addition, Tesco and Woolworths began to expand outside their home markets. For UK retailers (in 1992–3), the scale of their European business remained a small percentage of their total trade, Sainsbury's, for example, had approximately 18% of the UK grocery market but Europe-wide this dropped to 3%. So while leading UK supermarkets were used to dominating the home market they were only small fish in the Euro-pond. However, expansion did continue with the Burton Group in Spain and Germany, Boots in France, and Texas Homecare in Spain.

The SEM also saw the beginning of expansion by European retailers into other member states, e.g. Aldi, Netto, Naf Naf into the UK, and Ikea and Benetton across Europe. Developing retail operations within Europe meant extending communication lines and even more crucially managing the whole supply chain.

Market-place developments such as pan-European manufacturing and retailing concentration, product proliferation and technological developments should lead to less stockholding, more centralized warehousing, increased road transport and greater availability of products in Europe. In the future consumers will demand greater choice and food freshness Continent-wide, which should increase demand for sophisticated logistics skills, as pioneered by the leading UK companies. After the advent of the SEM, success in the domestic market will not necessarily ensure success in Europe – competition will come from both other national and international companies as well as independent operators from low-wage countries already used to operating in a more regulated environment.

Exel Logistics' strategy in mainland Europe

Food distribution entails the movement of large, physically bulky products with relatively low value when compared to say cars or computers and tends to have been operated on a local, national basis rather than global or international. Food logistics was seen as 'the art of the possible' for Exel Logistics.

As outlined earlier, having achieved UK market leadership by 1991, Exel Logistics faced several strategic options. Following successful moves in the USA, it was decided that the strategy would be parallel development in mainland Europe, concentrating on the food/grocery sector. This was mainly because other industrial sectors where they lacked strength were already international markets dominated by major international players, e.g. Shell, BASF and Ford. The food sector, however, was determined more by local tastes, local retailing and local markets.

The arrival of the SEM acted as a stimulus for expansion and Exel Logistics' first step was to follow existing UK customers into new markets. They decided on a priority sequence of countries by looking at the geography, the economic stage of development, market prospects and where existing clients wanted to develop their business. The first opportunity arose with Marks and Spencer when Exel Logistics built a distribution centre for them at Evrey near Paris to serve their stores in France. This strategy was not enough on its own, but it did allow them to establish initial credibility in the country – a 'footprint in the sand'. Although this was initially a low-risk way to develop a pan-European operation, it soon became necessary to decide whether being credible to existing clients in new countries was enough (reactive expansion), or should they also begin to look both at other domestic companies wanting to expand overseas and at acquiring existing distribution businesses in new countries (proactive expansion).

Again, the route of growth by acquisition in specific geographical areas was chosen and in 1991 the brand was launched first in Spain, then Germany, France and The Netherlands, and they aimed to be number one in food manufacturing and retail distribution in Europe by 1995. They proceeded with the rapid acquisition of businesses, seeking small- to medium-sized, but strategically important grocery distribution and warehousing companies. These were often family owned and required minimum investment on existing infrastructure since they were serving the needs of existing clients, although in new markets.

Overall, Exel Logistics' policy was to build on their successful development of dedicated distribution in the UK and to export it into mainland Europe, but where possible using experienced local management.

Spain

The first acquisition was Sadema (1990), Spain's third largest transport and distribution company. Turnover was £6.3 million, supplying chilled and ambient warehousing and distribution for leading Spanish food manufacturers from 15 locations. The business was owned by four manufacturers which were in effect clients with long-term contracts who had combined their operations. Sadema had national coverage, including the Balearic and Canary islands with 13 owned and two franchised operations. With large distances between population centres, Spain had few major international distribution operators and offered less competition than France or Germany. Exel Logistics saw easy market entry, in a growth area, with low risk:

> We believe that a high quality logistics service based on the UK model will be increasingly demanded by major national and multinational companies now growing so rapidly in Spain to meet rising consumer expenditure. (Robbie Burns, Exel managing director)

The major competitor, a Unilever subsidiary called SAD, had recently been bought by Swiss-owned Danzas. Unilever were actively pursuing a policy of outsourcing and seemed to be choosing a different third-party operator in each country – Exel Logistics had already acquired some of their distribution interests in the UK with SDP and Alpine. In Germany, Unilever had sold its frozen food business to Salvesen, another UK competitor.

Exel Logistics had to decide what service to offer in the Spanish market. They wanted dedicated business using their existing expertise in warehouse management to gain secure profits, but as in the USA there was some reluctance in the market to buy this service and Spain's physical size really required a network solution. However, since 1990 Exel Logistics have had some success in signing dedicated business, with Marks and Spencer expanding into Spain, Digsa, a Spanish grocery retailer, and Olympus. It was still difficult to get across the British concept of this method of distribution, which is about offering nation-wide delivery with economies of scale. Sadema was rebranded Exel Logistics–Iberica with its own corporate identity and image and became one of Spain's top three logistic companies. In 1992 successful expansion continued with a new contract with Oxford University Press and in 1993, Pirelli.

Germany

The first German acquisition was Hellweg Tiefkuhl (rebranded Exel Logistics Deutschland) in June 1991. A frozen product distribution company with trans-shipment operations, it had the ability to service all of Germany, including the old East, from a single cold storage centre near Dortmund in, a maximum of 48 hours. It was almost a parcels-style operation for frozen foods, a potential high added-value service. It fell within the buying criteria of being a small family-owned, low-risk food business, operating profitably.

In Autumn 1991, Exel Logistics bought from the liquidators a food products and catering distribution company called Restaurant Services. Rebranded Exel Logistics–Restaurant Services it was to seek new business and operate contracts aimed at developing deliveries to the restaurant and catering market. However, difficult trading and adverse economic conditions subsequently slowed business growth in Germany.

The most recent acquisition in January 1993 was a company called Macke & Son, another small family business, providing ambient food distribution for two clients aimed at the grocery market. With net assets of £2.1 million the company operated from a 59,000 m^2 site with 130 staff and 64 vehicles. It was rebranded Exel Logistics Kloppenburg on 1 January 1993.

France

October 1991 saw Exel Logistics' first acquisition in France, BOS Finances. This chilled and frozen distribution family business was a market leader in the chilled sector. It operated in the north-west region under regional company names, STM, STB and Frimotrans, and covered about one-third of the country. Concentrating on chilled distribution for meat, cheese and fish produce, it offered a service based on speed and quality providing fast overnight transport. Clients include Carrefour and Intermarche. The network of 13 temperature controlled locations gave Exel Logistics a sound geographical base, considering they already had the Fashionflow operation for Marks and Spencer near Paris. The new group continued to operate under the management of the Boucher family at the headquarters in Brittany, under the Exel Logistics–France brand name. The turnover was £17 million with 500 staff, 200 vehicles and 14,000 m^3 of warehouse capacity.

In 1992 Sodiaal, a temperature-controlled warehousing and distribution company, was acquired (also a producer of regional cheeses). Based in the central French region of Clermont Ferrand it brought 24 staff, 50,000 ft^2 of warehousing and ten vehicles to the company.

The Netherlands

In October 1991 Exel Logistics bought Food Express Intl BV, The Netherlands' largest independent food warehousing and distribution company, which served the Benelux countries. With a turnover of £7.3 million, 50 vehicles and 150 staff, it operated transport by owner–drivers on a subcontract basis. This was an ambient and chilled food distribution operation for grocery products operating from two centres covering all of The Netherlands, with Unilever as a major client. Rebranded as Exel Logistics–Nederland it was an important entry point into the Benelux countries. In 1992 Exel Logistics in The Netherlands moved outside the food sector by gaining contracts with Apple Computers and Texas Instruments.

By the end of 1991 Exel Logistics had a capability over a large area of mainland Europe, with access to local markets and local expertise. They had therefore achieved their initial goal of entering priority geographical markets and had to decide on their next step. They could continue to build a presence in new countries such as Austria and Portugal, proceed with further acquisitions in existing countries or slow down. The board advocated a period of consolidation. They decided to concentrate on their existing acquisitions, build on their initial presence, grow their businesses organically and acquire and develop the right people.

Nothing new was bought until November 1992 when they acquired two more French regional distribution businesses, Transports Pujos and Transports Martin, in Toulouse and Nice. Like BOS both were family owned and provided specialist transport for long- and short-life chilled products for manufacturers, retailers and restaurants. When linked with BOS they gave five regional companies but not quite national coverage for frozen and chilled foods.

Exel Logistics' strategy at the end of 1992 was still not complete, as they did not have credibility in all countries over all grocery product temperature ranges. The existing businesses offered:

- Spain – ambient and chilled
- Germany – frozen and chilled only
- France – mainly chilled, some frozen
- The Netherlands – mainly ambient.

Without networks at all temperature ranges, it would be impossible to link food networks between countries to become a true pan-European distributor. Even with this strategic gap, organic growth was beginning and new work was gained in both Spain and The Netherlands. Any organic development tended to be in warehouse contracts rather than transportation, which was often subcontracted out to owner–drivers.

Exel Logistics found that in mainland Europe most of the networked systems were not food oriented, but biased more towards industrial group haulage. The main pattern of movements was in a wide range of products without the hygiene, sanitation or temperature-controlled requirements of food. The food sector required technical expertise and was sensitive to legislative and temperature requirements. As for retailing, in the UK trends were dictated by what was happening in the move from town centre to out-of-town shopping, leading to huge changes in supply chain management. By experiencing and learning from both, Exel Logistics developed the strengths required to export overseas, but above all they built on the need for flexibility.

The position at the end of 1992

Growth in the UK has continued and in 1991 the company received awards for implementing successful environmental policies from the Worshipful Company of Marketeers and trade magazine *Motor Transport*. The company's commitment to quality of customer service has been recognized through the application of the Quest for Excellence quality campaign, culminating in 1992, 12 sites being awarded the international quality standard ISO9002.

NFC's target of reaching 50% of its revenue from overseas business by 1995 appears to be on course. These overseas earnings are derived from all divisions, not just distribution. But with Exel Logistics earning 40% of its income from overseas (and rising) whilst at the same time providing 47% of NFC profits, this represents almost 20% of overseas revenue for its parent company from Exel Logistics alone.

Exel Logistics has become one of the major supply chain service providers in the UK, USA and mainland Europe with world-wide sales in 1992 of £600 million and over 220 depots world-wide. Growth by acquisition alone will not be enough to ensure success, in either Europe or the USA. With an initial and fast-growing presence in Spain, France, The Netherlands and Germany the company is faced with yet more choices if it is to become a truly international brand.

Acknowledgement

The author acknowledges the assistance given by the Director of Sales and Marketing, Exel Logistics (1994). This case is available from European Case Clearing House, Cranfield, Beds, UK

International market-entry strategy*

Peter Dapiran
Faculty of Business and Economics, Monash University, Australia

Introduction

It was mid-1989 in Hershey, Pennsylvania, and Mr Roger Clarke, Vice-President International Sales of Hershey International, a division of Hershey Foods Corporation, was reviewing the Australian experience. He had a board meeting to attend in a week's time and had to present his assessment of what the cause of failure had been in Australia. Was it a strategic mistake or had implementation been the problem, and what strategy would be appropriate for re-entry?

Company background

In 1913 Milton Snavely Hershey sold his caramel confectionery business to establish a chocolate-making factory in what is now Hershey, Pennsylvania. His interest in chocolate making had been sparked by the new chocolate-making equipment he had seen at the Chicago exposition of 1893. His innovations in the mass production of chocolate confectionery and his emphasis on product quality ensured his success.

Milton Hershey's focus on quality remained a key emphasis for the corporation together with a strong focus on customer needs. Consumer value, new product development, a commitment to quality and strong trade relations remained high priorities for the firm. Its financial growth and success rested on a two-pronged strategy: high promotional and advertising expenditure (which in 1970 was 3.6% of consolidated net sales reaching 8.5% in 1981) and lowered manufacturing costs through improved productivity, plant modernizations and more efficient use of facilities (Table 31.1).

The corporation's objective was to become a major diversified food company. In trying to meet this objective it has rarely been tempted to stray from its core chocolate business. Its sharp focus has ensured that, for the American consumer at least, Hershey and chocolate have become synonymous.

*Data available on the Internet (see page xxii).

Table 31.1 Selected financial results of Hershey Foods Corporation (US$ millions)

	1984	1985	1986	1987	1988
Net sales	1423	1527	1635	1864	2168
Cost of sales	935	982	1032	1150	1326
Selling/marketing/administration	310	345	387	468	576
Income – continuing operations	88	97	107	124	145
Net income	109	112	133	148	214
Depreciation	23	28	31	35	44
Advertising	71	77	84	97	99
Promotion	95	105	123	171	230
Payroll	208	222	239	264	298
Working capital	188	225	174	190	274
Total assets	1052	1116	1262	1544	1765
Long-term debt	103	87	186	281	233
Stockholders' equity	661	728	728	832	1006

Source: Adapted from Hershey Inc. Annual Report, 1989.

To ease the uncertainty caused by fluctuating prices and the vagaries of the world sugar and cocoa bean markets, Hershey was tempted to diversify through the purchase of the Friendly Ice Cream Corporation in 1979. Friendly was a chain of over 700 family restaurants and ice cream shops. This change of strategic direction proved unsuccessful; the chain did not perform to expectations and in 1988 Friendly was sold to allow Hershey to concentrate on its expertise – the manufacture, marketing and distribution of packaged consumer foods, mainly chocolate, confectionery and pasta products. It pursued these tasks through its main operating divisions: Hershey Chocolate USA, Hershey International, Hershey Pasta Group, and Hershey Canada.

The costs of its other major chocolate-making raw materials, milk, almonds and peanuts, were all unaffected by international market fluctuations.

To pursue its diversification and growth objectives, Hershey embarked on a string of significant acquisitions in North America.

In late 1986 it purchased The Dietrich Corporation for US$102 million, thereby acquiring the Luden's and Queen Anne confectionery product lines. In mid-1988 the US confectionery operations of Cadbury Schweppes were bought for US$285 million. This purchase included the operating assets of the confectionery business and the licence to manufacture, market and distribute Cadbury brands in the USA. Integration of the Cadbury operations into the Hershey operations brought with it significant cost savings while catapulting Hershey into market leader position with 20.5% share of the US confectionery market. Arch rival Mars Inc. trailed with 18.5% share.

The mid-1987 US$162 million purchase of the Canadian confectionery and snack nut operations of Nabisco Brands Ltd allowed Hershey Canada Inc. to increase its market presence significantly. This acquisition was part of Hershey's strategy to become the low-cost producer in Canada and to rationalize the excess chocolate production capacity there.

The acquisition was followed by a year of consolidation and rationalization. Hershey closed its acquired Toronto plant, expanded the Smiths Falls, Ontario, facilities and introduced just-in-time philosophies in the plant. The closure of Sherbrooke, Quebec, was also planned. This would allow construction of a 110,000 ft^2 distribution centre at

Smiths Falls leading to reduced distribution costs but an increased concentration on customer service.

In late 1989, Hershey entered the refrigerated foods market with the introduction of chocolate-bar-flavoured puddings. Research showed that the majority of dry and refrigerated puddings sold were chocolate flavoured. Entry was reliant on the strong consumer association between Hershey and chocolate.

The United States confectionery market

The market was dominated by the two giants, Hershey and Mars Inc., who between them had the top ten selling chocolate bars and 39% of the confectionery market (Table 31.2). Jacobs Suchard and Nestlé, the Swiss multinational confectioners, came in a poor equal third with 6.7% each of the market. Fourth place, with 5.6%, was filled by Leaf Inc. owned by the Finnish company Huhtamaki Oy.

The all-important per capita consumption of confectionery had shown little growth over a number of years and seemed a long way short of the industry target of 25 pounds by 1995 (Table 31.3). Forecast demographic changes alone were not likely to help to achieve this ambitious target.

Expansion of the market hinged on strategies aimed at increasing per capita consumption especially through products developed for the adult market. Research showed that consumers over 18 years consumed 55% of all confectionery and that most consumption took place in the home. New products responding to customer health concerns would also help to increase consumption. Strategies to promote consumption of existing lines included increased shelf space, multiple store locations for confectionery sales points, manufacturing larger packs for take-home enjoyment and ensuring higher stock availability on the retail shelf.

Another effective strategy had been to position confectionery as a snack food, a market significantly larger than confectionery, alongside the traditional potato chips, cookies and pretzels. Mars scored a coup when it purchased the right to name Snickers and M&Ms the official snack foods of the 1984 Olympic Games.

Table 31.2 Top ten chocolate bars in the USA: sales by candy and tobacco distributors

| | | Rank | |
Product	Manufacturer	1988	1987
Snickers bar	Mars	1	1
Reese's Peanut Butter Cups	Hershey	2	2
M&Ms peanut chocolate candies	Mars	3	3
Kit Kat	Hershey	4	5
M&Ms plain chocolate candies	Mars	5	4
Hershey's milk chocolate with almonds	Hershey	6	6
Milky Way bar	Mars	7	7
Twix caramel cookie bars	Mars	8	12
Snickers bar, king size	Mars	9	13
3 Musketeers bar	Mars	10	9

Source: Adapted from Echeandia and Kitt (1989).

Table 31.3 US confectionery market consumption by weight

	1980	1982	1984	1985	1986	1987	1988
Annual (million pounds)							
Chocolate type	1845	2069	2317	2328	2333	2380	2400
Non-chocolate type	1576	1642	1945	2044	1909	1891	1900
Total*	3561	3886	4458	4570	4441	4472	4600
Per capita (pounds)							
Chocolate type	8.1	8.9	9.8	9.7	9.7	9.8	9.9
Non-chocolate type	6.9	7.1	8.2	8.5	7.9	7.8	7.8
Total*	15.7	16.7	18.9	19.1	18.4	18.3	18.5

*Totals do not equal the sum of the two components because of confectionery consumption not classified as either.
Source: Adapted from US Industrial Outlook (1989).

Hershey International

Although the North American market was of extreme importance to Hershey, it recognized the strategic importance of expanding into international markets and actively looked at international growth opportunities.

That an interest in the global market place was an integral part of its thinking was revealed in its mission statement, which read:

> Hershey Foods Corporation's mission is to become a major diversified food company and a leading company in every aspect of our business as:
> * The number-one confectionery company in North America, moving toward world-wide confectionery market share leadership.
> * A respected and valued supplier of high quality, branded consumer food products in North America and selected international markets.

Hershey's desire to participate in international growth was strongly motivated by the likelihood that any further high-growth opportunities in its own domestic market were severely limited following its purchase of Cadbury's.

The purchase in 1988 for US$4.5 billion of the British Rowntree by the Swiss Nestlé made Nestlé the second largest confectionery maker in the world trailing Mars Inc. This was followed by the purchase of Perugina (Italy) in 1988 and the remaining 50% of Allen Life Savers (Australia) in 1989. It was important that Hershey participated in this international activity.

In 1988 the value and volume of US confectionery exports grew significantly, aided by the weakened US dollar, tariff cuts (in Japan, Taiwan and Korea) and liberalized import policies of some Far Eastern countries, and aggressive promotion by the confectionery industry assisted by funding from the Department of Agriculture's Targeted Export Assistance (TEA) program. Japan, Canada, Taiwan, Hong Kong, and the Philippines accounted for 71% of export sales for the first six months of 1988. The European Community represented only 4% of total US confectionery exports despite that area's representing the world's largest confectionery-consuming population (Table 31.4).

Table 31.4 World per capita consumption of confectionery

	Consumption per person per year (kg)
Switzerland	13.2
UK	12.7
Germany	12.6
Belgium	10.6
The Netherlands	10.4
USA	8.5
Australia	8.1
Canada	5.7

Source: Adapted from *Retail World* (1986).

Hershey participated in this growth, experiencing record export sales in 1988. Major markets existed in Japan, South Korea and other Far East locations.

Hershey had used a range of strategies to penetrate the international arena. It had always relied heavily on direct exports to smaller markets but had also participated in acquisitions, joint ventures, licensing agreements and strategic alliances of various sorts. A licensing agreement operated in South Korea for chocolate products. Joint venture operations existed in Mexico and the Philippines.

In December 1986 a full ownership arrangement in Brazil was converted to a joint venture with the Bunge Born Group. Hershey retained 45% ownership of the jointly held pasta-making operations. This gave Hershey access to a finished goods distribution network and also to the raw materials of flour and fat for the pasta-making operations of the two venture partners.

In 1987 a leading Swedish sugar and chocolate confectioner, AB Marabou, was licensed to manufacture and market Hershey's Kisses chocolates with a distinctive European blend of chocolate. In 1988, this company purchased companies in Sweden and Denmark to strengthen access to the European market. In 1989, Hershey took out an equity interest in Marabou.

In July 1989, a licensing agreement was converted to a joint venture arrangement with Fujiya Co. Ltd to form Hershey Japan Co. Under the licensing arrangements, Hershey chocolate had been positioned as an exclusive imported product and sold through department stores and imported goods shops. The joint venture was established to broaden the market base by appealing to a larger consumer segment. Establishment of the joint venture was prompted by the results of market research undertaken at the end of 1988 to determine the most suitable products for the Japanese market.

In 1987 Hershey began exporting to Australia.

The Australian chocolate market

Generations of Australians had been raised on Cadbury's chocolate with 'a glass and a half of fresh dairy milk in every block'. To Australians, Cadbury's was chocolate and only those relatively few attuned to American culture could associate chocolate with Hershey.

In 1987 the AUS$1.1 billion Australian confectionery market for a population of under 17 million was dominated, as it had always been, by Cadbury Schweppes, which held a market share of 46%. Nestlé held a 36% share, with Mars at a low 10%. Such combined muscle provided a tight grip on distribution channels in Australia. New arrivals found it costly to access supermarket shelf space where the key success factor was to maximize the amount of space available to a company's products. This was especially important in such a high impulse-buying segment as confectionery. The dominance of these companies was reflected in the lucrative AUS$400 million chocolate bars segment of the market (Table 31.5). In 1987 Mars' Mars Bar was the undisputed leader, followed by Kit Kat, manufactured by Nestlé since that company's purchase of Rowntree (Table 31.6). Ironically, Kit Kat, a product that had dominated sales since the late 1950s in Australia and had held its market position consistently with continued sales growth, was owned by Hershey in the USA.

Restructuring of the world confectionery market, with its resultant significant concentration of ownership in Australia had created strong competitive pressures in the Australian market.

Mars Confectionery, the wholly owned subsidiary of Mars Inc., established a manufacturing plant in Victoria, Australia, in 1979. Mars had been active in Australia since the 1960s. At that time the products were made and sold by MacRobertsons, a long-established Australian confectioner. In 1967 Cadbury beat Mars to a takeover of Mac-

Table 31.5   The Australian confectionery market (AUS$ millions)

	1986	1987	1988
Chocolate bars	293	336	378
Block chocolate	179	199	220
Total chocolate	720	821	914
Total sugar	297	317	358
Total confectionery	1017	1138	1272

Source: Adapted from *Retail World*, 1 March 1989, p. 10.

Table 31.6 – Top ten chocolate bars in Australia, 1988

Rank	Product	Manufacturer	Market share (%)
1	Mars Bar	Mars	12.7
2	Cherry Ripe	Cadbury	8.1
3	Kit Kat	Nestlé	7.8
4	Crunchie	Cadbury	7.2
5	Flake	Cadbury	6.9
6	Aero	Nestlé	6.7
7	Picnic	Cadbury	5.3
8	Snickers	Mars	5.2
9	Violet Crumble	Nestlé	4.9
10	Milky Way	Mars	4.8

Total annual Australian chocolate bar market is AUS$378 million, which represents 26% of the total confectionery market.
Source: Adapted from Shoebridge (1988).

Robertsons. Cadbury continued to manufacture Mars products under licence until Mars established its own facilities. Mars concentrated on six brands of chocolate-enrobed bars, allowing it to minimize production costs through high-volume outputs.

Jacobs Suchard's move into Australia had been part of the company's global strategy to minimize reliance on its European markets. It had been beaten by Nestlé in its attempt to purchase the Rowntree group. In 1988 Jacobs Suchard set up an Australian subsidiary to handle its range of block chocolate products led by the well-accepted Toblerone line. The Toblerone range had been previously manufactured under licence by Red Tulip, a chocolate confectioner owned by Beatrice Confectionery. Red Tulip was sold to Cadbury in 1987. The licence agreement was cut short with the entry into Australia of the Jacobs Suchard subsidiary and the Toblerone range was subsequently imported from European manufacturing locations.

Jacobs Suchard's strategy for development of the Australian market was to provide a limited range of high-margin products supported by high advertising expenditures and to offer to the retail trade an alternative confectionery supplier to the two giants of the Australian trade, Cadbury and Nestlé. A factory to supply the Asia-Pacific region was being planned for the 1990s.

Hershey comes ... and goes

In 1985, Hershey signed an agreement with an Australian marketing company American Foods Pty Ltd for distribution in 1986 of a limited range of Hershey chocolate products, including Hershey Bar, Mr Goodbar, Krackel, Reese's Peanut Butter Cups and Reese's Pieces. American Hershey chocolate bars were to be introduced to the Australian market without a change in formulation. American Foods were planning to import the products from the USA with the result that retail prices were expected to be 30–40% higher than the competing products. Because of the premium pricing, the target market was to be the adult population segment.

Test marketing of Hershey products was limited to a trial through Grace Bros, a department store chain in Sydney, the largest city in Australia with a population of around 3.8 million. Although sales were not as successful as anticipated, the products were considered to be well accepted. A separate study was carried out to determine the awareness of the Hershey brand in Australia. A surprisingly high 37% of respondents was found to recognize the Hershey name and associate it with chocolate.

Following financial problems at American Foods, an arrangement which included a purchase of equity in American Foods by Hershey was finalized and the launch of the Hershey range was delayed until late 1987. Product was distributed to the grocery chains in August with a large TV advertising campaign launched in September–October with the advertising message 'You can't hide a Hershey smile'.

Distribution was to be through Streets Ice Cream, a company owned by the Dutch multinational Unilever, which allowed access to refrigerated logistics facilities including warehouses and delivery vehicles. Initial retail trade acceptance had been good.

At that time, the main competitors in the Australian confectionery market were Rowntree Hoadley (with a market share of 12%), Cadbury Schweppes (25.9%), Mars Confectionery (7.6%), Allen's Lifesavers (10%) and Beatrice (2.5%), all with long experience in the Australian confectionery market.

An advertising budget of at least AUS$3 million was expected to be necessary in the first year to gain product awareness in the face of such strong competition. This compared with an estimated annual advertising budget of AUS$5 million for Mars and AUS$6 million for Cadbury.

By early 1988 it became obvious to many in the retail trade that Hershey's sales expectations were not being met. Difficulties were being experienced achieving distribution to Brisbane and Perth (two of the states' capitals) and to some key supermarket chains in the states of New South Wales and Victoria, the two most densely populated states.

Retail chains suggested that the two main problems were the high retail prices and insufficient promotion by Hershey. Two large supermarket chains were considering dropping the Hershey line. The New South Wales supermarket chain of Coles Myer, the nation's largest retail organization, decided to distribute only five of the 16 product lines. The prices of Hershey products had an immediate dismotivating effect at the supermarket shelves where the impulse buying decisions were made. Hershey cut its prices to bring them to within 3 or 4 cents of the main Cadbury and Nestlé lines and reduced the number of lines from 16 to ten.

In February 1989 Hershey went home. However, it seemed that Australia was too lucrative a market to abandon. What had gone wrong? If the Australian market was valuable, what was the best way to re-enter it successfully? Roger Clarke had to find the answers for the forthcoming board meeting.

Acknowledgement

This case was published in Bowersox, D.J. and Bixby Cooper, M. (1992) *Strategic Marketing Channel Management*. McGraw-Hill, New York.

References

Echeandia, J. and Kitt, J. (1989) State of the Industry. *Candy Industry*, July, pp. H2–H18.
Retail World (1989) 12 March, p. 31.
Retail World (1989) 1 March, p. 10.
Shoebridge, N. (1989) Mars wants us to eat more bars a day. *Business Review Weekly*, 26 May, 111–3.
US Industrial Outlook (1989) US Department of Commerce, January, 39, pp. 17–21.

Further reading

Hershey Foods Corporation (1987, 1988, 1989) Annual Reports.
Flanagan, B. (1988) Hershey prices cut across the board, *Retail World*, 9 March.
Shoebridge, N. (1987) A middle-aged name with sweet appeal. *Business Review Weekly*, 24 April, 98–101.
Shoebridge, N. (1987) America's Hershey aims at Australian sweet-tooths. *Business Review Weekly*, 29 May, 77, 81, 84.
Shoebridge, N. (1988) Sweet dream fails in Australia. *Business Review Weekly*, 15 January, 54.
Weber, J. (1989) Why Hershey is smacking its lips. *Business Week*, 30 October, 140.

Modal choice decisions in international transport*

David Taylor
Department of Transport and Logistics, University of Huddersfield, UK

Introduction

Polymedic Ltd is a medium-sized company based in Sheffield, UK, the traditional home of Britain's high-quality steel industry. The company manufactures a range of steel surgical instruments such as forceps, bone-cutters and surgical scissors – all of which are used in hospital operating theatres. In 1994, Polymedic had a turnover of approximately £5 million with a net profit of £750,000 and employed a total of 150 people. Over the previous years the company had been reasonably successful and had built up a modest capital reserve of almost £1 million on which it earned bank interest of 10% per annum.

In 1995, following ten years of successful exporting to Turkey, Polymedic decided to use some of the capital reserve to establish a new, wholly owned marketing and stockholding subsidiary in Ankara (Exhibit 32.1). Management hoped that this would allow the company to exploit fully the expected rises in demand following an announcement by the Turkish government of its intention to increase the level of hospital provision in the country. The new subsidiary was planned to open in January 1996. Premises were leased that comprised an office, showroom space and a stockroom, which although small (90 m^2), was sufficiently large to accommodate at least a full year's stock, if so required.

Polymedic's marketing manager estimated that in 1996, total demand from Turkey would be in the order of £250,000 at cost price, with demand spread fairly evenly across the year. However, he was confident that sales volume would significantly increase once the company had 'a presence on the ground' in the form of the new marketing office.

In June 1995, Christine Mason, the company's distribution manager, was asked to determine the most appropriate method and schedule for transporting the 1996 product requirements from the factory in Sheffield to the subsidiary in Ankara.

*The names of the companies, personnel, and some of the data described in this case have been disguised for reasons of commercial confidentiality

Exhibit 32.1 Polymedic

Delivery alternatives

Christine was aware that there were various options in terms of both delivery schedules and modes of transport, but to get a feel for the costs involved she decided initially to consider three possible delivery alternatives:

1. shipment of the full consignment in one load in November or December 1995 ready for the opening in January
2. shipment of half the consignment in November/December 1995 and the rest in May or June 1996 or June 1996
3. regular monthly shipments of equal size commencing November/December 1995.

Production

The instruments were made from forged steel 'blanks' purchased from F.G. Poppyman, a drop-forging company in Sheffield. Raw materials represented approximately 25% of the total cost of manufacture and the manufacturing costs represented approximately 50% of the market price.

Once she had decided on the three delivery options, Mason held a meeting with Martin Decent, Polymedic's production manager, to discuss how the options would impact on manufacturing schedules. After some discussion, Decent eventually decided that manufacturing would take place as follows:

- for delivery options 1 and 2, all products would be manufactured in the four weeks prior to shipment
- for option 3, products would be manufactured at a constant rate throughout each month commencing four weeks prior to the first shipment.

Decent said that he thought manufacturing costs would be more or less the same irrespective of the manufacturing schedule adopted, but to obtain a 10% bulk purchase discount offered by Poppyman he would purchase all necessary raw materials to meet the 1996 Turkish demand in October 1995.

Transport

Mason next approached Woods International Forwarders, a local freight agent, for a quotation on transport rates and service levels by sea, land and air to Turkey. She told Steve, the agent at Woods, of the three delivery options under consideration and explained that Polymedic's standard method of packaging products for domestic or export shipment was to use tri-wall cardboard cartons measuring 50 cm × 50 cm × 40 cm. Instruments were individually packaged in plastic bags and then packed into the cartons between layers of tissue paper. On average, a fully packed carton would weigh about 10 kg and contain approximately £500 worth of instruments.

A few days later Steve called in response to the enquiry and Exhibit 32.2 shows the information noted down by Mason during the telephone conversation. Steve explained that he had not been able to obtain absolutely all the information needed, as there had been no reply to numerous faxes he had sent to their partner freight forwarder in Istanbul requesting details of certain transport charges within Turkey.

Reviewing her notes after the telephone call, Mason decided to start analysing the information she had to hand, as Steve didn't seem at all certain as to when, or even whether, a reply would be forthcoming from the Turkish agent. As she started the analysis, the thought crossed her mind as to whether the three alternative delivery schedules she had proposed were in fact the best options. However, she decided that, for the time being the best course of action was to evaluate fully the three options for which she now had data and then at least she would have a base point from which to compare any other ideas that might emerge.

Exhibit 32.2 Information received from Woods International Forwarders

Transport from Sheffield to Ankara

A. Sea transport

Option 1: Dedicated container

   20-ft container   capacity 250–300 cartons
   40-ft container   capacity 600 cartons
Container delivered to factory in Sheffield. (First three hours loading time no charge, thereafter £10 per hour.)
Delivered consignee Ankara
Sailing Felixstowe (UK) to Mersin (Turkey): voyage time 21 days
Sailings every ten days
Containers to be collected from consignor, minimum two days before advertised date of sailing
Total charge delivered to consignee:
   20-ft container   £1290
   40-ft container   £1935
Onward delivery time from Mersin to Ankara: two days by road (price unavailable)

Option 2: Container groupage service

No. of cartons	Cost (£)
<40	12.00 per carton
40	393.86 total
100	885.35 total
250	2044.69 total

Prices are for collection from Sheffield to delivery freight shed, Istanbul port. Sailing schedules, etc., as per Option 1. No information available as to on-cost from Istanbul to Ankara as Woods cannot obtain response to enquiry sent to their partner freight agent in Istanbul.

B. Overland road transport
Collection Sheffield delivery consignee Ankara
Journey time 8–12 days
(a) Full trailer load – capacity 600 cartons; cost £2975
(b) Road groupage service:

No. of cartons	Cost (£)
40	633
100	1070
250	1710

NB: Trucks travel direct from the UK to Turkey using roll-on/roll-off (Ro-Ro) ferries or the Channel Tunnel to cross the English Channel and Ro-Ro ferries to cross the Bosporus from Greece to Turkey. Quoted rates include allowance for ferry and all other charges *en route.*

C. Airfreight
Collection from Sheffield to arrival in freight shed, Ankara airport (pre-customs clearance)
Journey time 2–3 days
Flights daily London Heathrow to Ankara
Groupage rates:

No. of cartons	Cost (£)
1	97.50
2	132.55
5	229.48
10	396.80
40	1152.93

Onward transport from Ankara airport is the responsibility of the consignee (no prices available yet).

Additional information from the freight forwarder

Customs clearance

Time for customs clearance is very unpredictable in Turkey, on average varying between one and three days. For container, sea and air traffic it is necessary to employ a freight agent in Turkey to arrange the documentation for customs clearance at a cost of £30–40 per shipment. Agent can be arranged by Woods International Forwarders

Insurance rates

Sea groupage
Road groupage $\Big\}$ 0.5% of insurable value

Full container load (sea)
Full truck load (road) $\Big\}$ 0.425% of insurable value
Airfreight groupage

To calculate insurable value – the standard calculation is as follows:
Insurable value = (value of goods plus freight charges) plus 10%

Special documentation requirements

EUR1 form required for Turkey. This is the European Union (EU) 'Certificate of Origin', obtained from a local Chamber of Commerce in the UK at a cost of £15 and endorsed by them to vouch that the products are manufactured in the EU. An EUR1 must accompany each shipment.

Volume/weight ratio and airfreight charges

During the conversation with Steve, he happened to mention that it was a pity that the cartons used by Polymedic were not slightly smaller at 40 cm × 40 cm × 40 cm. If such a carton were used and could contain the same weight of product, i.e. 10 kg, then airfreight rates would be considerably cheaper and rates by other modes might be reduced. He explained that airfreight rates were set on the basis of either weight or volume. A standard ratio of 6:1 (cube to weight) is used and consignments are charged on whether the cube or the weight results in the greatest charge, i.e. 6 m^3 is regarded as the equivalent of 1 tonne for charging purposes.

The normal Polymedic cartons had a volume to weight ratio of 10:1 and as a result the 10 kg shipped in each carton actually incurred a charge equivalent to 16.7 kg because they were charged on the volume of the box rather than the weight.

If the smaller cartons (0.06 m^3) could be used, rates would be reduced as follows:

Sea groupage: Sheffield–Istanbul

No. of cartons	Cost (£)
40	260.43
100	594.18
250	1350.31

Air groupage: Sheffield–Ankara Airport

No. of cartons	Cost (£)
1	97.50
2	101.00
5	162.00
10	260.00
40	846.00

Road groupage

No. of cartons	Cost (£)
40	432.00
100	833.00

When Mason thought about this, she noted that packaging of cartons included a considerable, but arbitrary, volume of tissue paper to cushion the instruments, and perhaps the amount of tissue could be reduced without risking damage to the instruments.

Later she contacted the company's supplier of packaging materials and was told that cartons made to the smaller size would cost £0.40 each, the same as the existing cartons, but there would be a minimum order quantity of 5000.

The logistics of a Third-World relief operation

Andrew McClintock
Senior Logistics Officer with the UN in Zaire, 1994

Background

Political

In 1994 Rwanda had a civil war and political upheaval which resulted in a major refugee crisis. It began with the resurgence of tribal conflict in Rwanda, when the Tutsis re-asserted their control over the majority Hutus. This central African state (Figure 33.1) is about 750 miles inland from the Indian Ocean and was ruled by Belgium until 1960. During this crisis, it is estimated to have lost three million of its original seven million inhabitants: half a million killed, many internally displaced persons (DPs) and two and half million refugees, fleeing largely south-east into Tanzania and west into Zaire.

UN's position

United Nations became involved in the conflict through several of its agencies: chief among these were the World Food Programme (WFP) and the High Commission for Refugees (UNHCR). UNHCR employed Andrew McClintock, a British logistics consultant, as their senior logistics officer in Bukavu, Zaire. He arrived in Zaire on 2 September 1994. Bukavu is a place of uncommon natural beauty: situated at the south end of Lake Kivu, at an altitude of about 5000 feet, it has an idyllic curving waterfront and views of islands, fertile hills and the 10,000-foot peak of Mount Kauzi. The town is separated from Rwanda only by the narrow width of the River Ruzizi, and was the first asylum for between a quarter and half million refugees in July and August 1994. They had initially camped wherever they could find space, and were in need of relief supplies and transfer to camps with facilities.

Andrew's task was to act as the leader of a team responsible for co-ordinating the logistics efforts of all the relief agencies, for the supply of non-food items and for the

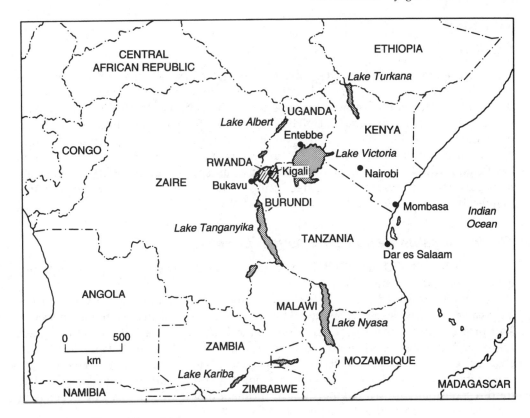

Figure 33.1 Map of East Africa.

transport of refugees in the Bukavu region. The job description, 'senior logistics officer', that he had been given with his initial briefing in Geneva, is reproduced as Appendix 33.1; but it was not an entirely exact statement of the actual job requirements.

Recruitment

Recruitment of staff to cope with such disasters is a considerable problem in its own right. UNHCR had about 35 international staff on site, and its office in Bukavu had probably as many local staff. The total number of expatriates (from a score of agencies) in the region of Bukavu was estimated at close to 500 and their accommodation provided its own logistical problem.

A further complication was that many personnel with the requisite specialist expertise were only available for short periods, because of the commitments of their normal employment. Andrew, with some juggling of his diary, had managed to make himself available at three weeks' notice, for three months. His predecessor, another Englishman, Chris Robertson, had been there little more than a fortnight since his arrival earlier in the emergency, during which time he had the task, under pressure, of finding facilities and setting up systems.

The task
UNHCR

The relief operation involved the combined efforts of UN agencies, and non-governmental organizations (NGOs), some of them well-known, and others less so (Appendix 33.2). In conjunction with other official bodies such as the World Health Organization and the World Food Programme, UNHCR had to direct the overall refugee effort by co-ordinating all activities with the local authorities, but at arm's length, often through NGOs. These 'implementing partners' were responsible for most of the executive action, e.g. Oxfam, who had a particular expertise in water supply, and CARE, who were the managing agent in several of the refugee camps, of which there were 23 during the time in question.

The logistics unit and its responsibilities

The Logistics Unit of UNHCR's Bukavu office worked under the direction of the emergency team leader (Exhibit 33.1).

The logistics unit had a staff of five, from Britain, Switzerland, the USA, the former Yugoslavia, and Zaire itself. Its own working language was English but among other HCR staff probably two thirds of conversation was in French. Two of the unit's three main responsibilities, the supply of non-food items, and refugee transport, were usually discharged on an operational basis through contractors; they, together with any subcontractors of their own were known as implementing partners (Exhibit 33.2). The third responsibility for overall logistical co-ordination of the 20 or so agencies active in the relief effort was handled directly.

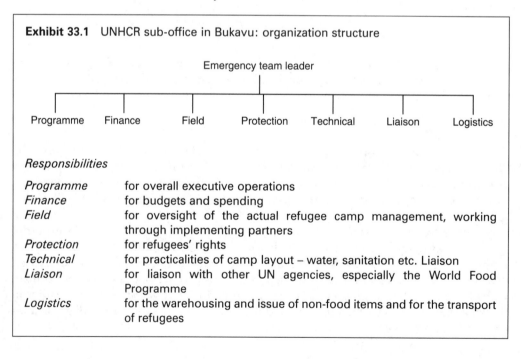

Exhibit 33.1 UNHCR sub-office in Bukavu: organization structure

Emergency team leader

| Programme | Finance | Field | Protection | Technical | Liaison | Logistics |

Responsibilities

Programme	for overall executive operations
Finance	for budgets and spending
Field	for oversight of the actual refugee camp management, working through implementing partners
Protection	for refugees' rights
Technical	for practicalities of camp layout – water, sanitation etc. Liaison
Liaison	for liaison with other UN agencies, especially the World Food Programme
Logistics	for the warehousing and issue of non-food items and for the transport of refugees

Exhibit 33.2 Implementing partners of UNHCR's logistics unit

At different times, UNHCR did also have both warehouses and certain trucks under its direct control, as well as occasional use of hired vehicles from local hauliers

UNHCR

Direct contractors (2)	**CARE**	**ACTION AID**
Responsibilities	Maintenance Warehousing Transport	Transport
Subcontractors for transport (3)	**WORLD VISION** **HELP INTERNATIONAL**	**UK ASSIST**

On a day-to-day basis, the transport operations of Action Aid/UK Assist were integrated with the transport activities that CARE supervised.

In more detail, the supply of non-food items, involved the receipt and storage of five standard items: blankets, water cans, kitchen sets, plastic sheets and soap. There had to be enough for perhaps 200,000 people, as some of those who had fled were either rich or armed, and so were not supported by UNHCR. The goods came by air and by road, and had to be stored in one of four warehouses which at the outset were managed directly by the logistics unit but were later handed over to one of the NGOs. Delivery of items to the site was usually organized not by HCR but by the implementing partner who ran the camp that needed them. The requirement for transport involved some movement of goods and the occasional loan of vehicles to other agencies with urgent temporary needs, but centred chiefly on refugees. In the town of Bukavu were some 50,000 people camped on roadsides, in churchyards and on other makeshift sites from which they needed to be moved urgently. The priority for use of trucks was therefore the removal of these people and their belongings to new camps as they were set up.

Incoming supply and storage of non-food-items (NFIs)
Routine supplies of food (350 g of cereal per day) were not HCR's responsibility, although certain supplementary foods were. The five non-food commodities, for once-only issue to each family, which were the Unit's business to make available, were the subject of detailed specifications and much figure work by UNHCR in Geneva: the ration for one family amounted supposedly to a total weight and space requirement of 3.08 kg and 0.368 m^3 (Exhibit 33.3).

Slick systems and accurate data were, however, battered by the time they reached central Africa. Remeasured with a tape measure, these standard items were found to need 50% more space than expected. The original number of beneficiaries was given as 200,000, who on Andrew's arrival were said already to have received 816 tonnes of supplies. From mid-September, a record was kept of issues to each camp and matched to a supposed total allocation derived from camp populations; but with the need for practical activity more pressing than the need for paperwork, no figures (for refugees, receipts or issues)

Exhibit 33.3   Standard rations for a family of five: non-food items (single issue)

Blankets	3	Plastic sheet 4 × 5 m	1
Water cans	2	Soap, per month	1 kg
Kitchen set	1		

Declared weight of one lot of standard rations:	3.08 kg
Declared cube requirement ditto:	0.368 m^3
Daily food allowance (cereal):	350 g per individual

It was the responsibility of the implementing partners to collect these items from the stores for distribution to their own camps.

---

were really dependable. At no time was it possible to answer the central question of any logistics system: 'can our stocks supply the expected demand?' The unit never knew with confidence either what the remaining demand from the camps for their allocation was likely to be, or the amount of potential stock: there was a figure for actual stocks, but no estimate of total quantities in the supply pipeline.

The NFIs came down 10,000-mile long supply lines. Geneva took the decisions, ordering supplies from its own depots in The Netherlands or Turkey, or buying wherever it could: kitchen sets were sourced in Egypt and Kenya, blankets in Zimbabwe and plastic sheets in Korea; personal vehicles for HCR staff, Toyota Landcruisers, had come earlier from the Arab Gulf. Some items came by sea via Mombasa on the Kenyan coast, and others by air via Entebbe and/or Kigali, Rwanda's capital, with a full-size international airport.

There was never any regular flow, as in a just-in-time system, but only irregular consignments of unpredictable size, almost always arriving without warning. Some materials sent for Bukavu's use were hijacked by other UN links upstream in the supply chain: five lorries destined for the unit were simply requisitioned by Kigali, the next stop up the line, convinced that their needs were more pressing.

In a situation that was often unpredictable, a typical problem faced by the stores manager was as follows. Waiting outside the gate of one of his depots one morning were two huge lorries than had come up, unannounced, from the coast, a 700 or 800 mile journey that had taken most of a week. With semi-trailers 76 feet long and a maximum gross weight of 75 tonnes, they each carried, as well as a load of 5000 boxed kitchen sets, 3000 litres of fuel for their own use. The unloading and storage of 10,000 boxes, thrown from hand to hand down a human chain, took 30 men 16 hours (Figure 33.2).

The supply lines changed as the situation settled down: in early September, most goods were coming by air, even though only half the runway was usable (Exhibit 33.4). As however both quantities and the political temperature abated, more goods came in by road, although this route was always less secure, with risks from a resumption of warfare, Third-World frontier bureaucracies and the weather: sometimes paved roads even were impassable with ankle-deep mud. The meal that came in for the World Food Programme was not HCR's responsibility, but its tortuous journey bears description: by sea to Dar es Salaam, by train to Kigoma on Lake Tanganyika, where it was transferred to lake steamer for either Bujumbura or Uvira; there it was put on lorries for the last 100 miles up the escarpment, making in all 25–35 days for a journey of less than 1000 miles.

Figure 33.2 Human chain: unloading kitchen sets from a lorry.

HCR's stocks (Exhibit 33.5) were stored in two large and two small warehouses, both with tolerable roofs but supplemented by 'rubbhalls' or 'wiikhalls', huge tents on steel frames, and inevitably extended by open-air storage. Their siting owed nothing to mathematical modelling of regular quantities and flow routes: instead, any feasible storage space was pressed into service, a hangar at the airport (Figure 33.3) – from which the owner had removed his half-repaired planes – and part of a former brewery in the town of Bukavu, for US$1800 per month. Even an old school kitchen was in use, though it succumbed in due course to an armed robbery. In total, UNHCR had nearly 6000 m^3 of warehouse space; rents, like other things (skilled labour, especially if bilingual or trilingual), escalated in price accordingly.

The local transport of goods and people
The local road system was basic, and bad roads would become worse with the onset of the rainy season. The territory served from Bukavu changed in size: initially it had extended south to Lake Tanganyika, but in its final form it measured perhaps 100 miles north to south, and 50 miles east to west. Only 35 km was paved with tarmac, from town along the lakeside to the airport. The location of the refugee camps in the vicinity of Bukavu is shown in Figure 33.4.

Resources at the disposal of the logistics unit varied: UNHCR's Handbook for Emergencies said that a camel could carry 250 kg; but it was not camel country! Trucks numbered between 30 and 40 (but with the bad roads, breakdowns depleted the fleet strength significantly); they are listed in Exhibit 33.6.

Exhibit 33.4 Transport capacities: aircraft; and airborne supply data

A. Transport capacities: aircraft

Aircraft type	Payload (tonnes)	Volume (m$^{3)}$)	Runway length (m)
Hercules C130	21	120	1500
Hercules C130 (US)	15		
Hercules C161	10		
Dakota DC3	3	40	1200
Boeing B 707	40	165	2100

Capacities vary with aircraft configuration, users, range and altitude. Source: *UNHCR Handbook for Emergencies*, p. 41.

B. Airborne supply data
Incoming goods through Bukavu-Kavumu airport:
Airport capacity (day flights only: no lights for night-flights):
Flights unloadable per day, with fork-lift truck   10
Flights per day, without fork-lift-truck   4

Fork lift trucks:
Original FLT (US): 10,000 lb capacity. Later FLT (ODA, UK): 7 tonne.

Actual inflow rates in first week of September 1994:
Flights/day   0–9   Total flights in the week   23
Tonnes/day   0–100
Main carriers: RNZAF and Luftwaffe (Hercules), ODA (Antonov).
Cost of flying in a vehicle (Land Cruiser type, value $25,000): $10,000.

Runway
Usable portion of runway: 1500 m
Cost of repair of remainder: $800,000 approx. (two tenders: from Strabag and Office des Routes).

The daily operation and maintenance of vehicles (under HCR direction and priority-setting) was handled by contractors, most of whom were NGOs who had come in from outside to assist in the emergency, but some of whom were local hauliers. Calculations of transport capacity requirements were based on the figures given in Exhibits 33.7 and 33.8. Inevitably, all planning of transport requirements was made more difficult by the knowledge that unforeseen events, both political and meteorological, would upset provisional ideas and change priorities. Effective capacity was also reduced by the requirement for lorries shifting refugees to operate in convoys of as many as 20 vehicles at a time. Administrative simplicity further introduced the assumption that each vehicle could only do one journey per day, which was often but not invariably true.

The drivers had a gruelling job. Some were recruited locally, some were unpaid volunteers sent by a group of English and American churches, and others were ex-soldiers, part of the peace dividend. Some lorries had no power steering, and a day at

Exhibit 33.5 Stocks of non-food items at HCR's four warehouses

(a) Flows and stocks for period ending 16 September 1994

	Received 10–16 Sept	Issued since 8 Aug	Stock held 16 Sept
Blankets	36,180	55,000	144,000
Jerry cans	–	24,549	4644
Kitchen sets	29,237	16,191	49,809
Plastic sheet 4 × 5 m	–	42,583	19,840
Soap, per month	–	25,929 kg	45,242 kg

(b) Flows and stocks for period ending 20 Oct 1994

	Received 10 July–20 Oct	Issued 8 Aug–20 Oct	Stock held
20 Oct			
Blankets	205,790	104,347	100,279
Jerry cans	52,553	47,970	3367
Kitchen sets	59,256	46,172	13,767
Plastic sheet 4 × 5 m	77,514	73,289	8654
Soap, per month	64,800 kg	52,043 kg	4716 kg

(c) Warehouses

Airport	Swala Hangar
Bukavu Town	Simba A (large)
	Simba B (small)
	School kitchen.

Total storage cube: 6000 m^3
Typical eaves height: 2–4 m
Typical rent: $80 m^2 per year

the wheel, fighting the potholes and the mud, was exhausting work: one driver, still not relaxed when home and in bed, dislocated his shoulder whilst asleep! No-one ever mentioned such safety considerations as statutory regulation of drivers' hours.

Co-ordination of all relief agencies logistics' activities

With approximately 20 NGOs active in the relief effort, alongside UNHCR, UNICEF, WFP, WHO, came the task of overall co-ordination. Regular meetings had already been set up with the logisticians of all the other agencies who either had or needed transport, and who could benefit from mutual communication. Matters of common interest included rates being paid to local hauliers (in Europe it might have been considered a cartel); representations to local government and military over the need for safe conduct for relief vehicles; routine administrative matters such as the constant change of staff; and the means of pooling resources so that empty trucks could be matched to unusual needs, sometimes without payment.

There were occasions when underlying rivalry between organizations with an eye to

Figure 33.3 Storage in airport hangar, Bukavu/Kavumu.

Exhibit 33.6 Vehicles available for the relief effort

Owning/operating agency	Quantity of vehicles			Cost ($)
	4 tonne AWD	7 tonne	Other	
HCR own		3		
Local double header (truck + trailer, 20-tonner)			1	$400/day
World Vision		30		
Action Aid/UK Assist	9			$2000/ week including fuel.
Help International	4			
Other six agencies' trucks rarely available for HCR.				

All agencies
Total – 150 lorries, (1/4 all-wheel drive) total capacity 950 tonnes.
150 Trucks, total capacity 950t, 25% AWD.

Vehicles off the road, all-wheel drive
Estimated portion of AWD vehicles off the road in rainy weather: 30%

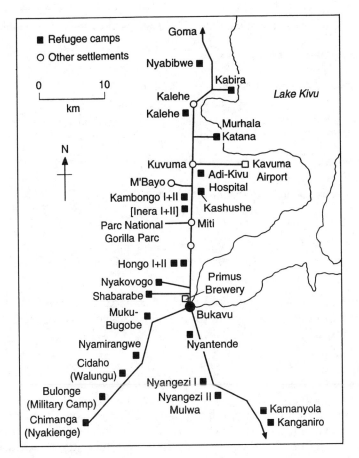

Figure 33.4   Location of refugee camps.

Exhibit 33.7   Transport capacities: surface carriers

Carrier	Payload	
	tonnes	m³
Standard railway truck	30	52
Container, 20 ft (6.1 m)	18	30
Container, 40 ft (12.2 m)	26	65
Lorry, articulated large	30	
Lorry, medium	6–8	
Land-Rover/Cruiser LWB pick-up	1	
Hand-drawn cart	300 kg	
Camel	250 kg	
Donkey	100 kg	
Bicycle	100 kg	

Source: UNHCR *Handbook for Emergencies,* p. 41.

Exhibit 33.8 Capacity and loading data of vehicles used by the logistics unit

Truck capacities, with different loads

4-tonner (Bedford)	People (and belongings): 50 (12/tonne)
7-tonner	Jerry-cans 1200
	Plastic sheets 1500
	Kitchen sets 500

Commodity figures

Blankets (in bales of 30)	700 blankets weigh 1 tonne, and occupy: $4.5\ m^3$ (compressed) $9\ m^3$ (loose)
Firewood	Requirement for one family for one month: 1 stere ($1\ m^3$)

---

their own supporters back home came to the surface. One independent comment, however, was that in this relief operation the general level of co-operation between all agencies was unusually good.

Costs

An early estimate of the cost to UN of the Rwandan relief operation was US$500 million. Budget setting was not the responsibility of the logistics unit, but the figures given were that logistics, as defined, came to about a quarter of the local operation's total. Relations with contractors were unlike those in the west. There was little opportunity for competitive quotations; it was more a question of using any resource that looked capable. Some of UNHCR's partners did, however, produce costings of their operations: for transfer of one refugee out of town $4.32 was quoted using 6 × 6 lorries, as against $7.53 for a different agency using 4 × 4s. That compared interestingly with an estimate of $3.50 for carrying people by boat to a lakeside camp, but the boat owner had disappeared when asked to provide his insurance certificate.

Particular features of the task: problems and freedoms

There were certain distinctive features to this logistics operation: as well as difficulties to tolerate, there were certain freedoms unavailable to anyone in the highly regulated west.

The infrastructure lacked almost all the features that materially developed countries take for granted. There was no postal system, telephone system, bank, dependable flow of electricity or water, local press, road or bridge maintenance or, underlying all these, effective civil authority or local government. Even the local military, it was said, were not really under the control of their officers, and when armed men in uniform hijacked relief vehicles, as they did (Appendix 33.3), complaints had little effect. The cost penalty of these problems was enormous. This cash economy, in which all large bills were settled in dollars rather than the local currency (*Nouveaux Zaires*), which halved in value in the three months did however have certain advantages: instead of prolonging credit at suppliers' expense, buyers knew that, at a certain fixed time, the creditors would turn up and expect their cash.

The need to use convoys for the transfer of refugees out of town carried its own considerable cost burden. The logistics unit considered the risk of letting individual lorries make their own journey as soon as they were loaded but, on the grounds of public profile, control and security, decided against it. The enormous delays associated with convoys, while loaded lorries awaited marshalling and unloaded lorries waited for the journey home were, on balance, thought justified. An example of the consequent loss of versatility was in coping with the confusion caused by bad weather on the roads. One of the refugee camps, Hongo, had been built in a hurry and without proper control on a slope above a road. When the rain came, the tents slid down the hillside with the mud, and the tarmac paving was buried under a foot of mud. One vehicle jack-knifed, not quite sliding into the lake, and everybody else tried to pass it and got stuck. With no police to take control of the situation it took half a day to sort out the jam of 70 or 80 vehicles (Figure 33.5).

In contrast to some of these maddening frustrations – and visitors to Africa either learn to adjust to the local tempo or have a nervous breakdown – there were certain freedoms to act without bureaucratic interference. The quasi-cartel between the agencies has already been mentioned, but there was much more. The employment of staff was simple: an agreement to pay warehouse workers $2 per day ($3 on Sundays) meant what it said: for six days $12 in the hand, with no stoppages and no paperwork. Planning law and transport regulation were other areas of greater freedom than in the west.

Figure 33.5 Hongo camp on the hillside, and blocked traffic on the muddy road.

The task

Within a week of arriving in Bukavu, Andrew McClintock, the new senior logistics officer, had begun to assimilate the information described above. The task facing him was to plan the overall shape of a three-month assignment, and the immediate steps to put in hand.

He was just outlining some initial ideas on paper when he heard his name on the radio: it was news from the airport 35 km away, that a Hercules C130 had just landed with 15 tonnes of biscuits, and with the message that two more flights were due later that day. He already knew that, at the airport, there was neither a secure compound nor spare covered storage.

Appendix 33.1: Job description/profile: senior logistics officer (L4)

1. Qualifications

 (i) University degree or equivalent in transportation or transport engineering (mechanical or civil). Training in business management desirable;
 (ii) Specialized diplomas or certificates from recognized sources (i.e. membership by examination of professional institutes).

2. Work experience

 (i) Minimum 8–10 years in transportation industry or five years in engineering industry plus 3–5 years in transportation or logistics field;
 (ii) Minimum two years' overseas work in a humanitarian relief organization, which will include logistical management field experience in developing countries.

3. Specialist knowledge

 (i) Field experience, similar to duty station (UN, NGO, ICRC/IFRC);
 (ii) Emergency/disaster work in country of recruitment or overseas.

4. General knowledge

 (i) Proven skills in emergency management, preferably in the logistics sector.
 (ii) Transportation management by modal type (i.e. air, land or sea), which will include fleet management experience (scheduling, maintenance, driver recruitment and training, etc.).
 (iii) Knowledge of procurement (local and international).
 (iv) Storage and distribution (including knowledge of commodity tracking systems, computerized stock control and electronic information data systems).
 (v) Management skills (including report writing, budgetary, accounting and forecasting, recruitment and training).
 (vi) Negotiating skills, particularly in the preparation of contractual arrangements.

(vii) Ability to manage and supervise international and local staff.
(viii) Knowledge of radio communication systems and the ability to establish a field radio communication network.

5. Language skills

(i)   English and French.
(ii) Other official UN languages.

6. Terms of reference (Emergency Assessment Missions)

A. Needs assessment

(i)   Assess logistical needs in terms of transport requirement.
(ii)   Assess conditions of local infrastructure, i.e. roads, bridges, airstrips, other communications systems, and determine the transport capacity of each of them.
(iii) Assess the availability, capacity and reliability of local transport facilities and companies.
(iv)   Assess the capacity of local warehouse and storage facilities.
(v)   Assess the availability of local facilities for staff, office space and workshops, etc.
(vi)   Assess the need and location of transit and/or reception centres and determine their size and requirements in terms of basic supplies and access to services.

B. Planning and design

(i)   Prepare an overall logistics plan of action for the delivery of assistance. The plan is to include the requirements for vehicles, warehousing and distribution.
(ii)   Prepare proposals for warehouse management, to include where appropriate a commodity tracking system and computerized stock control.
(iii) Prepare plans for the recruitment and training of staff, which will include specialized training for logistical and warehouse staff.
(iv)   Prepare plans for improvements to roads, bridges and airstrips.
(v)   Prepare plans for the establishment and improvements to warehouse and storage facilities.

C. Implementation

(i)   In conjunction with STS, negotiate mode, routing and delivery schedules with transporters, and monitor and co-ordinate the regular and timely supply of relief items.
(ii)   In conjunction with the STS, negotiate contracts for warehouse and storage facilities and recruit staff. Monitor the activities of the warehouse management and staff and implement training programmes.
(iii) In conjunction with PTSS and STS, negotiate contracts with local companies for road, bridge and airstrip improvements and supervise the contractual work.
(iv)   Co-ordinate and liaise with other UNHCR programme and field staff, NGOs and government agencies.
(v)   Write situation reports (sitreps) and send to HQ on regular basis.

Appendix 33.2: Agencies involved in the relief effort in Zaire (South Kivu)

The following agencies were involved not only in logistics, but also in camp management, health, children/orphans, water supply, etc. This list is not complete.

Official international organizations

Red Cross and Red Crescent
UNHCR (United Nations High Commission for Refugees)
UNICEF (United Nations International Children's Emergency Fund)
WFP/PAM (World Food Programme; Programme Alimentaire Mondiale)
WHO (World Health Organization)

National governments

Germany: Luftwaffe
United Kingdom: ODA (Overseas Development Agency)
New Zealand: RNZAF (Royal New Zealand Air Force)

Some NGOs (non-governmental organizations)

Action Aid – UK Assist
Action Internationale Contre le Faim
AMDA (Asian Medical Doctors Association)
American Jewish Joint Distribution Committee
Aviateurs sans Frontières
CARE Canada
CARE Deutschland
Caritas
GTZ (Gesellschaft der Technischen Zusammenarbeit) + IUCNZ
Help International
Islamic Relief
Lighthouse Doctors & Nurses International
Medecins du Monde
Medecins sans Frontières
Mennonite Central Committee
Ordre de Malte
Oxfam
Recherche Sauvetage Urgence International (ISRU)
Save the Children
World Vision

Appendix 33.3: Extract from *The Times* 29 November 1994

Missing aid worker 'survived for family' by Emma Wilkins

The British charity worker who was missing for five days after his aid convoy came under fire on Rwanda's border with Zaire described yesterday how thinking of his family inspired him to survive.

Don Reid, a former SAS soldier from Hereford and Worcester, fought through jungle, swam a swollen river and survived by eating berries and drinking rainwater until he reached a charity outpost in the Tongo mountains.

'I almost gave up a couple of times but was kept going by the thought that my wife and family would never know what happened to me,' he said. Mr Reid. 43, is expected to return to Britain today for a reunion with his wife, Lynn, and children, Andrew and Ian.

After his Assist UK aid convoy came under fire last Friday, Mr Reid fled into the bush. He kept his sights on the Tongo mountain range, where he knew Oxfam had an outpost. Using his T-shirt to collect rainwater which he found in rock depressions, Mr Reid managed to obtain a supply of drinking water. He eventually found a mountain track that took him to Oxfam's house, nine miles from where he abandoned his truck.

'The relief and joy of the Assist UK staff on hearing the news was heard as a huge roar went back over the air to Tongo,' a worker in the charity's headquarters in Goma said. Mr Reid had suffered only considerable weight loss and minor cuts.

Ian Henderson. a director of Assist UK, said charities had learnt vital lessons from Mr Reid's experience. 'Drivers will be issued with handheld radios in addition to their cab radios. We will identify predetermined rendezvous points and all staff will carry food and water wherever possible,' he said.

Relief operations, including transport and civil engineering work, had been suspended while a search for Mr Reid was carried out. Operations would restart immediately, Mr Henderson said.

Further reading

Davis, J. and Lambert, R. (1995) *Engineering in Emergencies*, RedR & Intermediate Technology, London. Chap. 6: Logistics, p. 106 (Chalinder, A.); Chap. 15: Vehicles.

UNHCR (1982) *Handbook for Emergencies, Part 1*, UNHCR, Geneva. Chap. 5: Supplies and Logistics (Butterworth, R.), pp. 31–54.

UNHCR (1989) *Supplies and Food Aid*, UNHCR, Geneva. Chap. 3: Purchasing and donations; Chap. 4: Receipt of shipments; Ch 5: Field logistics operations, pp. 93–122; Chap. 6: Vehicles; Chap. 7: Storage and warehousing.

Wood, D. F. *et al.* (1994) *International Transportation and Logistics*, Chapman & Hall, London. Chap. 15: Logistics of famine relief (Long, D.).

Sourcing retail merchandise from south-east Asia

David Taylor
Department of Transport and Logistics, University of Huddersfield, UK
and
Brian Shortland
Logistics Manager, Kingfisher Asia Ltd, Hong Kong

Introduction

In October 1993 Brian Shortland of Woolworths plc was considering the results of a 12-month project in which he had reviewed the supply chain systems operated by the company for sourcing merchandise from south-east Asia. It was clear that a major overhaul of the company's operation was required and he was contemplating how best to present the results of his review and his recommendations for improvements to the next Woolworths' board meeting which would be held in ten weeks' time.

Company background

Woolworths plc is a major retailer in Britain with some 800 outlets in the UK. The first store was opened in Liverpool, England, in 1909 by the F.W. Woolworth organization of the USA. The company under the FWW title was, by 1980, operating from 795 stores in all the major cities and towns in Britain. However, in 1982 the UK operation was bought from the American parent company by Kingfisher, a British consortium.

The main focus of the company is directed at young families with children. Five main product ranges are carried in store, these are: toys, children's clothing, entertainment (compact disks, tapes, videos), confectionery, and home & kitchen. Merchandise is priced in the low to medium range thus supporting the main customer base, and within the UK, Woolworths has a strong position in the market-place as is shown in Table 34.1.

Table 34.1 Woolworths' market position within the UK by value of sales 1993

Toys	Second place
Children's clothing	Second place
Entertainment	First place
Confectionery	First place
Home & kitchen	Not applicable

In 1993 some 33% of the merchandise sold, approximately £500 million at selling price, was manufactured in Asia, of which approximately £330 million was purchased from UK importers and £170 million was purchased direct from the Far East. This volume of merchandise entailed shipping some 3500 TEUs (20-ft equivalent container units), which made the company the largest importer by volume in the UK retail trade.

Importing process

Woolworths operated a shipping department, based at the London headquarters, to handle the order processing, customs clearance and payment for merchandise imported directly from overseas suppliers (Figure 34.1). Most merchandise was bought on cost and freight (C&F) terms from suppliers. Payment was mainly on the basis of 'documents against payment at sight' (D/P), with some letters of credit opened when certain suppliers insisted (see Appendix 34.1 for details of terms of trade).

There was very little co-ordination between the company's 25 merchandise buyers and the shipping department. Furthermore the buyers each independently arranged their own currency requirements from the company's central finance department in London, but there was no central control or reconciliation of the large number of currency contracts placed.

The shipping department was struggling to keep control of the situation and a number of problems were causing concern to senior management. The department was handling

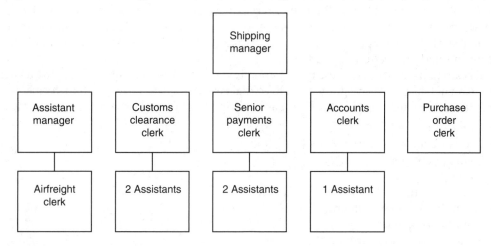

Figure 34.1 Structure of the shipping department.

some 6000 sets of shipping and bank documents per annum and preparing the same number of HMC&E (Her Majesty's Customs and Excise) declarations to clear goods for importing. The staff were knowledgeable and keen but had no authority to change company policy on importing or to challenge the buying function on their methods and practices.

The documentation procedure in place at this time was as follows. When buyers returned from their Far East sourcing trips, handwritten purchase orders were passed from the buying departments to the shipping department. This was because merchandise was purchased in various currencies and no systems within the organization could handle currencies other than Sterling, so import purchase orders could not be produced via the company's computerized purchase order management system.

Once received by the shipping department purchase orders were checked as to:

• latest shipment date
• payment terms
• correct country of origin
• correct currency
• supplier details
• customs tariff classification.

When checking and verification were complete, the import purchase order with shipping instructions would be mailed to the supplier. Where payment terms were by letter of credit, the application form would be completed manually and submitted to the company's bank in London. The bank would then issue the letter of credit to the supplier.

Once merchandise had been shipped from the port of export and bills of lading issued by the shipping company, the supplier would complete the various export documents. They would present the originals to their bank for onward transmission to Woolworths' bankers in the UK and at the same time send copy documents to the Woolworths shipping department.

Documents were received by Woolworths in London from their bank (on trust for 24 hours). These were then checked against the import purchase order and, if satisfactory, the bank was advised to pay the relevant bill of exchange if payment terms were D/P, or to accept the bill of exchange if terms were D/A (see Appendix 34.1). It is important to note that until the shipping documents were released to the importer by the bank, the importer had no title to the goods.

Declarations to HMC&E were then manually completed, which entailed copying all the relevant details of the consignment on to official HMC&E 'customs declaration' forms. The information required by HMC&E for each consignment of imported merchandise was:

• name of vessel
• arrival date at UK port
• name of UK port
• description of goods
• HMC&E tariff
• quantity of goods (numeric)
• quantity of goods (weight)
• value of goods in currency of invoice
• value of goods in Sterling (conversion rate is set each period by HMC&E)

- cost of freight
- duty payable (duty is payable on 'landed cost' i.e. cost of goods + ocean freight + insurance)
- country of origin
- insurance cost.

The HMC&E declaration was then sent to Woolworths' customs clearing agents at the port of import. They would present the declarations together with invoices, packing lists, GSP certificate and certificate of origin, for the goods to be cleared for import. This process took between five days and two weeks.

Once the goods had been cleared by customs, merchandise would be booked by the clearing agents for delivery from the port of import to the relevant Woolworths distribution centre (DC) in the UK. The company had two distribution centres, one in Swindon to serve the south and the other in Rochdale to serve the north of the country. On receipt at the DC, merchandise would be checked for quality against the standards set by the Woolworths quality assurance department. If acceptable, it would be issued to stores; if not, it would be held for return to the supplier.

Operation of the buying department

The company had three main merchandise divisions (Toys, Home Essentials and Kidswear) which all imported on a direct basis. Each division had a divisional director and a number of buying teams, which specialized in various lines within the product range for the division (Figure 34.2). The main processes in the company's buying cycle are shown in Figure 34.3.

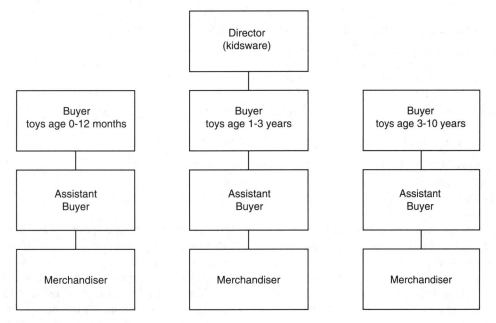

Figure 34.2 Typical divisional buying structure.

Range planning	Sourcing of potential suppliers	Selection of preferred suppliers	Samples received from suppliers	Buying decision	Purchase order placed
(step 1)	(2)	(3)	(4)	(5)	(6)

Goods ready for shipment from supplier	Goods on board vessel	Vessel departs port of export	Vessel arrives UK port	Documents received from bank	HMC & E declaration completed by Woolworth UK
(7)	(8)	(9)	(10)	(11)	(12)

HMC & E declaration presented to customs	Goods cleared for import	Bill of lading presented to shipping line for release of goods	Goods booked into Woolworths distribution centre
(13)	(14)	(15)	(16)

Figure 34.3 The buying cycle.

The buying cycle lead times varied for each division:

Children's clothing would typically be:

Buyers visit Far East	October/November
Orders placed	January
Delivery in UK	August/September

Toys would typically be:

Buyers visit Far East	September/October
Orders placed	January
Delivery in UK	May/June (for July sales promotion)

Woolworths, like many other retailers, considered efficient purchasing to be at the heart of successful retailing. As a consequence, the buying function was a particularly influential department within the company and was responsible for all purchasing activities from range planning and demand forecasting, through to placing the purchase orders and the specification of product volumes and delivery schedules. As one of the main elements in Woolworths' market position was price competitiveness, a key objective for the buyers was to minimize unit purchase price and as a consequence, the primary measure used to evaluate the effectiveness of buying was the gross margin. This was the estimated selling price of the product minus its landed cost at the 'back door' of the UK distribution centre (the latter being the price quoted by suppliers on a C&F basis).

On the whole, the buyers were very successful at meeting the gross margin objective because of their experience and expertise in negotiating and because the volumes required meant they usually had considerable purchasing power with suppliers. They would also order bulk quantities to receive further discounts and achieve economies in transportation costs. Most buyers had considerable experience in the business and had progressed to positions in buying through either the retailing or merchandising functions of the company. Buyers would pride themselves on their knowledge of the market and would be confident in their judgements about what would or would not sell and of the quantities that would be required for a particular season or period.

Buyers often made decisions on product selections, required quantities and approximate selling price on the basis of their 'feel for the market'. In practice, this required considerable skill but did entail some risk, particularly as Woolworths did not have an EPOS system in place in the stores and therefore had little in the way of computerized data on past sales from which to forecast demand. A further factor adding risk in purchasing was the fact that many of Woolworths products were either fashion items such as toys and clothing, or highly seasonal items such as garden furniture, the demand for which was notoriously difficult to predict. Such risks were exacerbated when merchandise was sourced from distant suppliers because of long and variable lead times of supply, fluctuations in currency values and the requirement to predict volumes, place orders and purchase often a whole season's requirements in one order, usually well in advance of the selling period. The normal pattern in purchasing from south-east Asia was to order the total quantity required for a season and for goods to be shipped in one bulk delivery or occasionally in phased shipments.

Identifying problems

As part of his investigation, Shortland held discussions with the following groups within the company, each of which had an involvement in the supply chain:

- buyers
- merchandisers
- shipping department
- finance department
- distribution management.

From these meetings a number of problem areas was highlighted by the managers within the respective sections.

Buyers

The buyers felt that one of the main problems lay with long lead times, particularly at the UK end of the supply chain. There was considerable uncertainty over the length of time taken between arrival of merchandise at the UK port and eventual clearance and delivery to the distribution centres. In practice this could vary between a few days and a few weeks and often resulted from delays due to documentation problems or customs procedures. Average port clearance time was about two to two-and-a-half weeks. In consequence buyers often added extra weeks to lead times to cover these periods, therefore those shipments that did clear the ports efficiently (e.g. in a few days) arrived at the distribution centres ahead of schedule and had to be stored for longer before distribution to the shops.

Buyers also expressed concern over the quality control system. In 1993 there was some £3.5 million owed to the company by major suppliers for faulty merchandise supplied over the previous 12-month period. The quality control system worked as follows.

Once a buyer had sourced a potential item, the supplier would be required to send samples for testing to the quality assurance (QA) department at headquarters in London. For many items this testing would be extremely rigorous, particularly for children's toys, for which European Union safety standards were very stringent. If the product met the required standards, it would be approved and an order confirmed. Staff from the London QA department would also visit the Far East on a number of occasions each year to inspect the factories of suppliers. Once a factory was accepted an agreed quality monitoring system was put into place, supervised by an external agency specializing in quality assurance management. However, suppliers would frequently despatch shipments before the QA agency had inspected the goods.

When products were delivered to the UK distribution centres, a rigorous, random sampling procedure was carried out and if the samples taken failed to meet the required standards, the whole shipment would be rejected. It was not at all uncommon to find that the quality of delivered products was below that of the samples originally sent to HQ in terms of either materials used or quality of workmanship. Resulting disputes with suppliers were often difficult to resolve and the only real lever Woolworths had was to withhold payment, either against the current shipment, if payment had not been made, or against future orders, e.g. when a letter of credit was involved.

Merchandisers

The role of merchandisers was to provide an interface between the buyers, the UK distribution centres and the administrative departments including the shipping department. Whilst the role of the shipping department was to organize the documentation and customs clearance of imported goods and arrange for delivery from the port to the appropriate DC, the merchandisers administered the disposition of goods. This involved allocating stock to the appropriate DC, informing DCs as to when to expect deliveries from suppliers and determining delivery volumes and schedules from the DCs to the stores. Merchandisers often worked in partnership with an individual buyer and would check that when a buyer placed an order, there was sufficient quantity to give stock coverage for each store.

The main complaint of the merchandisers was the lack of control over merchandise shipment programmes. Firstly, there was no control over when merchandise was actually shipped by suppliers, which often led to merchandise being received late in the UK. Secondly, as goods were normally purchased on C&F terms, the vendors supplied the merchandise, arranged the shipping and paid the freight, without any obligation to provide information about the vessel or shipping line used, or the date of departure from the port of export. Thus once an order was placed very little information was available until the shipping department received either the original documents from the bank or copy documents from the supplier. These were often received up to five weeks after merchandise was shipped from port of export by which time the goods could have arrived at the UK port.

Shipping department

The main problem here was that the department was working at full capacity to keep up with the flow of documents and in particular to complete the HMC&E declarations. The workload was such that there was a need to increase the number of staff employed.

Finance department

The company's finance managers considered that there was a serious risk element within the currency purchasing procedure. The finance department responded to the demands of the buyers. Each buyer independently ordered foreign currency to suit their own purchasing requirements and there was little overall control of the amounts purchased or the timing of purchases. Thus substantial deposits of foreign currencies were held by the company with the risk of losses being incurred if Sterling weakened.

Distribution management

Managers of the company's UK DCs voiced two main concerns. Firstly they were unaware of merchandise on order, or of delivery schedules until they received information from merchandisers about when goods were booked for receipt at the DCs. Often this was only a matter of weeks or even days before delivery, which meant that planning of staff and other resources within the DCs was difficult.

Secondly, if the volumes of merchandise purchased proved to be in excess of the amount sold in a particular season, the DCs were left holding the excess stock, sometimes for a whole year, until the next selling period. This could create problems of congestion in the warehouses and also added costs in excess of warehouse budgets. Warehouse managers resented these costs as they felt they arose as a result of inefficiencies in the buying process rather than from inefficiencies in the warehouse. Buyers were charged a fee for warehousing and distribution which was offset against their gross margin calculation. This distribution fee was calculated by allocating budgeted distribution costs on the basis of the proportion of total throughput accounted for by each line, but it did not include the cost of any long-term stocking of over-ordered lines, nor the cost of collecting and re-warehousing unsold stock from stores. Neither did it include any allowance for the cost of capital tied up in inventory. The latter cost was considered as part of the company's general overhead and was another issue of concern frequently raised by the finance department. On average, stock held by the company was in the in the order of £250–300 million, with the bulk held in stores, either on display (approximately 50%) or in back-of-store stockrooms (approximately 40%) and the rest held in the DCs (approximately 10%).

The need for change

Although the company's senior management did not have detailed knowledge of the day-to-day operations of the Far East supply chain, they had recognized that there were problems and hence had appointed Shortland to review and improve the situation. Following his investigations, Shortland had a much clearer picture of the various operational difficulties that existed; however, one area in which he had not found much information was in relation to the costs of operating the supply chain system. This was partly because these costs were split between various departments within Woolworths and also because a significant portion of the logistics costs was hidden in the C&F prices quoted by the majority of suppliers. Although he did not know the costs involved even in the delivery of product from suppliers into the DCs, his feeling was that the delivery costs alone might account for anything up to 15% of the C&F price. If this was the case, he was confident that there was scope for considerable saving.

Appendix 34.1: glossary

Term	Description
Shipping terms	
TEU	A count used in container shipping. One TEU equals one 20-ft container.
FEU	One FEU equals one 40-ft container.
Buying terms	
C&F (cost and freight)	The vendor quotes for supplying the merchandise, arranging shipment and paying the freight costs to a specific destination.
CIF (cost insurance and freight)	The vendor quotes for supplying the merchandise, arranging shipment, insuring the cargo, and paying the freight costs to a specific destination.
FOB (free on board)	The vendor quotes for supplying the merchandise and for all landside costs up to loading the cargo on board the ship. The buyer pays the freight costs.
Documents	
B/L (bill of lading)	When cargo is placed on board a vessel the B/L is given by the shipping line to the owner of the cargo (the shipper). This document is issued as a set, comprising three originals, which are signed by the shipping line or their agents, and three copies which are unsigned. Possession of an original of this document gives title to the cargo. This document is also a receipt for the cargo.

Invoice	The document giving details of the merchandise sold, with description, price and quantity.
Packing advice	Document giving details of number of cartons, carton numbers, marks, measurements and weights.
GSP certificate	Document issued in the country of export to support a claim that the merchandise is within the GSP (general system of preferences) enabling less or nil duty to be payable in the country of import.
Certificate of origin	Document issued in the exporting country stating the origin of the goods.

Payment terms

Letter of credit (L/C)	This method of payment gives safeguards to both the vendor and the buyer. A letter of credit is issued by the buyer's (applicant's) bank (issuing bank) via the vendor's bank (advising bank) to the vendor (beneficiary). The L/C is a bank guarantee that the Issuing Bank will make payment, or accept and pay bills of exchange drawn by the beneficiary, providing all documentation and conditions stated in the L/C are met.
Bill of exchange	A written obligation to pay at sight or at some specific future date a sum certain, to the drawee.
Drawee	The person or company requiring payment.
Acceptance	The act of signing the bill of exchange accepting responsibility for the debt. Once a bill is accepted there is no defence in law against non-payment.
Acceptor	The person or company acknowledging the debt.
Documents against payment (D/P)	Documents granting title to the goods will be handed to the buyer upon payment of the bill of exchange.
Documents against acceptance (D/A)	Documents will be handed to the buyer on acceptance of the bill of exchange for payment at some future specified date.

General terms

HMC&E	Her Majesty's Customs and Excise Department, i.e. UK customs
ICC	International Chambers of Commerce
Period entry	This is a concession allowed by HMC&E after auditing the importer's computer software. It

Local import

allows the importer to make monthly returns to HMC&E of all imports made within the period. The local office (relative to the DC) into which the 'control' merchandise will be delivered receives notice of the contents and time and date of delivery. If HMC&E wish to inspect the cargo they will attend the DC site at the time of arrival. If they do not appear the merchandise is deemed 'cleared' for customs purposes.

Reference maps

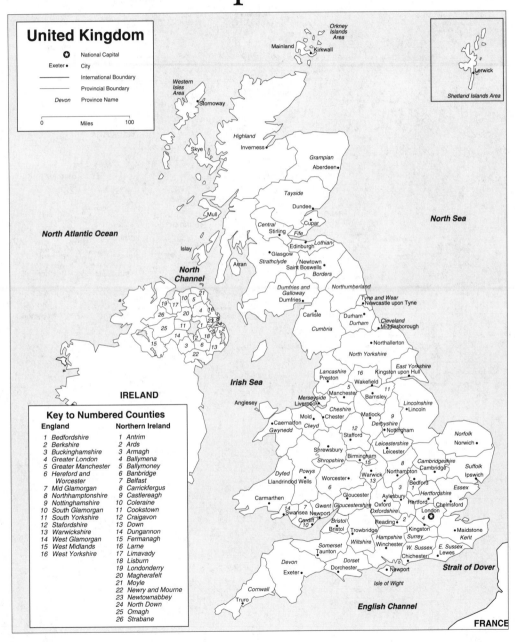

United Kingdom

⊛	National Capital
Exeter •	City
———	International Boundary
———	Provincial Boundary
Devon	Province Name

0   Miles   100

Key to Numbered Counties

England

1 Bedfordshire
2 Berkshire
3 Buckinghamshire
4 Greater London
5 Greater Manchester
6 Hereford and Worcester
7 Mid Glamorgan
8 Northhamptonshire
9 Nottinghamshire
10 South Glamorgan
11 South Yorkshire
12 Stafordshire
13 Warwickshire
14 West Glamorgan
15 West Midlands
16 West Yorkshire

Northern Ireland

1 Antrim
2 Ards
3 Armagh
4 Ballymena
5 Ballymoney
6 Banbridge
7 Belfast
8 Carrickfergus
9 Castlereagh
10 Coleraine
11 Cookstown
12 Craigavon
13 Down
14 Dungannon
15 Fermanagh
16 Larne
17 Limavady
18 Lisburn
19 Londonderry
20 Magherafelt
21 Moyle
22 Newry and Mourne
23 Newtownabbey
24 North Down
25 Omagh
26 Strabane

Shetland Islands Area

Orkney Islands Area

Mainland • Kirkwall • Lerwick

Western Isles Area • Stornoway

Highland
Skye
Inverness •

Mull

North Atlantic Ocean

Islay

North Channel

Arran

Grampian
Aberdeen •

Tayside
Dundee •
Cupar •
Central
Stirling   Fife
Edinburgh • Lothian
• Glasgow
Strathclyde   Newtown
Saint Boswells
Borders

North Sea

Dumfries and Galloway
Dumfries •

Northumberland
Tyne and Wear
• Newcastle upon Tyne

Carlisle •

Durham
• Durham
Cleveland
Middlesborough •

Cumbria

• Northallerton

North Yorkshire

Lancashire
Preston •   16   East Yorkshire
Kingston upon Hull •
5   Wakefield •
Manchester •   11
Merseyside   Barnsley •
Liverpool •
Lincolnshire
• Lincoln
Cheshire
Anglesey   Chester •   Matlock •   9
Mold •   Derbyshire
Caernarfon •   12   Nottingham •
Gwynedd   Clwyd
Stafford •   Norfolk
Norwich •
Shrewsbury •   Leicestershire
Shropshire   Leicester •
Birmingham •   8
15   Cambridgeshire   Suffolk
Dyfed   Powys   Warwick   Northampton   Cambridge •   Ipswich •
Worcester •   13   3   Bedford •
Llandrindod Wells •   6   1   Essex
Gloucester •   Aylesbury   Hertfordshire
14   7   Gwent   2   Oxford •   Hertford •   Chelmsford •
Carmarthen •   Swansea Newport •   Gloucestershire   Oxfordshire   London   • Maidstone
Cardiff •   Bristol •   Reading •   Kingston •   Kent
10   Bristol   Surrey   W. Sussex   E. Sussex
Trowbridge •   Hampshire   Lewes •
Somerset   Wiltshire   Winchester •   Chichester •
Taunton •   Strait of Dover
Devon   Dorset   • Newport
Exeter •   Dorchester •   FRANCE
Isle of Wight
Cornwall
Truro •   English Channel

IRELAND

Irish Sea

19
10   17
5
26   20   4
16
25   11   21   23 24
14   1   9
18
15   12   7   2
3   6   13
22

Europe

ICELAND
Reykjavik

Norwegian Sea

North Atlantic Ocean

SWEDEN
Kiruna
Hammerfest
Murmansk
Oulu
NORWAY
Trondheim
FINLAND
Sundsvall
Gulf of Bothnia
Bergen
Tampere
Gavle
Helsinki
Oslo
St. Petersburg
RUSSIA
Stockholm
Tallinn
ESTONIA
Moscow

North Sea
Goteborg
Riga
LATVIA
Aberdeen
DENMARK
Baltic Sea
LITHUANIA
Belfast
Edinburgh
Copenhagen
Vilnius
Minsk
IRELAND
Newcastle
Tver
Dublin
Rostock
Gdansk
BELORUSSIA
Liverpool
Hamburg
U.K.
NETH.
Poznan
Cardiff
Amsterdam
Hannover
Berlin
Warsaw
London
BELGIUM
Bonn
POLAND
Kyiv
English Channel
Bruxelles
Leipzig
UKRAINE
GERMANY
Le Havre
LUX.
Frankfurt
Prague
Krakow
Lvov
Paris
CZECH REP.
Strasbourg
Nantes
Munich
SLOVAKIA
MOLDOVA
FRANCE
Vienna
Bratislava
Chisinau
Odesa
SWITZERLAND
AUSTRIA
Budapest
Bern
HUNGARY
Cluj-Napoca
Bay of Biscay
Geneva
Ljubljana
Pecs
ROMANIA
Bilbao
Lyon
Zagreb
SLOVENIA
Bordeaux
Milan
Constanta
CROATIA
Bucharest
Porto
Venice
BOSNIA
Belgrade
Varna
Black Sea
Marseille
Florence
Sarajevo
SERBIA
PORTUGAL
ANDORRA
BULGARIA
Lisbon
Madrid
MONTENEGRO
Sofiya
Barcelona
ITALY
Titograd
Skopje
Istanbul
SPAIN
Rome
Adriatic
MACEDONIA
Valencia
Tirana
Thessaloniki
TURKEY
Naples
ALBANIA
Sevilla
Tyrrhenian Sea
GREECE
Aegean
Malaga
Cagliari
Ionian Sea
Palermo
Patrai
Athens
Mediterranean Sea
CYPRUS
CRETE

250 Km
250 Mi.

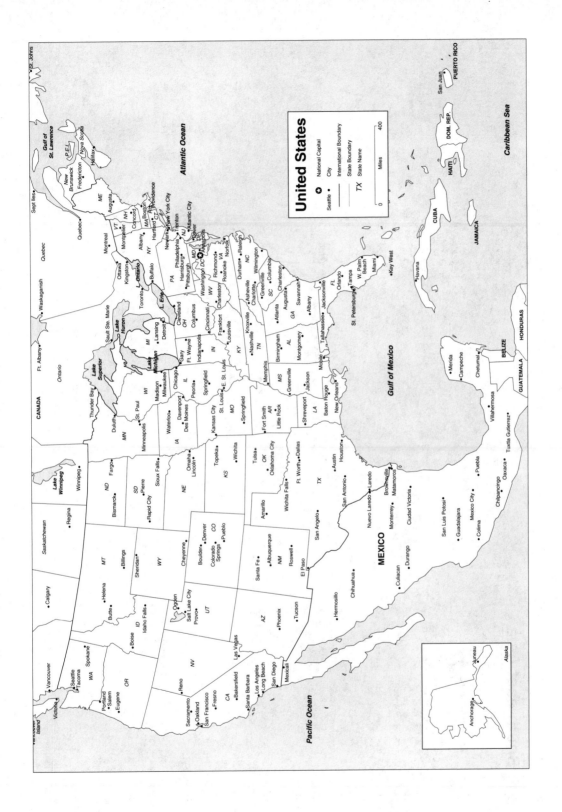

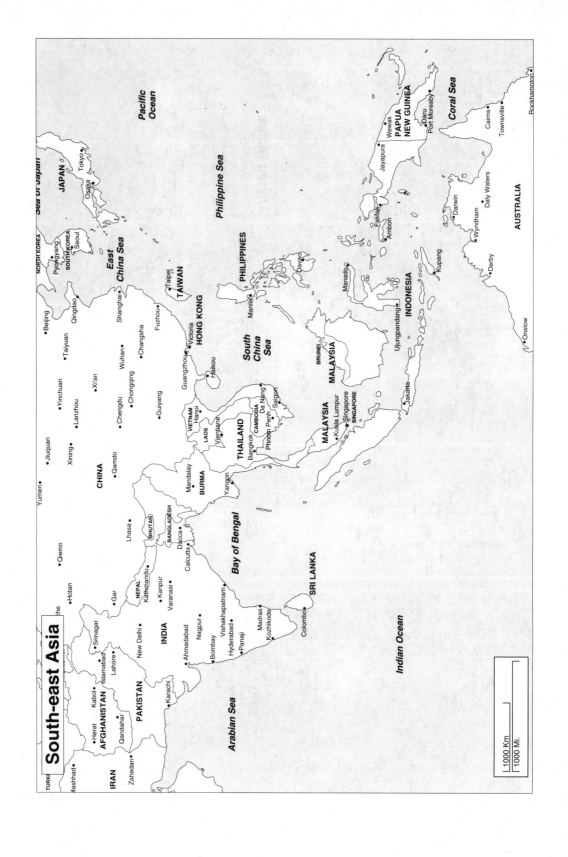

South-east Asia

Pacific Ocean

Sea of Japan

JAPAN
Tokyo
Osaka

NORTH KOREA
Pyongyang
SOUTH KOREA
Seoul

East China Sea

Beijing
Qingdao
Shanghai
Taiyuan

Taipei
TAIWAN

Philippine Sea

HONG KONG
Victoria
Guangzhou
Fuzhou
Changsha
Wuhan

Haikou

PHILIPPINES
Manila
Davao

Wewak
PAPUA NEW GUINEA
Daru
Port Moresby
Jayapura

Coral Sea
Rockhampton
Cairns
Townsville

Yumen
CHINA
Yinchuan
Xining
Lanzhou
Xi'an
Chengdu
Chongqing
Guiyang
Qamdo
Jiuquan

South China Sea

BRUNEI
MALAYSIA

INDONESIA
Manado
Ujungpandang
Kupang
Jakarta

Fakfak
Ambon

AUSTRALIA
Darwin
Daly Waters
Wyndham
Derby
Onslow

che
Hotan
Gar
Lhasa
NEPAL
Kathmandu
BHUTAN
Kanpur
Varanasi

Qiemo

VIETNAM
Hanoi
LAOS
Vientiane
THAILAND
Bangkok
CAMBODIA
Phnom Penh
Da Nang
Saigon

MALAYSIA
Kuala Lumpur
SINGAPORE
Singapore

Mandalay
BURMA
Yangon

BANGLADESH
Dacca
Calcutta

Bay of Bengal

SRI LANKA
Colombo

TURK
Mashhad
IRAN
Zahedan
Herat
Kabol
AFGHANISTAN
Qandahar
Srinagar
Islamabad
Lahore
PAKISTAN
Karachi
New Delhi
INDIA
Ahmadabad
Nagpur
Bombay
Hyderabad
Panaji
Vishakhapatnam
Madras
Kozhikode

Arabian Sea

Indian Ocean

1000 Km
1000 Mi.

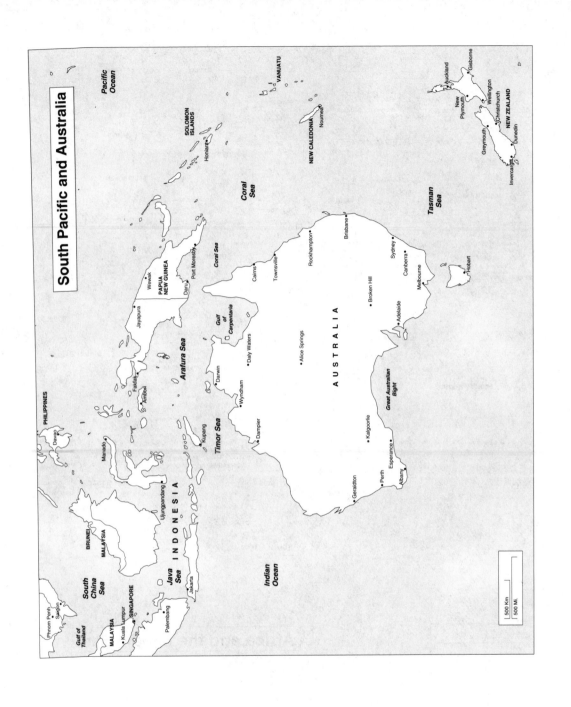

South Pacific and Australia

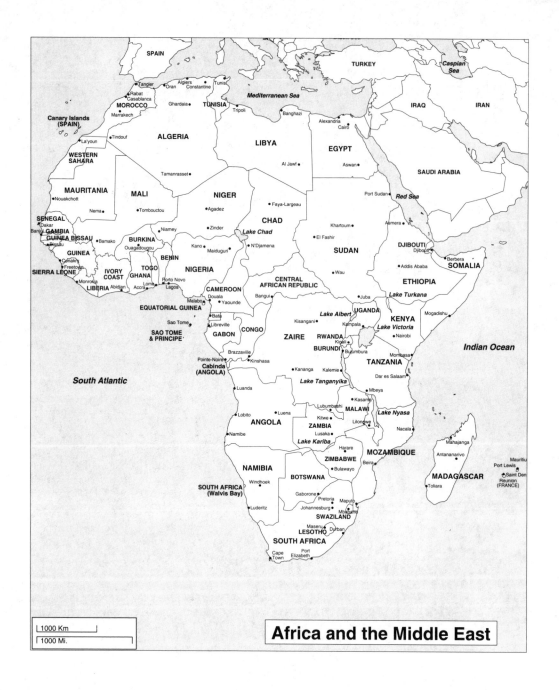

Africa and the Middle East

1000 Km

1000 Mi.